ANALYZING FINANCIAL STATEMENTS

George E. Ruth

AMERICAN
BANKERS
ASSOCIATION ®

This publication is designed to provide accurate and authoritative information in regard to the subject matter covered. It is sold with the understanding that the publisher is not engaged in rendering legal, accounting, or other professional service. If legal advice or other expert assistance is required, the services of a competent professional person should be sought.

From a Declaration of Principles jointly adopted by a Committee of the American Bar Association and a Committee of Publishers and Associations.

The American Bankers Association is committed to providing innovative, high-quality products and services that are responsive to its members' critical needs.

To comment about this product, or to learn more about the American Bankers Association and the many products and services it offers, please call **1-800-BANKERS** or visit our Web site: www.aba.com.

This textbook has been approved by the American Institute of Banking for use in courses for which AIB certificates or diplomas are granted. The American Institute of Banking is the 102-year-old professional development and training affiliate of the American Bankers Association. Instructional materials endorsed by AIB have been developed by bankers, for bankers.

American Institute *of* **Banking**

AMERICAN **BANKERS** ASSOCIATION ®

ii

Table of Contents

LIST OF EXHIBITS

ABOUT THE AUTHOR

George E. Ruth is Senior Vice President and Chief Credit Officer for Klein Financial Corporation. Klein Financial owns nine community banks in central Minnesota. Ruth, who began his banking career in 1965, has extensive experience in commercial lending, credit, and operations. He is a 1988 graduate of ABA/AIB's Stonier Graduate School of Banking.

Ruth is an accomplished writer on banking topics. For the ABA, he has authored *Analyzing Financial Statements* and *Commercial Lending*. He, as well, is the author of *Lending Principles*, published by The Schools of Banking. Teaching is another of Ruth's contributions to the banking industry. In addition to teaching at the ABA's National Commercial Lending school and various graduate schools, he is the lead instructor for several state Commercial Lending Schools.

ACKNOWLEDGMENTS

Many individuals have supported the writing of this textbook. In particular, I am appreciative of the assistance I received from the members of the committee that reviewed the manuscript for this edition. They provided many comments and ideas throughout the process

Finally, I would like to thank my wife, Linda, who has supported my career and encouraged me along life's way!

William C. Barksdale, Jr., Principal
Barksdale & Associates
Columbia, SC
Retired Senior VP of Wachovia

Susan N. Daniel
Private Client Credit Advisor
Wealth Management
Sun Trust Bank
Jacksonville, FL

Ernestine L. Keiser
CPA Accounting Manager
Integic Corporation
Chantilly, VA

Susan L. McMullen
Assistant Vice President - Credit Officer
Blue Ball National Bank
Blue Ball, PA

PREFACE

One of may favorite sayings is "Numbers talk and banker's need to listen." The purpose of *Analyzing Financial Statements* is to provide commercial lenders with the knowledge and skills they need in order to analyze and interpret financial information. The goal of this textbook is to emphasize "listening" to the interpretation, not merely calculating the numbers. A number of practical exercises are located at the end of each chapter.

The primary audience of this text includes trainees in credit training programs, small business lenders, loan review staff, and those who need to understand the analysis of business financial statements as part of their job. Although most banks now use computer programs to spread financial information and make calculations, bankers need to understand how the numbers came together and what they mean. To accomplish this, a lender must

- understand the source of the information,
- determine the quality of the financial statement received,
- know the legal structure and type of business organization,
- be able to interpret the data, and
- apply this understanding to make a good credit decision.

Turner Electronic Corporation and Designs by Dezine, Inc., fictitious companies, are used throughout the textbook to help students learn the analysis process. The analysis process begins with an understanding of the types of financial information the lender may receive, the components of the financial statements, and other management reports. The process continues with an understanding of the various forms of business organization and legal structure, types of loan structures, and competing and complementing sources of financing. Whether a business is a manufacturer, wholesaler, retailer, service company, or agricultural, its business organization and legal structure affect its income statement and balance sheet.

Nest in the process is the analysis of the income statement. The income statement is analyzed first because of its impact on the balance sheet. While analyzing an income statement, a lender must consider sales, cost of goods sold, fixed and variable expenses, and the net profit margin. In addition, a lender should consider break-even and operating leverage, concepts that are important in income statement analysis.

With an understanding of the income statement, the balance sheet is analyzed next. The various balance sheet accounts are classified as assets, liabilities, or net worth. Accountants and bankers classify these accounts differently. This textbook clarifies how bankers classify each account.

Next ratios are calculated. Ratios are categorized as liquidity, financial leverage, coverage, or profit in nature. The textbook explains how to calculate each ratio and then what the ratio means. Because cash, and only cash, repays loans, two chapters are devoted to cash flow. The first chapter focuses on the accountants, lender prepared direct method, abbreviated method, and traditional cash flow methods used to analyze business financial statements. The second chapter focuses on personal cash flow and financial statements.

The final two chapters explain cash budget and pro forma financial statements. Again, practical application exercises are used to demonstrate these concepts.

The new addition features a *Master Case Book* that includes blank forms you may want to use. A summary of business and personal financial statement components, listing accounts as current and noncurrent, is provided to give consistent account classifications. A summary of various ratios, how to calculate them, and what they mean is also provided. Blank forms to calculate a cash budget and personal cash flow are also provided.

Analyzing financial statements is a process in which a systematic procedure must be followed step-by-step in order to assess and monitor credit risk. With this in mind, the new edition of *Analyzing Financial Statements* was expanded to include:

- how to calculate break-even
- emerging technologies
- how to calculate and interpret traditional and global cash flow, and
- new cases and exercises to apply what you have learned.

1

FINANCIAL STATEMENT ANALYSIS: AN OVERVIEW

LEARNING OBJECTIVES

After studying *Financial Statement Analysis: An Overview,* you will be able to

- define financial statement analysis,
- explain technical versus interpretive aspects of credit analysis,
- explain differences between accrual and cash accounting,
- identify and describe types of internally and externally prepared financial statements,
- identify and describe common types of internally prepared management reports,
- understand limitations of financial statement analysis, and
- define key terms that appear in **bold** type in the text.

INTRODUCTION

The profitability and soundness of any bank depend on the quality of its loan portfolio. Funds are acquired (at a cost) via deposits and then "rented" to borrowers. It is the responsibility of the loan officer to see that money lent is rented for a higher cost than it took to obtain it. This requires the loan officer to understand the bank's cost to acquire funds and the methods of pricing loans fairly. Prior to renting the money, the lender needs to interview the applicant, investigate references and background information, visit the company, and analyze past, current, and projected financial performance. The lender then needs to properly structure and document the loan. Once funds are disbursed, the lender monitors the loan by analyzing the borrower's financial performance on a regular basis. The financial statement analysis and the risk that the loan will not be repaid remain until the individual or business makes final payment.

Despite precautions taken by a lender, risk remains an inescapable part of commercial lending. If, for example, the borrower does not meet the loan terms, secondary repayment sources, such as collateral, often are insufficient to cover the losses. For this and other reasons, banks depend on commercial loan officers to make sound judgments about the financial stability and capacity of businesses applying for loans.

Credit risk—the risk that a loan will not be repaid—can be managed in the lending portfolio by establishing policies for analyzing the financial soundness of customers, structuring loans to match repayment sources, monitoring the performance of customers after the loan is made, and identifying problem loans early. Assessing the degree of risk includes financial statement analysis. The loan officer can lessen the hazard of a loan loss by accurately appraising a customer's creditworthiness and ability to repay and by ensuring that the loan is properly secured, structured, and monitored.

Financial statement analysis involves both technical and interpretive considerations. The scope of the analysis will vary, depending on the amount and terms of the loan.

When conducting a financial analysis, the lender usually follows a four-step systematic approach:

1. obtain financial information;
2. process, spread, and common-size financial statements;
3. analyze and interpret information; and
4. complete trend, comparative, and continuity analyses.

To evaluate credit risk, the lender attempts to identify the uncertainties a commercial borrower may face. A lender must confirm, for example, that a borrower's financial strengths and weaknesses are balanced. If its strengths exceed its weaknesses by a margin sufficient to cover perceived uncertainties, the borrower represents an acceptable credit risk. Often, this concept is expressed in the formula:

$$\text{Strengths} - \text{Weaknesses} > \text{Uncertainties} = \text{Acceptable Credit Risk}$$

Financial statements provide a standardized way to record and communicate important financial information about the operations and financial conditions of businesses, other types of organizations, and individuals. To obtain detailed information about companies and individuals, banks generally rely on three components of financial statements:

- **balance sheet**—a detailed list of assets, liabilities, and owner's equity, showing a company's or individual's financial position at a given date
- **income statement**—a summary of a company's or individual's income and expenses over a given period of time (also referred to as a profit and loss statement, operating statement, and earnings statement)
- **cash flow statement**—a summary of a company's operating, financing, and investing activities (cash receipts and payments) over a specific period of time (also referred to as a sources and uses of funds statement)

The balance sheet, income statement, and cash flow statement together are referred to as a financial statement. If, however, the company or accountant does not prepare a cash flow statement, the balance sheet and income statement together are referred to as a financial statement

Financial information may be prepared internally or externally. Internally prepared information and reports include financial statements, business plans, accounts receivable aging, inventory analysis, operating and capital budgets, and tax returns. Most companies, through an accounting firm, prepare their financial statement externally at least once per year. These statements may be compilations, reviews, and audits.

A BRIEF HISTORY OF FINANCIAL REPORTING

Prior to the Great Depression, businesses had fewer outstanding debts than they do today. To obtain capital funds, most businesses depended on the equity markets or on short-term lending from commercial banks. The unregulated stock market experienced cyclical swings, and, in the absence of diligent analysis by lenders, these swings created severe financial distress. Because consistent or reliable financial information was difficult to obtain, a drop in investor confidence could sweep throughout the economy and adversely affect the stock market.

The stock market crash of 1929 dealt a tremendous blow not only to individual stockholders but to numerous businesses seeking additional working capital. The collapse precipitated an adverse chain reaction that carried throughout the commercial banking industry. Prior to the crash, banks had extended short-term credit against planned stock issues, which, given the situation, never took place. Commercial banks, then, were faced with undercapitalized borrowers and, in many cases, defaulting loans. Banks nervously called in loan portfolios. Widespread bank and business failures brought a halt to the booming economy, caused tremendous economic loss, and thereby precipitated the Great Depression of the 1930s.

As a consequence of the Great Depression, the federal government established the **Securities and Exchange Commission (SEC)**, which publishes and oversees regulations that govern financial information submitted by businesses reporting their financial condition and their operations. One of the SEC's regulations required the accounting profession to create standardized rules for business accounting principles. From this program, the accounting profession established guidelines called **generally accepted accounting principles (GAAP)**. Initially, the American Accounting Association and the American Institute of Certified Public Accountants coordinated GAAP. Today, however, the **Financial Accounting Standards Board (FASB)** in Norwalk, Connecticut, runs GAAP. Nearly 1,000 corporations, banks, and other organizations, including nearly 7,000 public accounting firms and individual certified public accountants, hold membership in FASB. (Additional information about FASB is available on their Web site). Examples of FASB's rules include:

- FASB No. 116 addresses how to account for contributions to nonprofit organizations,
- FASB No. 117 addresses the preparation of financial statements for nonprofit organizations,
- FASB No. 141 addresses the counting of Business Combinations, and
- FASB No. 142 eliminates the amortization of goodwill associated with business combinations.

GAAP provides a reasonable and consistent method to analyze financial statements. Although it does not eliminate personal interactions vital to the bank and borrower relationship, GAAP makes it possible to thoroughly examine a business's past performance. GAAP also enables different companies to use the same concepts in their accounting activities. Even though many companies today do not issue financial statements backed by an independent audit, most banks require companies to prepare statements in accordance with GAAP.

FINANCIAL STATEMENT ANALYSIS: A DEFINITION

Financial statement analysis is a systematic examination and interpretation of a business's past performance in order to predict the business's future profitability and capacity to repay debt. Financial statement analysis helps the lender decide whether a loan should be made, determine possible terms and conditions, and identify the monitoring needed until the loan is repaid. It is a critical component of the commercial lending process, which begins with an interview between the commercial customer and the lender, then moves on to the stages of credit investigation, financial statement analysis, loan structuring and pricing, loan negotiation, loan documentation and closing, and loan follow-up. Financial statement analysis focuses on the company's past, current, and projected financial performance as reflected in its financial statements, rather than on its management style or credit history. Nevertheless, such non-financial considerations do help establish the frequency and the depth of the financial statement analysis.

Thus, financial statement analysis is fundamentally important to the lending decision and to the monitoring process that begins once the loan is closed. It is also critical to early identification of problem loans. Early detection of a problem situation enables the lender to determine immediately what action a company needs to take to rectify the situation.

Technical Versus Interpretive Analysis

Technical manipulation of the data is only a small part of a comprehensive and effective financial statement analysis. Once the technical analysis of a company and its industry has been completed, the lender must interpret the results to determine whether to make a loan.

Technical

Whenever they examine available financial information, commercial lenders apply research techniques based on sound business logic and generally accepted accounting principles. Technical applications include spreading information for clarity, comparing ratios with those of other businesses, preparing cash flow calculations for analysis, and projecting future operating results.

Interpretive

The goal of interpretive analysis is to learn not only *what* is happening, but also *why* it is happening. In this process, how past events and current trends might affect a company's future repayment ability are important considerations. Here, the lender first must obtain complete background information on the company, including:

- ownership
- management
- lines of business
- competition (domestic and foreign)
- markets in which the company operates
- timing of the operating cycle
- characteristics of the industry
- position within the industry
- pertinent government regulations
- susceptibility to inflation or other changes in the general economy
- the extent to which demographic trends and consumer preferences might affect operations

Understanding these organizational and environmental factors gives meaning to the numbers used in the interpretive examination. This information, along with the financial information, helps the loan officer determine the risks of a proposed loan.

FOCUS OF FINANCIAL STATEMENT ANALYSIS

The focus of financial statement analysis depends on the specific purpose of the examination. For example, a loan request to fund a temporary increase in inventory or to acquire new equipment will be analyzed in a different way than interim data to monitor an existing loan. The purpose of the analysis will affect the nature and depth of the investigation.

The size of the requested loan (relative to the size of the bank) and its terms also affect the range of financial statement analysis. A large loan requires more effort by the bank than a small loan because a loss would have a greater impact on bank earnings. This is not to say that small loans do not involve a considerable amount of uncertainty concerning repayment, but the smaller interest income does not always profitably allow for extensive analysis. A $50,000 loan for 90 days, adequately secured with a defined source of repayment, for example, involves less analysis than a $350,000 loan for five years to finance an equipment purchase.

Sequential Steps

Financial statement analysis (exhibit 1.1) starts with a preliminary investigation of the company, its background and history, and its current relationship with the bank. The analysis then moves to an in-depth examination of the company's operating performance and financial structure, as evidenced by its historical and projected financial statements. Most banks use a systematic approach to obtain the needed documents: processing, spreading, and common-sizing the information, and, finally, completing written trend, comparative, and continuity analyses.

1. *Obtaining Information*
   Reliable and current financial information is critical to the analysis. Most banks require annual financial information to be no more than 15 months old. Even

---

Credit Scoring Versus Credit Analysis

A large regional bank may credit score loans up to several million dollars. Credit scoring is the process of giving points for length of time in business, the number of years of consecutive profits, the amount of debt versus equity, the type of collateral, and the term of the loan. The total of the points helps estimate the repayment probability, based on the information in the financial statements. An applicant who scores high enough is granted the loan. A full credit analysis is completed on larger loan requests *only*.

Community banks typically perform a full credit analysis on all commercial loans, taking into consideration such *non-financial factors* as character, number of jobs in the community, and length of time in business. The full credit analysis process involves interviewing the business to understand the "story" behind the numbers. In contrast, when credit scoring is used, the story behind the loan request is not told. The decision is made based on the numbers.

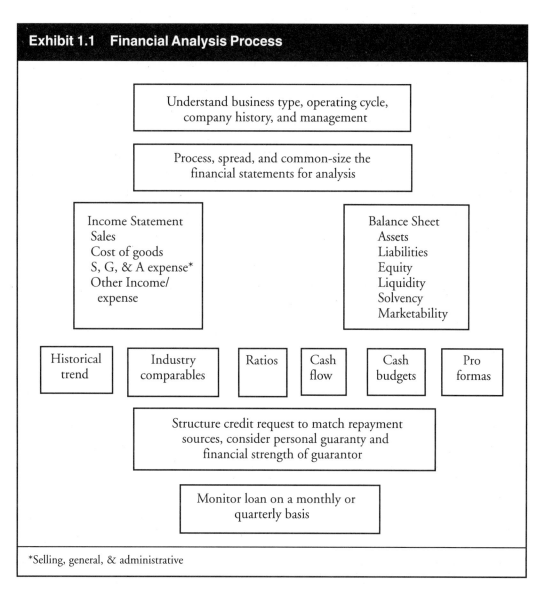

Exhibit 1.1   Financial Analysis Process

Understand business type, operating cycle, company history, and management

Process, spread, and common-size the financial statements for analysis

Income Statement
Sales
Cost of goods
S, G, & A expense*
Other Income/
  expense

Balance Sheet
Assets
Liabilities
Equity
Liquidity
Solvency
Marketability

Historical trend | Industry comparables | Ratios | Cash flow | Cash budgets | Pro formas

Structure credit request to match repayment sources, consider personal guaranty and financial strength of guarantor

Monitor loan on a monthly or quarterly basis

*Selling, general, & administrative

then, the bank should obtain **interim financial statements,** that is, monthly, quarterly, or semiannual financial statements. If the information is outdated, credit may be approved on a short-term basis but be subject to receiving current annual reports. To determine comparisons and trends for well-established companies, the lender should obtain at least three consecutive years of annual financial statements. If the business is new, the bank should obtain two years of projected financial statements.

2. *Processing the Statements*
   Whether mailed to the bank or delivered personally, financial statements must be signed and dated by the customer or the customer's accountant. By signing the statement, the customer is saying that the information is true and correct. The lender then spreads, summarizes, and places the financial statement in a credit file. Some banks use a log sheet to record the type of statement, the date received, and so forth. A tickler file indicating when the next statement is due helps ensure follow-up.

3. *Spreading the Statements*

Statement spreading is when financial statement information is extracted and listed in a consistent format so a lender can quickly spot trends and make comparisons. (See exhibit 1.2, Income Statement and Balance Sheet Spreadsheet.) Various types of spreadsheets are available, and the type used depends on the source of the information to be spread, the number of statements to be spread, and the nature of the analysis (such as comparative analysis versus trend analysis). Spreading financial statements demands attention to detail, and it requires the ability to perform complex mathematical tasks. Needless to say, it can be a time-consuming, costly process. Today, most banks use computer software programs to calculate statement spreading.

Exhibit 1.2   Income Statement and Balance Sheet Spreadsheet

Income Statement	Date Amount	%	Date Amount	%	Date Amount	%
Net sales						
Cost of goods sold						
Gross profit						
Operating expenses						
Operating profit(loss)						
Other income						
Interest expense						
Other expense						
Net profit before tax						
Taxes						
Net profit after tax						
Assets	Date Amount	%	Date Amount	%	Date Amount	%
Cash						
Accounts receivable						
Inventory						
Other current assets						
Total current assets						
Land						
Buildings						
Equipment						
Other fixed assets						
Depreciation						
Net fixed assets						
Prepaid expenses						
Other noncurrent assets						
Total assets		100		100		100

Exhibit 1.2 Income Statement and Balance Sheet Spreadsheet (continued)

Liabilities	*Date* *Amount*	*%*	*Date* *Amount*	*%*	*Date* *Amount*	*%*
Notes payable bank short term						
Accounts payable-trade						
Accrued expenses						
Current maturities long-term debt						
Other current liabilities						
Total current liabilities						
Long-term debt bank						
Other long-term debt						
Subordinate debt						
Total liabilities						

Net worth	*Date* *Amount*	*%*	*Date* *Amount*	*%*	*Date* *Amount*	*%*
Common stock						
Retained earnings						
Paid in capital						
Treasury stock						
Total net worth						

4. *Common-sizing the Statements*

   When spreading a statement, the numbers are common-sized, a process that gives the lender a deeper understanding of the financial statement. When statements are **common-sized,** each number on the income statement is expressed as a percentage of net sales, and each number on the balance sheet is expressed as a percentage of total assets. For example, if net sales are $100 and operating expenses are $35, common-sized operating expenses are expressed as 35 percent.

Spreading and Common-sizing Forms

The format and detail of spreadsheets used to common-size financial statements varies greatly. Most forms do not list all balance sheet or income statement accounts. For example, exhibit 1.2 in the textbook and exhibits 1 and 2 in the *Master Case Book* are sample forms that bankers may use to manually spread a financial statement. Exhibits 3 and 4 in the *Master Case Book* are common-sized spreadsheets using a computer-generated form. If a financial statement does not contain an account classification, such as those in exhibit 8 of the *Master Case Book,* the account is not listed on the manual or computer-generated form.

When financial statements are common-sized, the lender may compare related information quickly and note changes over time. For example, if a shoe retailer remodels the company-owned building, the value of those improvements as a percentage of total assets will increase. When a company remodels space, sales often are expected to increase. Depending on what type of inventory is carried in the new space, the mix of sales may change. If the sales mix changes, the cost of inventory as a percentage of sales will probably change. Common-sized statements show these percentages in a readable format.

5. *Written Analysis*

   After the statements are spread and common-sized and other mathematical calculations (such as ratios, cash flow figures, or projections) are completed, the lender writes an objective, not speculative, analysis or interpretation. The interpretation should include an explanation of what actually caused any changes and avoid the so-called *elevator technique* of just stating that something went up or down. For example, the analysis should not be worded, "sales increased 4 percent." Rather, the analysis should read, "sales increased 4 percent due to a 3 percent price increase and a small increase in product volume sold."

6. *Trend Analysis*

   Two basic analytical techniques are trends and industry comparisons. When determining trends, lenders compare information during similar periods or at comparable times for the same company. Trend analysis is used to detect favorable or unfavorable changes in the financial position of a company, as reflected in revenues, expenses, assets, or liability accounts. Making industry comparisons enables the lender to see where the competition stands in relation to the business of the loan applicant. Industry comparisions, too, are used to detect favorable or unfavorable conditions, but on an industry-wide basis.

7. *Comparative Analysis*

   Comparative analysis parallels the financial information of at least two companies, preferably of the same size and industry. This allows the lender to draw conclusions about the relative performance of the companies. By using The Risk Management Association (RMA) *Annual Statement Studies,* a lender can match many companies to the subject company and draw statistical conclusions. *Annual Statement Studies* data are taken from financial statements of more than 130,000 customers of RMA-member financial institutions.

8. *Continuity Analysis*

   The concept of continuity assumes a company will remain in business, in its present form, for a period long enough to use its assets for their intended purpose, which is to generate cash flow to repay liabilities in the ordinary course of business. This concept also is known as a going concern. If a company is not *a going concern,* then the immediate practical problem for the lender is to determine whether the company's assets are properly valued for financial presentation. If the assets are not properly valued, the lender will need to determine whether the net worth is overstated.

The underlying assumption of continuity is that assets will be used for their original purpose—to generate future revenues and long-term net cash flow. If a business fails, the assets could be liquidated for the sole purpose of immediately repaying debt. This would produce a result substantially less than any value appearing on the financial statements under a set of distressed circumstances. If there is reason to question the ability of the business to maintain its status as a going concern, the accountant must bring this question to the attention of the reader of the financial statements; however, such a statement by accountants is rare unless the company already is in default on its obligations.

Accrual Accounting Versus Cash Accounting

It is important to understand a company's operations in terms of its accounting methods. Most medium- to large-size companies prepare financial statements using accrual accounting rather than cash accounting.

Accrual accounting recognizes revenues when earned (that is, when sales are transacted), regardless of when the company receives cash from the sale. All expenses (that is, the costs to produce a product or provide a service) are recognized when costs are incurred rather than when cash payment is made.

Cash accounting recognizes revenues as earned when payment is received, regardless of the timing of the transaction. Likewise, the company recognizes the cost associated with producing these revenues only when the cash is actually paid out. For example, if a company with a calendar-year fiscal period sold $2,000 worth of products on December 20, 20x3, with payments collected on January 20, 20x4, the $2,000 would be recognized as 20x3 revenues under the accrual method, but as 20x4 revenues under the cash method.

Although cash accounting is of special interest to the lender, because loans are repaid in cash, most companies use accrual accounting for financial reporting purposes because it matches related revenues and expenses and, thus, provides a more accurate measure of the company's ability to generate profits. Profits are the primary source of cash flow to repay term debt. To illustrate, assume that Photo Dealer, a retailer of photographic equipment, opened for business on November 1, 20x3. The company buys cameras for $125 each, paying for them at the time of purchase. It rents office and warehouse facilities for $500 per month and pays an average of $200 per month for utilities. The company pays the rent and utility bills in cash on the 15th day of each month.

On November 1, Photo Dealer purchases 40 cameras for $125 each (for a total of $5,000). The next day, the company sells 30 cameras at $200 each to a commercial business. The cameras will be delivered to Photo Dealer's customer during November. The cameras are sold on 30-day terms, due December 2. Between December 8th and 20th, Photo Dealer sells 10 cameras to consumers at $100 each—a 50 percent year-end discount intended to sell the remaining inventory. These cameras are delivered at the time of purchase in December, with payment due upon receipt of the merchandise. On a cash basis, the business appears to have lost money in November, whereas profits in December were excellent. Exhibit 1.3 on the following page shows the company's interim income statement, prepared on a cash basis, for November and December.

Exhibit 1.3   Cash-Basis Income Statement

Photo Dealer
Income Statement (Cash Basis)

Item	Month Ended 11/30/x3	Month Ended 12/31/x3
Sales (revenues)	--	$7,000*
Purchases**	$5,000	--
Gross profit	(5,000)	7,000
Utilities and rent expense	700	700
Profit (loss)	(5,700)	6,300

* 30 cameras at $200 and 10 cameras at $100
** 40 cameras at $125 each

Accrual accounting, which matches revenues with expenses, tells quite a different story. It shows that November was a profitable month for Photo Dealer, whereas December was unprofitable. Recall that during November, Photo Dealer sold 30 cameras for $200 each, resulting in a $75 profit on each camera. In December, the company sold 10 cameras for $100 each, for a $25 loss per camera. Although the business had excess cash in December (as shown in the cash-basis statement), the extra cash was not the result of an effective sales strategy. Exhibit 1.4 shows the company's interim income statement calculated on an accrual basis.

In the two income statements for Photo Dealer, the total profits for the two-month period equal the amount of cash generated ($600 in each case). In an actual situation, the amount of profit or loss shown on an accrual-basis income statement normally would be quite different from the company's cash flow. Analyzing cash flow allows the lender to understand the timing and amount of a company's cash requirements over

Exhibit 1.4   Accrual-Basis Income Statement

Photo Dealer
Income Statement (Accrual Basis)

Item	Month Ended 11/30/x3	Month Ended 12/31/x3
Sales (revenues)	$ 6,000*	$ 1,000**
Purchases	3,750***	1,250****
Gross profit	2,250	(250)
Utilities and rent expense	700	700
Profit (loss)	1,550	(950)

* 30 cameras at $200
** 10 cameras at $100
*** 30 cameras at $125
**** 10 cameras at $125

time—information that may not be evident from examining a company's accrual-basis financial statements. Nevertheless, the income statement, constructed using the accrual method, is a better reflection of true company profits.

The components of the income statement involve a company's recognition of income and related expenses as well as the resulting profit or loss. It is important to understand that recognition of profit does not generally coincide with a company's cash flow. In fact, although all companies seek to maximize cash flow in order to pay loans, salaries, dividends, and so on, not all companies try to maximize profits.

Many small businesses use cash accounting. The lender can determine which method is used from the financial statements and the company's tax return. Cash basis financial statements will not have accounts receivable or accounts payable because the sale is not recognized until collected and the related expense until paid. The income tax return should reflect lower taxes if cash accounting is used. Many privately held companies try to minimize reported earnings to reduce taxes. However, this is only a temporary situation. Eventually, revenues will be recognized with no offsetting expenses. The lender needs to be aware of this future tax liability and to determine whether the company is reserving sufficient money for taxes.

TYPES OF FINANCIAL STATEMENTS

Whether or not financial statements are prepared either internally or externally, the critical consideration is the quality and consistency of the information. Depending on how the financial statements were prepared, this information can vary greatly. Financial statements are a report card on the business. They help the lender understand the business's capacity for repaying debt, and they form the basis for monitoring the borrower once the loan is made. Statements also document the company's management decision over time, including how managers deal with changes in the industry.

Internally Prepared Financial Statements

Internally prepared statements are the least reliable because most business owners do not possess the accounting expertise necessary for preparing them. Further, many businesses do not employ an outside accountant or accounting firm to prepare financial statements because company owners claim they cannot justify the cost of a compilation, review, or audit. In today's market, the cost of compilations start at approximately $3,000; audits cost about $10,000 to $15,000. In most companies, these amounts are not high in relation to sales and, therefore, are a justified expense. They are a cost-of-business tax consideration as well. Statements generated in-house from books and records that have not been independently verified may or may not be accurate.

The following questions must be considered when an owner has the financial statements prepared internally by an employee of the company:

- How experienced or competent is the preparer?
- Are the financial records of the company accurate and complete?
- Have all the liabilities been identified and reported?
- How did the preparer recognize income and expense?
- How did the preparer value the inventory?

- What procedures did the preparer use to validate the accounts receivable?
- How were the fixed assets depreciated and valued?
- Can the business owner unduly influence the preparer?
- Even if the person who prepares the information is qualified and the data are available and reliable, how independent is the preparer?
- Is the preparer a day-to-day employee of the company?

Internally prepared information includes interim and fiscal financial statements and may include company tax returns.

Tax Returns

Tax returns may be prepared internally or externally. On occasion, internally prepared tax returns can be used in place of a financial statement. These occasions should be limited to when the lender is lending money to purchase small parcels of commercial real estate, when someone other than the business will repay the loan, or when the amount of the loan is relatively small. Even in these cases, and depending on the risk involved, the lender may want externally prepared tax returns or financial statements.

Information reported in tax returns can be more reliable than that reported in management reports because it is prepared according to rules set by the Internal Revenue Service (IRS) code. A tax return is signed directly under the admonition that: "Under penalties of perjury, I declare that I have examined this return and accompanying schedules and statements and, to the best of my knowledge and belief, they are true, correct, and complete. Declaration of preparer (other than the taxpayer) is based on all information of which preparer has any knowledge."

Tax returns also provide insight into the character and competence of management. Trying to avoid taxes by liberally interpreting IRS guidelines may be acceptable, but evading taxes by deliberately underreporting income is unacceptable and obviously fraudulent. There is little reason to believe the information reported in a customer's income statement, balance sheet, or other document is correct if the information in the customer's tax returns has been doctored. The following tax returns can be useful to a loan officer:

1. *U.S. Individual Tax Return Form 1040*
   This return can be used to verify information contained in personal financial statements. This form is requested for larger consumer loans or for guarantors of corporate loans, or when the borrower is a sole proprietorship. In a sole proprietorship or partnership, personal income tax returns are used to verify sources of income.

2. *Schedule C of Form 1040*
   This form, which is filed with the personal income tax form, contains information about sources of revenue and expenses resulting from profit or loss in a sole proprietorship. The income reported on this schedule is added to any other source of personal income, and from that, the total taxable income is calculated. In several respects, the information in Schedule C parallels the information found in an income statement.

3. *The U.S. Partnership Return Form 1065*

   This is similar to the corporate tax return, except income tax is not calculated or paid by the partnership. The income reported on the return may or may not be available for personal use. The lender will need to verify whether the income was paid out to the partners or retained in the partnership.

4. *U.S. Corporation Income Tax Return Form 1120 or 1120S*

   All corporations are required to file a Form 1120, and S corporations are required to file Form 1120S. A corporate tax return contains an income statement, balance sheet, and supplemental schedules.

5. *Employer's Quarterly Federal Tax Return Form 941*

   This form is required if the net taxes due each quarter are $500 or more, or under certain other conditions. The lender will want to receive a copy to ensure that quarterly taxes are paid on time.

6. *Tax Information Authorization Form 8821*

   This form authorizes the Internal Revenue Service to provide copies of tax returns to third parties.

Interim Financial Statements

Occasionally, only fiscal year-end statements are adequate when considering a loan request. Fiscal year-end statements are prepared for a complete year and should be received within 90 days of the year's end.

When a lender needs more current information, however, he or she can review interim financial statements to see the high and low points of a company's operating cycle. Interim financial statements often are prepared internally on a monthly or quarterly basis. If a company makes annual year-end adjustments, the lender will want to keep this in mind, because adjustments could distort the interim statements. For example, many companies calculate contributions to profit sharing or bonuses during the last month of the fiscal year. Therefore, earnings may be lower at the fiscal year's end than reported in the 11-month interim statement. Interim financial statements usually are received within 20 days of the month's end. Most companies automatically send interim statements to the bank. Timely financial statements are essential to financial analysis.

External Financial Statements

A certified public accountant (CPA) usually prepares external financial statements. To be designated a CPA, an accountant must meet the standards of the profession and be certified or licensed. Each of the 50 states offers certification, and the professional standards are virtually identical nationwide. Even though standards are rigorous, not all CPAs are equally qualified or have the years of professional experience necessary to meet an industry's specific requirements or a client's overall needs. Financial statements prepared by CPAs must conform to GAAP, as discussed earlier. GAAP requires financial statements to be presented fairly and accurately.

"Presents Fairly": A Definition

The phrase *presents fairly* in an audit opinion is not precise. According to GAAP, principal assumptions should be disclosed, their form and substance should be comparable to those of the prior year, and all matters should be noted by certified public accountants. GAAP's stated responsibilities and its members' base of knowledge have evolved to address increasingly complex business environments.

Throughout the history of accounting, there has been a consistent trend toward conservative presentation of financial information. If an asset's value on the open market declines, the accountant typically writes it down to its realizable value. A significant loss of a fixed asset's value due to economic obsolescence constitutes an appropriate reason for a write-down. If, however, an asset increases in value, the accountant does not show the increase but continues to reflect the asset according to GAAP. This custom of writing assets down to net realizable value is applied typically to marketable securities and inventories, although it is sometimes extended to other assets.

Financial Statement Components

CPA-prepared financial statements contain the following components:

- opinion
- balance sheet
- statement of income
- statement of retained earnings
- statement of cash flows
- footnotes

Footnotes

Footnoted disclosures that accompany a financial statement provide significant information to a company's creditors and the lender. In effect, footnotes allow the auditor to comment on the statements relative to GAAP standards. Comments commonly disclose the following: type and location of business; amount of lines of credit and terms; term debt structure; pending lawsuits; unfunded pension liability; terms of leases; and taxable events. Three years of footnotes for Turner Electronic Corporation are provided in the *Master Case Book*.

Types of Externally Prepared Financial Statements

Externally prepared statements are prepared as a compilation, review, or audit.

Compilation Financial Statements

A **compilation** financial statement presents the financial data obtained from the borrower in a basic financial statement form. The CPA does not express any degree of assurance regarding the data. A compilation, which may include footnotes, is available to nonpublic companies only. Exhibit 1.5 summarizes the CPA's requirements for a compilation statement.

Most externally prepared financial statements received by lenders are compilations. Because of the limited process used by the CPA, the lender must take the time to understand thoroughly all entries and how they were prepared. For example, the lender will need to determine if there is a reserve for bad debts or if bad debts are expenses, what type of inventory valuation method is used, and so forth. Exhibit 1.6 illustrates a compilation opinion.

Review Financial Statements

In a **review** financial statement, the CPA expresses no opinion of the financial statements. Exhibit 1.7 on the following page summarizes the CPA's requirements.

Review financial statements are the second most common form of statement received by lenders. These statements offer additional assurances to lenders and allow the lender to focus on the financial statements. Lenders still must have a good understanding of the various entries to the statements and the accounting techniques applied. Exhibit 1.8 on the following page illustrates a sample of a review opinion.

Audited Financial Statements

With an **audit,** the CPA expresses an independent opinion on the fairness of the financial statements. To render an opinion, the CPA must evaluate the quality of the customer's accounting systems. The CPA also must test the numbers by verifying the accounts receivable, inventory, and accounts payable. The lender usually requires an audit when:

Exhibit 1.5   Compilation Statement Requirements

- Possess a general understanding of the client's business transactions and the form of its accounting records
- Be familiar with stated qualifications of the client's account personnel to consider the need for adjustments to the account records
- Read the financial statements and consider whether they are appropriate in form and content and free from obvious material errors
- Does not have to be independent but must disclose the fact that he/she is not independent

---

Exhibit 1.6   Compilation Opinion

We have compiled the accompanying balance sheet of Turner Electronic Corporation as of December 31, 20x2, and the related statements of income, retained earnings, and changes in financial position for the year ended, in accordance with standards established by the American Institute of Certified Public Accountants.

A compilation is limited to presenting information, in the form of financial statements, that is the representation of management. We have not audited or reviewed the accompanying financial statements and, accordingly, do not express an opinion or any other form of assurance about them.

Exhibit 1.7 Review Statement Requirements

- Obtain knowledge of the accounting principles and practices of the client's industry.
- Acquire a general understanding of the client's business, including its organization and how it functions.
- Make inquiries about the client's personnel accounting policies, record keeping procedures, actions of owners and management that may affect financial statements, subsequent events, changes in business, activities, and related party transactions.
- Perform analytical procedures to identify and explain unusual items or trends reflected in the financial statements.
- Determine, on the basis of information furnished to the CPA, that financial statements conform to generally accepted accounting principles.
- Be independent.

Exhibit 1.8 Review Opinion

We have reviewed the accompanying balance sheet of Turner Electronic Corporation as of December 31, 20x2, and the related statements of income, retained earnings, and cash flows for the year ended, in accordance with standards established by the American Institute of Certified Public Accountants. All information included in these financial statements is the representation of the management of Turner Electronic Corporation.

A review consists primarily of inquiries of company personnel and analytical procedures applied to financial data. It is substantially less in scope than an examination in accordance with generally accepted auditing standards—the objective of which is the expression of an opinion regarding the financial standards taken as a whole. Accordingly, we do not express such an opinion.

Based on our review, we are not aware of any material modifications that should be made to the accompanying financial statements in order for them to conform to generally accepted accounting principles.

- loan policy dictates
- the loan is large
- risk is high relative to financial strength of the borrower
- the term of the loan is long

Examining the Auditor's Opinion

Audited financial statements are prepared using tests that determine whether the statements are in accordance with the principles and policies promulgated by the SEC and the FASB. Management often is tempted to construct internally prepared financial statements in a manner that puts the company's performance in the most favorable light. Tests performed by auditors are designed to reveal practices, should they exist, that may not present the company fairly. Another factor that may make the results of an audit relatively muddy is the auditor's desire to continue to be the accounting firm for the business it is auditing. Because of these factors, the word *fair* more appropriately describes the result of an audit than the word financial lenders would like to see—*accurate*. As discussed earlier, in accordance with GAAP standards, financial statements must be presented fairly and accurately. However, a fair presentation is not always accurate.

The most famous case of an unqualified opinion of a company that submitted financial statements was Enron Corporation. On December 2, 2001, Enron, a $700 billion company, filed for bankruptcy. The bankruptcy filing came after the company announced it had overstated earnings by approximately $600 million dollars. Later, the on-site accountant was charged with shredding work documents related to the audit. This example makes it clear that relying solely on audited statements will not prevent or protect a bank from lending to a company that may have significant problems. The audit itself, as in the Enron case, does not prevent misrepresentation to either company management or potential lenders. This and other factors make the accountant's job complicated. Although regulatory authorities attempt to keep financial reporting to investors at a high standard, financial statements need to be technically interpreted by the lender, as discussed earlier.

In audited financial statements, the CPA may express an unqualified opinion, a qualified audit opinion, an adverse audit opinion, or a disclaimer opinion. The first page of the audit will contain the opinion of the auditor.

For analysis, the qualified opinion is comparable to an unqualified opinion and, depending on the reason for the qualification, is usually suitable. A financial statement with a disclaimer opinion would be considered unaudited, but it could have been prepared in accordance with GAAP. An adverse opinion is of questionable value.

Audited financial statements differ from unaudited statements in one highly important aspect—the degree of confirmation of asset, liability, sales, and expense account balances. For example, in the normal course of an audit engagement, inventory levels are physically sampled and statistically selected accounts receivables are confirmed. In the preparation of compilation or review statements, confirmation is not done, or is not done with the same thoroughness or independence as for an audited financial statement.

The professional standards of certified public accountants require CPA's to be independent from the customer or to disclose business or family relationships that might inhibit the exercise of independent judgment. The presence of audited financials (and their implications) gives a certain comfort level to the creditors of the company. The reliance on analysis of less-than-audited statements by creditors needs to be clearly understood, and the bank should be protected with collateral, personal guarantees of the owners, or other appropriate considerations.

With audited financial statements, a CPA usually issues a **management letter.** Sent to the Board of Directors or management of the company, the letter expresses operational concerns or deficiencies not expressed in the audit (see exhibit 1.9 on the following page). Because it is not part of the audit, the lender must request a copy of the management letter.

Unqualified Audit Opinion

In an **unqualified audit opinion,** management receives the highest accolade for "presenting fairly the financial position and results of operations and changes in financial position for the period involved." The three paragraphs of the unqualified opinion describe what the auditors found, how the auditors found it, and what the auditors think about the findings. Exhibit 1.10 on page 21 illustrates an unqualified opinion.

Exhibit 1.9 Management Letter

To the Board of Directors of Turner Electronic Corporation:

In planning and performing our audit of the financial statements of the Turner Electronic Corporation for the year ended December 31, 20x2, we considered its internal control structure in order to determine our auditing procedures for the purpose of expressing our opinion on the financial statements and not to provide assurance on the internal control structure. However, we noted certain matters involving the internal control structure and its operation that we consider to be reportable conditions under standards established by the American Institute of Certified Public Accountants. Reportable conditions involve matters coming to our attention relating to significant deficiencies in the design or operation of the internal control structure that, in our judgment, could adversely affect the organization's ability to record, process, summarize, and report financial data consistent with the assertions of management in the financial statements.

NOTE: The auditor would include paragraph(s) to describe any reportable conditions noted. Internal controls include such items as the accuracy of computer-generated information due to obsolete software, lack of dual control over certain procedures, and operational procedures that need to be corrected. If a material weakness in the internal control structure were noted, the auditor would include the following discussion:

A material weakness is a reportable condition in which the design or operation of one or more of the internal control structure elements does not reduce the risk of errors or irregularities to a relatively low level that would be material to the financial statements being audited. Employees in the normal course of performing their assigned functions may not be able to detect a material weakness within a timely period.

Our consideration of the internal control structure would not necessarily disclose all matters in the internal control structure that *might* be reportable conditions and, accordingly, would not necessarily disclose all reportable conditions considered to be material weaknesses as defined above.

NOTE: The auditor would include paragraph(s) to describe any material weaknesses noted. For example: Inventory is not monitored properly and is subject to employee theft.

This report is intended solely for the information and use of the audit committee (board of directors, board of trustees, or owners in owner-managed enterprises), management, and others within the organization.

Qualified Opinion

In a **qualified audit opinion,** the statements fairly present the financial position and results of the operations—with reservations. These reservations could include certain qualifications about the **scope of the auditor's engagement** (i.e., the range of action and inquiry used in the audit) at the audited company or uncertainties about the future, which cannot be resolved or the effects of which cannot be estimated. These reservations, usually phrased "except for" and "subject to," are exemplified in exhibit 1.11.

Disclaimer Opinion

In a **disclaimer opinion,** accountants cannot express an opinion because of limitations in the scope of the auditing firm's engagement or uncertainties about the future that cannot be resolved or the effect of which cannot be estimated. For example, a lawsuit may be pending against the business that, in the accountant's opinion, might cause the

Exhibit 1.10 Unqualified Audit Opinion

We have audited the accompanying balance sheets of Turner Electronic Corporation as of December 31, 20x2, and December 31, 20x1, and the related statements of income, retained earnings, and cash flows for the years then ended. These financial statements are the responsibility of the company's management. Our responsibility is to express an opinion on these financial statements based on our audits.

We conducted our audits in accordance with generally accepted auditing standards. These standards require that we plan and perform the audit to obtain reasonable assurance about whether the financial statements are free of material misstatement. An audit includes examining, on a test basis, evidence supporting the amounts and disclosures in the financial statements. An audit also includes assessing the accounting principles used and significant estimates made by management, as well as evaluating the overall financial statement presentation. We believe our audits provide a reasonable basis for our opinion.

In our opinion, the financial statements referred to above present fairly, in all material respects, the financial position of Turner Electronic Corporation at December 31, 20x2, and December 31, 20x1, and the results of its operations and its cash flow for the years then ended in conformity with generally accepted accounting principles.

Exhibit 1.11 Qualified Audit Opinion

We have audited the accompanying balance sheets of Turner Electronic Corporation as of December 31, 20x2, and December 31, 20x1, and the related statements of income, retained earnings, and cash flows for the years then ended. These financial statements are the responsibility of the company's management. Our responsibility is to express an opinion on these financial statements based on our audits.

We conducted our audits in accordance with generally accepted auditing standards. These standards require that we plan and perform the audit to obtain reasonable assurance about whether the financial statements are free of material misstatement. An audit includes examining, on a test basis, evidence supporting the amounts and disclosures in the financial statements. An audit also includes assessing the accounting principles used and significant estimates made by management, as well as evaluating the overall financial statement presentation. We believe our audits provide a reasonable basis for our opinion.

In the accompanying balance sheets, the company has excluded from property and debt certain lease obligations that, in our opinion, should be capitalized in order to conform to generally accepted accounting principles. If these lease obligations were capitalized, property would be increased by $X thousand and $X thousand, long-term debt would be increased by $X thousand and $X thousand, the current portion of long-term debt would be increased by $X thousand and $X thousand, and retained earnings would be increased by $X thousand and $X thousand as of December 31, 20x2, and 20x1, respectively. Additionally, net income would be increased by $X thousand and $X thousand and earnings per share would be increased by $X.XX and $X.XX, respectively, for the years then ended.

In our opinion, except for the effects of not capitalizing certain lease obligations as discussed in the preceding paragraph, the financial statements referred to above present fairly, in all material respects, the financial position of Turner Electronic Corporation at December 31, 20x2, and December 31, 20x1, and the results of its operations and its cash flows for the years then ended, in conformity with generally accepted accounting principles.

business to be liquidated if lost. A disclaimer opinion includes the **review** and **compilation opinions**. This means that auditors consolidated the statements and prepared acknowledgments without independently verifying data—an important part of any audit, as illustrated in exhibit 1.12.

Adverse Audit Opinion

In an adverse audit opinion, statements do not fairly present the financial position or results of operations in conformity with generally accepted accounting principles, as illustrated in exhibit 1.13. The company illustrated in exhibit 1.13 has poor accounting procedures because it carries its property, plant, and equipment at current appraised value. GAAP requires the company to carry these items at cost less depreciation. An adverse opinion is rarely encountered.

OTHER COMPONENT ANALYSIS

After examining the opinion and footnotes, the lender should analyze management reports, the income statement, balance sheet, statement of retained earnings, and statement of cash flows and complete other calculations based on the financial statements.

Management Plans and Reports

Information from business and personal financial statements is, by itself, insufficient to measure performance because the information may not be adequately detailed. Management plans and reports can provide additional insight, but the usefulness of these reports varies among companies.

Business and Strategic Plan

Many businesses prepare an annual business and strategic plan that summarizes the company's goals in the market, types of product, management structure, sales growth, and financial results for the coming year. The details of a business and strategic plan vary by the size of the business and the organizational ability of the owner.

Exhibit 1.12   Disclaimer Opinion

We have been engaged to audit the accompanying balance sheets of Turner Electronic Corporation as of December 31, 20x2, and December 31, 20x1, and the related statements of income, retained earnings, and cash flows for the years then ended. These financial statements are the responsibility of the company's management.

The company did not make a count of its physical inventory in 20x2 or 20x1, stated in the accompanying financial statements at $X thousand as of December 31, 20x2, and $X thousand as of December 31, 20x1. Further, evidence supporting the cost of property and equipment acquired prior to December 31, 20x1, is no longer available. The company's records do not permit the application of other auditing procedures to inventories or property and equipment.

Because the company did not take physical inventories, and we were not able to apply other auditing procedures to satisfy ourselves as to inventory quantities and the cost of property and equipment, the scope of our work was not sufficient to enable us to express, and we do not express, an opinion on these financial statements.

Exhibit 1.13 Adverse Audit Opinion

We have audited the accompanying balance sheets of Turner Electronic Corporation as of December 31, 20x2, and December 31, 20x1, and the related statements of income, retained earnings, and cash flows for the years then ended. These financial statements are the responsibility of the company's management. Our responsibility is to express an opinion on these financial statements based on our audits.

We conducted our audits in accordance with generally accepted auditing standards. Those standards require that we plan and perform the audit to obtain reasonable assurance about whether the financial statements are free of material misstatement. An audit includes examining, on a test basis, evidence supporting the amounts and disclosures in the financial statements. An audit also includes assessing the accounting principles used and significant estimates made by management, as well as evaluating the overall financial presentation. We believe our audits provide a reasonable basis for our opinion.

As discussed in Note X to the financial statements, the company carries its property, plant, and equipment accounts at appraisal values, and provides depreciation on the basis of such values. Further, the company does not recognize deferred income taxes with respect to differences between financial income and taxable income arising because of the use, for income tax purposes, of the installment method of reporting gross profit from certain types of sales. Generally accepted accounting principles require that property, plant, and equipment be stated at an amount not in excess of cost, reduced by depreciation based on such amounts, and that deferred income taxes be recognized.

Because of the departures from generally accepted accounting principles discussed in the preceding paragraph, as of December 31, 20x2, and December 31, 20x1, inventories have been increased $X thousand and $X thousand by inclusion in manufacturing overhead of depreciation in excess of that based on cost; property, plant and equipment, less accumulated depreciation, are carried at $X thousand and $X thousand in excess of an amount based on the cost to the company; and deferred income taxes of $X thousand and $X thousand have not been recognized, resulting in an increase of $X thousand and $X thousand in retained earnings and in appraisal surplus of $X thousand and $X thousand, respectively. For the years ended December 31, 20x2, and December 31, 20x1, cost of goods sold has been increased $X thousand and $X thousand, respectively, because of the effects of the depreciation accounting referred to above, and deferred income taxes of $X thousand and $X thousand have not been recognized, resulting in an increase in net income of $X thousand and $X thousand, respectively.

In our opinion, because of the effects of the matters discussed in the preceding paragraphs, the financial statements referred to above do not present fairly, in conformity with generally accepted accounting principles, the financial position of Turner Electronic Corporation at December 31, 20x2, and December 31, 20x1, or the results of its operations or cash flows for the years then ended.

Operation and Capital Budgets

Almost every well-run company develops operation and capital budgets that specify how the company funds are to be spent in the upcoming year. Operation budgets provide insight into a company's plans for allocation of its resources. Capital budgets provide insight into future financing needs for fixed-asset purchases.

Accounts Receivable Aging

This report lists individual customer accounts and the amounts due by billing dates in aging categories. This includes accounts whose balance is current and those that are 30, 60, or 90 days past due. This report also identifies amounts that may be uncollectible.

Inventory Analysis

Companies often analyze inventory from a number of different perspectives, for example, age, type, location, and quantity. A schedule of inventory aging or turnover often identifies slow-moving products. Depending on the type of company, inventory may be raw material, work-in-process, or finished goods. Many companies have multiple locations, and the quantity of inventory needed will vary by location.

Income Statement Analysis

The **income statement**—also called a profit and loss statement (P & L statement) or earnings statement—is one of the most important sources of information about a company. The income statement influences most balance sheet components. The following chart shows the components of a balance sheet that are taken from the income statement:

Income Statement	Balance Sheet
Cash sales	Cash
Credit sales	Accounts receivable
Cost of goods sold	Inventory, accounts payable
Depreciation	Fixed assets
Net profit (loss)	Retained earnings

Over a period of time, the income statement reflects how total revenues (or sales) and expenses lead to the net profit (or loss) for that period. The terms "revenue" and "sales" often are used interchangeably. Sales generally refer to companies that sell a product. Revenues generally refer to companies that provide a service.

The analysis consists of examining the quality and consistency of sales/revenues and accuracy of the expenses. The income statement identifies a company's growth as evidenced by the increases in sales/revenues and also reveals the company's viability through profitable operations. A consistently unprofitable company would not be considered viable.

Income statement analysis includes analyzing the break-even point of the company. Break-even analysis is the point at which the sum of fixed and variable costs meet.

Balance Sheet Analysis

The **balance sheet** is a point-in-time financial picture of the company, usually as of the last day of a month, a quarter, or the company's fiscal year. The basic structure of the balance sheet can be stated as a simple equation:

$$\text{Assets} - \text{Liabilities} = \text{Net Worth}$$

Balance sheet analysis entails a line-by-line evaluation of the company's assets and liabilities (or debt) and the difference between the two—its net worth (or equity). *Net worth* and *equity* are used interchangeably. The purpose of balance sheet analysis is to determine the liquidity and solvency of the company. Liquidity is the ability of the company to convert its assets to cash in time to pay its liabilities as they become due. Solvency is the ability of the company to sell its assets for sufficient cash to pay all of its liabilities.

Statement of Cash Flow Analysis

The third component of a financial statement to be analyzed is the statement of cash flows. As its name implies, this statement of a company's business operations shows how a company obtains and uses its cash resources. The data to construct a statement of cash flows come from the income statement and the balance sheet.

Because debt is repaid with cash, the statement of cash flows helps the lender assess both the company's funding needs and its sources of repayment. The statement of cash flows shows inflows and outflows of cash categorized as operating activities, investing activities, and financing activities. If the financial statement is an audit, the accountant includes a statement of cash flows. In compilation and review statements, the cash flow statement may or may not be included.

If possible, borrowers should be required to submit a statement of cash flows as part of their financial documentation in accordance with SFAS No. 95. Some borrowers, especially those submitting statements that have not been prepared by outside auditors, cannot or will not prepare a statement of cash flows. In this case, the lender can calculate the information in the spreading process.

Ratio Analysis

Ratios are not only the best known and most widely used of all financial statement analysis tools, they are the most overrated and most widely misused as well. Ratios allow the lender to study the relationship and trends over time between various components of financial statements, such as assets and liabilities or expenses and revenues. Although ratios are easily calculated, their correct interpretation is problematic. The primary classes of ratios are liquidity, financial leverage, coverage, and profit.

Preparing Forecasts

Forecasts, basic to loan analysis, are presented in numerical form. When forecasting, it is assumed that the borrower will be able to repay the principal and interest. Two tools used in this analysis are **cash budgets** and **pro formas**. A cash budget projects the cash position of a company during a short period of time (usually less than one year). Using revenues/sales as its primary basis, a pro forma statement forecasts what a company income statement and balance sheet will look like after any new debt is added.

Presented in the form of a monthly financial forecast, a cash budget forecasts a company's cash receipts and payments on a month-to-month basis. This enables the lender to gauge a business's peak credit needs and its ability to generate sufficient cash to repay short-term loans during the term of its operating cycle. The cash budget also helps a lender determine whether a company's borrowing needs are long- or short-term. Cash budgets are particularly useful in determining the financial needs of borrowers with seasonal operating cycles (such as a toy store that rings up half of its total sales in the last two months of each year). Because management controls the outflows of cash, a company's management should prepare cash budgets.

Creating one- to three-year forecasts (referred to as pro forma statements) forces the lender to apply information gathered from historical financial statements to estimate future level of sales. Examining a company-provided forecast involves evaluating the company's underlying assumptions as well as the expected economic, competitive, and regulatory environments in which the company will operate. For example, if the company is forecasting sales growth of 10 percent per year and the expected economic and industry growth is 4 percent, the lender clearly will want to understand why the company expects to grow faster.

Normally, the projections depend on the size and term of the requested loan. Because management-submitted pro formas tend to be biased, however, commercial lenders often create their own prognosis for a company, based on what they consider to be more likely assumptions (such as lower profit margins).

Limitations of Analysis

Although financial statement analysis is a critical tool in commercial lending activities, it has some important limitations. First, its success depends on the reliability and completeness of the information being analyzed. Yet, even with unqualified audit opinions, financial statement analysis is not an exact science providing absolute conclusions. Because analysis deals with future uncertainties, it is better at formulating questions and projecting possibilities than it is at providing definitive answers.

Technical analysis alone cannot provide a complete understanding of the borrower. Banks do not base loan decisions on financial statement analysis alone; a borrower's nonfinancial strengths and weaknesses must be considered. Nonfinancial strengths include the company's plant capacity, pending lawsuits, technology changes, and industry trends. These concerns are not always apparent in the financial statement. In addition, pricing, negotiation of specific terms, the bank's willingness to assume risk, and the availability of funds are important aspects of the decision to extend or deny credit.

SUMMARY

Financial statement analysis is used to determine the amount of risk involved in a lending situation. It involves the technical calculation and interpretation of financial information to assess a company's past performance, present condition, and future viability. This assessment is expressed in the formula

$$\text{Strengths} - \text{Weaknesses} > \text{Uncertainties} = \text{Acceptable Credit Risk}$$

The depth of the analysis may be influenced by the size, purpose, and term of the loan or, in the case of a problem loan, the specific circumstances surrounding that loan. Financial statement analysis involves the following:

1. Obtaining reliable and current financial information
2. Processing the statement by spreading and common-sizing the information
3. Completing trend and comparative analysis
4. Preparing written trend, comparative, and continuity evaluations of the historical statements by focusing on the company's operations (as seen in its income statement), its financial structure (as seen in its balance sheets), and its sources and uses of cash (as seen in the statement of cash flows).

After completing all of these analytical steps, the lender must interpret the information in light of the company's nonfinancial strengths and weaknesses and the total environment in which the company operates.

Financial statements may be prepared internally or externally. Internal statements include interim and fiscal year statements. Tax returns may be prepared internally or externally. External statements include compilations, reviews, and audits. Compilations are the most common form of externally prepared financial statements received. Audited financial statements express an opinion by a CPA. The four types of opinion are unqualified, qualified, disclaimer, and adverse. Audits also include a management letter about the operations of the company.

To supplement the analysis, the lender needs to consider various management reports. Management reports vary from business and strategic plans to capital budgets to accounts receivable aging reports. Financial analysis also involves using ratios to determine liquidity, financial leverage, coverage and profit trends, analyzing cash budgets for short-term requests, and preparing pro forma projections for long-term requests.

QUESTIONS FOR DISCUSSION

1. Give an example of the difference between accrual and cash accounting.
2. Define the balance sheet equation.
3. How is a compilation statement different from an audited statement?
4. The local pizza shop is requesting a loan to purchase a new oven. What management reports would you request and why?
5. A company values its equipment at current market value on its financial statement. What type of audit opinion would you expect to receive?

Exercise 1

Match the following terms with the following definitions.

Terms

1. ___ FASB		6. ___ Fiscal year-end statement	
2. ___ Interim statement		7. ___ Balance sheet	
3. ___ Accrual accounting		8. ___ Compilation	
4. ___ GAAP		9. ___ Income statement	
5. ___ Cash accounting		10. ___ Unqualified opinion	

Definitions

A. The rules, conventions, practices, and procedures that form the foundation for financial accounting.

B. The degree of work that is less in scope than a review or audit performed by a public accounting firm in conjunction with the issuance of financial statements of a nonpublic entity. As such, the accountant does not express an opinion or give any other form of assurance on the financial statements.

C. Financial statements issued for periods shorter than one year.

D. An opinion rendered by an independent auditor of financial statements that says that the financial statements fairly present the financial position, the results of operations, and the changes in financial position for the company.

E. Organization that coordinates the preparation of and changes to generally accepted accounting principles.

F. A detailed list of assets, liabilities, and owners' equity (net worth) showing a company's financial position at a specific time.

G. An accounting system in which revenues and expenses are recorded and realized only when the accompanying cash inflow or outflow occurs, without regard to the actual period to which the transactions apply.

H. A method of accounting in which revenue is recognized when earned, expenses are recognized when incurred, and other changes in financial condition are recognized as they occur, without regard to the timing of the actual cash receipts and expenditures.

I. A financial statement prepared as of the company's legal year-end.

J. A financial statement that shows a summary of a firm's or individual's income and expenses for a specific period.

Exercise 2

The local retail hardware store purchases a riding lawnmower for $300 on May 3 for cash. On May 10, the lawnmower is sold for $500 on credit due in 30 days.

- What would the *accrual* financial statement show for sales, costs, and profit in May? In June?
- What would the *cash* financial statement show for sales, costs, and profit in May? In June?

2

BUSINESS STRUCTURE AND ORGANIZATION

LEARNING OBJECTIVES

After studying *Business Structure and Organization*, you will be able to

- define the basic types of legal structure of a business entity,
- explain the operating cycle for a manufacturer, wholesaler, retailer, service, and agricultural company,
- identify the reasons each type of business borrows money, its sources of repayment, and the lending risk,
- explain how a company's cash flow cycle can affect debt requirements and repayment sources,
- identify the various borrowing arrangements used to structure a business loan,
- describe the way alternative lending sources complement or compete with banks, and
- define key terms that appear in **bold** type in the text.

INTRODUCTION

A company's ownership can be structured legally as a sole proprietorship, a partnership, a corporation, an S corporation, or a limited liability company. Each structure influences the net worth section of the balance sheet and therefore affects the approach the lender takes in analyzing financial statements.

Business entities can be classified as manufacturers, wholesalers, retailers, service, or agricultural companies. Each type of business has **working assets** and a unique **operating cycle**. Working assets—accounts receivable, inventory, and equipment—are the primary assets used to generate revenue or the primary assets on the balance sheet. The operating cycle explains how the business uses cash and the working assets to produce a product or service for sale. By understanding the operating cycle of each type of business, the lender can identify the purpose, repayment possibilities, and risks in lending to that type of business. The operating cycle also assists the lender by providing a mental picture of the possible income statement and balance sheet components.

Cash, and only cash, repays loans. Understanding cash flow cycles and how cash is generated and used are key to the financial analysis process. The cash flow cycle explains the purpose of the loan and the sources of repayment. Businesses use loans to purchase inventory, fund accounts receivable, pay labor, and finance equipment. Additional sources of financing include initial capital, accounts payable, bank debt, and additional capital provided by the owners.

Matching the purpose of the loan and repayment sources identifies the possible loan structures. Possible loan structures include:

- special commitment loans
- revolving lines of credit
- seasonal lines of credit
- permanent working capital loans
- letters of credit
- term loans
- leases

When a lender, due to either the loan amount or the type of credit risk, cannot meet a client's loan requirements, the lender may refer the client to a competing or complementing source, such as:

- trade creditors
- commercial finance companies
- commercial sales finance companies
- leasing companies
- insurance companies
- brokerage firms

LEGAL STRUCTURES

Sole Proprietorships

Most businesses in the United States are set up as sole proprietorships. More often than not, when a carpenter, physician, electrician, or other service professional operates a small business, it is structured as a sole proprietorship.

A sole proprietorship is the easiest business structure to set up because there are virtually no documents to file (some states, however, may require a certificate of assumed name to be filed). Typically, there is no government approval to seek other than federal, state, or local licenses. However, federal, state, and local filings related to payroll, sales, and property taxes could all be useful documents for purposes of credit analysis.

In a sole proprietorship, the owner controls the business and is completely responsible for its operations. Regardless of how the business's income is used, all business profits and losses are those of the proprietor. For example, if the 20x3 net income of a sole proprietorship is $50,000, of which $25,000 is reinvested in the business, the company is taxed on the whole $50,000. Tax is calculated at the individual rate and not at the corporate income tax rate. The assets, debt, and income of the owner and the business are one and the same. Any legal claim against business assets is treated as a claim against the owner's personal assets.

Although the personal liability of a sole proprietorship poses a risk for the owner, this liability is of some benefit when trying to collateralize a loan. A loan officer can take personal and business assets into account when evaluating the potential collateral of a sole proprietorship. When analyzing a sole proprietorship, a lender requests and reviews a personal financial statement, personal tax return, and financial statements of the sole proprietorship business entity. The Internal Revenue Service (IRS) does not require a sole proprietorship to prepare a balance sheet. A balance sheet, however, will be included with the personal financial statement of the owner. To properly analyze the business performance, business assets and liabilities are separated out.

General Partnerships

A business jointly owned by two or more persons is a **general partnership**. All that is necessary to set up a general partnership is a written agreement. The agreement includes, for example, how the partners would buy each other out if necessary, how the profits will be divided, and who is authorized to borrow on the partnership's behalf. In theory, each partner has a right to participate in the management of the company. In practice, control and authority usually are divided according to areas of expertise. The division of responsibility frequently falls between the technical and management aspects of the business operation.

To meet tax-reporting requirements, the general partners file a balance sheet and income statement at least once per year. Profits or losses are divided among the partners according to the terms of the agreement. The value of each partner's capital is found in the net worth section of the balance sheet under the partner's capital account. Each partner lists capital accounts separately. All business income from a general partnership is regarded as the income of the owners. It is taxed at individual income tax rates and not at corporate tax rates. All partners are, separate and without limitation, liable for the indebtedness of the general partnership. When one partner obtains debt in the name of the partnership, all partners are personally liable for the debt. Therefore, personal and business assets are considered collateral for partnership loans.

A variation of a partnership, in which a partner's liability is limited to the amount invested, is called a limited partnership. A limited partnership has a general partner and then a number of limited partners who participate as minority investors. Their share of profits or losses is limited by agreement. A limited partner cannot be involved in managing the concern. The general partner of a limited partnership may have unlimited liability. Most banks, nevertheless, do not lend to limited partnerships.

Corporations

A **corporation** is a legal entity that has a distinct existence apart from its owners. Corporations pay taxes, buy and sell assets, incur liabilities, and can sue or be sued. Unlike sole proprietorships, a corporation is highly regulated by the federal government and the state in which it conducts business. Corporations are either privately held by one or more persons or publicly held by thousands of shareholders. For the latter, a stock certificate is issued to establish individual corporate ownership.

Because a corporation is recognized as an entity, separate from its owners, it is entitled to all net income. And corporate income is taxed at corporate tax rates. The portion of net income paid out to shareholders is called dividends, which reduce retained earnings and therefore reduce total equity. Dividends are not an allowable expense deduction for a corporation and therefore are subject to double taxation— once at the corporate rate and again at the rate paid by the owner of the stock. Due to the double taxation of dividends, most privately held corporations do not pay dividends. The net profit of a privately held corporation usually is managed by the owner's salary or other benefits, such as company vehicles, which are expenses on the income statement.

One advantage of a corporation is that it protects its owners from personal exposure to indebtedness. If a corporation is sued or fails to pay an obligation, the personal liability of the owners is limited to the owners' holdings in the company. Personal assets are not at risk. Only business assets are pledged to secure loans. Because of this, many banks require the owners of privately held corporations to personally guarantee any debt. On occasion, the bank may request that an owner's personal assets be used to secure a personal guaranty.

Corporations retain their legal existence regardless of any changes in ownership. A sole proprietorship or a general partnership ceases to exist upon the death of the owner or partners.

S Corporations

S corporations are a popular form of business structure. Their popularity and subsequent growth coincided with the enactment of the Tax Reform Act of 1986, which eliminated several corporate and personal tax deductions and significantly lowered marginal income tax rates for individuals. As a result, corporate income is taxed at a higher tax rate than personal income. With an S corporation, however, all net income from the corporation is taxed at the individual income tax rate. A dividend is usually taken for the amount of the taxes. The amount of profit withdrawn as a dividend from an S corporation to pay income taxes should not be greater than the individual tax liability. Although the income appears on the personal tax return, lenders should not assume it is available for personal use.

S corporations also differ from corporations in two major respects: they may not have more than 75 shareholders and they may issue one class of common stock only.

Limited Liability Companies

A limited liability company (**LLC**), which is authorized in most states, offers several advantages to business owners. Like S corporations, LLCs are taxed at the individual income tax rate and, as with a corporation, owners of LLCs have no personal liability. Also, the number of shareholders in an LLC is not limited; owners may include corporations, trusts, and partnerships. Unlike corporations, however, LLCs have a limited life, and ownership interest is not freely transferable. LLCs terminate at a specified termination date or after the death, withdrawal, expulsion, bankruptcy, or dissolution of a member. LLCs must have more than one owner.

Some states have a variation of the LLC, called a Limited Liability Partnership (LLP). With more states authorizing LLCs and LLPs, and with each state setting its own laws, the commercial loan officer must understand the documentation process and how to structure loans peroperly for all types of business legal structures (see exhibit 2.1 on the following page). LLCs and LLPs have not been listed in exhibit 2.1 because the legal structure, taxation, and transfer ownership vary from state to state. Once the lender understands the company's legal structure, the next step is to identify and examine the operating structure.

TYPES OF BUSINESS OPERATING STRUCTURES

Before examining specific financial data, the lender should understand the company, its operating cycle, and environment. This knowledge provides a context for the financial statement analysis and enables the lender to put the figures in a meaningful perspective. To learn about the basic qualities of an individual business, a lender can take the following steps:

- *Understand the **working assets***—assets primarily used to generate revenue are key components on the balance sheet. Accounts receivable is the working asset for a lawyer who provides services sold on credit. Inventory is the working asset for a retailer of linens who sells products for cash. For a restaurant that sells food for cash, the working asset is equipment.

- *Identify the **operating cycle***—define the time it takes a business to add value to raw materials, purchase finished products, hire labor to produce and sell the product or service, and collect the cash from the sale. The operating cycle defines how the working assets are used in the business.

- *Analyze the **cash flow cycle***—understand how cash is used and generated, and the timing of financing and loan repayment.

Exhibit 2.1   Business Legal Structures

Type of Business	Sole Proprietorships	General Partnerships	Sub Chapter S Corporations	Corporations
Ownership	1 person	2 or more people personally own	1 or more people by owning shares of stock	1 or more people or other corporations by shares of stock
Liability	All at risk: business and personal assets	All at risk: business and personal assets	Only investment amount at risk	Only investment amount at risk
Taxation	Taxed personally only. All income flows to single owner to be taxed	Taxed personally only. Income may flow to parteners by distribution formula	Taxed personally only. Income remains in corporation but dividend is paid to owners for taxes	Corporation taxed as entity and dividends paid to shareholders are taxed personally
Number of owners	1 person	Infinite number of people	No more than 75 people	Infinite number of people and/or corporations
Transfer of ownership	Voluntarily, bankruptcy, or upon death	Voluntarily, bankruptcy, or upon death	Voluntarily by sales of stock, bankruptcy	Voluntarily by sales of stock, bankruptcy
Life	Stops with death of owner	Stops with death of any partener	May go on forever	May go on forever
Management	Limited mostly to sole owner	Limited to parteners	Unlimited	Unlimited
Continuity	Limited by life of owner	Limited by life of any one partener	Unlimited	Unlimited
Size	Normally small	Small to large	Small to large	Small to gigantic

The primary factor a lender should take into consideration from the onset is the type of business in which the loan applicant is engaged—that is, whether it is a manufacturing, wholesaling, retailing, service, or agricultural company. Each category of business operation has particular operating cycles, unique types of credit needs, and various sources of financing or repayment.

The role each business operating structure plays in producing and distributing a product illustrates the distinctions among manufacturers, wholesalers, retailers, service, and agricultural companies. Before canned peas reach a consumer's dinner table, one or more manufacturers, wholesalers, retailers, and service companies have been involved in the process that began with the growing of fresh peas. A manufacturer of canned goods first buys fresh peas from an agricultural company (the farm), with the ultimate destination being thousands of neighborhood grocery stores. Rather than form an account relationship with each grocery store, the manufacturer turns to a wholesaler, which buys large quantities of canned goods for eventual distribution to its customers.

The wholesaler distributes the canned peas to the grocery stores, which are retailers. On occasion, the wholesaler overestimates the grocery stores' demands for canned goods and ends up with more inventory than needed. Due to a lack of storage space, the wholesaler stores the canned goods with a storage company until needed. The storage company, which has no direct hand in the manufacturing, wholesaling, or retailing of the canned goods, is a service company.

Businesses of the same type tend to have certain similarities, such as operating cycles of the same duration, requirements for cash or credit, and asset and liability structures. The fact that many businesses today are diversified—that is, they operate in more than one type of business—complicates the examination significantly. For example, if a company manufactures and wholesales canned goods, the lender should review the various components of the company separately. The company should provide unconsolidated or separate statements by division at the request of the lender. And, most importantly, the lender needs to commit extra time and analysis to gain an understanding of the credit risk associated with the borrower.

Operating Cycle

Each type of business entity—a manufacturer, wholesaler, retailer, service, or agricultural company—has different operational characteristics. A close look at a business's operating cycle can reveal information about the amount and purpose of the financing needed, the various sources of repayment, the timing of the repayment, and the risks associated with repayment.

The operating cycle begins with an infusion of **capital** (the funds invested in a business on a long-term basis), in the form of cash, used to buy inventory such as raw materials (in the case of a manufacturer) or finished goods (in the case of wholesalers and retailers), to pay labor (in the case of a service company), or to purchase equipment (for all types of companies). This capital, available from a variety of sources, includes equity from the owners, trade credit, or a bank loan. Most banks require initial operating capital to be cash supplied by the owners.

The length of the operating cycle varies among industries and businesses and affects the amount of capital needed. The longer the operating cycle, the greater the financing needed to complete the cycle. For example, a retailer of diamonds would have a greater financing need than a retailer of ice cream.

The successful and profitable completion of the operating cycle results in the generation of cash, which is used to start the cycle over again and to repay bank debt. Multiple operating cycles are needed to repay long-term debt. Short-term debt is generally repaid from the completion of one cycle.

Manufacturers

A **manufacturer** makes products to sell. Some manufacturers buy raw material and change its form. A Styrofoam manufacturer, for example, changes foam pellets into sheets of Styrofoam to be used as insulation. Other manufacturers purchase parts such as wood, screws, and upholstery material to make furniture.

The manufacturer's operating cycle (see exhibit 2.2) starts with cash that is used to finance the purchase of raw materials. Using these raw materials, the company manufactures a finished product, sells the finished goods on credit, and records the sales as increases in accounts receivable. When the accounts receivables are collected, cash is generated. This cash is then used to repay trade creditors or the bank debt, or to purchase more raw materials, thus beginning the cycle again. The working assets are accounts receivable, inventory, and equipment.

Historically, banks have given manufacturers excellent lending terms. They considered accounts receivable derived from physical products shipped, inventories of raw materials, and finished goods as **collateral** that easily could be liquidated. Lending institutions also considered buildings and equipment as collateral that maintained or even increased its value over time. Collateral is often referred to as the secondary source of repayment. Excess cash generated from a successful operating cycle is the primary cash source to repay most loans.

In general, manufacturers, who normally hold most assets in accounts receivable, inventory, and fixed assets, carry significant debt to fund operations (which typically entails equipping a plant). For example, before the fresh peas can be canned, the manufacturer must obtain substantial capital to build or lease a plant and purchase processing and canning equipment. The 2002/2003 composite balance sheet for manufacturers of canned fruits, vegetables, preserves, jams, and jellies in exhibit 2.3 on page 38 illustrates this mix.

Accounts receivable, inventories, and fixed assets fall in the range of 60 to 85 percent of the total assets for nearly every manufacturer. Comparing a company's assets with industry averages helps the loan officer determine whether or not the composite of a company's assets falls within acceptable boundaries. The balance sheet components of canned fruit, vegetables, preserves, jams, and jellies manufacturers, for example, are typical for this type of organizational structure.

Manufacturers request loans to

- fund raw material purchases
- fund work in process and labor
- carry accounts receivable
- make plant improvements
- purchase equipment related to production processes

Loans to manufacturers are repaid from the excess cash generated during the operating cycle. Most loans to manufacturers are repaid from the completion of multiple operating cycles. However, the more operating cycles there are to complete and the more complex the operating cycle, the greater the lending risk.

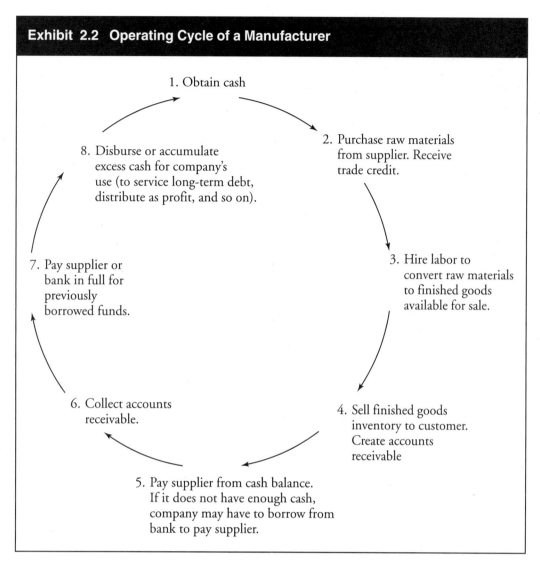

Exhibit 2.2 Operating Cycle of a Manufacturer

1. Obtain cash

2. Purchase raw materials from supplier. Receive trade credit.

3. Hire labor to convert raw materials to finished goods available for sale.

4. Sell finished goods inventory to customer. Create accounts receivable

5. Pay supplier from cash balance. If it does not have enough cash, company may have to borrow from bank to pay supplier.

6. Collect accounts receivable.

7. Pay supplier or bank in full for previously borrowed funds.

8. Disburse or accumulate excess cash for company's use (to service long-term debt, distribute as profit, and so on).

The risks that may disrupt the completion of a manufacturer's operating cycle are

- inability to sell the product
- quality of the raw material used
- labor costs and availability
- collection of the accounts receivable
- efficiency of the plant operation

Wholesalers

A **wholesaler** does not produce a product but resells finished goods to retailers, other wholesalers, or major users of the product. The main risk for wholesalers is purchasing inventory that is no longer in demand by the market or is available elsewhere at lower prices.

The operating cycle (exhibit 2.4 on page 39) begins with a cash payment to purchase finished goods inventory. Suppliers may finance a portion of the inventory. When the inventory is sold, accounts receivable is created, which is converted to cash

Exhibit 2.3 Manufacturers—Canned Fruits, Vegetables, Preserves, Jams, and Jellies (Composition of 2002–2003 Assets and Liabilities)

Assets

Cash and equivalents	4.9%
Accounts receivable	15.5%
Inventory	35.4%
All other current	2.1%
Total current assets	57.8%
Fixed assets (net)	34.0%
Intangibles (net)	2.4%
All other noncurrent	5.9%
Total assets	100.0%

Liabilities

Notes payable short-term	15.0%
Current maturities long-term debt	2.8%
Trade payables	13.6%
Income taxes payable	0.2%
All other current	5.7%
Total current	37.3%
Long-term debt	18.2%
Deferred taxes	0.7%
All other noncurrent	5.4%
Net worth	38.5%
Total liabilities and net worth	100.0%

upon payment, completing the cycle. A notable characteristic of the wholesaler's operating cycle is the large amount of inventory purchased and sold. This high rate of inventory turnover means that a wholesaler's gross profit and net profit, as a percentage of sales, are usually low.

RMA COMPOSITE BALANCE SHEETS

The RMA composite balance sheets—exhibits 2.3, 2.5, 2.7, 2.9, and 2.10—list the major balance sheet accounts. Because only the major balance sheet accounts are listed, percentages do not add up to 100 percent. However, total assets are always listed as 100 percent and, therefore, the numbers given are correct.

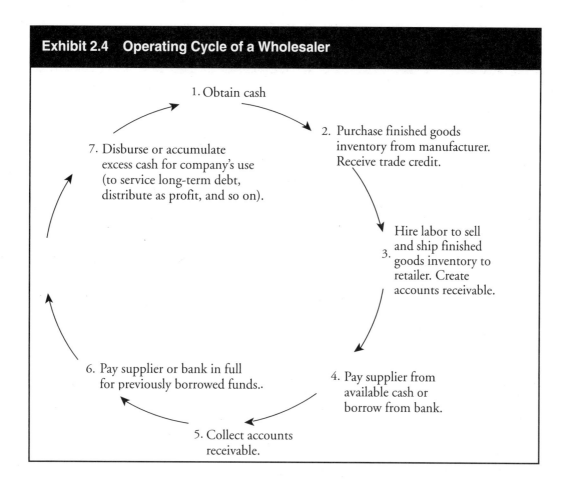

Exhibit 2.4 Operating Cycle of a Wholesaler

1. Obtain cash

2. Purchase finished goods inventory from manufacturer. Receive trade credit.

3. Hire labor to sell and ship finished goods inventory to retailer. Create accounts receivable.

4. Pay supplier from available cash or borrow from bank.

5. Collect accounts receivable.

6. Pay supplier or bank in full for previously borrowed funds..

7. Disburse or accumulate excess cash for company's use (to service long-term debt, distribute as profit, and so on).

Accounts receivable typically constitutes another important asset for wholesalers, and accounts payable constitutes an important liability. Most wholesalers lease space and therefore do not require substantial amounts of fixed assets. The majority of loans needed by wholesalers are to carry the key working assets, namely, inventory and accounts receivable. Exhibit 2.5 on the following page illustrates the composite for wholesalers of general groceries for 2002/2003.

In 2002, accounts receivable and inventory accounted for 57 percent of the total assets for wholesalers of groceries. For a wholesaler, 23.3 percent of fixed assets is in the normal range. However, certain wholesalers, such as wholesalers of fish, may have significant fixed assets. They need to invest in refrigeration coolers to keep the product fresh.

Wholesalers request loans to

- purchase finished goods
- fund new product offerings
- carry accounts receivable
- purchase equipment
- fund plant expansions or purchases

Loans may be for short or long terms. For example, a wholesaler of fish requests a loan to purchase a new refrigeration unit. The loan would be structured on a long-

Exhibit 2.5 Wholesalers—Groceries and Related Products—Composition of 2002–2003 Assets and Liabilities

Assets

Cash and equivalents	7.1%
Accounts receivable	28.7%
Inventory	28.3%
All other current	2.0%
Total current assets	66.2%
Fixed assets (net)	23.3%
Intangibles (net)	4.7%
All other noncurrent	5.8%
Total assets	100.0%

Liabilities

Notes payable short-term	17.7%
Current maturities long-term debt	5.1%
Trade payables	21.3%
Income taxes payable	0.2%
All other current	7.4%
Total current	51.8%
Long-term debt	12.9%
Deferred taxes	0.3%
All other noncurrent	5.9%
Net worth	29.1%
Total liabilities and net worth	100.0%

term basis and repaid from the successful completion of multiple operating cycles. Short-term loans to wholesalers are usually seasonal or related to a one-time large sales order.

Risks that may disrupt the successful completion of a wholesaler's operating cycle include

- quality of the product
- ability to market the product
- credit approval policies
- collection of accounts receivable
- relationship of accounts payable

Retailers

A **retailer** purchases finished products from wholesalers or directly from manufacturers for resale to consumers. Retail businesses are diverse, ranging from national department stores to small specialty boutiques. The operating cycle (see exhibit 2.6) begins with cash used to purchase a finished product that then is sold directly to the public on credit or for cash. Suppliers may finance some of the inventory. Thus, accounts receivable is usually minimal, as illustrated in the composite statement of retailers of grocery stores in exhibit 2.7 (on the following page).

For grocery stores, accounts receivable is low, which is typical for retailers, because food is paid for in cash. Fixed assets are higher, due to the high cost of leasehold improvements and equipment. As with wholesalers, a key factor in evaluating a retailer is inventory turnover. Turnover is the number of times a complete stock of goods is sold in a given period. Depending on the type of retailer, either inventory or fixed assets can be the working asset. Retailers of groceries and meats are unusual because their working assets are inventory and fixed assets, which total 69.6 percent of total assets.

The amount of capital required to finance a retail operation varies greatly according to sales volume and the particular industry involved. Rapidly growing sales volume usually requires a significant amount of inventory.

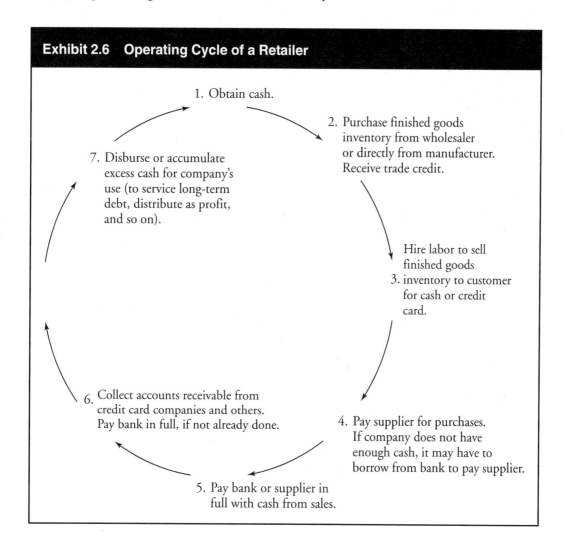

Exhibit 2.6   Operating Cycle of a Retailer

1. Obtain cash.

2. Purchase finished goods inventory from wholesaler or directly from manufacturer. Receive trade credit.

3. Hire labor to sell finished goods inventory to customer for cash or credit card.

4. Pay supplier for purchases. If company does not have enough cash, it may have to borrow from bank to pay supplier.

5. Pay bank or supplier in full with cash from sales.

6. Collect accounts receivable from credit card companies and others. Pay bank in full, if not already done.

7. Disburse or accumulate excess cash for company's use (to service long-term debt, distribute as profit, and so on).

Exhibit 2.7 Retailers—Grocery Stores—Composition of 2000–2001 Assets and Liabilities

Assets

Cash and equivalents	11.6%
Accounts receivable	4.8%
Inventory	25.5%
All other current	2.4%
Total current assets	44.3%
Fixed assets (net)	44.1%
Intangibles (net)	5.1%
All other noncurrent	8.4%
Total assets	100.0%

Liabilities

Notes payable short-term	4.1%
Current maturities long-term debt	4.5%
Trade payables	17.3%
Income taxes payable	0.1%
All other current	9.8%
Total current	35.8%
Long-term debt	32.2%
Deferred taxes	0.3%
All other noncurrent	6.3%
Net worth	25.4%
Total liabilities and net worth	100.0%

Retailers request loans to

- purchase permanent inventory
- purchase seasonal inventory
- purchase equipment
- fund leasehold improvements

Inventory loans increase at peak seasons, especially during the fourth quarter. Seasonal loans are repaid from selling seasonal inventory and consequently are short-term.

Risks that may disrupt the successful completion of the operating cycle for a retailer include:

- product quality and mix
- service provided by employees
- relationship with accounts payable

Service Industry

Unlike manufacturers, wholesalers, or retailers, companies in the service industry do not sell a tangible product. Their product is a service and may come in the form of financial consultation, legal advice, or a variety of other types of services.

Because little or no inventory is involved, the operating cycle of a **service company** is different from a manufacturer, wholesaler, or retailer. Cash is used in the performance of service, which, in turn, may generate cash or accounts receivable. For example, the medical profession provides a service on credit. Customers of insurance companies are billed, which creates accounts receivable. When the accounts receivable is paid, cash is created, beginning the cycle again. A different example is a car wash. Car washes provide a service that is paid for in cash. Exhibit 2.8 illustrates the operating cycle of a service company.

Because service industries produce intangibles, they generally have few physical assets and comparatively low-term debt requirements. There are exceptions, such as the storage industry, where the costs of fixed assets are high. Accounts receivable (dental) or fixed assets (warehousing and storage companies, as exhibit 2.9 on the following page illustrates) are generally the working assets on the balance sheet of a service company.

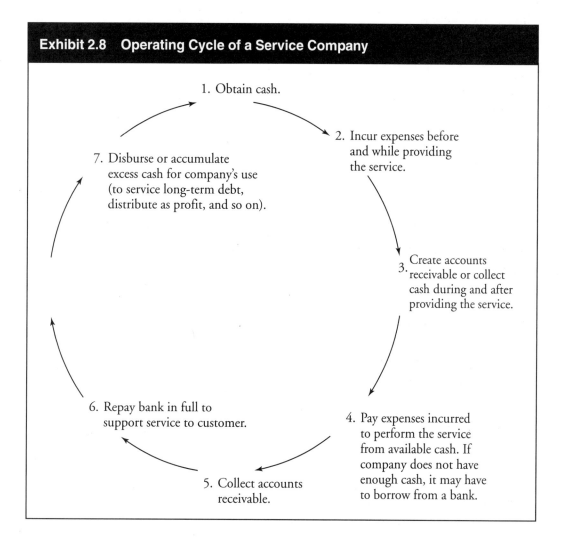

Exhibit 2.8   Operating Cycle of a Service Company

1. Obtain cash.

2. Incur expenses before and while providing the service.

3. Create accounts receivable or collect cash during and after providing the service.

4. Pay expenses incurred to perform the service from available cash. If company does not have enough cash, it may have to borrow from a bank.

5. Collect accounts receivable.

6. Repay bank in full to support service to customer.

7. Disburse or accumulate excess cash for company's use (to service long-term debt, distribute as profit, and so on).

Exhibit 2.9 Transportation—General Warehousing and Storage—General Composition of 2000–2001 Assets and Liabilities

Assets

Cash and equivalents	9.0%
Accounts receivable	17.5%
Inventory	2.3%
All other current	4.1%
Total current assets	32.9%
Fixed assets (net)	54.8%
Intangibles (net)	3.1%
All other noncurrent	9.20%
Total assets	100.0%

Liabilities

Notes payable short-term	7.3%
Current maturities long-term debt	4.1%
Trade payables	7.5%
Income taxes payable	0.2%
All other current	11.0%
Total current	30.1%
Long-term debt	45.1%
Deferred taxes	0.2%
All other noncurrent	5.4%
Net worth	19.2%
Total liabilities and net worth	100.0%

A warehouse company is unusual for a service company because of the low amount of accounts receivable and the high fixed asset requirements. The cost of land, buildings, and fixed assets for storage is high compared to that of accounts receivable.

A growing service area is the technology industry. Tech companies vary from software developers to Internet providers. The operating cycle for these companies is unique because large amounts of cash are needed to pay labor to research and develop products. Because no tangible product is produced and the length of time to develop the product is long, large amounts of capital are needed. Also, the general composition of assets is usually a mix of accounts receivable and fixed assets. Often, however, accounts receivable are a work-in-process of completion and the fixed assets are computers—which have little value to the lender. The summary composition (exhibit 2.10) of Professional Services—Computer Programming Services—demonstrates this relationship.

Exhibit 2.10 Professional Services—Computer Programming Services— General Composition of 2002–2003 Assets and Liabilities

Assets

Cash and equivalents	15.0%
Accounts receivable	44.6%
Inventory	3.6%
All other current	4.3%
Total current assets	67.5%
Fixed assets (net)	14.9%
Intangibles (net)	8.0%
All other noncurrent	9.5%
Total assets	100.0%

Liabilities

Notes payable short-term	16.8%
Current maturities long-term debt	3.6%
Trade payables	10.5%
Income taxes payable	0.7%
All other current	25.2%
Total current	56.8%
Long-term debt	13.9%
Deferred taxes	1.1%
All other noncurrent	13.4%
Net worth	14.8%
Total liabilities and net worth	100.0%

Service and technology companies request loans to

- carry accounts receivable
- fund fixed asset purchases
- fund leasehold improvements
- finance research and development

Again, the loans are repaid from the completion of multiple operating cycles. Risks that may prevent successfully completing a service or technology company's operating cycle include:

- quality of service provided
- credit approval process
- accounts receivable collection system
- length of time to develop product

Agriculture

The agricultural industry bears special mention because of its importance to the economy of many communities. Numerous companies fall under the umbrella term *agricultural industry*, and they can be manufacturing, wholesaling, retailing, or service businesses. In this textbook, the term specifically refers to farming that produces crops or livestock.

The operating cycle of an **agricultural business** is similar to that of a manufacturer in some aspects. Cash is used to purchase seeds, fertilizer, livestock, or other materials for the production of inventory. Unlike manufacturing, however, the inventory of an agriculture entity is not a finished good but is a crop, milk, livestock, or other farm product. For example, canned peas are a finished good but pea pods are a crop. The product is sold for cash or credit, creating accounts receivable which, when paid, generate cash. The cash is then used for the next operating cycle.

The primary working assets for farmers are crops, livestock, or dairy products that will turn to cash within one year. Financial statements include a category called "intermediate assets," which are assets with a useful life of less than ten years. For example, livestock and certain equipment would be classified as intermediate assets. Long-term assets include land and buildings.

Agricultural businesses borrow short- and long-term. Most farmers borrow each spring to fund the cost of planting a crop and pay off the loan from the sale of the crop. Long-term loans for land, buildings, and equipment are partially repaid seasonally from the excess cash.

Risks that disrupt the successful completion of an agricultural company's operating cycle include:

- weather
- disease
- commodity prices
- equipment costs

CASH FLOW CYCLES

The various characteristics of a business operating cycle are important to financial statement analysis because they affect cash flow, which in turn affects a company's need for bank financing and its ability to repay debt. Most businesses rely on accounts payable or bank loans or cash as their sources of financing. This cash may be used to purchase inventory, which in turn is used to produce goods or deliver services, and then returns to cash (or accounts receivable, and then cash). This cash enables the company to purchase more inventory to begin the **cash flow cycle** again.

Understanding cash flows, including how cash is generated and used, is a critical and difficult part of the financial statement analysis process. Exhibit 2.11 shows a comparison of the cash flow cycles of the different types of business operations, each selling a product or providing a service for $1.00. This exhibit also shows the effect on the timing of cash needs.

Exhibit 2.11 Cash Flow Cycle Comparison

Manufacturer

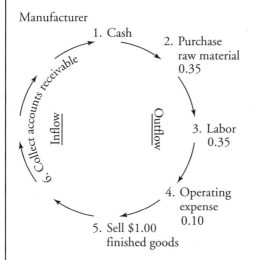

Raw material costs less than finished goods.
Labor adds significant costs.
Operating cost lower due to labor manuf. cost.
High profit margin

Wholesale

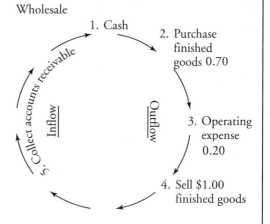

Finished goods cost more than raw material.
Low labor cost.
Operating cost higher than manufacturer.
Low profit margin.

Retail

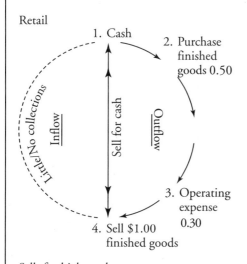

Sells for high mark up.
Operating costs high.
Sales for cash.
Good profit margin.

Service

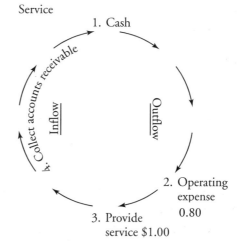

No cost of sales.
High operating expenses.
High profit margin.

Cash flow in financial statement analysis includes all of the economic resources available to a company—not just the balance in the cash account. Although most business transactions do involve cash or cash equivalents, lenders also consider such seemingly non-cash economic resources as accrued expenses (accruals) and accounts payable (trade credit) as part of the cash flow. Trade credit results from the common practice of purchasing goods on account, meaning that the goods are paid for some time after they are received. During the time between the purchase of and payment for a supplier's goods, trade credit serves as a source of cash.

Salary, vacation, and bonus accruals are non-cash resources involving a promise to pay later for a service performed now. A bank, for example, may pay employees weekly for work performed the previous week. Such owed, but unpaid, labor costs constitute another source of cash. The concept of cash flows, therefore, includes not only cash and cash-equivalent accounts, but also other tangible resources or assets (such as inventory or machinery) and intangible economic power (such as the ability to incur debt in the form of trade credit and accruals). Because loans are repaid in cash, a company's cash flow cycle is of particular importance to the lender. By measuring the amount of cash allocated in each step of the operating cycle, the lender can evaluate the success of the company's ability to manage the business and the risks associated with any loans made to the company.

Uses of Cash

To illustrate a simple cash flow cycle, consider the Harris Table Company, a manufacturing business that assembles all types of tables and resells them at a profit.

Assume the Harris Table Company buys unassembled table parts, employs a person to assemble the tables in its shop, and then sells the completed tables.

Exhibit 2.12 shows that on Day 1, the Harris Table Company has $50 in its account. On Day 2, the company pays $35 for table parts. On Day 3, the employee assembles the table and places it on the showroom floor. The employee is paid $15. On Day 4, the table is sold for $75 cash. Harris Table makes a $25 profit on its original $50 investment.

As exhibit 2.13 on page 50 illustrates, the length of the company's cash flow cycle further increases if the table is sold on credit. In the example, a table is sold on Day 4 on 30-day terms. This creates accounts receivable and lengthens the cash flow cycle, assuming the customer waits until Day 34 or longer to pay for the table. In the meantime, the company has no cash for purchasing parts for more tables or for paying its employee.

The preceding examples illustrate that the cash flow cycle reflects the type of operation in which a company engages. It also illustrates how management decisions can affect the cash flow cycle (in this case, by management's decision to sell the tables on credit).

Sources of Cash

The initial source of cash for most businesses is the owner's original equity and loans. On-going sources of cash include collection of accounts receivable, selling inventory for cash, receiving credit from suppliers, additional loans, and profit retained in the

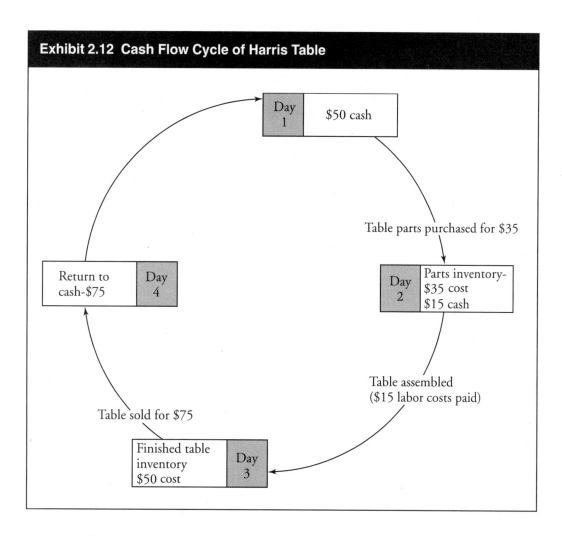

Exhibit 2.12 Cash Flow Cycle of Harris Table

Day 1 — $50 cash

Table parts purchased for $35

Day 2 — Parts inventory-$35 cost $15 cash

Table assembled ($15 labor costs paid)

Day 3 — Finished table inventory $50 cost

Table sold for $75

Day 4 — Return to cash-$75

company. Up to this point, Harris Table Company's use of cash in its operations (to buy inventory and pay for labor) has been considered, but the question of where the cash came from (the sources of cash) has not been addressed. It was assumed that the company had sufficient cash to purchase parts, pay for labor, and wait 30 days to collect the proceeds of a sale.

Capital

Capital, one of the major sources of cash available to businesses, may be the only source of cash available to a new business. The amount of money invested in the Harris Table operation by the company's owner (the original $50) is considered capital. But what happens if a company does not have sufficient capital to sustain its entire cash flow cycle? Specifically, what would happen if, for example, the Harris Table Company started out with only $40 worth of capital? Exhibit 2.14 on page 51 illustrates this situation.

After spending $35 on table parts, the company has only $5 left, whereas labor to assemble the table costs $15. The Harris Table Company faces a classic business dilemma—a shortage of cash. The shortfall is only $10, but the company needs that money to hire the labor to assemble the table. Once assembled, if the table is sold for cash, the worker can be paid. But if the company cannot complete its operating cycle, it will fail. Failure to complete the operating cycle is a common cause of problem loans.

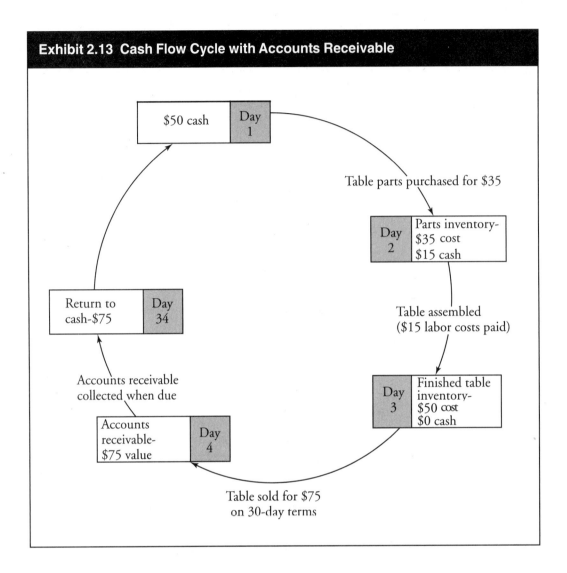

Exhibit 2.13 Cash Flow Cycle with Accounts Receivable

$50 cash | Day 1

Table parts purchased for $35

Day 2 | Parts inventory–
$35 cost
$15 cash

Table assembled
($15 labor costs paid)

Day 3 | Finished table
inventory–
$50 cost
$0 cash

Table sold for $75
on 30-day terms

Accounts
receivable–
$75 value | Day 4

Accounts receivable
collected when due

Return to
cash–$75 | Day 34

How can a company with insufficient capital raise money to enable it to complete its operating cycle? It could go to its bank and request a short-term loan. However, because loans cost money in the form of interest payments and thus reduce the company's profits, the company might want to consider other sources of cash first, such as trade credit, labor accruals, a reduction of selling credit terms, or starting a company with more capital.

Trade Credit

The Harris Table Company can try to negotiate credit terms with its supplier of table parts. If its supplier will allow 30-day payment terms, for instance, the resulting cash flow cycle is like the one illustrated in exhibit 2.15 on page 52.

In that scenario, the Harris Table Company has $40 in its account on Day 1. The next day, the company purchases $35 worth of table parts and promises to pay for them in 30 days. Thus, the company still has $40 cash at its disposal. On the third day, Harris Table Company uses $15 of its cash reserve to hire a laborer to assemble the table parts. On the fourth day, the table sells on 30-day terms. On Day 32, the bill for table

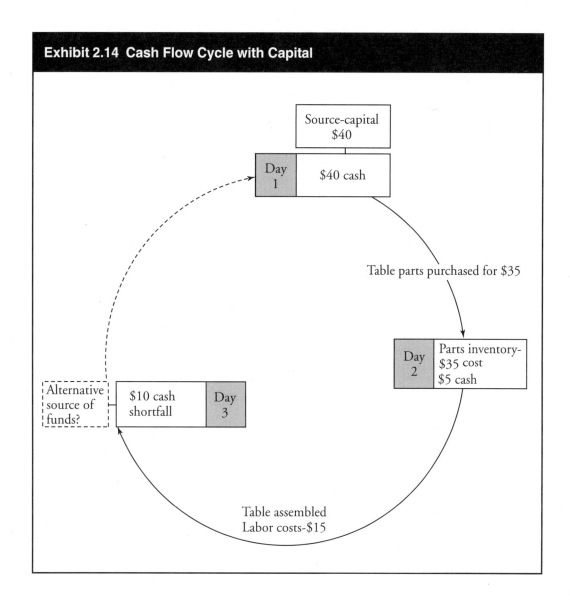

Exhibit 2.14 Cash Flow Cycle with Capital

Source-capital
$40

Day 1 — $40 cash

Table parts purchased for $35

Day 2 — Parts inventory-
$35 cost
$5 cash

Table assembled
Labor costs-$15

Alternative source of funds?

$10 cash shortfall — Day 3

parts is due, and Harris Table Company faces a $10 shortfall again. Unless the company can raise the additional $10, its supplier must wait for payment until Day 34, when the customer's payment of $75 becomes due. If this fails to satisfy the supplier, the company may still need to request a short-term loan or inject more cash into the operating cycle. However, the company now needs to borrow the $10 for only two days, rather than for 30 days (as required in the previous scenario).

Accruals

Another strategy Harris Table Company might use to complete its cash flow cycle would be to defer the payment of its labor for a week. This is, in effect, a source of cash called accrued expenses–salaries. The company's cash flow cycle would then look like the one in exhibit 2.16 on page 53.

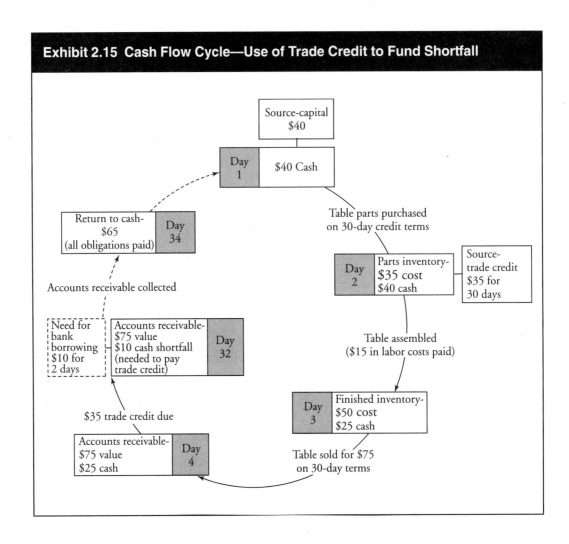

Exhibit 2.15 Cash Flow Cycle—Use of Trade Credit to Fund Shortfall

Again, Harris Table begins with $40 in capital and spends $35 for table parts. Since it pays cash for the supplies, it now has a $5 balance. On Day 3, the employee assembles the table but agrees to be paid one week later. On the fourth day, a customer purchases the table on 30-day terms. On Day 10, the $15 salary expense comes due, but the company has only a $5 cash balance. Again, the company finds itself $10 short and must borrow from the bank for 24 days, or extend trade credit, or inject more capital into the company until the customer's $75 payment comes due. Although this strategy is preferred over borrowing for 30 days, it is not as effective a solution as is negotiating extended trade credit terms.

Reduction of Credit Sale Terms

Another strategy Harris Table Company could adopt to alleviate its cash shortfall would be to reduce the credit terms offered to its customers. Suppose the company reduced the credit terms extended to its customers from 30 days to 18 days and was also able to negotiate a 20-day trade credit with its supplier. The company's cash flow cycle would now look like the one depicted in exhibit 2.17 on page 54.

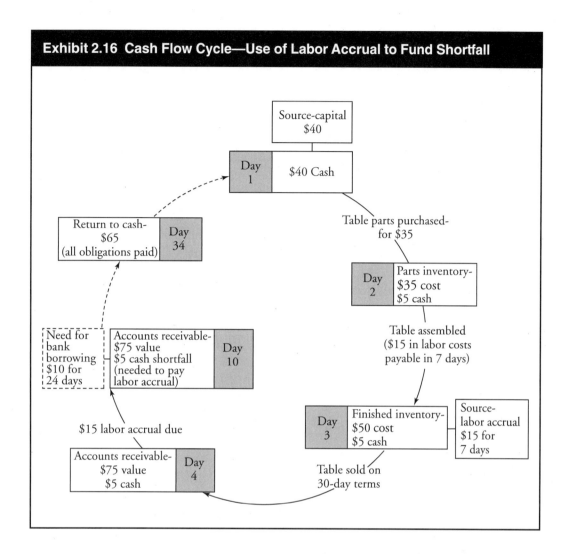

Exhibit 2.16 Cash Flow Cycle—Use of Labor Accrual to Fund Shortfall

Source-capital
$40

Day 1 — $40 Cash

Table parts purchased-
for $35

Day 2 — Parts inventory-
$35 cost
$5 cash

Table assembled
($15 in labor costs
payable in 7 days)

Day 3 — Finished inventory-
$50 cost
$5 cash

Source-labor accrual
$15 for
7 days

Table sold on
30-day terms

Accounts receivable-
$75 value
$5 cash

Day 4

$15 labor accrual due

Need for bank
borrowing
$10 for
24 days

Accounts receivable-
$75 value
$5 cash shortfall
(needed to pay
labor accrual)

Day 10

Return to cash-
$65
(all obligations paid)

Day 34

On Day 1, the company has $40 in its account. The next day, the company purchases $35 in table parts on credit, promising to pay for them in 20 days. The employee assembles the table on the third day and receives $15 in payment. On the fourth day, a customer purchases the table for $75 on 18-day terms. On Day 22, both the company's $35 bill for table parts and the customer's $75 payment for the table come due, enabling Harris Table to meet its debt obligation (assuming the customer pays by the due date). Moreover, the company still makes a $25 profit on its original investment, which may be used to start the operating cycle once again.

Long-term Uses of Cash

The discussion of cash flow thus far has been concerned with the current operating cycle, which involves the conversion of cash into working assets and then back into cash within a short period. But that cash conversion process does not take place in a vacuum. Businesses need facilities to house their operations and equipment to perform their tasks.

The Harris Table Company, for example, might need offices for its sales and administrative staff, space for the assembly process, and a warehouse for its inventory. It

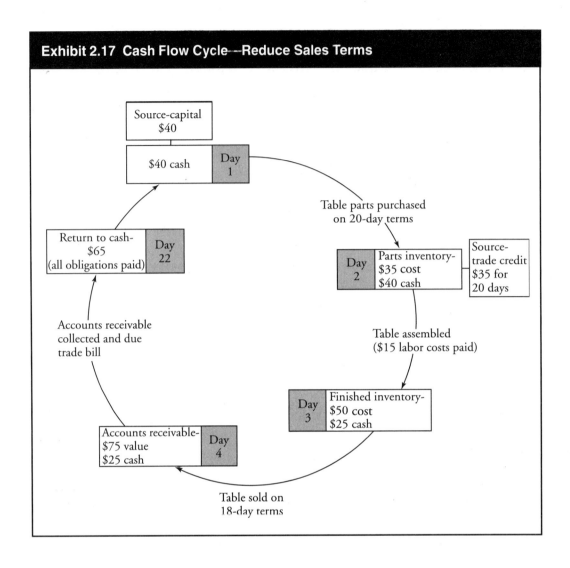

Exhibit 2.17 Cash Flow Cycle—Reduce Sales Terms

Source-capital
$40

$40 cash | Day 1

Table parts purchased
on 20-day terms

Return to cash-
$65
(all obligations paid) | Day 22

Day 2 | Parts inventory-
$35 cost
$40 cash

Source-
trade credit
$35 for
20 days

Accounts receivable
collected and due
trade bill

Table assembled
($15 labor costs paid)

Day 3 | Finished inventory-
$50 cost
$25 cash

Accounts receivable-
$75 value
$25 cash | Day 4

Table sold on
18-day terms

also might need production equipment (such as a drill press) and other equipment (perhaps a delivery van). Assets needed to support, rather than be consumed by, a company's operation are referred to as fixed assets. The acquisition, funding, use, and replacement of fixed assets is called the fixed asset cycle (illustrated in exhibit 2.18) because the company reuses the assets throughout a number of operating cycles rather than expending them or converting them to cash within a single operating cycle. Most fixed assets, however, are eventually expended through their repeated use in the production process and must be replaced. Because replacement usually occurs several years after the initial purchase, replacement costs become higher and need to be considered in cash flow analysis.

The fixed asset cycle, like the operating cycle, begins with the expenditure of cash to acquire an asset, such as a drill press. The company does not, however, directly convert the fixed asset back into cash by selling its drill press to create an accounts receivable later collected to produce cash. Nevertheless, fixed assets do play a critical part in the operating cycle. The company's products cannot be created and its services cannot be delivered without the support of the company's fixed assets. The company does recover the original cash expenditure for the fixed asset, but only over time and

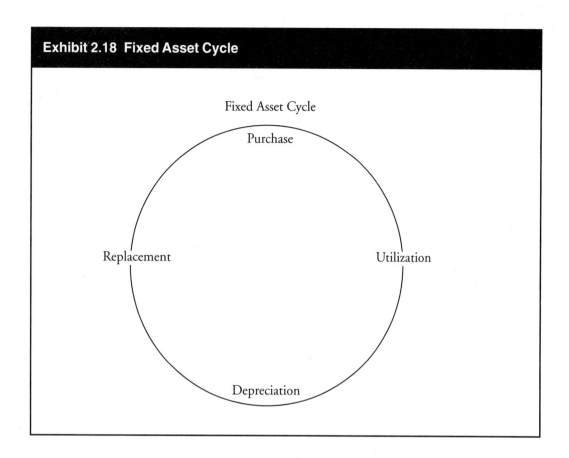

Exhibit 2.18 Fixed Asset Cycle

Fixed Asset Cycle

Purchase

Replacement

Utilization

Depreciation

only through the profitable sale of the products that the fixed asset helped create. During this time, the fixed assets generally have declined in value. Fixed assets are financed over the life of the asset, which generally exceeds one year. The loan is repaid from successfully completing multiple operating cycles.

Long-term Sources of Cash

A company must have adequate accounts receivable, inventory, and fixed assets to support its current operating cycle. Additionally, the company must structure its payments for accounts receivable, inventory, and fixed assets to avoid disrupting the current operation of the business. Initial payment for the permanent accounts receivable, permanent inventory, and fixed assets can come from three sources: excess cash, capital contribution, or debt. Of these, debt and excess cash are the most common. Permanent accounts receivable are those amounts the company will carry on average each month. Permanent inventory is the amount of inventory the company needs to maintain to generate a constant level of sales. The company's current operating cycle generates the cash to repay the debt.

However, cash generated through the current operating cycle must first be used to replenish the company's inventory and accounts receivable. Accounts receivable includes all cash due to a company for goods or services sold to customers on credit.

To the extent that it is not used for some other purpose, the cash generated from operations is normally available to purchase fixed assets or to service debt. Therefore, the lender should structure payment terms on loans for the purchase of permanent accounts receivable, permanent inventory, and fixed assets in such a way that companies can repay these debts with cash generated from multiple completions of the operating cycle. Exhibit 2.19 summarizes business functions, working assets, operating cycles, and capital requirements for the various business types. With an understanding of the legal structure, business type, and cash flow cycle, the lender can now begin to identify possible lending arrangements.

TYPES OF BORROWING ARRANGEMENTS

As exhibit 2.20 illustrates (see page 58), choosing the correct borrowing arrangement requires matching the purpose of the loan, the source of repayment, the required loan amount, and the term of the loan. Borrowing arrangements may be special commitment loans, seasonal lines of credit, a revolving line of credit, permanent working capital loans, a letter of credit, term loans, or lease financing.

Special commitment loans support isolated increases in current assets needed for unusual circumstances. The loans are disbursed all at once and repaid from the sale of the assets financed. Repayment is required within a designated period, usually 30, 60, or 90 days. These loans are repaid with the cash generated by the conversion of non-cash current assets to cash.

For example, a retailer of sporting goods has an opportunity to sell basketballs and jerseys to the local school district. This is a one-time opportunity. The loan will be structured as a special commitment loan disbursed to pay for the basketballs and jerseys and repaid when the funds due from the school district are collected.

A **revolving line of credit**, used to fund daily operations, is repaid by converting current assets to cash. Because the line of credit usually has a principal balance outstanding, this type of loan is often referred to as asset-based lending. The outstanding amount will vary by the daily collection of cash. The maturity is for one year, or less for monitoring purposes. The principal portion of the loan will never be repaid as long as the company's sales volume requires a level of accounts receivable and inventory in excess of the company's internally generated capital. The primary users of revolving credit are rapidly growing companies that have inadequate cash flow and trade credit to finance the accounts receivable and inventory necessary to support their growing sales volume. A loan agreement with specific terms, such as an accounts receivable aging and inventory list, usually support the loans.

For example, a manufacturer of plastic pipe needs to finance inventory and fund accounts receivable growth. The sales growth is due to increasing the product line and territory, and it is expected to continue for some time. Due to the sales growth, the company does not generate sufficient cash to fund the increases in accounts receivable and inventory. It needs a revolving line of credit. As long as sales increase at a rapid rate, the principal portion of the loan will not be repaid in full. Interest is usually collected monthly.

A **seasonal line of credit** is used to support a seasonal increase in current assets. Funds are used to purchase seasonal inventory, which is sold for cash or credit. If sold on credit, a seasonal line of credit is needed until the accounts receivable are paid. The loan is repaid when the inventory is sold or accounts receivable are collected. The loan

Exhibit 2.19 Summary of Business Functions

Type	Working Asset	Stages in Operating Cycle	Capital Required	Invest Fixed Assets	Typical Financing Needs
Manu-facturer	Plant and equipment	Purchase raw materials Hire labor to manufacture finished goods inventory Sell on credit, creating receivable to cash	Large	Large	Long-term to finance fixed assets or permanent investment in inventory and accounts receivable. May require short-term financing for temporary build-ups in receivables and inventory.
Whole-saler	Inventory and accounts receivable	Purchase inventory (finished goods) Sell creating receivable Conversion receivable to cash	Function of volume and length of operating cycle	Limited	Long-term to finance permanent investment in inventory and accounts receivable. May require short-term financing for tempory build-ups in receivables and inventory.
Retailer	Inventory and real estate	Purchase inventory (finished goods) Sell inventory for cash	Function of volume and length of inventory cycle plus required investment in real estate	Modest or large	Long-term to finance per-manent invest-ment in inventory and real estate. May require seasonal financing to support tempory build-ups in inventory.
Service	Accounts receivable and fixed assets	Perform service Receive payment in cash or short-term receivable	Limited or large	Nominal or large	Accounts receivable or long-term to finance fixed assets

Exhibit 2.20 Summary of Borrowing Arrangements

Type	Purpose	Repayment	Terms
Special commitment	support isolated increases in current assets	sale of current assets	short
Revolving lines of credit	support increases in accounts receivable and inventory	conversion of current assets to cash	interest monthly, principal outstanding until sales growth slows
Seasonal line of credit	inventory purchases, support accounts receivable	sale of current assets purchased or collection of accounts receivable	short
Permanent working capital	permanent increases in accounts receivable and inventory	excess cash generated from increased sales	long with short-term ballon payments for review
Letter of credit	facilitate inventory purchases	cash flow or sale of collateral	not technically a loan
Term Loan	fixed assets	cash flow generated from assets purchased	useful life of assets purchased or cash flow, whichever is shorter
Lease	fixed assets	cash flow	useful life of asset(s) or lease term, whichever is shorter

is usually structured with a short-term maturity to match the completion of the operating cycle. For example, a retailer of lawn mowers and garden equipment needs to purchase seasonal inventory in late winter. The loan will be repaid over the spring and summer months from the sale of inventory for cash.

Permanent working capital loans should be considered when a company's current debt and equity are not sufficient to meet its working capital requirements. Working capital is defined as current assets minus current liabilities. Such loans may be amortized over several years, but often they have a one- or two-year maturity. The loan is used to fund permanent growth in accounts receivable and inventory. Repayment is structured to match the company's cash flow. The cash flow consists of profits generated from multiple completions of the operating cycle.

For example, a wholesaler of machine tools wants to expand into an adjacent state. The company needs a permanent working capital loan to purchase permanent inventory for the new location. The loan will be repaid from the monthly cash flow generated at the new location.

A **letter of credit** is not technically a loan. With a letter of credit, a bank guarantees payment for goods or services purchased by a customer on contract from a third party. Because the bank is guaranteeing the funds, letters of credit usually are issued for the bank's best customers only. For underwriting and monitoring purposes, a letter of credit is treated as a loan. Because the bank is required to pay on the letter of credit even if the business no longer exists, most letters of credit contain promissory note provisions secured by collateral.

For example, a retailer of computers purchases large orders of inventory from Asia. The seller wants to be guaranteed payment when the computers are shipped. The bank customer requests a letter of credit guaranteeing payment upon shipment.

Term loans are used to finance fixed assets—namely equipment, land, and buildings. Repayment comes from multiple completions of the operating cycle. The term of the loan matches the life of the asset purchased and the cash flow generated by the borrower. The longer the life of the fixed asset, the longer the term of the loan. For example, real estate has a longer life than telephone systems.

Assume that a local pediatrician wants to expand her practice to include a new examination room. She requests a loan to remodel the existing building and purchase new equipment. She repays the loan using the excess cash flow generated from the new patient load and increased procedures.

Lease financing is used to finance fixed asset additions. Leasing offers many advantages. For example, leases are 100 percent financing, whereas a loan requires a down payment. Leases are also attractive to new or growing companies with little capital.

For example, the owners of a movie theater desire to extend their area of operation and build additional screens. They wish to lease new audio equipment as well. The lease will be repaid from the growth of sales and existing cash flow of the business.

COMPETING AND COMPLEMENTING COMPANIES

Banks no longer enjoy exclusive domination of the commercial lending market. The commercial customer can now turn to a variety of sources for financing. The source of financing a customer chooses depends, to some extent, on what the loan will be used for and the type of financing desired. Nonetheless, in today's competitive financial services environment, there are many alternatives to commercial bank loans. The following sources of financing either complement, or compete with, those offered by community banks.

Trade Creditors

Manufacturers and wholesalers often extend credit to purchasers of their inventory. The terms, usually 30 days or fewer, depend on the type of industry and the nature of the items being purchased. Trade creditors generally do not charge customers interest on the amount owed. However, they may charge interest or a late fee if payment is not received on time. Trade credit is known as **accounts payable** on the balance sheet. The terms "trade creditors" and "accounts payable" are used interchangeably.

Commercial Finance Companies

Commonly known as asset-based lenders, **commercial finance companies** specialize in making working capital or investment capital loans to small businesses. The loans are secured by the businesses' accounts receivable, inventory, or, on occasion, equipment.

Asset-based lenders make loans based on the value of the collateral the borrower agrees to pledge, not the financial condition of the company. Assets commonly considered are accounts receivable and inventory. The loans usually are monitored daily. Banks often work with asset-based lenders in order to offer better pricing. For example, an asset-based lender may originate a loan at 8 percent, and the bank will buy a participation at 6 percent. The effective yield is lower for the borrower, but the bank receives the added monitoring benefit provided by the commercial finance company. This type of arrangement is particularly useful when lending to a start-up business or to rapidly growing companies, which are often more of a credit risk to banks. Larger banks may have a separate commercial finance company subsidiary.

Commercial Sales Finance Companies

Commercial sales finance companies are generally involved in financing large industrial or agricultural equipment, either by purchasing the finance paper from equipment dealers or by directly financing the equipment themselves. They offer competitive terms by financing the purchase price for a longer term than the bank.

Leasing Companies

Leasing companies are a major source of credit for financing equipment for businesses. Leasing is an attractive alternative because the initial capital outlay is small and there are often tax benefits, that is, the lease payments may be tax-deductible. Equipment with quickly changing technology is often leased. Companies with rapid growth can choose to lease equipment in order to use their capital to fund the growth.

Insurance Companies

Insurance companies extend loans for large equipment and commercial real estate projects. Hard assets, such as the equipment or commercial real estate, usually secure these loans. They have long maturity dates. Insurance companies also compete with banks in the retail credit market, offering, for example, auto loans.

Brokerage Firms

In today's financial services marketplace, brokerage firms have become strong competitors of banks. They compete with banks for personal and small business loans, typically offer quick servicing of loan requests, and are staffed with professionally trained sales representatives. Brokerage firms may set up lines of credit to fund their loans or have sufficient cash on hand.

SUMMARY

It is important for the lender to thoroughly understand the applicant company's legal and organizational structure. Companies may be sole proprietorships, partnerships, corporations, Sub S corporations, or limited liability companies. Understanding each of the five basic types of businesses—manufacturers, wholesalers, retailers, service companies, and agricultural businesses—and how each has a characteristic operating cycle that creates differing funding needs are key to understanding the purpose, repayment source, and risk of a loan.

The operating cycle and the fixed asset cycle explain the cash movements related to a company's basic operations. Those cycles must generate sufficient cash to replenish current working assets, provide for growth, and repay debt. Any other cash requirements are outside of the company's primary operation, and management should consider these needs only after the company has adequately provided for the funding requirements of the operating and fixed asset cycles.

Understanding the company's business operations will also help a lender understand its cash cycle. As illustrated by the Harris Table Company examples, cash flow cycles may use various sources of cash—including capital, trade credit, accrued expenses, and bank loans.

With an understanding of a loan applicant's legal and organizational structure, and its operating, cash flow, and fixed asset cycles, the lender can then consider possible lending arrangements. These include special commitment loans, seasonal lines of credit, revolving lines of credit, permanent working capital loans, letters of credit, term loans, and lease financing. With the current changing financial environment, the lender must also know possible alternative sources of financing that may complement or compete with the bank. These include trade creditors, commercial finance companies, commercial sales finance companies, asset-based lenders, leasing companies, insurance companies, and brokerage firms.

QUESTIONS FOR DISCUSSION

1. How would the net worth section of a balance sheet for a proprietorship, a partnership, and a corporation differ?
2. Diagram the operating cycle for a floor-covering retailer. Identify the various loan purposes, sources of repayment, and lending risk.
3. What are the differences among trade credit, accruals, and capital as sources of funding?
4. A car dealer needs to purchase new diagnostic equipment. What are the possible lending sources that would compete with bank financing?
5. List the reasons a photography studio would borrow money. What could disrupt the operating cycle of a photography studio?

Exercise 1

What type of lending arrangement would you recommend for the following loan purposes?

1. purchase winter coats and gloves
2. purchase a printing press
3. open a new location in an adjacent city
4. import German auto parts
5. gradually expand existing customer base

Exercise 2

Identify the potential problems that could disrupt the operating cycle of the following businesses (exclude the economy, the weather, and so forth, from your answers). Focus on what is within the control of the owner.

1. a local gas and grocery retailer
2. a bowling alley
3. a wholesaler of dried cereals
4. a manufacturer of plows

3

INCOME STATEMENT ANALYSIS

LEARNING OBJECTIVES

After studying *Income Statement Analysis*, you will be able to

- list the basic components of an income statement,
- spread and common-size an income statement,
- identify issues that affect revenue analysis,
- differentiate among expenses that are in cost of goods sold, operating expenses, other income, interest expense, and other expense on an income statement,
- explain the difference between LIFO, FIFO, and weighted average-cost inventory valuation methods,
- explain how the inventory valuation method affects a company's profitability,
- apply the concepts of comparison, break-even, and trend analysis to the income statement, and
- define the key terms that appear in **bold** type in the text.

INTRODUCTION

As an integral part of a financial statement, the income statement reflects a firm's revenues from sales and its costs of doing business. In preparing income statements, businesses usually use accrual accounting concepts to match revenues with expenses over a stated period of time (usually 12 months). Income statements also may be prepared using a cash-basis method, which recognizes income when received and expenses when paid in cash. An income statement is called a profit and loss (P&L) statement or earnings statement as well.

Income statements consist of revenues and expenses. When revenues exceed expenses, companies are profitable. Because income statements are a gauge of a company's ability to convert its resources to cash flow, lenders regard these statements as an important tool for evaluating a company's long-range profitability. A company's earnings are the primary component of the cash available to repay creditors (principal and interest). Therefore, the analysis of a company's income statement is a major factor in the lender's decision to extend credit.

The evaluation of an income statement requires an understanding of the company's industry. To achieve this, lenders must identify both internal and external factors—factors that the company can control and those it cannot—that contribute to the demand for a company's products or services. For example, most companies cannot control the economy but can control how much they spend on operating expenses, such as advertising.

To analyze an income statement, a lender starts with a complete understanding of how a company achieved sales or revenues. Next, the lender calculates and analyzes the cost of goods sold based on the type of business and industry. Inventory, a key component of cost of goods sold, is valued by using the last-in first-out basis, the first-in first-out basis, or the weighted average cost method. Finally, a lender reviews operating expenses (also called selling, general, and administrative expenses (S, G, & A)).

Some costs are fixed and others are variable. The relationship of fixed costs to total costs is called *operating leverage.* Comparison, trend, operating leverage, and break-even analysis are additional tools used to analyze the income statement.

CONCEPT OF THE SPREADSHEET

Financial statement analysis typically begins with reviewing the accounts on the financial statements, then placing that information into a spreadsheet—a format that is used for credit analysis within the bank. Three advantages of using spreadsheets are the

- ease of dealing with rounded and common-sized numbers,
- consistent treatment of accounts for all borrowers, and
- ease of spotting trends.

On a spreadsheet, income statement and balance sheet accounts are grouped under the same line categories year by year, to provide a consistent presentation of the account over a period of time.

Rules

Before analyzing a company's financial statement, a lender should review the basic rules for analyzing a spreadsheet:

1. *Numbers are rounded off to four or five digits.* This convention makes the spreadsheet easier to read. If financial statement entries are in the millions, the numbers are rounded to the thousands on the spreadsheet. If financial statement entries are in the thousands, the spreadsheet components are rounded to the hundreds. For example, if sales were $4,385,289, the spreadsheet would show $4,385 with the label "000s omitted" at the top.

2. *Spread and analyze annual and interim statements separately.* Compare interim statements with interim statements of the same date from previous years. If quarterly or monthly statements are available, make multiple spreadsheets that contain fiscal years, first quarters, second quarters, third quarters, and fourth quarters. The spreadsheet allows the lender to review several years of financial performance at once.

3. *Read the CPA's opinion and footnotes before spreading the statement and beginning the analysis.* Because footnotes generally detail the basic methods used to construct financial statements, it is essential that they be read before spreading the statement. Some footnotes contain information that does not appear on the balance sheet, income statement, statement of cash flows, or reconciliation of equity. This information may pertain to potential lawsuits, warranties, and events that will take place after the statement date. The footnotes for Turner Electronic Corporation, located in the *Master Case Book*, serve as an example.

4. *Determine the intangibles.* Identify, research, and evaluate intangibles. These include patents, trademarks, goodwill, deferred charges, and organizational costs. The amortization expense of intangibles appears on the income statement, whereas the items themselves appear on the balance sheet. **Amortization** is the expensing of an intangible asset over its life period. Generally, intangibles have little or no value to the lender in the event of liquidation. They are deducted from the net worth to calculate a tangible net worth.

5. *Consider the following factors before and during the analysis:*

    - the type of business and its management objectives
    - external factors
    - whether the statements are fiscal year or interim
    - methods the company uses to recognize revenue and expenses
    - sales volumes, sales trends, product or service mix, order back logs, discounts, allowances, returns, large nonrecurring sales, seasons, and cyclical factors
    - cost of goods calculation and the method used to value inventory
    - fixed and variable operating expenses
    - other income and other expense components
    - taxation issues
    - who prepared the statements

TYPES OF BUSINESSES AND MANAGEMENT OBJECTIVES

The financial characteristics of manufacturers, wholesalers, retailers, and service companies are distinctly different. In producing a product, manufacturers have high fixed expenses (building, labor, and equipment). Because of high fixed expenses, a decline in sales quickly affects a manufacturer's net profit margin. Wholesalers sell large volumes of finished products at prices slightly higher than the products actually cost. In order to remain profitable, wholesalers must manage and control operating expenses. Retailers move numerous products and have high personnel costs. To remain profitable, retailers must understand how to control product and inventory turnover by department. Service companies, in contrast, do not produce a finished product but, to be profitable, must control personnel costs while providing quality service.

Management objectives also influence the income statement. For example, if a company wanted to capture a larger market share, it might decide to lower the selling price of its products or to introduce new products. If it lowers selling prices without lowering other expenses, profits would decrease in the future. And if the new products were priced low when compared to the production or acquisition costs, this, too, would lower profits.

EXTERNAL FACTORS

Competitive, regulatory, and economic conditions affect a company's income statements. Newly enacted tax laws can affect everything from tax rates on profits to depreciation of fixed assets. These changes may appear as lower net profits on the income statement. Regulatory changes, such as new environmental requirements, increased health and safety standards, or decreased import quotas (the amount of goods that may be imported annually), also affect profits.

For example, a company may import parts from the Far East for internal components. Changes in quotas could affect its sales and, ultimately, net profits. Consumers may spend less during periods of poor economic performance. This lack of consumer confidence can translate into lower sales and possibly less profit. Also, changes in unemployment rates will have almost an immediate impact on many types of products. The lender must thoroughly understand the economic environment of a company and factors that influence the company's profitability.

METHOD OF ACCRUING REVENUE AND PERIOD OF INCOME STATEMENT

Before analyzing the income statement, the lender reviews the method of accruing revenue and the period covered by the statement. This information helps the lender analyze the type of information summarized in each of the various income statement categories.

Method of Accruing Revenue

Although many small companies use a cash-basis method of accounting, financial statements generally are prepared on an accrual basis. **Accrual-based financial statements** recognize revenues (used interchangeably with sales) when sales are made—not when payment is received—and expenses when they are incurred, not necessarily when payment is made.

Different types of expenses are recognized in distinct time periods. On accrual-based financial statements, expenses that relate directly to sales of tangible items are called **cost of goods sold** on the income statement and are not recognized until the inventory item is sold. A buildup in inventory (for a wholesaler or retailer) or in raw materials, works-in-process, or unsold finished goods (for a manufacturer) will reduce profits whether or not the LIFO (last-in, first-out) or FIFO (first-in, first-out) method is used. However, the effect is greater when LIFO is used. (LIFO and FIFO approaches to inventory costing will be discussed later.) Furthermore, the cost related to the purchase of fixed assets, such as equipment, is not recognized at the time of the purchase or upon delivery of the equipment. Instead, the company recognizes depreciation expense, derived from the cost of fixed assets, over a period equal to the expected useful life of the asset. Depreciation is a non-cash expense that reduces the fixed asset value over the life of the asset.

Period of Income Statement

An income statement that spans a year is called an annual statement or **fiscal year-end statement.** Income statements prepared for periods of less than 12 months are called **interim statements.** Although some businesses experience a production cycle of more than one year, they still have to prepare income statements every 12 months to meet the requirements of most lenders and the Internal Revenue Service. The most common interim periods are semiannual, quarterly, and monthly. Year-to-date figures prepared at the end of any month during the year also serve as interim statements. Therefore, the time represented by an interim statement can be from one to 11 months. Lenders generally require existing companies to submit annual income statements for at least the past two or three years, as well as current interims. A company owner or controller prepares most interim statements. An accountant usually prepares annual statements. Lenders may encounter difficulties when comparing interims with year-end statements prepared by an accountant because the accountant might have made year-end adjustments or used different accounting methods.

The *Master Case Book* shows the common-sized income statements on a computer-generated spreadsheet for Turner Electronic Corporation for the last three years. These comparative data will be used for analysis in examples throughout this chapter.

Sales Analysis

Most financial statements do not list gross sales. The first item on the income statement is net sales. Discounts, returns, and allowances are subtracted from gross sales to obtain net sales.

Discounts, Allowances, and Returns

Not all sales result in full payment. Discounts, allowances, and returns must be deducted from gross sales. In some industries, it is common to offer **discounts** for large volumes of purchases. A company also may offer a discount to improve the collection time period of the accounts receivable. For example, a company may offer a discount of 2 percent if payment is received in 10 days, but no discount if payments are received after 10 days. If the timing of the accounts receivable collection does not improve, the lender should question the reason the company offers a discount. Many times when a company offers a discount, customers do not pay within the terms to get the discount. The lender is concerned if discounts are being given to customers who are paying within terms. The discount lowers the gross profit and ultimately the net profit the company earns. If a customer pays within terms and takes the discount, the company will have quicker use of the cash, which then can be used for continuing operations and repaying bank debt.

Allowances result when customers are compensated for faulty goods by being given credit on future bills. **Returns** result when merchandise is returned and the bill is canceled.

Discounts, allowances, and returns are considered when analyzing a company's profits and collateral. For example, if a company earns a 2 percent net profit margin and provides a 2 percent discount, the earnings would have been 4 percent if this discount had not been provided. Alternatively, if returns and allowances represent 2 percent of sales, earnings would have doubled to 4 percent if there had not been product problems or returns. Increasing allowances and returns can be an indicator of a decline in the quality of a company's products or services.

After analyzing gross sales, discounts, returns, and allowances, the lender then calculates net sales, which is the first entry on most income statements.

Gross sales
− sales discounts
− sales returns
− allowances
_____
= net sales

Exhibit 3.1 illustrates the calculation of net sales for the last three years for Turner Electronic Corporation.

An analysis of the discounts, returns, and allowances, suggests that the sales growth in 20x1 affected product quality. The number of returns and allowances increased. Also, the company gave more discounts to achieve the sales. The amount of discounts, returns, and allowances dropped in 20x2, indicating that the company's product quality probably returned to previous levels.

Net Sales

When analyzing net sales, the lender considers sales volume and price trends, sales mix, order back-logs, large nonrecurring orders, sales to marginal customers, seasons, and cyclical factors.

Exhibit 3.1   Net Sales—Turner Electronic Corporation (000s omitted)

	20x0	20x1	20x2
Gross sales	$6,425	$7,804	$7,439
– discounts	112	178	92
– returns	41	93	56
– allowances	12	51	21
= net sales	$6,260	$7,482	$7,270

Sales Volume and Price Trends

A good indicator of a company's performance is the change in sales levels over several years. By scanning an income statement spreadsheet, a lender can readily note and compare the dollar value in sales. However, numbers can be misleading. A consistent 6 percent to 8 percent increase in sales may not indicate a good performance when the competition and industry are growing at a 10 percent rate during the same period. Also, if the inflation rate (for the industry or the national economy) is 4 percent, a 2 percent increase in sales may actually be a loss when compared to the increased costs of 4 percent.

Good lenders focus on comparison analysis, not on the technical number changes. Revenues on the income statement should be compared with current sales, sales in previous periods, and competitors' sales growth. A company's annual sales figures are easier to evaluate when they are compared with previous years' sales. This type of comparison is called **trend analysis.** When sales figures are compared to companies in the same industry during the same period, it is called **comparison analysis.**

Sales volume and price also can be affected by how the company pays its sales personnel. Some companies pay sales personnel based on sales volume. This may result in large sales with less profit. Other companies pay commission based on gross profit, which encourages the sales personnel to sell the more profitable items.

Turner Electronic Corporation's net sales for the last three fiscal income statements are as follows:

Year	Sales (000s omitted)
20x0	$6,260
20x1	$7,482
20x2	$7,270

On a dollar and percentage basis, the change from year to year would be:

	% Change	$ Change (000s omitted)
Period 20x0–20x1	19.50%	$ 1,222
Period 20x1–20x2	(2.80%)	$ (212)

Taking the dollar amount of change, year to year, and dividing it by the base year, derive the calculation. For example, the dollar change between 20x0 and 20x1 was an increase of $1,222. Dividing that amount by the 20x0 base of $6,260 equals 19.5 percent.

When analyzed technically, sales grew from 20x0 to 20x1 and then decreased the following year on a percentage basis. The percentage average during the three years shows a growth of 16 percent. If during the three years, the industry and competition grew at a 20 percent rate, then Turner Electronic Corporation has not done as well as its competition. However, if the competition and industry grew only 8 percent, then the company did better.

Another way to look at sales is on a unit basis. Sales revenue is determined by volume and price. Referring back to Turner Electronic Corporation, if 20x0 sales were achieved by selling 1,000 DVD players at $3,000 each and 1,630 speakers at $2,000 each, then the average sale was $2,380. If prices and product mix in 20x1 remained the same, then the increase in revenues came from increasing the number of sales units. But if the company instituted a price increase of 25 percent, the number of units sold in 20x1 declined, since sales grew only 19.5 percent. These potential product and price changes are illustrated in the following examples.

20x0 Sales by Product

Product	Number of Units	Price	Total Sales	Average Sale
DVD players	1,000	$3,000	$3,000,000	$3,000
Speakers	1,630	$2,000	$3,260,000	$2,000
Total	2,630		$6,260,000	$2,380

20x1 Sales by Product with No Price Changes

Product	Number of Units	Price	Total Sales	Average Sale
DVD players	1,200	$3,000	$3,600,000	$3,000
Speakers	1,941	$2,000	$3,882,000	$2,000
Total	3,141		$7,482,000	$2,382

In the example of 20x1 sales with a 25 percent price increase, the company sold fewer units in 20x1 than in 20x0, and its sales increase was strictly due to the price increases.

20x1 Sales by Product with 25 Percent Price Increase

Product	Number of Units	Price	Total Sales	Average Sale
DVD players	960	$3,750	$3,600,000	$3,750
Speakers	1,552	$2,500	$3,880,00	$2,500
Total	2,512		$7,480,000	$2,978

Sales Mix

Businesses often differentiate sales by new customers, old customers, operating divisions, product lines, sales territories, and so forth. Companies that carry numerous products for sale, such as a retailer of sporting goods, are often best analyzed by looking at average dollar sales and number of customers per department. Such breakdowns can help the loan officer focus on the precise factors influencing sales. If Turner Electronic Corporation realizes 60 percent of its revenues from speaker sales and 40 percent from DVD players, but devotes equal manufacturing equipment and other resources to making both, the loan officer may question management's decisions.

Order Backlogs

One indicator of future sales is order backlogs. Trends in order backlogs can provide insight into future revenue streams and the company's capacity to supply its product or service. For example, if Turner Electronic Corporation had order backlogs of $500,000 in 20x1 and $800,000 for 20x2, the lender might reasonably assume sales will increase in 20x3. However, excessive order backlogs could also create customer dissatisfaction, which might decrease future sales.

Large Nonrecurring Sales

A one-time sale may contribute to a substantial increase in the level of sales from one year to the next. For example, if Turner Electronic Corporation sales grew from 20x0 to 20x1 due to a one-time order of $500,000, then the decrease in sales in 20x2 is not as dramatic as it might appear.

Sales to Marginal Customers

Businesses sometimes yield to temptation by relaxing normal credit terms in order to obtain sales and grow profits. Lenders can detect this by looking for slowing payment trends in accounts receivable and rapid new customer growth. Lenders need to know whether future profits could be affected because some of the accounts receivable may actually be a bad debt expense.

Seasonal and Cyclical Factors

When making either internal or external sales comparisons, lenders should use income statements that cover comparable periods because seasonality and other cyclical factors may cause wide variations in sales from period to period. It is pointless to compare revenues for a three-month period during a company's peak selling season with sales for a three-month period during the low point of a company's seasonal cycle. The key issue in the analysis is peak versus low point, not specific months of the year. A year-round golf course in the South could not be compared validly with a course in the North that conducts business during the summer months only.

Sales trend comparisons of companies in cyclical industries are misleading if different time periods are compared. In an economic downturn, sales figures of a cyclical company are expected to be lower than in prosperous years. And as the economy emerges from a recession, such a company's sales will show dramatic increases. As a result, it can be difficult to assess the performance of a cyclical company. A good assessment would compare a company's annual statements of similar time periods with those of competitors.

For a complete sales analysis, the lender must understand what questions to ask. A summary of key questions regarding the income statement is found in the *Master Case Book*.

EXPENSE ANALYSIS

After probing the changes in revenues shown on the income statement, the lender's next step is to consider the corresponding expenses incurred. The evaluation of expenses in relation to revenues begins with a consideration of the company's cost of goods sold, inventory valuation method, and gross profit margins, followed by a detailed analysis of its operating expenses.

Cost of Goods Sold

The second entry on the income statement is **cost of goods sold**. Whenever a product is manufactured or purchased for sale, certain direct costs are incurred. The cost of goods sold is based on the products purchased or manufactured during a business's operating cycle or interim period that are available for sale. However, in accrued financial statements, costs of goods sold are not recognized until the company sells the inventory. When calculating the cost of goods for the products that were sold, a company's beginning and ending inventories need to be taken into consideration. A service company has little or no inventory and, therefore, generally has no cost of goods sold.

Cost of Goods Sold—Manufacturer

For a manufacturer, the cost of goods calculation is complex because three different types of inventory must be identified: raw materials, work-in-process, and finished goods. For example, a manufacturer of wine mixes water and grape juice (raw materials) and then begins the process of fermenting (work-in-process) before the wine (finished goods) is made.

Manufacturing expenses (direct labor costs and certain overhead expenses) also must be added to determine the true cost of the finished products. Again, these costs are recognized as expenses only when the company sells its inventory, which means that beginning and ending inventory amounts must be considered.

The analysis of a manufacturer's cost of goods sold must include not only pricing considerations, but also an evaluation of the company's cost controls. Understanding manufacturer's efficiency in controlling productivity (that is, manufacturing as much product as possible from a given amount of labor and related overhead expenses) is critical for a lender.

Cost of goods for a manufacturer is calculated as follows:

> Beginning inventory
> + raw materials used
> + labor expense
> + manufacturing overhead
> − work-in-process
> − ending inventory
> _____
> = cost of goods sold

The formula can be expanded to analyze the various components using the following calculations:

> Beginning raw materials
> + purchases
> − ending raw materials
> _____
> = raw materials used

> Beginning work-in-process
> + raw materials used
> + labor
> + manufacturing overhead
> − ending work-in-process
> _____
> = cost of goods manufactured

> Beginning finished goods
> + cost of goods manufactured
> − ending inventory
> _____
> = cost of goods sold

The formula does not assume inventory is sold. It assumes that inventory was present at the beginning of the period, was gone at the end of the period, and that something happened to cause the difference. That difference could have resulted from loss, theft, or sales. The term *shrinkage* is used to describe inventory that has been written off due to loss or theft.

Purchasing lower quality **raw materials** can affect finished product quality overall and potentially affect sales and profits. Obtaining competitive bids may help control the cost of raw materials. Some industries have many potential suppliers of raw material, whereas others are limited to a few. A lender can determine whether a manufacturer is purchasing inferior raw materials by examining the returns and the visiting the plant to inspect finished goods. This is important because ultimately it may affect the customer's ability to sell the product.

Labor costs comprise the wages paid to production workers. Manufacturing overhead expenses usually are allocated according to a percentage of space. For example, if 60 percent of a manufacturer's facilities are used in the manufacturing process, then 60 percent of the total utilities, rent, general managerial expenses, and building depreciation (a noncash expense) would be allocated to manufacturing overhead. Equipment depreciation also is allocated on some basis, either by time or hours used, predicated on the original useful-life estimated by management.

Maintenance and replacement of fixed assets are items that management can easily stall or control to smooth the variations in income from period to period. Maintenance can be cut back in a period of high-volume production or competition. Unless it is prolonged, such a cutback usually will not seriously harm the future operations of the company. For analysis, depreciation is less important than overhead expenses. Because it is a noncash charge that does not affect cash flow, depreciation is of less concern. Nevertheless, its effect on profits can be quite dramatic. The analytical problem relates to estimating the useful life of the asset. Briefly, management can select a life that is conservatively short, thereby lowering profits, or choose one that is aggressively long, which would increase profits. For the lender, it is important that income be stated consistently each year.

The cost of goods sold for Turner Electronic Corporation in 20x0, 20x1, and 20x2 is calculated in exhibit 3.2. Each cost of goods sold category is expressed in dollars and as a percentage of net sales.

The costs of raw materials and manufacturing overhead have risen faster than sales. Raw materials have risen from 35 percent to 39 percent of net sales. The lender will want to understand why the company is not passing on to its customers the costs of raw materials and what is causing the company to purchase more raw materials. Manufacturing overhead has risen from 11 to 14 percent of net sales. A detailed list of these expenses should be obtained and analyzed.

Cost of Goods Sold—Wholesaler and Retailer

Adding the company's inventory purchases to the beginning inventory for that period and then subtracting the ending inventory calculates the cost of goods sold for a wholesaler or retailer. This gives the cost of the merchandise sold (or lost or stolen) during the period. The basic formula for calculating the cost of goods sold for a retailer or a wholesaler is:

$$
\begin{array}{l}
\text{Beginning inventory} \\
+ \text{ net cost of purchases} \\
\underline{- \text{ ending inventory}} \\
= \text{cost of goods sold}
\end{array}
$$

The net cost of purchases, which includes shipping costs, can be further refined by subtracting volume discounts, returns, and allowances on purchased goods.

Exhibit 3.2 Cost of Goods Sold Calculation—Turner Electronic Corporation (000s omitted)

	20x0		20x1		20x2	
Net sales	$6,260	100%	$7,482	100%	$7,270	100%
Beginning inventory	1,696	27%	1,787	24%	1,980	27%
+ raw materials	2,194	35%	2,722	36%	2,853	39%
+ labor costs	1,187	19%	1,324	18%	1,285	18%
+ manufacturing overhead	699	11%	807	11%	1,022	14%
= cost of goods available for sale	5,776	92%	6,640	89%	7,140	98%
− ending inventory	1,787	28%	1,980	26%	2,392	33%
= cost of goods sold	3,989	63.7%	4,660	62.3%	4,748	65.3%

This is shown by:

$$\frac{\text{Purchases} - \text{(purchase discounts, returns, and allowances)}}{\text{= net purchases}}$$

$$\frac{\text{Net purchases} + \text{transportation costs}}{\text{= net cost of purchases}}$$

Determining Physical Inventory

Inventory is a key component in the cost of goods sold for all companies. For some retailers, a perpetual inventory system keeps a daily count of inventory for accounting purposes. When a business sells an item, it immediately deducts that item's cost from the inventory account. Companies usually use this system for very expensive or large inventory items that do not sell quickly and can be easily identified (serial numbers, color, size, and so forth). Automobile dealers, heavy equipment dealers, and jewelers are examples of companies that traditionally use a perpetual inventory system.

The perpetual inventory method is impractical for most companies because of the large number of low-value items in inventory. These companies use a periodic method of inventory instead. Even with computers to track sales, companies need to take a physical count of inventory on a scheduled basis to get a better estimate of their inventory, taking into account possible posting errors, damage, waste, and theft. Since inventory counts are normally taken once a year, or at the end of an operating cycle, interim statements usually are based on estimates of inventory.

A physical count might ensure an accurate account of inventory, but determining the value of the inventory is much more difficult. Balance sheets show the dollar value of the inventory. A loan officer must realize that this dollar value is an estimate based on the cost of a number of inventory items being purchased by the company over a period of time and having different prices because of various factors, including inflation. Therefore, it is important to remember most companies use an estimate to identify the value of inventory on interim balance sheets.

Inventory Value Methods

The two most common methods of valuing inventory are known as **last-in, first out (LIFO)** and **first-in, first-out (FIFO)**. FIFO uses the cost associated with the oldest remaining unit in inventory being recognized first as sold. Turner Electronic Corporation uses the FIFO method.

Unfortunately, the FIFO method also assumes that the currency used to set inventory value is stable from one statement period to the next. In times of rising inflation rates, FIFO assigns the dollar value of the older inventory to cost of goods sold, which usually happens to be valued at lower costs, resulting in a balance sheet that contains ending inventory valued at current cost. The result on the income statement is twofold: the statement's cost-of-goods-sold entry indicates costs lower than those required for the business to replace old inventory and remain in business, but the statement shows a higher gross profit. This type of profit is called *inventory holding gains profit*, since it is derived from the holding of inventory, not from the operating skills of management.

In contrast, LIFO uses the cost associated with the last—the newest—unit of inventory purchased to determine the expense charged in the income statement when any unit is sold. As a result, ending inventory is valued at old, rather than recent, prices. In inflationary periods, this valuation method causes the ending inventory item in the cost-of-goods formula to be lower relative to the purchases indicated. Unfortunately, the balance sheet contains old-cost inventory, but the income statement contains the more recent and higher costs, which in turn produces lower gross profits. The positive aspect is that the higher cost-of-goods-sold value under LIFO is in line with the replacement inventory costs the company faces to stay in business.

A LIFO windfall can occur when a company sells more than it purchases. As a company reduces older inventory valued at lower prices, inventory profits are created when the inventory is expensed through cost of goods sold—the very event that occurred over time using FIFO. Hence, FIFO produces inventory-holding gains over time, while LIFO avoids them as long as inventory is not declining, which is a typical situation. To illustrate the impact that inventory valuation has on ending inventory, cost of goods sold, gross profit, and net profit, consider a simple example in which inflation is running high. A new company has made the following inventory purchases over a three-day period. There is no beginning inventory because the company is new.

Inventory Purchases

Day	Number of Units	Unit Cost	Total Purchases
1	5,000	$1.00	$ 5,000
2	3,000	1.50	4,500
3	6,000	2.00	12,000
Total	14,000		21,500

If 8,000 units were sold on Day 3 for $4 per unit, and 6,000 units remained in inventory at the end of Day 3, the accounts on the two income statements—one prepared with the LIFO method and one prepared with FIFO—would appear as illustrated in exhibit 3.3.

As this example illustrates, the choice of inventory valuation method can significantly affect income statement accounts. Two companies might have identical sales revenue and expenses. However, by using the FIFO method, one company would appear to earn $3,630 more in profits ($14,850 versus $11,220).

A lender also should consider LIFO and FIFO from a collateral standpoint. Because LIFO inventory is carried at a lower cost on the balance sheet, a lower loan amount potentially may be advanced. For example, assume a lender uses a 50 percent advance rate on inventory. The lender will advance 50 percent of the cost of the inventory. As seen in exhibit 3.3, the ending inventory for LIFO is $6,500 and the ending inventory for FIFO is $12,000. If the 50 percent advance rate were used in each case, one borrower would receive $3,250 and the other $6,000. Lenders should not use the same advance rate for FIFO and LIFO values of inventory.

Weighted-average Cost Method

Along with the use of computerized inventory tracking, the weighted-average cost method is becoming more popular. Companies that have fluctuating inventory levels use weighted-average inventory accounting because it combines the other two methods, thereby reducing the inventory-holding gains of FIFO and limiting the gains in a LIFO windfall.

Exhibit 3.3 LIFO and FIFO Comparison

LIFO	LIFO	FIFO	FIFO
Sales (8,000 units @ $4.00)	$32,000	Sales (8,000 units @ $4.00)	$32,000
Opening inventory	$ 0	Opening Inventory	$ 0
Purchases	$21,500	Purchases	$21,500
Cost of goods available for sale	$21,500	Cost of goods available for sale	$21,500
Less ending inventory (6,000 units)		Less ending inventory (6,000 units)	
5,000 units @ $1.00	$ 5,000	6,000 units @ $2.00	$12,000
1,000 units @ $1.50	$ 1,500		
Subtotal	$ 6,500		
Cost of goods sold	$15,000	Cost of goods sold	$ 9,500
Gross profit	$17,000	Gross profit	$22,500
Gross margin	53%	Gross margin	70.3%
Income taxes @ 34%	$ 5,780	Income taxes @ 34%	$ 7,650
Net profit	$11,220	Net profit	$14,850

The weighted-average unit cost is calculated as the cost of goods for sale (beginning inventory and net purchases) divided by the units available for sale. A comparison of the weighted-average method with the FIFO and LIFO in exhibit 3.3 follows:

Weighted Average

Sales (8,000 units at $4.00)	$32,000
Purchases	$21,500
Goods available less ending inventory	$21,500
6,000 units at $1.54 ($21,500/14,000 = $1.54)	$ 9,240
Cost of goods sold	$12,260
Gross profit	$19,740
Gross margin	61.7%
Income tax @ 34%	$ 6,712
Net profit	$13,028

As one might expect, the weighted-average method shows results approximately halfway between the LIFO and FIFO methods.

The retail method is another inventory value method. It is used by retailers as a way of estimating the cost of their ending inventory. The retailer can either take a physical inventory at retail prices or can estimate ending retail inventory and use the cost-to-retail ratio to convert the ending inventory at retail to its estimated cost. This eliminates going back to original invoices or other documents to determine the original cost of each inventory item. The retail method can be used under any of these cost-flow assumptions: FIFO, LIFO, or weighted-average costs. The lender should understand which method is used because the valuation method affects net profits and the collateral value of the inventory.

Gross Profit and Gross Margin

Often, the cost of goods sold is expressed as a percentage of net sales. The difference between this percentage and 100 percent is the **gross margin. Gross profit** represents a company's profitability in dollars, based only on its sales, compared to its cost of goods sold. For a retailer or wholesaler, gross profit reflects the markup applied to the company's purchases, as reflected in its selling price. For a manufacturer, gross profit represents the value added to the raw materials or parts and labor in the manufacturing process. Gross profit is calculated

$$\text{Net sales} - \text{Cost of goods sold} = \text{Gross profit}$$

Gross margin is calculated

$$\frac{\text{Gross profit}}{\text{Net sales}} = \text{Gross profit margin}$$

Common-sizing and Gross Profit

The gross profit margin represents the percentage of each dollar of sales that is available to cover the company's other operating expenses. Expressing each component of the income statement as a percentage of net sales is called **common-sizing**. Although the concept is simple, its application in the actual operation of a business can be difficult. For instance, most companies sell several products, each of which may have a different cost-of-goods-sold percentage and gross profit margin. These percentages may vary not only for different products, but also for the same products over time, depending on the competition and general market conditions. Therefore, the lender only knows how the company's products are doing on average. Because a company's sales mix changes annually and the gross profit margin usually varies by product, the gross profit margin changes. For example,

- A retailer has 600 products, 300 of which are quite profitable and 300 of which are losing money, with the overall average being a relatively low profit margin
- A retailer has 600 products, all of which are marginally profitable, with the overall average being a relatively low profit margin

Without knowledge of product mix, both report low profits on sales of 600 units. With knowledge of sales mix, the lender could determine that discontinuing products sold at a loss would result in higher profits in the first bullet above. A lender would have to know the business better than the company's own management in order to reach a conclusion more correct than the one reached by management. Nevertheless, a lender needs to analyze a company's gross profit and gross margin in order to determine the dollar impact on the net profit.

Cost of Goods Sold Comparative Analysis

Based on the discussion above, it is evident that in order to compare cost of goods sold (or profit margins), a lender needs to know what inventory valuation method a company uses and must be aware that comparisons of companies using different valuation methods can be misleading. Since a change in the valuation method used can significantly affect the cost of goods sold and gross profit margin percentages, a lender must be alert to such a change and take it into account when examining a significant improvement or deterioration in the cost of goods sold as a percentage of total sales. A company can switch from FIFO to LIFO inventory valuation without Internal Revenue Service (IRS) approval. A switch from LIFO to FIFO requires IRS approval. Any gain realized from the switch must be amortized over twice the number of years the company used LIFO.

As long as a company consistently uses the same valuation method over successive operating periods, improvement or deterioration in the company's profit can be a meaningful indication of the company's performance. Nevertheless, using FIFO in a company with stable or growing inventories may indicate that management is artificially boosting profits in inflationary times. In view of the higher taxes being paid, this practice is detrimental to the company's shareholders and creditors. Because of the higher taxes being paid, the creditor is being harmed in the long run because there is less of an equity cushion.

The disparity between the two methods also opens the door to converting between the two to get more comparable figures. Generally accepted accounting principles (GAAP) require companies to provide information concerning the LIFO reserve in the footnotes so that the balance sheet may be updated with more current costs of the remaining inventory. This is done because LIFO charges current costs to the income statement—the proper approach to reflect current income unaffected by inventory holding gains.

With two years of GAAP financial statements, it is possible to combine the effects of the LIFO reporting and convert it to FIFO. Unfortunately, there is no information available to convert from FIFO to LIFO—the method that reports income with greater consistency in times of changing inflation rates. Thus, converting LIFO to FIFO is not recommended, even if doing so would make it easier to compare one company to another. Instead, when reviewing a company that uses LIFO, the lender should find a comparable company that uses LIFO because this method is a more adequate estimator of the current cost of goods sold.

The lender can perform the same types of examinations of gross profits and gross margins that previously were performed for sales. The lender can look at trends over time, industry comparisons, and breakdowns of profitability by product line and location. For example, by common-sizing the income statements for Turner Electronic Corporation, as shown in exhibit 3.4, it becomes clear that at the same time that sales were increasing between 20x0 and 20x2, the company's gross margin was decreasing.

In 20x2, the gross margin as a percentage of net sales is at a three-year low. The lender will want to determine what is causing the change and why sales declined, specifically:

Lenders should learn to look at the income statement in terms of 1 percent changes. For example, in 20x2, each 1 percent change is $72,700. The 3 percent decline in gross profit from 20x1 to 20x2 cost Turner Electronic Corporation $218,100 in lower gross profits. Without a corresponding decrease in other expenses, Turner Electronic Corporation's profits in 20x2 will surely decline.

Continued deterioration in Turner Electronic Corporation's gross margin, concurrent with sales remaining level, will mean greater risk to the lender, since net profits will probably decline.

Exhibit 3.4 Gross Profit Analysis—Turner Electronic Corporation (000s omitted)						
	20x0		*20x1*		*20x2*	
Net sales	$6,260	100.0%	$7,482	100.0%	$7,270	100.0%
Cost of goods sold	3,989	63.7%	4,660	62.3%	4,748	65.3%
Gross profit	2,271	36.3%	2,822	37.7%	2,522	34.7%

Operating Expenses

Operating expenses are those incurred by a company in the normal course of conducting its business, other than the just-mentioned expenses of purchasing inventory and direct manufacturing expenses (which constitute cost of goods sold). These operating expenses often are categorized on the income statement as **selling, general, and administrative expenses (S, G, & A)**. The last is a category that includes everything from salaries of office staff to postage stamps. Operating expenses are calculated:

> Selling expenses
> + general and administrative expenses
> _____
> = operating expenses

Factory workers' wages are included in cost of goods sold, whereas management's salaries are considered an operating expense. Manufacturing companies normally allocate a portion of the company's total overhead and administrative costs to cost of goods sold, and the remainder of those costs to operating expenses. Wholesalers, retailers, and service companies keep all of these expenses under operating expenses. The lender may find that a manufacturer has changed the allocation of certain manufacturing costs from cost of goods sold to operating expenses, or vice versa, thus distorting trend comparisons between costs of goods sold and operating expenses. In such cases, the lender must be cautious about evaluating large swings in gross profit margins, either positive or negative, until a detailed review of the company's expense allocations is made.

If it is available, a detailed breakdown of operating expenses is very useful in analyzing a company's operating expenses. Ideally, operating costs will be shown for two or more years. These costs—generally considered fixed costs—can be further categorized for in-depth analysis as controllable costs and noncontrollable costs. Controllable costs—which include bonuses, profit-sharing contributions, and a company's travel and entertainment budget—are usually higher in the years that the company expects higher earnings and are directly managed by the company management. These types of expenses can escalate because they directly benefit the persons controlling them—the managers. For example, charging excessive rental or lease payments to the company for facilities owned by the owners or managers of the company is clearly controllable.

Noncontrollable costs include utility payments, office salaries, and long-term lease obligations—all the necessary costs of doing business that cannot easily be changed by management. For example, once an equipment lease is signed, that expense cannot be altered, at least not in the near future. Identifying noncontrollable expenses and controllable expenses, especially in a small, privately held company, helps the lender identify the costs that must be met if the company is to remain in business, as opposed to those that could possibly be reduced to improve profitability. Presumably, if management has shown consistent and effective restraint over its controllable expenses in the past, it is likely to continue doing so during a debt repayment period. Exhibit 3.5 on the following page lists expenses by controllable and noncontrollable categories.

Exhibit 3.5 Types of Controllable and Noncontrollable Expenses

Controllable Expenses	Noncontrollable Expenses
Selling expense	Utilities
Advertising	Rent
Research and development	Salaries
Travel and entertainment	Insurance
Officer salaries	Lease payments
Profit sharing	Taxes (other than income, i.e., real estate,
Bonuses	sales, unemployment, withholding)

Operating Expense Analysis

Another way to evaluate a company's effectiveness of control is to look at operating expenses as a percentage of net sales. When sales increase faster than operating expenses, the operating expenses as a percentage of net sales decreases, thus showing good expense control. Consistency should also be analyzed by comparing a company's expenses in relation to net sales over time. In addition, comparing a company's operating costs to net sales with that of similar companies, or with an industry average, may be instructive.

Applying these concepts in an analysis of the operating expenses of Turner Electronic Corporation produces the conclusions shown in exhibit 3.6.

Exhibit 3.6 Operating Expense Analysis—Turner Electronic Corporation (000s omitted)

	20x0		20x1		20x2	
Net sales	$6,260	100.0%	$7,482	100.0%	$7,270	100.0%
Gross profit	2,271	36.3%	2,822	37.7	2,522	34.7
Personnel expenses	936	15.0	1,076	14.4	1,086	14.9
Occupancy expense	275	4.4	285	3.8	286	3.9
Selling expense	676	10.8	632	8.4	648	8.9
Office expense	239	3.8	245	3.3	332	4.6
Other expenses	8	0.1	22	0.3	8	0.1
Bad debt expense	40	0.6	8	0.1	2	
Total operating expenses	2,174	34.7	2,268	30.3	2,362	32.5
Operating profit	97	1.5	554	7.4	160	2.2

Note: Each component is expressed as a percentage of net sales.

Analysis of Turner Electronic Corporation Operating Expenses

The lender is now ready to analyze the major accounts listed as operating expenses. For Turner Electronic Corporation these include: personnel, rent, selling, office, and bad debt expenses.

Personnel Expenses

Personnel expenses have remained stable as a percentage of sales. The company has been able to increase its sales without additional personnel expense (such as office, bookkeeping, and so forth). The lender will want to know how long this can continue and what future costs are expected to be. The owner's salary of $360,000 is divided into cost of goods sold (manufacturing overhead) and personnel expenses. The owner's salary has been $360,000 per year for three years. The lender will need to determine how much of this is necessary to meet the owner's debt and living expenses and what, if any, is excess.

Rent

Rental expenses for Turner Electronic Corporation's facilities are $456,000 annually ($204,000 in cost of goods sold for the plant and $252,000 of the occupancy expenses for administrative offices). The owner of the company owns the building. The lender will want to know the monthly costs the owner needs to pay and if the rent is in line with the market. Other occupancy expenses included in the rent are for the maintenance of the building. The sales growth during that period indicates an increasingly efficient use of the facilities. Because commercial rents for manufacturers, wholesalers, and service companies are usually based on a long-term lease, a business's rent may not increase or decrease with changes in sales volume. For retailers, many long-term leases have a fixed cost plus a percentage of net sales. As net sales increase, the rent increases.

Selling Expenses

The selling expenses are for commissioned sales personnel. The lender will want to know how many sales personnel are employed and if they are paid on sales or gross profit as a percentage commission.

Office Expenses

The assembly personnel are under cost of goods sold and office personnel are under personnel expense. Office expenses have increased $87,000 in one year without a corresponding increase in sales. Upon further examination, the lender determined that legal expenses were included in office expenses, which increased by $78,000 in 20x2 in order to sue a competitor. The lender will need to determine the expected outcome and future legal expenses.

Bad Debt and Other Expense

The lender might also question the unusual charge to bad debt in 20x0 ($40) and in other expenses in 20x1 ($21). Will these recur in the future or were they one-time events?

Operating Profit or Loss

Operating profit represents the profit from the basic operation of the company—that is, manufacturing or acquiring products and then selling them. Operating profit is a key figure in analyzing how efficiently and consistently management has used the company's resources in its primary operations to generate profits. In closely held companies, the size of the owner's salary and other expense items that could be forms of owner's compensation can affect operating profit. These items might include rent paid on buildings actually owned by the owner of the company, profit sharing, pension fund payments, automobile expenses, and travel expenses.

An operating loss results if a company's expenses exceed its gross profit. Operating profit or loss is calculated

$$
\begin{array}{l}
\text{Gross profit} \\
- \text{ operating expenses}^* \\
\hline
= \text{ operating profit or loss}
\end{array}
$$

* Selling, general, and administrative

Operating Profit Analysis

The operating profit for Turner Electronic Corporation (shown in exhibit 3.6) has decreased 5.2 percent in one year. The cause of the decline is the decline in gross profit mentioned earlier and a 2.2 percent increase in operating expenses. Operating profits for Turner Electronic Corporation have been inconsistent for three years, and the lender will want to understand the cause and the potential effect on future earnings. Again, operating profit should be viewed as a percent of sales, and the lender should watch for one-percent changes. Each one-percent change in the year 20x2 is $72,700 per year. In the year 20x2 the company earned $34,000 in net profit after tax. Therefore, a one-percent decrease in operating expenses could almost triple company earnings, whereas a one-percent increase in operating expenses would cause a net loss from operations.

BREAK-EVEN ANALYSIS

With an understanding of a company's total costs, the lender should next consider the company's break-even point. A company's **break-even point** is the point where the revenue from sales equals total costs. Below the break-even point, the company is losing money. At the break-even point, the company has neither a profit nor a loss; its net income is zero. It also is unable to repay any current maturities of long-term debt. Three factors affect the break-even point: fixed costs, variable costs, and selling price.

Fixed Costs

Company costs that do not vary with increases or decreases in sales or production levels are called fixed costs. Examples include property taxes, rent, insurance, salaries of office staff, utilities, maintenance cost, and interest and principal payments. Although payments of loan principal are not shown as an expense on the income statement, they are

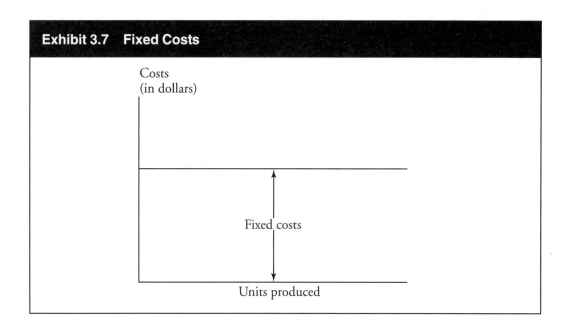

Exhibit 3.7 Fixed Costs

treated as a fixed cost in **break-even analysis.** Exhibit 3.7 shows that fixed costs remain constant regardless of the company's production or sales level.

Variable Costs

Company costs that vary relative to the level of sales or production are called variable costs. Examples include purchases of raw material (for a manufacturer) and inventory (for a retailer or wholesaler), hourly employee wages, and sales commissions. For many companies the variable costs are close to the cost of goods sold. Manufacturers and other labor-intensive companies usually have high variable costs. Exhibit 3.8 shows that variable costs rise as the production level or sales level increases.

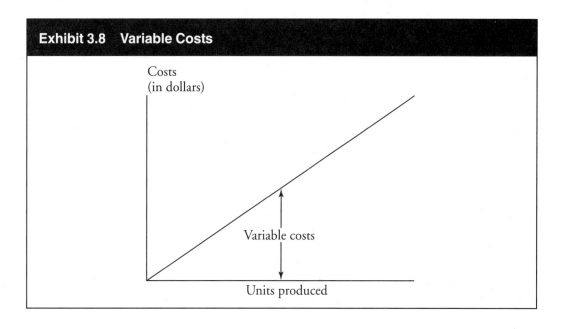

Exhibit 3.8 Variable Costs

In times of declining sales, some variable costs become fixed, which could change the break-even point. For example, a manufacturer keeps the machinists on payroll when machines are not running because of declining sales. The payroll then becomes fixed. It is very hard for small companies to lay off these workers, as they may have worked there for years and a "family" atmosphere exists. Also, if a company lays off the better-skilled workers, they will be able to find jobs quickly. When sales increase again, the company might have to replace them and good replacements might or might not be available. The expense of keeping the workers on the payroll as a fixed cost is less than the risk of not finding good workers later.

Selling Price

The selling price is important when analyzing break-even points because if the company does not sell its products for more than they cost, the company will not be profitable. Companies may sell some products for less than cost or at cost in order to obtain other product sales. For example, a grocery store may sell bananas at less than cost with the expectation the purchaser will buy other items with profit margins. When a company has high fixed costs, the selling price is even more important because the fixed costs must be covered before the company will be profitable.

Simple Break-even Analysis

For an illustration of the impact of fixed costs, variable costs, and selling price on a company's break-even point, examine Turner Electronic Corporation. The company purchases certain repair parts, such as speaker wires, and resells them. Individual wires were purchased for 75 cents and resold for $1.25. The cost of the wires is considered variable because if no repair speaker wires are needed none should be purchased. Variable costs are generally the cost of goods sold. The company's contribution margin is defined as that portion of the sales available to cover fixed costs and produce net income. It is calculated as:

Selling price per unit	$1.25
− variable cost per unit in dollars	$0.75
= contribution margin per unit in dollars	$0.50

The contribution margin also can be expressed as a percentage of the selling price. In this case, the contribution margin percentage is 40 percent (0.75/1.25). At present there are no fixed costs, so the company's break-even point cannot be calculated. Now, suppose that sales improve dramatically and Turner Electronic Corporation has to hire a part-time office worker for $5,000 per year. This is a fixed cost (it does not vary with the company's sales) that needs to be covered by the 50 cents of each sales dollar (the company's contribution margin in dollars). The company must now sell 10,000 speaker wires to reach its break-even point.

This is calculated as:

$$\frac{\text{Fixed costs}}{\text{Contribution margin in dollars}} = \text{Break-even point in units}$$

For our example, the calculation would be:

$$\frac{\$5,000}{0.50} = 10,000 \text{ units}$$

The fixed costs divided by the contribution margin in dollars equals the number of units that need to be sold. The fixed costs divided by the contribution margin as a percentage equals the net sales volume that must be obtained.

$$\frac{\$5,000 \ (\text{fixed costs})}{0.40 \ (\text{contribution margin})} = \$12,500$$

This can be verified as follows:

Sales*	$12,500
− variable costs**	$ 7,500
− fixed costs***	$ 5,000
= break-even point	$ 0

*10,000 units @ $1.25; **10,000 units @ 0.75 cents; ***salaries and rent

Eventually, more space is needed to store records and handle correspondence, so the company rents a building for $1,000 per year (another fixed cost). The company's fixed costs are now $6,000 per year, further increasing the break-even point. The company now must sell 12,000 speaker wires to reach the break-even point. This is calculated using the same formulas as before.

Break-even using the contribution margin in dollars:

$$\frac{\$6,000}{0.50} = 12,000 \text{ units}$$

Break-even using the contribution margin as a percentage:

$$\frac{\$6,000}{0.40} = \$15,000$$

Again, this can be verified:

Sales*	$15,000
− variable costs**	$ 9,000
− fixed costs***	$ 6,000
= break-even	$ 0

*12,000 units @ $1.25; **12,000 units @ 0.75 cents;
***$5,000 in salaries plus $1,000 in rent

As sales grow, Turner Electronic Corporation hires a commissioned sales person so the owner can stay in the office to fill orders and manage shipments. The salesperson is paid 5 cents on all sales (a variable cost). Variable costs are now 80 cents per unit (75 cent cost of each speaker wire and 5 cent commission per sale). This reduces the company's contribution margin from 50 cents on each speaker wire sold to 45 cents ($1.25 − 0.80), and further increases the break-even point. If the fixed costs remain at $6,000, then 13,333 speaker wires must be sold to break even.

The break-even point in units is calculated:

$$\frac{\$6,000}{0.45} = 13,333 \text{ units}$$

The break-even point in net sales dollars is calculated:

$$\frac{\$6,000 \text{ (fixed costs)}}{0.36 \text{ *}} = \$16,667$$

*(0.45/1.25)

This can be verified as:

Sales*	$16,667
− variable cost**	$10,667
− fixed costs***	$ 6,000
= break-even	$ 000

*13,333 units @ $1.25
**80 cents (75 cent cost, 5 cent commission) (13,333 × 0.80)
***$5,000 for office worker and $1,000 for rent

This sequence of events demonstrates how fixed costs, variable costs, and selling price influence a company's break-even point. As shown, the break-even point is calculated by dividing the company's total fixed costs by the contribution margin in dollars or as a percentage. The contribution margin represents that portion of the sales dollar available to cover fixed costs and to produce net income.

The lender might ask the question, how many units must the company sell to cover all fixed costs and earn $1,000 net profit? The calculation would be

$$\frac{\$6,000 \text{ Fixed costs} + \$1,000 \text{ Profit}}{0.50 \text{ (contribution margin in dollars)}} = 14,000 \text{ Units}$$

Of course, throughout this process, the lender also should be considering the market and whether or not the company can sell 14,000 units.

Applications of Break-Even Analysis

Break-even analysis is very useful in financial analysis. Lenders use break-even analysis to test assumptions about the levels of fixed costs, variable costs, and selling price that a company's break-even sales levels support. As such, break-even analysis depends on a realistic determination of the amount and nature of a company's costs. In summary, break-even analysis helps the lender and company management determine:

- the level of sales at which no profit or loss exists
- whether the company's projected sales can support its fixed and variable costs
- the level of sales necessary for the company to repay debt
- the effect of changes in the company's cost structure or sales price on break-even sales

Finally, break-even analysis provides an important link between a company's income statement and balance sheet. Through pro forma analysis, the lender can determine the level of assets and the amount of debt and capital needed to support the break-even point for sales.

OPERATING LEVERAGE

Operating leverage is another analytical technique that is based on an understanding of a company's cost structure. **Operating leverage** is the ratio of fixed costs to total costs.
   The formula for calculating operating leverage is

$$\frac{\text{Total fixed costs}}{\text{Total costs}} = \text{Operating leverage}$$

This variable should not be confused with financial leverage (total debt/net worth). As explained in the discussion of break-even, a high ratio of fixed costs to total costs implies low variable costs, which results in a high contribution margin. As sales move above the break-even point, the profits of a company with a high proportion of fixed costs (that is, a high level of operating leverage) increase dramatically. Since fixed costs are covered at the break-even point, the company then takes the full contribution margin to the bottom line. This is otherwise known as economies of scale.
   To illustrate, assume that a company has fixed costs of $50,000 and a variable cost percentage of 43 percent and a fixed cost percentage of 57 percent. Using the formula of fixed costs divided by the contribution margin (one minus the variable cost percentage), the break-even point is calculated as follows:

$$\frac{\text{Fixed costs}}{(1 - \text{variable cost percentage})} = \text{Break-even point (dollars)}$$

The calculation would be:

$$\frac{\$50,000}{(1 - 0.43)} = \$87,719$$

As sales increase above the $87,719 level, 57 cents of each additional sales dollar becomes profit. The amount is 57 cents because the fixed costs (57 cents) have been covered at the break-even point—only the variable costs (43 cents) need to be paid.

If the company's cost structure has fixed costs of $25,000, a variable cost percentage of 71 percent, and a fixed cost percentage of 29 percent, the break-even point would be approximately the same. It would be calculated as:

$$\frac{\$25,000}{(10 - 0.71)} = \$86,207$$

In this case, each dollar of sales above the break-even point provides only 29 cents of profit. A company with high operating leverage and a low variable cost percentage, as in the first example, experiences a much greater increase in profitability as sales increase than a company with low operating leverage and high variable costs.

Above the break-even point, a company with high operating leverage performs admirably. But when sales decrease below the break-even point, the company loses a significant amount on each dollar of sales, and net losses mount rapidly. In the preceding example, the company with a variable cost percentage of 43 percent will lose 57 cents on each dollar of sales if its sales are below break-even.

Exhibit 3.9 illustrates the effects of high and low operating leverage. It is apparent that an equal increase in unit sales beyond the break-even point produces greater profitability for a company with high operating leverage than for a company with low operating leverage. However, an equal decrease in sales volume also produces greater losses. An understanding of operating leverage and the potential impact of sales increases and decreases on companies with different cost structures suggests the following conclusions:

- A company with high operating leverage and high vulnerability to decreased sales represents a greater potential loan risk.
- A company with high operating leverage may be able to earn its way out of an unprofitable situation by increasing sales only moderately.
- A company with low operating leverage may be unable to earn its way out of an unprofitable situation. The additional sales required to reach the break-even point may be so great that the company's balance sheet cannot support its working asset requirements.
- A company with low operating leverage can withstand substantially greater sales decreases before becoming unprofitable.

Operating leverage is a critical concept in financial analysis because it influences profits and cash flow and, thus, a company's ability to grow and repay debt.

OTHER INCOME, INTEREST EXPENSE, AND OTHER EXPENSE ANALYSIS

Some companies have income sources in addition to sales, and expenses other than those included in cost of goods sold or operating expenses. Exhibit 3.10 on page 92

Exhibit 3.9   Effects of High and Low Operating Leverage

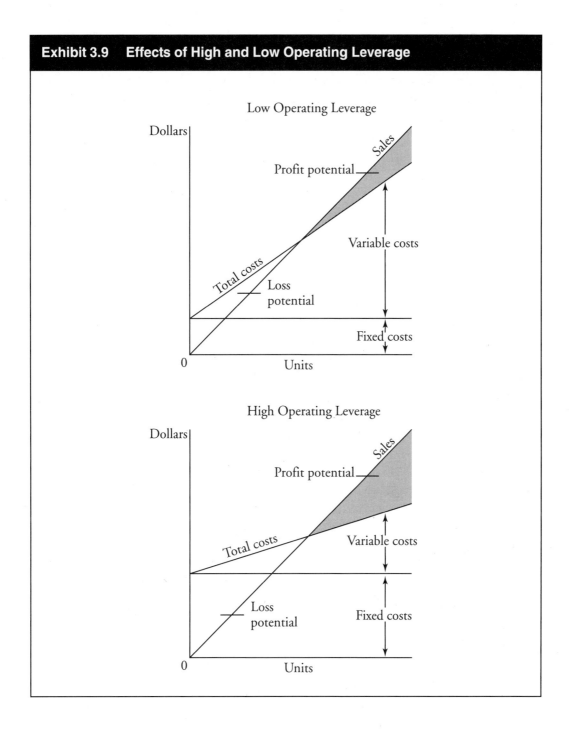

illustrates the calculation of other income, interest expense, and other expense for Turner Electronic Corporation. After evaluating the operating profit or loss of the company, a lender should look at the income and expense items that lie outside of the normal operations of a business. This enables the lender to determine if these items significantly affect the overall net profit or loss of the company, and whether or not these are consistently recurring items.

Exhibit 3.10 Other Income and Other Expense Analysis—Turner Electronic Corporation (000s omitted)

	20x0		20x1		20x2	
Net sales	$6,260	100.0%	$7,482	100.0%	$7,270	100.0%
Operating profit	$ 97	1.5%	$ 554	7.4%	$ 160	2.2%
Interest expense	$ 66	1.1%	$ 86	1.1%	$ 109	1.5%
Net profit before tax	$ 31	0.5%	$ 468	6.3%	$ 51	0.7%
Tax	$ 10	0.2%	$ 119	1.6%	$ 17	0.2%
Net profit after tax	$ 21	0.3%	$ 349	4.7%	$ 34	0.5%

Note: Each component is expressed as a percentage of net sales.

The calculation for the remainder of the income statement is

Operating profit (loss)
+ other income
− interest expense
− other expense
_____
= net profit or loss before tax
− taxes
_____
= net profit or loss

Other Income

Other income is income generated outside the normal operating activities of the company. This income does not result from sales of the company's products or services, but from other, unrelated activity. Some companies have a dependable source of other income that should be analyzed as a recurring income source. Typical sources of other income include the following:

Rental Income

Rental income is often generated from excess building facilities or equipment. A company with excess capacity that can be rented or leased without interrupting the efficient flow of normal operations is wise to do so. The lender needs to consider whether the income will be a continuing income source or whether the company will soon need to use the space or equipment itself.

Interest Income

Interest income can be generated from excess cash invested in savings deposits or from other investments, such as a loan to another company. If such investments recur, the level of market interest rates will affect the level of income generated.

Profit on the Sale of Fixed Assets

A company can generate additional income by selling its excess fixed assets at a profit. For instance, after upgrading its fixed assets with more efficient equipment, a company may want to sell its used equipment. A profit results when the sale price exceeds the net book value of the asset sold. The net book value is the asset's cost less accumulated depreciation.

Dividend Income

Many companies own stock in related operating companies or in publicly traded companies. Any dividends received constitute a source of nonoperating income. Because dividends are based on the profitable operation of another company, without independent evaluation, the lender may not assume that they constitute a dependable source of income in the future. The lender might also investigate the reason for the investment. Was it a temporary use of excess funds, some form of speculation, or to gain a business advantage?

Discounts Earned

Suppliers often offer cash discounts for prompt payment of money owed. This can benefit companies that have the ability to generate cash on a timely basis to meet their maturing obligations, but the level of discounts offered by suppliers is a factor over which the company has little control. Although any discounts earned by the company should be included as nonoperating income, or other income, some companies just deduct it from cost of goods sold.

Other Expenses

A company may have other expenses (also called nonoperating expenses) as well as nonoperating income. Such expenses might include interest expense (often shown as a separate item), loss on a sale of fixed assets, loss on a sale of stock or discontinued operations, and discounts allowed.

Loss on the Sale of Fixed Assets

If a company sells any of its fixed assets below book value, the loss associated with the sale is recognized as a nonoperating expense. When such losses appear on the income statement, a lender needs to determine if additional losses are to be expected. Additional losses are more likely if the company has consistently underestimated depreciation on the used equipment by overestimating its useful life.

Loss on Discontinued Operations

A company also can choose to discontinue some of its operations. This usually occurs when certain products or services have not been as profitable as management would like and the assets could be more efficiently used in some other area of the business. For example, if a company determined a certain product is unprofitable, it might decide to discontinue selling it. When it decides to discontinue an operation, a company usually establishes a reserve on the balance sheet by estimating what losses will occur when liquidating the related assets and contracts. For the lender, the analytical problem is to determine whether the company will face additional losses in the future—something that even might not be within management's control.

Interest Expense

Interest expense is shown as nonoperating expense because not all companies borrow money, or, at least, not the same amount at the same time. Because this cost is discretionary, it is listed separately so that operating expenses can be comparable. This way of listing the interest expense also highlights the amount of interest paid, which can be compared to the bank's records or can be used to measure the extent of interest costs on bottom-line profits.

The cost of borrowing money depends both on the company's overall level of borrowing and whether debt is at a fixed or floating rate. In the latter case, the market interest rate at any particular time can have serious consequences. Therefore, interest expense can fluctuate dramatically, depending on the company's borrowing requirements and interest rates.

Because it usually amounts to only a small fraction of revenues or of major expenses, interest expense rarely is a deciding factor in the success or failure of a company. However, when making a new loan, the lender should consider the increased interest expense and its effect on the company's profits.

Income Taxes

The provision for income taxes is deducted from a company's profit figures to get to net profit after tax. If the financial statements are prepared using GAAP, the provision for taxes shown on the income statement and the actual cash taxes paid or payable usually differ. When this happens, a deferred tax liability is listed on the balance sheet.

Because many factors affect the amount of taxes reported on the income statement, making useful comparisons between companies is difficult. To review a company's ability to manage its tax burden and to project the impact of taxes on future profitability, a loan officer must understand in detail many complex tax issues.

Tax expense is one item that should be looked at as a percentage of sales. The computation of the cash-paid tax rate provides a starting point for investigation. The cash-paid tax rate is the actual amount of taxes paid by the company. For example, a stated tax rate might be 15%, but the actual cash-paid tax rate was 4% of sales. The stated tax rate is the amount of taxes on net income before tax and is not a percentage of sales. Some lenders would like to refer to this percentage as the "effective tax rate," but GAAP standards mandate that the word *effective* be used for the stated tax percentage, as dictated by the IRS, and reduced only for items like investment tax credits (ITC) or credits for foreign income taxes paid.

S corporations, partnerships, and sole proprietorships are taxed at individual income tax rates. Individual income tax rates are lower than corporate tax rates. Unfortunately, this circumstance makes comparing corporations after taxes less valid. The lender must make sure that companies under comparison are in the same tax status. If the company is a sub S corporation, the lender should verify that the amount paid to the owners is no greater than their individual tax liability. Excess amounts decrease the company's total equity and should be viewed as a bonus, distribution, or dividend to the owners.

By tracing the trend in net profits during a number of years, a lender gains insight into the consistency with which management has operated the company. This provides some basis for assessing the likely future profitability of the business. A company's profit record also should be compared with that of similar businesses and with industry averages. This comparison can help the lender put the company's results in perspective.

SUMMARY

The income statement is of key importance in any examination because it shows sales, which are the basis of a company's existence, and profits, which determine a company's long-term viability (profitability). Spreading and common-sizing a company's past income statements facilitates comparisons over time and with industry averages. In common-sizing, income statement accounts are shown as a percentage of net sales. Before beginning an in-depth review of a company's revenues and expenses, the lender should already have a good understanding of the type of business in which the company is engaged and the marketplace, including sensitivity to economic cycles, seasonality, and product life cycles.

Income statement analysis begins with revenue analysis. This entails determining the methods a company uses to recognize revenues and expenses. First, net sales are calculated by subtracting discounts, returns, and allowances from gross sales. The lender then must consider sales volume, sales trends, product or service mix, order backlogs, large nonrecurring sales, seasons, and cyclical factors.

Expense analysis involves assessing two basic categories of expenses: cost of goods sold and operating expenses. The cost of goods sold consists of inventory purchases for a wholesaler or retailer and of expenses for raw materials, direct labor, and certain manufacturing expenses, depreciation, and overhead for a manufacturer. Most service companies do not have cost of goods sold. In analyzing a company's cost of goods sold, the lender should consider how the company counts its inventory (perpetual versus periodic inventory systems) and how it values the inventory (FIFO versus LIFO methods). The calculation of cost of goods sold enables the lender to calculate the company's gross profit margin, a key figure in assessing the company's efficiency and consistency of operation. The weighted-average cost and retail method are two other inventory methods used.

Next, the lender should consider the company's operating expenses, also called selling, general, and administrative expenses, to see whether any expenses appear excessive and to capture trends over time by comparing changes in sales to changes in expenses. The lender also will analyze a company's expenses in terms of controllable versus noncontrollable costs. Once changes are isolated, the lender must seek explanations for the changes.

Break-even is that point where the sum of fixed and variable costs meet. The higher the fixed costs, the higher the break-even point for a company. When a company has high fixed costs, it has high operating leverage. Operating leverage is the relationship of fixed costs to total costs. The higher the operating leverage, the greater amount of sales needed before a company begins to be profitable.

Next, any nonoperating income and expense items unrelated to the company's basic operations are analyzed to determine whether any significant amounts are likely to be recurring or nonrecurring. Interest expense, often shown separately on the income statement, is an expense to which the lender should pay particular attention. Finally, the company's income tax expense and its after-tax profits are analyzed.

QUESTIONS FOR DISCUSSION

1. A computer retailer brings in its fiscal year-end income statement to review with you. The statement indicates sales have declined 5 percent per year for two years. What questions do you have for your customer?
2. Use an example to explain the difference between the LIFO and FIFO method of valuing inventory.
3. How is the cost-of-goods-sold calculation different for a retailer versus a service company?
4. A chiropractic clinic brings its year-end statement for review. The income statement indicates revenues are increasing 15 percent per year and operating expenses are decreasing as a percentage of revenue. What are the possible causes of this decrease?
5. A retail lighting company sells lamps for $30. The lamps are purchased from a wholesaler for $18. What is the company's contribution margin? If the company's fixed expenses are $25,000 per year, what is the company's break-even point in sales dollars and units sold?

EXERCISE 1

Use the following form to spread and common-size Topper's income statement.

Toppers, Inc. Income Statement (in thousands of dollars)

	20x0	20x1	20x2
Sales	$5,015	$7,296	$10,743
Cost of goods sold	3,527	5,163	7,348
Gross profit	1,488	2,133	3,395
Selling, general, and administrative expenses	1,456	1,770	2,409
Operating income	32	363	986
Interest expense	8	7	3
Interest income	3	8	29
Other income	135	55	106
Net profit before tax	162	419	1,118
Tax	0	0	0
Net profit after tax	162	419	1,118

Income Statement Spreadsheet						
	20x0		20x1		20x2	
	Amount	%	Amount	%	Amount	%
Net sales						
Cost of goods sold						
Gross profit						
Operating expenses						
Operating profit (loss)						
Other income						
Interest expense						
Other expense						
Net profit before tax						
Taxes						
Net profit after tax						

EXERCISE 2

Refering to your spreadsheet for Toppers, answer the following questions:

1. What do you think is causing the sales changes?
2. Do you think the company bids projects properly? Why or why not?
3. What is causing the operating expenses to decline as a percentage of sales?

EXERCISE 3

The sales mix of a retail gift shop is shown below. Inflation is running about 3 percent per year. What questions would you have for the company, based on its sales history?

	000s Omitted		
	Year 1	Year 2	Year 3
Cards	$115	$148	$112
Gift wrap	$121	$124	$222
Miscellaneous	$106	$205	$110
Total sales	$342	$447	$444

4

ANALYZING BALANCE SHEETS

LEARNING OBJECTIVES

After studying *Analyzing Balance Sheets*, you will be able to

- define the balance sheet equation,
- evaluate asset accounts in terms of liquidity and value,
- explain the difference between current assets, fixed assets, and noncurrent assets,
- identify and define the types of liabilities,
- explain the various equity or net worth components,
- apply balance sheet analysis to the Turner Electronic Corporation case study, and
- define the key terms that appear in **bold** type in the text.

INTRODUCTION

The balance sheet, like a photograph, provides a financial picture of a company on a given day at a given time. It categorizes all of a company's resources as **assets**, all of its debts as **liabilities**, and all of the owner's investment as **equity**. A company uses its assets, including accounts receivable, inventory, and equipment, for manufacturing or purchasing products for sale or to provide a service. A company's assets are financed by its liabilities (also called debt) and the owner's equity (also called net worth or, simply, equity).

A simple equation represents the basic structure of the balance sheet:

$$\text{Assets} - \text{Liabilities} = \text{Net Worth}$$

This equation helps the lender understand constant changes in a business's financial structure. Because the equation must always be in balance, a change on one side must be offset by an equal change on the same or the other side to maintain the balance. For example, an increase in assets must be balanced by a decrease in another asset account or by an increase in liabilities or equity. A company can obtain assets (inventory or fixed assets) by selling or collecting other assets (accounts receivable), using its cash to pay for the asset at time of purchase, creating new liabilities, or raising additional equity. Selling inventory on credit, for example, creates accounts receivable, another current asset.

Purchasing inventory on credit creates debts, thereby increasing liabilities. Purchasing inventory for cash received from an owner's injection of new equity increases net worth. Liabilities can be paid by selling or collecting assets or by increasing other liabilities or increasing equity. For example, accounts payable can be repaid by selling inventory for cash, which decreases an asset, or by borrowing from the bank, which increases a liability. The inventory also could be paid from a cash injection of equity from the owners. Any combination of increasing or decreasing assets, liabilities, and equity can complete a transaction—provided the equation remains in balance.

In assessing a business's financial condition, an accountant is concerned with assets (what is owned), liabilities (what is owed), and the owner's equity (the investment by the owner or stockholder). For commercial businesses, fixed assets normally are recorded at historical cost—that is, the market value at the time of purchase. In periods of inflation or deflation, recording assets at historical cost may produce differences between carrying value (in terms of accounting) and current value (in real economic terms), because increases or reductions in value are not reflected.

Assets are listed first on the balance sheet and spreadsheet in descending order of liquidity. The balance sheet review is an evaluation of the value and liquidity of each asset account. Liquidity is the ability to convert assets to cash at or near market value in time to meet all debt payments as they come due. Illiquidity refers to the situation in which the "true" value of the assets when converted to cash is less than the liabilities due. "True" value is defined as book, market, or liquidation value—whichever is greater. Overall, high liquidity reduces the risk of illiquidity, which is the inability to pay bills as they come due. Thus, each asset is considered potential collateral in a lending situation.

Assets may be current, fixed, or noncurrent (other). Current assets are expected to be converted to cash within the operating cycle (usually one year or less). GAAP's rules for determining current status are not consistently based on the operating cycle. A company's current position is analyzed in terms of the difference between current assets and current liabilities. The difference is called net working capital, but is usually shortened to working capital, and is calculated as

$$\text{Current assets} - \text{Current liabilities} = \text{Working capital}$$

Liabilities, classified as current or long term, are listed in order of priority of payment. The lender should know whether the liability is secured or unsecured, its original loan purpose, its interest rate, the principal repayment due each year, and the expected sources of repayment.

The owner's equity account or net worth can be viewed from two perspectives:

- *Accounting*—the owner's initial and subsequent investments and what ever net income has been retained in the business from its inception
- *Financial*—the net difference between the value of assets and the obligations of liabilities

The financial perspective of net worth raises a lender's awareness of the "true" value of the assets in the marketplace, which is important for collateral protection and potential revenue that may be produced from a company's assets.

Lenders and accountants may classify balance sheet accounts differently. For example, accountants classify notes receivable as a current asset and lenders classify them as noncurrent assets. A summary of how a lender should classify account classification is located in the *Master Case Book*.

ANALYTICAL ISSUES

In reviewing a balance sheet, a lender keeps in mind that the distribution of assets, liabilities, and equity on a company's balance sheet depends on the type of business, the industry, and the company's managerial decisions. A summary of distribution of the primary assets, liabilities, and equity by type of business follows.

These factors, as well as conditions in the company's markets, the company's development stage, and the availability of financing—debt and equity—also affect the company's balance sheet structure. The common-sized, computer-generated spreadsheet for Turner Electronic Corporation's balance sheet for three years is located in the *Master Case Book* and will be referred to in this module.

ASSETS

Assets are classified as current and noncurrent and are listed in order of liquidity.

	Manufacturers	Wholesalers	Retailers	Service Companies
Assets	Accounts receivable, inventory, and fixed assets	Accounts receivable and inventory	Inventory	Accounts receivable or fixed assets
Liabilities	Short-term debt to finance raw materials, work-in-process, finished goods, and accounts receivable. Long-term debt to finance equipment	Primarily short-term debt to finance or support the generally high levels of accounts receivable and inventory	Primarily short-term debt to finance inventory	Short-term debt for accounts receivable, long-term debt for fixed assets

Current Assets

Current assets are expected to be converted to cash by normal operations of the company within a period that does not exceed one year. The four primary current assets are cash, marketable securities, accounts receivable, and inventory. Current assets are shown on the balance sheet in order of their liquidity—cash first, followed by marketable securities, accounts receivable, inventory, and other current assets.

Cash

In keeping with the priority of liquidity, **cash** is listed first on the balance sheet. Companies can hold cash in various forms, some of which are restricted for special purposes. For example, some companies may keep only a small amount of petty cash on the premises to take care of small disbursements that cannot be paid by check or credit card. Some retailers need a lot of cash to make change; therefore, their cash position may not be an advantage. The time that elapses between the disbursement and collection of cash helps determine a company's cash requirements. For example, if the time between purchasing inventory for cash and selling inventory for cash is only ten days, a short time frame needs to be funded.

Cash is represented most often by deposits in checking accounts that are available for use in a company's operations or in temporary interest-bearing accounts. In analyzing a company's cash account, the availability of cash is the most important consideration. For example, restrictions may apply if interest-bearing deposits are pledged against debt. If a company pledges its interest-bearing accounts, the cash becomes unavailable for daily operations. Compensating balances, which may be required for support of bank credit facilities, also may be unavailable for operations.

A company with foreign bank accounts may find that other governments make it difficult to transfer deposits to domestic operations. Moreover, deposits of foreign currency are subject to exchange fluctuations.

Overdrafts are not considered cash. They are unsecured loans and, therefore, are listed as current liabilities.

Marketable Securities

The second category of assets on a balance sheet is **marketable securities**. Lenders must analyze carefully the current value of a company's marketable securities account, as well as its types of investments and their relative liquidity.

Accounts Receivable

When it sells merchandise or services on credit, a company provides payment terms to allow the purchaser to pay within a specified time. As an incentive for early payment, a company may offer a discount as well. Until they are collected, credit sales are shown as **accounts receivable** on the balance sheet. Other receivables, such as those created by credit extended to company officers, employees, affiliates, or by the sale of other assets, should not be included in this account. The accounts receivable account is for trade accounts receivable. In other words, accounts receivable should reflect only unpaid amounts due to sales of product or services provided as part of a business's normal operations.

Both the size and quality of the accounts receivable is important. The size of a company's accounts receivable is influenced by the

- amount of credit sales
- company's credit terms and collection policies
- customers' payment habits

Liberal credit terms may result in larger accounts receivables. For example, if a company's sales total $125,000 per month with terms of net 30 days, accounts receivable should technically never exceed $125,000. But if the company extended its terms to 60 days, its accounts receivable would technically double to $250,000. Increasing terms always increases the likelihood of losses because unexpected events could occur with the passage of time (within the extended payment schedule). For the same reason, lax collection practices often result in delayed or lost payments. For example, suppose the company ignored overdue accounts and allowed customers to pay in 90 days rather than the required 60-day terms. Its accounts receivable could increase by another $125,000 to $375,000.

Liberal extension of credit to customers who are not creditworthy and lax collection policies can undermine the quality of a company's accounts receivable and result in uncollectible accounts receivable. Uncollectible accounts receivable are expensed to

BANKERS ACCEPTANCE, U.S. GOVERNMENT SECURITIES, AND COMMERCIAL PAPER

Companies with revenues over $5 million often temporarily invest their excess cash in bankers' acceptances, U.S. government securities, or high-grade corporate commercial paper. These investments earn income as interest or dividends until the cash is needed in the business. To have the full confidence of the lender, these securities should

- be readily marketable,
- have a short-term to maturity, and
- pose limited risk of losing principal.

Other securities do not meet these criteria. If a company has temporary investments in other securities (some stock traded on a major stock exchange, stocks not actively traded, stocks in privately held companies, and stocks held in affiliates), accountants usually classify these investments as marketable securities. For the lender, they should be classified as other noncurrent assets for the following reasons:

- Some stocks traded on major exchanges are subject to wide swing in value. Generally, stocks that trade at less than $10 per share have wider swings in value. Also, the potential number of purchasers will be lower.
- Stocks held in privately held corporations do not have a readily available market or price.
- Stocks in privately held affiliates represent ownership interest in companies, and there is no established market or price.

Therefore, these stocks should be listed not as marketable securities, but as noncurrent assets by the lender. Companies with revenues under $5 million typically invest short-term funds in savings or certificates of deposit at their local bank.

the income statement as bad debt expense or deducted from the allowance for doubtful accounts, which decreases the net profit from operations.

A lagging economy also can result in slowed payments on accounts receivable. Generally, when an overall downturn in economic activity occurs, companies earn less profit and their liquidity is reduced. A chain reaction results: companies paid more slowly by customers slow down the payments to creditors. Less cash is generated for the business's operations, because the company's liquidity is reduced when its receivables convert to cash less quickly.

If accounts receivable has increased or decreased rapidly, the lender should examine the income statement to see if there has been a corresponding increase or decrease in sales. If not, the increase in accounts receivable may suggest that credit terms are being extended to stimulate sales, or the decrease in accounts receivable may signal a change in customers or products.

From the lender's standpoint, accounts receivable represent a good source of collateral because they are generally more liquid than the inventory they replaced. A company's credit terms can indicate the approximate time accounts receivable converted into cash. Accounts receivable also are considered good collateral because they usually convert to cash quickly. However, accounts receivable are a good source of collateral only as long as a business is in operation. If a business fails, the bank generally will have a hard time collecting the accounts.

Aging of accounts receivable statements are listings of a company's customers showing the amount owed by each company for goods shipped or services performed and the length of time the amount is outstanding since the original billing date. Access to this listing assists the lender in evaluating the quality of the receivables. By studying this summary, the lender can determine the punctuality of a company's credit accounts in relation to the credit terms allowed, the success of the company's collection efforts, and the overall quality of the accounts receivable. The company can supply a list showing the aging of each account receivable, both individually and by category. This information is important because the older receivables also may have amounts due currently. The accounts receivable are usually listed by days: current, 30, 60, and more than 90 days old, by account.

For example, Turner Electronic Corporation accounts receivable aging, illustrated in exhibit 4.1, show that 70 percent of the accounts are current (less than 30 days), 17 percent are due in less than 60 days, 5 percent are due in 61 to 89 days, and 8 percent are more than 90 days past due. The foreign accounts receivable total 14 percent of the accounts but are supported by letters of credit. With accounts this current and limited bad-debt expense, it seems that the company does a good job managing the approval and collection of its accounts receivable. With a large customer base, the repayment risk is spread out. However, if it is too large, the time to collect numerous small accounts receivable may be too costly.

The lender also can use the accounts receivable aging statement to identify any concentration of accounts receivable in one or a few accounts. Such concentration

Exhibit 4.1 Partial Accounts Receivable Aging—Turner Electronic Corporation

Customer	Total	Current	30-59 Days	60-89 Days	Over 90 Days
XYZ Inc.	$ 53	$ 40	$ 13		
MAKCO	80		40	30	10
TEF	18	18			
		Continued listing of all accounts			
Total	$772	$540	$132	$38	$62

usually means increased repayment risk, although this depends on the quality of the customer representing the concentration. Turner Electronic Corporation shows no concentrations of accounts receivable. However, the MAKCO accounts receivable represent about 11 percent of total receivables and 2.3 times 20x2 net profits after tax. MAKCO is showing deteriorating payment habits as well.

To monitor the quality of their receivables over time and to spot current repayment trends, companies should age their accounts periodically. In many service industries, accounts receivable are broken into completed work and work-in-process. For example, a law firm may list accounts receivable for large lawsuits in process and work (wills) completed. Analyzing different aging statements of receivables for the same company enables the lender to detect whether the past-due receivables have improved or deteriorated. If the trend is negative, the lender must determine the causes and investigate what action management has taken to reverse the slowing trend.

Allowance for Doubtful Accounts

Some accounts receivable remain uncollected and, therefore, constitute a loss or bad debt. A company prepares for this by calculating the percentage of bad debt over recent years and creating an allowance for doubtful accounts. This amount is then deducted from its accounts receivable. The company increases this allowance by regularly expensing for bad debts through the income statement. When an account becomes uncollectible, it is charged against the accounts receivable **allowance for doubtful accounts** instead of directly to the income statement. This cushions the income statement from a sudden loss that is the sole result of poor credit judgment. It also avoids charging one accounting period for an activity that took place in another. By expensing bad debts in the year credit sales took place, revenues and expenses are better matched.

In assessing a company's accounts receivable, a lender considers the adequacy of a company's bad-debt allowance. If credit term policies do not change, the reserve should be a set percentage of the company's receivables. In normal sales growth, as accounts receivable increases, the allowance should increase proportionally.

By using the following formula, the lender can calculate the amount of bad-debt losses:

Beginning allowance for doubtful accounts
+ current year bad-debt expense from income statement
– ending allowance for doubtful accounts
_____

= bad-debt losses

For example, Turner Electronic Corporation's bad-debt losses for 20x2 would be:

Beginning allowance for doubtful accounts	$10,000
+ current year bad-debt expense from income statement	$ 2,000
– ending allowance for doubtful accounts	$10,000
= bad-debt losses for 20x2	$ 2,000

If the quality of the company's accounts receivable deteriorates because of a change toward more aggressive financial policies, the allowance should be increased. For example, if losses historically have been 1 percent of average accounts receivable, the allowance should represent at least 1 percent of average receivables. When losses in a particular year begin to escalate and this higher level is expected to continue, the company should increase the amount expensed on the income statement for bad debts to better match the revenues with expenses.

If a company does not have an allowance for doubtful accounts, the bad debts are expensed directly to the income statement as they are recognized. This can result in large profit variations, if a large accounts receivable is charged off in one year.

Inventory

The three components of **inventory** are raw materials, work-in-process, and finished goods. There are two major methods to value inventory: last-in-first-out (LIFO) and first-in-first-out (FIFO). LIFO and FIFO applications are discussed under the inventory valuation heading.

Raw Materials Inventory

Manufacturers typically purchase **raw materials** inventory to be used in the manufacturing process. Wholesalers, retailers, and service companies generally do not have raw materials. Lenders should evaluate raw material inventory on the same basis as they do finished goods—that is, in terms of marketability. The end use of raw materials determines their marketability. Raw materials that have multiple uses and can be liquidated by being sold to various industries have a marketability that is much better than that of a raw material used in a single manufacturing process. For example, a manufacturer of window coverings has bolts of material for drapes and materials for pleated shades. The bolts of material are readily salable to fabric retailers, but the pleated shade material can be sold only to another manufacturer of window coverings.

A large raw materials inventory account can result from speculation in inventory, due to expected price increases or concern over the potential loss of a supplier. A company may try to hedge on prices by buying inventory in bulk at a low price with hopes of selling it later at a higher price, or to avoid having to purchase it at a higher price in the future. A large loss can result if the price of the raw materials decreases unexpectedly. Companies often are unable to hold onto excess inventory because they need liquidity. Holding onto inventory can be expensive during periods of high interest rates, if bank financing is required. A company may decide to purchase large quantities of raw material if it is concerned about the material's ongoing availability. For example, Turner Electronic Corporation purchases raw materials from several European countries. If the company were concerned about the United States' relationship with the supplier's country, it might decide to stockpile raw material if no other source were available. In most cases, accounts payable should move in the same direction as inventory. Therefore, if the company is stockpiling inventory, the accounts payable may get stretched.

Work-in-Process

Generally, manufacturing companies are the only type of businesses that have work-in-process. From a lender's viewpoint, this inventory account is the most problematic; it may be difficult to sell in case of liquidation. The amount of **work-in-process** inventory depends primarily on the length of the production process. If the production process is short, the value of the company's work-in-process is small in relation to its raw materials and finished goods inventories. But if the process is long and complex, as in manufacturing large or heavy equipment, a more significant proportion of a company's assets may be tied up in work-in-process.

Partially completed products not only require additional investment before they reach the value of finished goods, they also have a market value that is less than the invested costs. Therefore, the lender should assign no value to work-in-process inventory for loan collateral.

Usually, a company that makes customized products has a large work-in-process inventory but no finished goods inventory; its products, on completion, are delivered immediately to the buyer. Because the general marketability of custom-made products is low, a manufacturer should require substantial deposits or progress payments while manufacturing the products, to reduce the risk of custom orders not being accepted. In the eyes of a lender, custom-made inventory usually has almost no collateral value.

Finished Goods Inventory

Finished goods are salable merchandise. Wholesalers' and retailers' **finished goods** are purchases of product for resale and are the inventory. For a manufacturing company, the finished goods inventory includes any finished products not yet shipped or, possibly, sold. In a service company, consumable supplies used to provide a service are considered finished goods inventory and are limited in value.

For most businesses, the risk that the finished goods inventory will not sell is related primarily to the style sensitivity of the merchandise. Therefore, lenders assess a company's inventory account in terms of the present and future marketability of its inventory. Some kinds of merchandise have predictable and long-term marketability. For example, an office retailer sells paper and pens that hold their value because they are staple items subject to continuous demand. But if the company's inventory included specialized software that is subject to obsolescence, a sudden drop in market demand could render the inventory valueless. In evaluating a company's inventory account, the lender determines whether it includes obsolete inventory that fails to meet market demand. If so, the value of the company's inventory and its profits in recent years may be overstated. Inventory is not expensed until sold or written off as obsolete. Obsolete inventory does not represent liquidity for the company or good collateral value for a lender to liquidate to repay debt. Most companies write off obsolete inventory annually—as part of taking the physical count of the inventory.

Whenever management decides to compete more aggressively by keeping inventory stock high, the risk is that demand for the product will drop suddenly. Sometimes companies keep large inventories because obtaining supplies is difficult or entails lengthy waits before delivery, as is the case with orders from overseas.

Inventory Valuation Methods

The choice of the accounting method is important in determining the collateral value. The two basic methods of valuing inventory—last-in, first-out (LIFO) and first-in, first-out (FIFO). LIFO charges to expenses the most recent (last-in) cost of inventory because the company has to replace the used inventory at current value. This leaves ending inventory, a balance sheet asset, at the oldest, lower value, assuming rising prices. The actual physical inventory is not an issue when choosing an accounting method. FIFO expenses the old inventory cost first; this method places the current value of inventory on the balance sheet.

If the company uses LIFO to value inventory, the lender should look at the footnote on inventory that states the difference between FIFO and LIFO valuations. This difference (after taxes), known as the LIFO reserve, should be commented on in the inventory analysis and in the retained earnings analysis. In this way, the current costs of the inventory value will be identified. Some lenders recommend writing up (or down) inventory as an asset and retained earnings in order to present current value and profits. Although this may be valid, only CPA-prepared audits and reviews provide adequate footnotes to make this adjustment. Also, interim statements—monthly, quarterly, and semiannually—generally do not reflect a LIFO reserve and will result in a distorted comparison from period to period. Therefore, a comment regarding the LIFO reserve and its effect on profits and ratios is appropriate. Over time, inflation and growing inventories complicate this situation.

Sometimes an interim statement uses a plug number or an unchanged year-end number for inventory. If so, the lender should question the income statement. The listed cost of goods sold will be wrong, and it will not be possible to determine the correct net profit or loss.

Other Current Assets

Other current assets usually are an insignificant account. Lenders list an income tax refund due in this account on the spreadsheet. Other so-called current assets, such as prepaid expenses and cash value life insurance, need to withstand the test of intending to be converted to cash during the operating cycle. The lender does not classify these accounts as current assets.

Exhibit 4.2 on the following page gives a summary of Turner Electronic Corporation's current assets. The company may be getting more liquid because cash is at a three-year high. Accounts receivable are down from 20x0 to 20x1, yet sales are level. It appears that the company is doing a good job collecting the accounts receivable. This was confirmed in the earlier accounts receivable aging analysis. Raw materials that are increasing considerably are of concern. With sales level and the raw materials account growing, a lender will need to understand what is causing raw materials to increase. It could be due to new products, large pending orders, stockpiling of raw materials, or poor controls. Work-in-process, however, would have no value to the bank, because it would have to hire someone to complete the assembly of DVD players and speakers. The bank would then have to sell them, which it may or may not be able to do. Finished goods represent products that can be sold or should sell quickly. They also

Exhibit 4.2 Current Assets—Turner Electronic Corporation (000s omitted)

Assets	20x0		20x1		20x2	
Cash	$ 37	1.4%	$ 51	1.6%	$ 74	2.1%
Accounts receivable-trade	650	23.7%	915	28.2%	782	22.0%
Less: allow for doubtful accounts	0	0.0%	10	0.3%	10	0.3%
Total accounts receivable-net	650	23.7%	905	27.9%	772	21.7%
Raw materials	1,200	43.8%	1,411	43.5%	1,513	42.6%
Work in process	354	12.9%	304	9.4%	439	12.3%
Finished goods	233	8.5%	265	8.2%	440	12.4%
Total inventory	1,787	65.3%	1,980	61.0%	2,392	67.3%
Total current assets	2,474	90.4%	2,936	90.5%	3,238	91.1%

represent good collateral to the bank. Overall, current assets have increased to 1 percent of the total assets (from 90.4 percent to 91.1 percent)—not a large increase in three years.

Noncurrent Assets

Up to this point, assets described are classified as current assets. Unlike current assets, however, noncurrent assets are not expected to convert to cash within 12 months. The principal category of noncurrent assets is fixed assets. Other noncurrent assets are cash-value life insurance, prepaid expenses, accounts receivable officers and owners, investments in other companies, deferred charges, and intangible assets.

Fixed Assets

Fixed assets include land, buildings, vehicles, machinery and equipment, leasehold improvements, and furniture—any items of a fairly permanent nature required for the normal conduct of a business. The fixed-asset account may be highly significant or small, depending on the type of business. In analyzing this account, the book value of fixed assets is important.

Financial statements, prepared according to GAAP, show the value of fixed assets at book value. Book value is calculated by taking the original historical cost (the purchase price paid by the company) minus allowable depreciation to date. Unfortunately, historically based book values may be of little worth to lenders. Lenders are concerned primarily with liquidation value, the amount a company or creditor could realize if it had to dispose of the assets in less than 90 days. Most assets have much less value in liquidation than in their book or market value. Market value is the price a company could expect to receive for an asset sold in the open market under normal economic conditions, without the pressure of time. Thus, the liquidation value of assets may be more or less than book value.

The lender should assess the capacity, efficiency, and specialization of a company's fixed assets. Capacity is how much additional sales volume a company's existing fixed assets can support. For example, if a retailer of children's clothing does $500,000 of sales from its rented 2,000 square foot store, the lender will want to know how much sales can increase before more space is needed. Because retailers are open limited hours per day and the store's space allows only a certain amount of inventory, capacity will be limited.

A company's efficiency depends on the cost-effectiveness of the equipment it uses. More efficient equipment may or may not reduce the cost of manufacturing and selling products or providing services to a point where replacing existing equipment is cost-effective. However, as less efficient equipment nears the end of its economic life, it may be best to replace it with state-of-the-art equipment. Old equipment can become technologically obsolete because of new production methods or because more advanced equipment comes on the market. A company with inefficient equipment and the resulting higher costs may become less competitive in its pricing, leading to a decline in sales.

Specialized equipment may have a lower resale value than more commonly used equipment. The marketability of a company's fixed assets, rather than their book value (cost minus depreciation), determines the assets' value as collateral for a loan. Multiuse fixed assets normally have more buyers and therefore have higher collateral value when liquidated than single-purpose, specialized assets. For example, an engineering company's computer software is specialized and changes frequently, which makes it difficult to liquidate. But other office equipment, such as desks and chairs, could be used by many companies and, thus, could be liquidated more easily.

Certain expenses, recorded as fixed assets, are referred to as **capitalized expenses**. For example, costs incurred in overhauling a major piece of equipment normally would be capitalized, whereas minor repairs to the machine typically are treated as expenses. Treatment depends on when benefits will be received. Benefits from a complete overhaul will be received for several years. As a result, the expenditure is added to the cost basis of the machine and allocated by charges for depreciation. For a minor repair, benefits are derived in the current period. As a result, the expenditure is charged against current income.

Costs to improve a leased building such as carpeting, special lighting, general renovations, and decorating are not directly expensed on an income statement. They are capitalized on the balance sheet as **leasehold improvements** and amortized. **Amortization** is expensing the costs of these fixed assets on the income statement over their useful life. However, leasehold improvements usually stay with the building and become the property of the building's owner should the company move to a new location. For this reason, banks give leasehold improvements no value as collateral. For certain types of retail and service companies, it is not unusual for leasehold improvements to constitute the major category of fixed assets. Some lenders discount leasehold improvements when calculating tangible net worth. Tangible net worth will be discussed later in the chapter.

Capital leases of equipment, as defined by Statement of Financial Accounting Standards (SFAS) No. 13, also are considered a fixed asset on the balance sheet. However, since the company does not legally own the equipment, a capital lease fixed asset has no liquidation value. When considering whether to make a loan, lenders must find out about any leased assets in the fixed asset account. They are listed in a footnote on leases. The accountant preparing the financial statements will suggest a value based on the present value of the future contracted-for lease payments, limited by the original cost of the equipment.

If there is no footnote on leases, a value can be approximated by referring to the long-term debt footnote. Here, the debt associated with capital leases is identified and quantified. At the inception of a capital lease, the amount incorporated into the debt section is usually a good estimate of the purchase price of the equipment. Eventually, the company accounts for the "debt" by amortizing it throughout the life of the lease. Unfortunately for lenders, the debt payment schedule does not match the depreciation taken against equipment. Therefore, at some time during the term of the lease, the equipment may have no book value and no depreciation to provide tax benefits. Nevertheless, the remaining debt shown on the debt schedule usually is the best available approximation of the equipment's value.

One of the best ways to value fixed assets is to look to credible independent appraisers who have experience in identifying the proper value range of an asset. If a loan applicant has recently arranged for such an appraisal of its physical assets, the appraiser's value can be a starting point. However, lenders should do their own independent valuation. This may be done by

- randomly verifying the values presented by calling companies in the same industry,
- using specialized appraisers with experience valuing similar types of fixed assets, and
- contacting the company's insurance agent for current values.

The lender must be able to explain to the appraiser precisely what type of valuation is sought. Valuations may be done on a liquidation basis, auction basis, market, or replacement value.

Depreciation Methods for Fixed Assets

Except for land, fixed assets are assumed to lose their economic value over their estimated useful life for financial statement analysis and for GAAP and Internal Revenue Service reporting. A fixed asset is initially valued at cost when purchased and then depreciated over time. The accounting issues for depreciating fixed assets are the

- costs at which the assets are recorded on the balance sheet, the
- amortization period at which the cost should be allocated to future periods, and the
- salvage value of the fixed assets.

All costs required to bring the fixed asset into operating condition are recorded as part of the cost of the asset. Examples include sales taxes, freight costs, installation costs, and set-up costs. These costs may or may not add value to the asset. When assessing the asset as collateral, the lender will need to figure out the asset value, which may require deducting some of these costs.

Each year after a fixed asset has been purchased, it is depreciated—that is, it is partially expensed on the income statement and valued at a progressively lower amount (called book value) on the balance sheet. Finally, it is considered to be without value or to have reached a salvage value below which it cannot fall. Because there are several ways to calculate depreciation, a company may figure **depreciation** differently for financial reporting purposes than for tax purposes. The primary methods of calculation are straight line and double-declining balance.

- Straight-line depreciation is calculated by dividing the cost of a fixed asset less salvage value by its initially estimated useful economic life and recording that amount on the financial statements each year. For example, an asset that costs $50,000 and has a salvage value of $10,000, depreciated over five years, would have depreciation of $8,000 per year ($50,000 – $10,000= – $40,000/ 5= – $8,000).
- The double-declining balance depreciation method is calculated as two times the straight-line rate multiplied by the declining asset balance.

Exhibit 4.3 shows the calculations for depreciating a fixed asset that costs $100,000 and has a useful life of five years, using both the straight-line and double-declining methods. The annual depreciation expense, which is recognized on the company's income statement as an operating expense, and the value of the asset are reduced to zero during a five-year period.

Exhibit 4.7 (page 127) will demonstrate the continuing effects of double-declining balance depreciation on cash flow and deferred taxes. Unlike other expenses on the income statement, depreciation is a noncash expense. That is, the company does not pay out cash for the expense.

Exhibit 4.3   Depreciation Calculation

	Straight-Line Depreciation		Double-Declining Method	
Cost of asset	$100,000		$100,000	
Useful life	5 years		5 years	
Salvage value	$10,000		N/A	
Depreciation	20%		20%	

	Straight-Line		200% Decline	
End of Year	Depreciation	Book Value	Depreciation	Book Value
1	$18,000	$82,000	$40,000	$60,000
2	18,000	64,000	24,000	36,000
3	18,000	46,000	14,400	21,600
4	18,000	28,000	8,640	12,960
5	18,000	10,000	5,148	7,776

	Straight-Line	Double-Declining
	$100,000	Two times the straight-line
	– 10,000	rate (20%) multiplied by the
	= 90,000	declining balance

The accounting entry to record depreciation is

- debit depreciation expense (as is the case with any other expense), and
- credit allowance for depreciation (no cash, as is the case with most other expenses).

The company pays out cash only when the fixed asset is purchased. Since depreciation is a noncash, yet tax-deductible, expense, it is a tax advantage to write off the value of an asset as quickly as possible, assuming the company has taxable income or can carry back the current-year losses to the previous year's taxable income and receive a refund. Because of this possibility, the IRS has published guidelines for how quickly companies can depreciate fixed assets for tax purposes. The current rules, promulgated by the Tax Reform Act of 1986, are called MACRS—Modified Accelerated Cost Recovery System. MACRS allows more cost recovery in the earlier years of the recovery period, hence its name.

Using accelerated depreciation methods for tax purposes and the straight-line method for financial reporting purposes would distort income reporting in the current year. Theoretically, MACRS initially would produce low taxes, but would end up giving the company higher taxable income in the future, if the company did not continue to purchase equipment and it ran out of depreciation expense. To prevent this occurrence, GAAP requires the creation of a reserve for deferred taxes to offset the actual tax savings. This reserve, which appears on the balance sheet as a liability, is identified as "deferred taxes." This topic will be discussed under long-term liabilities later in the chapter.

Nondepreciable Fixed Assets

Land is one fixed asset that normally does not depreciate on the balance sheet. If it is used in the normal course of operations, it is considered a fixed asset; otherwise, it is considered an investment. Since land is valued at cost on the company's balance sheet, its appreciation can represent hidden value. The same is true of buildings that depreciate on the financial statements, even though the buildings might appreciate over time. Lenders should not list these appreciated values on the spreadsheets. As part of the analysis summary, however, the lender may comment on land values.

Exhibit 4.4 illustrates the fixed assets for Turner Electronic Corporation. The company does not own its land or building. The fixed assets are primarily company vehicles and equipment used to manufacture products. With the fixed assets heavily depreciated, the lender will want to find out what the company's future equipment needs will be.

Dividing the annual depreciation of $48,000 in 20x1 and $56,000 in 20x2 into the net fixed assets of $237,000 in 20x1 and $215,000 in 20x2 yields the remaining useful life, which is 4.9 years in 20x1 and 3.8 years in 20x2. Therefore, any loans against these assets as collateral would be at the risk of full depreciation and no book value for the asset in about four years. The lender might determine the loan does not exceed the useful life of the asset.

Exhibit 4.4 Fixed Asset Summary—Turner Electronic Corporation (000s omitted)

	20x0		20x1		20x2	
Furniture and fixtures	$113	4.1%	$ 113	3.5%	$ 113	3.2%
Machinery and equipment	659	24.1	703	21.7	741	20.8
Leasehold improvements	25	0.9	25	0.8	37	1.0
Transportation equipment	154	5.6	159	4.9	144	4.0
Gross fixed assets	951	34.7	1,000	30.8	1,035	29.1
Less accumulated depreciation	715	26.1	763	23.5	820	23.1
Total fixed assets net	236	8.6	237	7.3	215	6.0
Percent depreciated	75%		76%		79%	

Other Noncurrent Assets

Other noncurrent assets are not expected to turn into cash within a year. Although CPAs consider some of these to be current assets, most bankers consider them to be noncurrent, due to their lack of real liquidity.

Cash Value Life Insurance

Cash value life insurance represents cash deposits built up in a whole-life insurance policy. Some accountants classify this as other current assets, but bankers consider cash value life insurance a noncurrent asset because the intent is not to cash the policy in the current year. If the cash value is unencumbered by a loan from the insurance company or another financial institution, a company can use this available cash.

The insurance policy's real liquidity depends on the death of the insured. The lender must determine who is insured and the face value of the policies. The lender also evaluates the adequacy of the insurance coverage based on the importance to the company of the insured persons and the liabilities that would need to be paid from the proceeds of the insurance policy.

Prepaid Expenses

Other outlays of cash that have neither produced benefits nor been expensed on the income statement are capitalized as **prepaid expenses**. The expense is paid but not recognized until the benefit is received. Examples include insurance premiums paid annually and lease rentals paid in advance. Prepaid expenses provide little liquidity, although they do provide a future reduction in current cash outlays. Accountants usually list prepaid expenses as current assets.

Notes Receivable

Notes receivable are outstanding notes with a specific repayment agreement, are not a normal part of operations for most businesses, and do not constitute a significant asset account. However, some businesses accept notes for the sale of merchandise. For instance, a heavy equipment dealer might accept notes with extended payment terms for the sale of large pieces of equipment.

An evaluation of the quality of notes begins with their payment status. If a customer took the note out to pay a past-due accounts receivable, then a collection problem already exists and the note may be of questionable value. This type of conversion to notes receivable makes the accounts receivable aging look better when, in reality, it is not as good as it appears. The company's liquidity is reduced if it cannot collect the note on a timely basis. If the company's notes receivable start to become a significant account, the lender should investigate the company's credit policies.

The next step is to evaluate any built-in interest rate charged to the customer. Since GAAP assumes that the rate being charged corresponds to the market rate, only a sharp deviation will raise a warning. The problem with this limited concern for the notes-receivable rate of interest is that an interest rate lower than market can reduce the value of this asset to the company. For example, consider the automobile companies that induce potential purchasers by offering zero percent annual rate of financing on a three-year car loan when the prevailing rate is 6.5 percent. Clearly, the purchaser sees this as an inducement for the same reason that the lender would find the value of the note compromised below the face value. In effect, the automobile manufacturer is giving a discount to the buyer and reducing the value of the note. If these notes are sold, the company may have to account for them at a discount from face value.

Companies also assign notes as collateral. However, before a bank accepts notes as collateral, it should obtain financial information about the debtor to determine whether the note will be paid within its specified terms.

Accounts Receivable Officers or Owners

This noncurrent asset account represents a company loan to one of its officers or owners. Although it is usually shown as "accounts receivable other" on financial statements, such a loan does not represent a liquid asset that is convertible to cash and available for business operations. Company officers may pay the company last because they control the company. Therefore, all such loans are spread in the noncurrent asset category and not in current accounts receivable.

The lender should determine why the loan was made and the prospects for repayment. For example, an officer may have taken a loan from the company instead of a salary or bonus. This loan is, in effect, an expense not recognized by the company, thus improving its profitability. Because of this, most banks deduct any amount due from officers or owners from total equity. Moreover, the company officer need not claim the loan as income, thus avoiding additional personal taxes—assuming the loan does not stay on the books too long. Lenders should closely examine loans to company officers to determine whether the officer has sufficient personal liquidity to repay this receivable. Most lenders discount "notes receivable officers" from the net worth when calculating tangible net worth. Tangible net worth will be discussed later in the chapter.

Due from Affiliated Companies

Affiliated companies are related by common ownership—either one owning the other, or both companies owned by the same individual or another company. On a company's financial statements, amounts **due from affiliates**, like accounts receivable from officers or owners, is shown as accounts receivable other. This receivable is frequently nonliquid because of the nature of the affiliation and the absence of pressure to pay such debts. Therefore, lenders consider it as a noncurrent asset and determine the purpose. The lender should find out whether

- normal sales exist between the companies,
- one company has lent money to the other one, and
- if the affiliate has the ability to repay the receivable, regardless of the reason behind the account.

If a company wants to borrow money from the bank and lend it to an affiliated company, the lender obtains financial statements on the affiliate and the company to evaluate the company's ability to back up repayment. Extensive inter-company borrowings or investments bear watching, particularly in a closely held company where the distinction between the owner's and the company's finances may be blurred.

Investments in Affiliates

When one company owns less than 20 percent of another, the affiliate status of the two companies is not always recognized. Ownership of debt or equity may be carried into the other securities account. A lender should know the extent of management's involvement in the investment. The investment is carried on the books at the lower of cost or market. If the investment is short-term for income purposes only, the value is the current market.

Ownership of 20 to 50 percent of the common stock of another company normally requires the equity method of accounting for the investment. This method reflects the original amount of investment in the affiliate, plus (minus) the owner's accumulated share in the earnings or losses of the affiliate since the investment was made. This account represents the net historical value of the investment. Any earnings or dividends will show up as other income on the income statement. Because the investment cannot be reduced below zero, accounting for an affiliate in this manner can disguise how much the other company may be losing.

Prior to January 1, 1997, GAAP required consolidation of the entities if management controlled or owned 50 percent or more of the company, since the most important issue is control or influence by management. Since January 1, 1997, companies have been permitted to remove qualifying financial assets from their consolidated balance sheets and place them in special-purpose nonconsolidated subsidiaries that incur debt to third parties backed by those assets. Once financial assets have been properly segregated in a special-purpose subsidiary for the benefit of unaffiliated investors, the corporate parent of the subsidiary is deemed as no longer "controlling" those assets. Accordingly, these assets will not be consolidated for GAAP, even if 100 percent of the entity of the subsidiary is owned by the corporate parent that transferred the assets to the subsidiary. As a result, GAAP will now avoid circumstances where the balance sheet of a company could be inflated by assets that had been segregated in the control of unaffiliated parties. Both the assets and the liabilities or interest funded by those assets will be excluded.

Deferred Charges

Deferred charges are services that already have been performed and on which payment has been made, carried as accounts payable or accrued. However, even though there is little or no possibility of a refund, these expenditures have been capitalized and not yet expensed. This occurs when GAAP's accrual accounting tries to match the expense outlay to the future anticipated benefit. An obvious example would be a fee paid to a banker for committing to a three-year revolving loan. Such a commitment would provide value to the company throughout the entire three years and should be expensed (charged against income) during those years.

The examples above show that deferred charges are different from prepaid expenses. For prepaid expenses, either the services have not been performed or the products have not been delivered. Prepaid expenses are like a deposit—cash has been paid out against the benefits of future services or products. If the service or product is not used, prepaid expenses are totally or partially refundable. This is not so in deferred expenses, where the outlay is irreversible and the service or product has been received. As a result, the company's balance sheet overstates its assets and equity when deferred expenses are incurred but not expensed.

Some companies show their start-up expenses as deferred charges because they will result in future sales benefits. However, from a liquidation viewpoint, the value of start-up expenses is questionable. Developmental expenses related to real estate, such as architectural fees and surveys, are carried as deferred charges. Whether or not this account represents value in liquidation or liquidity for operations depends on the company's expense deferred. Lenders must thoroughly investigate any sizable amount in the deferred charges account.

Deferred Taxes

When **deferred taxes** appear on the balance sheet as an asset, it is because of GAAP's attempt to eliminate the differences between tax and GAAP depreciation accounting. According to the latest rules (SFAS No. 109), losses in operations can create future tax benefits that are shown as assets. This does not affect the company's operations, except to reduce GAAP's provision for taxes. Therefore, when spreading the statement, an analyst should directly offset these losses against deferred taxes on the liability side of the balance sheet.

Intangibles

Intangibles are one of the most misunderstood accounts on the balance sheet. It is standard procedure to categorize all intangibles as noncurrent assets and deduct the total from the stated net worth. Deducting intangibles from the book net worth produces tangible net worth. However, this procedure compounds the problem of calculating net worth based on assets at historical cost. Intangible assets can have value.

Therefore, disregarding the intangibles account can obscure important information about the company, its operations, and its real value in liquidation.

For a proper evaluation, lenders must identify the items in the intangibles account, such as goodwill, patents, trademarks, or operating rights. **Patents** give a company the exclusive right to manufacture a product. The intangibles account reflects only the purchase price of the patent or the legal cost of recording internally developed patents, although the value of a patent for a highly successful product may be greater than these costs. A **trademark** is the registered name of a product or service. Trademarks can be bought and sold or licensed in exchange for royalty payments. Again, the balance sheet account reflects only the purchase price or legal cost of recording the trademark, although the current value of a trademark may be greater.

Operating rights are special rights granted by government regulatory agencies. For example, telephone companies, airlines, and television stations must obtain operating rights for their areas of business. Because companies can sell or lease these rights, the rights often represent a value greater to a company than is shown on the balance sheet.

Another intangible that frequently shows up on balance sheets is called **goodwill**, an accounting term used for capitalizing acquisitions when the price paid to purchase another company exceeds the book value of its physical assets. Goodwill represents payment in consideration of the acquired company's established customer base, reputation, and future earnings potential. Again, traditional credit theory discards the possibility of evaluating such a figure.

In theory, the amount a company pays in excess of book value when acquiring another company should lose value over time because the new owners will make their own imprint on the acquired company. Effective June 2001, FASB No. 141 Business Combinations and FASB No. 142 Goodwill and Other Intangible Assets changed the accounting procedures for goodwill.

FASB No. 141 requires that all business combinations initiated after June 30, 2001, be accounted for under the purchase method of accounting. FASB No. 142 eliminated the amortizing of goodwill associated with business combinations completed after June 30, 2001. Effective, January 1, 2002, goodwill amortization expense ceased and goodwill is assessed for impairment at least annually at the reporting unit level by applying a fair-value-based asset test. These changes should lower the amortization expense of goodwill on the income statement.

Some banks and accounting firms classify assets differently than earlier categorizations. Exhibit 4.5 on the following page categorizes assets as current, fixed, and noncurrent other assets. Fixed assets are considered noncurrent assets; however, because of collateral considerations, most lenders view them separately.

LIABILITIES

Unlike assets, which can fluctuate in market value, most liabilities are fixed and must be paid at that value. Lenders consider assets to be the tools with which a business entity functions, whereas liabilities and net worth represent sources of cash to finance those assets.

Lenders evaluate a company's liabilities in terms of their repayment requirements, their continued availability as a source of financing for the company, and their

Exhibit 4.5 Asset Categories

Current	Fixed	Noncurrent
Cash	Land	Other securities
checking accounts	Buildings	stocks not actively traded
savings accounts	Equipment	stocks in privately held companies
petty cash	Leasehold	stocks not traded on major
	improvements	exchange
Marketable securities	Furniture	Accounts receivable from officers
certificates of deposit	Vehicles	and owners
banker's acceptance		Cash value life (if assigned may be
U.S. government securities		current asset)
high-grade commercial paper		Notes receivalbe
Accounts receivable		Deferred charges
trade accounts only		Investment in affiliates
Inventory		Deferred taxes
raw materials		Intangibles
work-in-process		patents
finished goods		trademarkes
Other current		operating rights
income tax refund		goodwill

anticipated sources of repayment. Liabilities also are evaluated in terms of their present and future interest costs to the company and the assets that may secure them. Normally, short-term or revolving debt is incurred to finance current assets that grow with sales (such as accounts receivable and inventory), whereas long-term loans are used to finance fixed assets that lose value within the payment schedule. This matching maturities concept is important for evaluating debt capacity.

During the review of any liability, the lender determines to whom the money is owed, why it was borrowed, its repayment terms, whether assets have been pledged, and whether or not any restrictive loan agreements are in force.

Current Liabilities

Current liabilities are liabilities due in one year or less. A company's current liabilities include notes payable to banks, commercial paper, accounts payable, accrued expenses, notes payable officers, and current-year income taxes. The liquidity of the borrower's assets and the relationship between current assets and current liabilities may change significantly during a long period. To pay short-term liabilities, however, the company will need to have sufficient cash on hand or be able to convert current assets to cash in a timely enough fashion to pay the current liabilities as they come due.

Because borrowers know they are frequently the focus of the banks analysis, current liabilities and their relationship to current assets are a sensitive issue. Therefore, borrowers take care to arrange the end of the fiscal year to occur at a time when short-term financing needs are lowest. If the lender or accounting firm suggests to the owner of a retail store that financial statements be closed on November 30, the effect could be very misleading. At that time of year, most of the retailer's assets are invested in inventory; the retailer is just beginning to enter its busiest season, when about 35 percent of its total sales occur in just 30 days. Thus, short-term borrowings are bound to be high as the company strains to provide the amount and variety of merchandise demanded by its customers. Liquidity will look very low.

Notes Payable to Banks

Notes payable to banks frequently represent the short-term financing of a company's current assets (accounts receivable and inventory). A company with seasonal financing needs may have a seasonal line of credit. For example, a retail lawn and garden company may use a bank loan to increase its inventory before spring. As the company sells its inventory, it creates accounts receivable or cash. When accounts receivable are collected, or cash sales accumulate, the bank loan is repaid. Therefore, short-term bank debt may fluctuate depending on when a company prepares its balance sheet during the cash conversion cycle. Most banks expect that during the slow part of the year, the borrower will repay all lines of credit. This period is called a cleanup period.

If a company's bank debt represents a seasonal or revolving line of credit, the lender must determine its terms, including payout requirements, if applicable. Since the company may have loans from more than one bank, the evaluation should cover the purpose, expiration date, interest rate, and security pledged on each credit line. The evaluation also should assess the adequacy of these lines of credit for the company's needs.

When a company's sales grow rapidly, the increases in accounts receivable and inventory cannot always be funded internally. Permanent rapid growth of these current assets needs to be funded long term. A permanent working capital loan that finances these assets over a period of time longer than one year is needed. The loan is secured by short-term assets, but has a long-term amortization. A lender, who requires the company to report the current asset values, closely monitors the loan. This is to ensure that the collateral (accounts receivable and inventory) does not fall below the balance of the loan. If the collateral value does fall, the lender may require the company to make mandatory prepayments. These long-term amortizing notes may be structured to balloon each year and appear as notes payable to bank. The cash to repay these loans comes from multiple completions of the operating cycle, and the principal portion of these loans is rarely repaid in one year.

Accounts Payable

Accounts payable, also called trade payable, represent normal credit extended by suppliers for purchasing inventory and services. A lender reviews the normal credit terms and then decides if the borrower has the ability to take advantage of discounts. Discounts may be given if a debt is paid earlier than the due date. For example, a company offers a 2 percent discount if the debt is paid within 10 days but requires full payment if the debt is paid in over 10 days. This 2 percent discount per month is close to 24 percent per year—a very high effective rate of interest. Therefore, the company often borrows from the bank short term to take advantage of discounts.

The terms of accounts payable vary by industry. For example, the wholesaler grocery industry has short trade terms (usually 7 to 10 days), whereas a furniture retailer receives 30- to 45-day terms from its suppliers.

Accounts payable represents a permanent source of "interest-free" funding for the company because, as the company pays its accounts, financing remains available for new purchases. When a company does not pay its accounts payable on a timely basis, its suppliers may refuse to extend credit for new purchases. The company then has to pay cash or it may not have a source of inventory to continue its operations. Stretching the time between making purchases and paying for them is called "riding the trade" and could suggest mismanagement or inadequate liquidity.

Accrued Expenses

Accrued expenses, also called accruals, represent unpaid costs a company has expensed through the income statement. These expenses include salaries, utilities, withholding taxes, profit-sharing contributions, and year-end bonuses. For example, if a balance sheet is prepared in the middle of a pay period, the wages owed as of that date are shown as an accrued expense. If the accrued expense is a large dollar amount, such as bonuses, a lender will want to determine the timing of the payment and the source of funding. Lenders look for significant amounts in this account. If a comparative analysis reveals any unusual buildup, a liquidity crisis could be in the making.

Current Maturities of Long-term Debt

Current maturities of long-term debt represent the principal portion of installment payment on long-term debt due in the coming year. For example, if a borrower owes $50,000, payable $10,000 principal plus interest annually, the current maturities long-term debt would be listed as $10,000 and the long-term debt as $40,000 the first year. Assuming the first year payments were made on time, the second year $10,000 would be listed as current maturities long-term debt and $30,000 long-term debt. Principal payments may be due on an annual, quarterly, or monthly basis within the next 12 months. Unlike other current liabilities, which depend on the conversion of current assets for repayment, these current maturities are paid from a company's cash flow cycle.

The analytical problem with this account is that some companies have cash flow cycles shorter than one year. This means that all of the other current asset and liability accounts mentioned above will likely be of shorter maturity than this account. Comparing the current maturities of long-term debt for a whole year to those shorter accounts may be misleading with regard to the liquidity problems of the company.

A lender's analysis of amortizing debt includes identifying its terms, conditions, security, and to whom it is owed. Some loans are structured so that no principal repayments are made until the end, when the entire balance of the loan becomes due. A lender must be alert to "bullet" loans or other "balloon" payments (substantial and irregular principal repayments), because they may require refinancing. If refinancing is needed, a lender needs to determine the availability of refinancing.

Income Taxes Payable

Income taxes payable, also called accrued taxes, represent the actual tax liability due, probably by the next tax payment date. The tax liability shown in this account seldom matches the income tax expense from the income statement for two reasons.

First, companies pay estimated income tax for the current year on a quarterly basis. Other taxes, such as payroll withholding, may require payment weekly or monthly. The year-end tax liability is far less than the total tax liability. Any taxes owed for previous quarters should put the lender on notice for potential IRS liens. Accruals of prior quarters' withholding taxes are especially crucial, because the IRS has priority when liens are placed on a company's assets. Most banks do not lend money to companies with delinquent tax liabilities.

Second, the income taxes payable account does not include noncurrent deferred taxes that may be recorded on the income statement—as provision for taxes—but are not due because they are only a theoretical liability for a future period.

Notes Payable Officers and Affiliates

Any amounts owed to company officers, partners, or other owners, as well as debts owed to affiliated companies, are properly carried as current liabilities if they are not subordinated. Subordination means that the holder agrees to have a junior status to other creditors when it comes to payment. The amounts are considered current because management controls repayment and could pay such debts at will. Lenders need to find out how this liability to officers or affiliated companies arose, and its terms.

Notes Payable to Others

Notes payable to others includes any amounts borrowed from creditors other than banks. Lenders determine the identity of such creditors, including the reasons for creating the note, its terms, and the security pledged. Because such notes may represent a significantly past-due trade account, the existence of this account on the balance sheet signals caution.

Commercial Paper

For companies with revenues over $5 million, commercial paper is often listed as a liability. Commercial paper usually represents unsecured debt of the issuer for short-term borrowings from investors for up to 270 days in amounts of $100,000 or more. This form of financing is only available to well-regarded companies with established credit ratings (as conferred by investment services such as Moody's Investors Service or Standard & Poor's). Another alternative is a bank's issuing a letter of credit to back the commercial paper issue of a smaller company that cannot obtain such a rating. In any case, the credit rating agencies always require open bank credit lines to back up outstanding commercial paper.

Other Current Liabilities

Other current liabilities usually are insignificant in relation to total current liabilities. This account is made up of reductions to asset accounts as deferred or unearned income, or as deposits of some kind. For example, if a company manufactures custom-made or high-priced products, it may require deposits before processing or shipping orders. Such deposits, which are classified as a current liability, can be an important source of financing for these companies. In liquidation, customer deposits also can affect the value of inventory, especially if the deposits were for inventory in stock and the inventory was pledged as collateral to the depositor.

Any company that operates under contracts and calculates its income on the percentage-of-completion basis, like a construction company, may have deferred income. Under percentage-of-completion accounting, profits in excess of the originally budgeted amount are not recognized until the contract is completed. Assuming the contract is completed without unexpected expenses, this liability will become part of net worth.

The current liabilities illustrated in exhibit 4.6 for Turner Electronic Corporation are notes payable short-term bank (the company's line of credit), current maturities long-term debt, accounts payable-trade, and accrued expenses. The line of credit has decreased in the last year. The lender will want to know the high and low amounts owed on the line during the year and when the line of credit matures. The current maturities have increased each year to finance the company's fixed-asset purchases. The accounts payable trade has increased significantly to finance raw material purchases. The lender will want to determine the number of accounts, the amount of credit available to the company, the payment terms, and what raw materials were purchased. The accrued expenses have remained level and may not be a concern.

Long-term Liabilities

Long-term liabilities include long-term debt, subordinated debt, reserves, and deferred taxes. Repayment of long-term debt principal normally involves a series of payments over a period of time. The lender prepares a schedule of the principal repayments required by the reported debt and confirms that the repayments can be made within the company's normal net cash flow expectations.

Exhibit 4.6 Summary of Current Liabilities—Turner Electronic Corporation (000s omitted)

	20x0		20x1		20x2	
Liabilities	$	%	$	%	$	%
Notes payable short term-bank	647	23.6	634	19.5	508	14.3
Current maturities long-term debt	60	2.2	70	2.2	78	2.2
Accounts payable-trade	357	13.0	507	15.6	969	27.3
Accrued expenses	117	4.3	163	5.0	161	4.5
Total current liabilities	1,181	43.1	1,374	42.4	1,716	48.3

Repayment of long-term liabilities comes from net cash flow and not just from converting current assets to cash. Again, debt analysis covers the terms, purpose, interest rate, and security pledged for all outstanding loans.

Long-term Debt

Long-term debt represents liabilities with maturities greater than 12 months. It is usually used to finance land, buildings, equipment, permanent increases in inventory levels, and accounts receivable. Usually, terms are tied to the useful or depreciable life of the asset—whichever is less. For example, a company may purchase a piece of equipment that has a ten-year useful life but depreciates the equipment over seven years. The asset would be amortized over seven years. Long-term debt usually is payable to banks or commercial finance companies for equipment, or others.

Subordinated Debt

Subordinated debt is a liability (usually held by company officers or affiliated companies) that can be repaid only when specified terms of the subordination agreement have been met.

Owners of privately held companies frequently lend funds to their business for tax purposes. The source of the funds is usually from officer salary or bonuses received from the company. Subordinated debt pays the owners interest that companies can deduct as an expense. In contrast, no deduction may be taken for dividends paid to common stockholders. From the bank's point of view, these liabilities are the equivalent of equity. A bank may extend a loan to a company if any debt held by the owner or stockholders is subordinated to the bank debt. If debt is subordinated to the bank, the bank should require the holder to sign the bank subordination form, hold the original agreement and notes, and thoroughly understand their terms.

The bank may allow regularly scheduled principal and interest payments to be made, provided the bank loan is current, but the debt may not be paid off early. If the loans are secured, the collateral may also be subordinated. When calculating tangible net worth, most lenders add subordinated debt due to officers to the equity. Tangible net worth will be discussed later in the chapter.

Reserves

Reserves represent a liability that will become due in the future. Although reserves, like contingent liabilities, are not a formal debt currently owed to a creditor, their cost has been estimated by a method approved by GAAP and recognized on the balance sheet as a liability that theoretically will become due in the future.

For example, if a corporation decides to discontinue operations or to offer substantial severance payments to encourage reduction of staff, a reserve for discontinued operations can be created. Liquidating discontinued operations may create a loss in an amount that the company can estimate and recognize in advance. If equipment is part of the liquidation, the company, by creating a reserve through the income statement, can recognize the difference between the book value of the equipment and the actual selling price.

When it liquidates the assets, the company charges any loss to the reserve rather than to its income statement. In severance reserves, the outlay will be paid in cash, but the reserve will be present for a short time only.

Deferred Income Taxes

Deferred income tax liability, the most common reserve item, is created to reconcile discrepancies that arise from using different fixed-asset depreciation methods for tax purposes and for financial reporting purposes. Many companies depreciate fixed assets faster for tax than for financial reporting. But in the long term, both methods result in expensing 100 percent of the cost of the fixed asset. From GAAP's viewpoint, evening out the reported profits after taxes is better than showing the actual cash that flows to the government. GAAP records an "extra" tax liability incurred by reporting the straight-line rather than the accelerated depreciation method for financial reporting. Because it is not paid out in cash, deferred income is segregated from the normal net worth accounts and carried as a reserve for deferred taxes. Exhibit 4.7 illustrates the effect of the first-year book and tax reporting being different for a fixed asset costing $100,000 depreciated over five years.

Deferred Tax Account Posting

If the value of the company's fixed assets continues to increase, the reserve remains stable or increases because additional depreciation is figured on an accelerated basis. Thus, this tax liability can be deferred indefinitely, unless there is a substantial drop in the company's fixed asset purchases. The latter easily could occur for a small company that had just built a new plant filled with new equipment. The company is unlikely to purchase additional equipment in the immediate future; its large increases in depreciation from the new fixed assets will initially increase its deferred income taxes, but the lack of new purchases will not add to it. Here, the deferred tax account serves a justifiable purpose in smoothing income over the life of the equipment.

As a result of a substantial drop in asset purchases, the reserve may convert to a current liability (income tax debt) that requires payment in the current year. A company going through such a transition probably would not request new loans, but would have cash available to repay existing loans.

Leases and Other Off-Balance-Sheet Liabilities

Perhaps the most problematic change for lenders in the past 25 years has been the increasing use of off-balance-sheet financing by corporations. Three major factors are behind this increase:

- acquisition or creation of captive finance and real estate subsidiaries,
- acquisition of less than a 50 percent interest in, or joint venturing with, affiliates, and
- growth of the equipment leasing industry.

Exhibit 4.7   Depreciation and Deferred Taxes

Depreciation and Deferred Taxes	Book		Tax
Cash	$100,000		$100,000
Salvage value	10,000		0
Depreciation base	90,000		100,000
Depreciable life	5 years		5 years
Depreciation method	Straight Line		Double Declining
Profit before tax and depreciation*	$40,000		$40,000
First year depreciation	18,000		40,000
Pretax profit	22,000		0
Tax (30%)	6,600		0
Net after tax	15,400		
Deferred tax		6,600	
Cash flow (net profit & depreciation)	33,400		40,000
Second year depreciation	18,000		24,000
Pretax profit	22,000		16,000
Tax (30%)	6,600		4,800
Net after tax	15,400		11,200
Deferred tax (year 1 + year 2)		8,400	
Cash flow	33,400		35,200
Third year depreciation	18,000		14,400
Pretax profit	22,000		25,600
Tax (30%)	6,600		7,680
Net after tax	15,400		17,920
Deferred tax (year 2 -year 3)		7,320	
Cash flow	33,400		32,320
Fourth year depreciation	18,000		8,640
Pretax profit	22,000		31,360
Tax (30%)	6,600		9,408
Net after tax	15,400		21,952
Deferred tax		4,512	
Cash flow	33,400		30,592
Fifth year depreciation	18,000		5,184
Pretax profit	22,000		34,816
Tax (30%)	6,600	667	10,445
Net after deferred tax	15,400		24,371
Cash flow	33,400		29,555

*Assume for illustration that profits and tax rate remain consistant over the five years.

As of December 1998, with the implementation of the Statement of Financial Accounting Standards (SFAS) No. 89, captive "other purpose" subsidiaries were eliminated as a form of off-balance-sheet financing. A company, however, can form up to a 50-percent-owned joint venture with another party and account for it on an equity basis. Ignoring the debt, the subsidiary itself can be a source of off-balance-sheet financing.

Operating leases of equipment and real estate (under SFAS No. 13) are popular with highly leveraged companies because the leases may be long-term commitments not identified on the balance sheet. They allow substantial off-balance-sheet financing because SFAS No. 13 considers them to be agreements signed in the ordinary course of business rather than liabilities.

The lender's responsibility involves calculating the extent of the fixed commitments that companies have off the balance sheet and understanding lease repayment terms and purposes. Thus, lenders closely examine each element of a company's funding structure, as detailed in the footnotes, rather than just transfer numbers from the balance sheet to the spreadsheet. Any off-balance-sheet obligations need to be added to the total liabilities for correct analysis. When determining debt repayment ability, lenders must consider the amounts needed to service the debt.

Contingent Liabilities

Contingent liabilities pose a significant threat to the viability of a company's operation. They include legal commitments, lawsuits, letters of credit, warranty claims, and guarantees.

Legal commitments can bankrupt a company; for example:

- In a construction company, legal commitments could arise from a simple error in estimating costs on a particular fixed cost job.
- For an importer, signing a letter of credit to import materials commits payment whether or not the products shipped were the correct ones, were salable, or were otherwise usable.

To enable a supplier to obtain credit, large purchasers occasionally guarantee the obligations of the smaller supplier to assist the latter in obtaining needed working capital. Advance payment would use up cash and be reflected on the balance sheet, while the contingency is not.

The analytical problem is that contingent liabilities are not placed on the balance sheet because no specific amount can be feasibly estimated. Careful reading of any contingency footnotes is important. Lenders must stay abreast of news events concerning their borrowers, their borrowers' customers and suppliers, the relevant industries, and any pending government regulations or public policy issues that might affect a borrower.

NET WORTH OR EQUITY

The difference between a company's total assets and its total liabilities is its equity or **net worth** (also called owners' equity or shareholders' equity). The amount of equity represents the cushion available to a lender in liquidating assets to repay liabilities. Equity can consist of capital stock, paid-in surplus, retained earnings, and treasury stock. Net worth or equity is calculated

$$\text{Assets} - \text{Liabilities} = \text{Net Worth}$$

A company's liabilities to its creditors do not shrink if asset values are reduced. Therefore, to obtain a true picture of the relationship between a company's debt and equity, the lender should compare the reduced value of the assets with its liabilities. The equity gives the lender a closer picture of a company's financial cushion in the face of shrinkage in its asset values. The amount of debt versus equity varies by industry and type of business within the industry. Industries with heavy dependencies on fixed assets tend to have higher debt to equity ratios than do industries with low fixed asset needs.

Stockholders, like creditors, have a claim against the assets of a company. However, stockholders can make their claims only after all of the company's creditors have been paid. Stockholders must absorb any shrinkage in a company's asset values, and they take the most risk in financing a company. However, the stockholders also have potential for the greatest return on their investment.

A recent concern regarding stocks is that some stocks have aspects of debt, given certain circumstances or occurrences. The best-known example is employee stock ownership trusts (ESOT). In these plans, the company loans money to the employees to buy back stock in the company. Only when the employees pay off the loans does the equity created have any meaning in financial statement analysis. Depending on the particular ESOT agreement, which is based on tax advantages to the company and the employees, there may be little equity cushion in these companies. Determining the nature of some of these stock hybrids is more important than a detailed reconciling of the net worth section. Any listing of multiple classes of stock deserves legal attention to determine the various rights and triggers that may accompany each class.

Stock (Common Stock, Par Value, Paid-in Surplus, and Preferred Stock)

Common stock is the minimum legal value of the company's outstanding shares of stock, usually called par value. Common stock entitles the holder to vote at shareholders' meetings and provides potential income to the investor through declared dividends and appreciation in value. Dividends are declared at management's discretion.

Par value—usually one dollar—is an arbitrary value established when a company authorizes shares to be issued.

Paid-in surplus represents additional equity generated when the company sells stock because the stock's price is usually more than the par value.

Preferred stock does not entail voting rights, but dividends accrue at a set rate (which is fixed at the time of issuance). However, unless it has a net profit or has declared common stock dividends, the company may not have to pay the set rate. Dividends may be cumulative, which means they accumulate if not paid in a given year. Most often, if cumulative, common dividends may not be paid until all past and accrued dividends are paid. In liquidation, preferred stockholders have preference over common stockholders to the company's assets. The lack of mandatory annual cash payments removes the debt aspect from preferred stock, which also departs from debt, in that it may not have to be redeemed at par value unless management so wishes.

Retained Earnings

Retained earnings represent after-tax net profits or losses kept in the company as a source of financing. Most companies retain some of their earnings to reduce their dependence on borrowing money. Many companies pay dividends to their owners (stockholders). Paying out a high portion of earnings in dividends, however, provides less support for future growth of the company, given the high cost of common stock issuance and the requirements by most lenders that the equity base remain proportionate to the debt level. Retained earnings may be negative if the company has experienced more net losses than net profits over time. Negative retained earnings also are called retained deficits.

Treasury Stock

Treasury stock is stock issued and then later repurchased by the company. The value of treasury stock is subtracted from the other accounts that make up a company's equity. In closely held companies, one owner can buy out the other owner using treasury stock. The company purchases the stock from the selling owner. This entry decreases the amount of total equity in the company.

Reconciliation of Net Worth

As part of the financial statement presentation, GAAP require a detailed reconciliation of net worth. If the statements are not audited, the lender should prepare a reconciliation showing any changes in the equity accounts (net worth) from the last statement. A company's net worth increases as after-tax profits are added to retained earnings. Increases also may result from new equity investments when additional stock is sold to shareholders.

Sometimes a company's equity accounts decrease. For example, equity will decrease if there is a net operating loss after taxes or if excess earnings are paid out as dividends to stockholders. Decreased equity also may result from the repurchase of outstanding shares of stock as treasury stock.

Exhibit 4.8 illustrates the reconciliation of net worth for Turner Electronic Corporation.

Tangible Net Worth

As stated earlier, some assets are considered intangible, for example, patents, trademarks, and goodwill. Many lenders, when calculating the tangible net worth, also discount notes receivable officers and leasehold improvements. On the plus side, many lenders add subordinated debt to equity when calculating tangible net worth. The tangible net worth is an indication of the borrowing capacity or strength of a company.

Exhibit 4.8 Reconciliation of Net Worth—Turner Electronic Corporation (000s omitted)

	20x0	20x1	20x2
Net profits	$ 21	$ 349	$ 34
Dividends	0	0	0
Change in net worth	21	349	34
Beginning net worth	1,377	1,398	1,746
± change in net worth	21	349*	34
= ending net worth	$1,398	$1,746	$1,780

*Does not add up due to rounding.

SUMMARY

Gaining a thorough understanding of a company's balance sheet is an essential first step in financial statement analysis. By knowing the type of company, its industry, and its managerial policies, the lender should have a general idea of what the company's balance sheet will look like. By reviewing asset values, liability repayment terms, and the relationship between debt and equity, lenders can predict the consequences of liquidating a company that has failed.

An evaluation of each asset account in terms of value and liquidity—the ability to convert an asset to cash at or near market values—assists the lender in determining the company's debt repayment capability and the need for collateral to secure debt. Furthermore, an evaluation of each liability account helps determine the current repayment requirements of the company in relation to its possible new financing requirements. When a company's total liabilities exceed the "true" value of assets, the company is said to be insolvent. If insolvency is not cured, usually by increasing equity, it may lead to bankruptcy. An evaluation of a company's liabilities in relation to its equity accounts enables the lender to compare the bank's overall risk as a creditor to the risk faced by a shareholder.

Assets, classified as current, fixed, or noncurrent are listed in order of their liquidity. Current assets, which include cash, marketable securities, accounts receivable, inventory, and other current assets, are expected to be turned into cash in less than one year.

Noncurrent assets are fixed assets and other noncurrent assets. Fixed assets include land, buildings, vehicles, equipment, and leasehold improvements. Fixed assets are depreciated based on their useful life. The net book value may be more or less than the market value, depending on the type and age of the fixed assets. Other noncurrent assets are cash value life insurance, prepaid expenses, notes receivable officers and affiliates, and investments in affiliates. These noncurrent assets are not liquid. Intangibles such as patents, trademarks, and goodwill also are noncurrent assets. Lenders deduct intangibles from equity to determine a tangible net worth.

Liabilities are listed as current or long-term. Notes payable bank is an amount due on short-term notes and lines of credit. The maximum amount available and the terms are important for the lender to know. Accounts payable or trade payable represent amounts owed for inventory purchases. This interest-free financing is important to the ongoing viability of the company. The lender will want to determine the number of trade relationships, length of relationships, and maximum credit available to the company. Other current liabilities include current maturities of long-term debt, accrued expenses or accruals, and notes payable other.

Long-term liabilities include notes to banks and others due in more than one year. Subordinated debt is an amount owed to the company's owners. If debt owed to an owner is subordinated, the lender considers this equity when calculating tangible net worth. Additional considerations when analyzing long-term liabilities are leases, off-balance sheet liabilities, and contingent liabilities.

Net worth or equity is made up of common stock, preferred stock, paid in surplus, retained earnings, and treasury stock. To determine if dividends have been paid, the net worth should be reconciled to current year earnings. The tangible net worth may be compared to the book net worth.

QUESTIONS FOR DISCUSSION

1. What is the difference between accounts receivable and notes receivable?
2. How is the inventory of a manufacturer different from that of a retailer?
3. If the local retail drug store purchases the local equipment rental company, what are the possible effects on the balance sheet? Assume the purchase price is greater than the net book value of the assets.
4. Define subordinated debt and give an example.
5. How can lenders determine if a company pays out its profits as dividends?

Exercise 1

Select items from the following list of accounts to construct the equity portion of a financial statement for Challenge All, Inc.

	(000s omitted)
Cash	$ 8
Provision for income tax	7
Accumulated depreciation	34
Notes payable bank	367
Prepaid expense	22
Current maturities long-term debt	56
Accrued expenses	25
Raw materials	36
Building	568
Retained earnings	286
Accounts payable	355
Finished goods	147
Paid-in surplus	200
Treasury stock	20
Work-in-process	22
Operating expenses	953
Common stock	1
Net profit after taxes	33

EXERCISE 2

Select items from the following list of accounts to construct the current assets portion of a financial statement for Douglas Auto, Inc.

	(000s omitted)
Net accounts receivable	$ 90
Accounts payable	38
Accrued salaries	8
Accrued taxes	10
Accumulated depreciation	34
Building	61
Common stock	13
Cash	7
Certificate of deposit	11
Finished goods	22
Work-in-process	30
Land	3
Equipment	50
Net profit after taxes	6
Operating expenses	228
Prepaid expenses	10
Raw materials	19
Term loan payable	44
Treasury stock	22

5

Using Ratios to Analyze Financial Statements

LEARNING OBJECTIVES

After studying *Using Ratios to Analyze Financial Statements*, you will be able to

- calculate and explain the meaning of liquidity, financial leverage, coverage, and profit (also called operating) ratios,
- apply these ratios to the analysis of financial statements,
- explain the concepts of working capital, working investment, and Z score,
- calculate select technology industry ratios,
- use ratios for industry comparison and trend analysis, and
- define the key terms that appear in **bold** type in the text.

INTRODUCTION

Ratios are among the best known and most widely used financial statement analysis tools. By presenting information in a manageable form, ratios allow a lender to study relationships between various but related components in a set of financial statements. As comparative tools, ratios are used to measure a company's performance over time (trend analysis) and to compare it with that of its competitors or industry averages (comparative analysis).

Often, ratios are misused in financial statement analysis. Unless interpreted correctly, ratios can be misleading. They should be used as measuring devices that lead to instructive questions and as building blocks in the construction of a company's total financial picture. They never should be used as the primary basis for approving a loan or rejecting loan applications.

The figures used in calculating ratios primarily come from income statements and balance sheets. Thus, ratio analysis is an extension of other financial statement analytical techniques.

In this module, you will examine the arithmetic computation and meaning of four types of financial ratios: liquidity, financial leverage, coverage, and profit (also called operating). You also will consider how ratios are selected and used to spot trends and compare a company's performance in key areas with other companies in its industry.

USES AND LIMITATIONS OF RATIOS

Ratios show the relative size of things. For example, if you want to compare two baseball players, you might consider their batting averages. If one is hitting 400 and the other's average is 250, you know which one is doing better, even if you do not know how a batting average is calculated. A batting average is a measure of productivity. Financial ratios measure a company's productivity.

In financial statement analysis, ratios help the lender measure relationships or proportions between related accounts included in a company's financial statements. For example, a ratio will show that the relationship of $336 of assets and $118 of liabilities is the same as the relationship between $109,487,094 of assets and $54,743,952 of liabilities. Moreover, ratios usually are expressed in their simplest form. The ratio of both examples could be expressed as 2:1, 2 to l, or 2/1. Generally, balance sheet ratios are expressed in numbers or dollars such as 2:1 (2 to 1) or $2 to every $1. Income statement relationships are usually expressed as percentages. For example, if a company earns five cents for each dollar of sales, the return on sales ratio may be expressed as 5 percent.

Relationship

Ratios are comparisons between two related accounts or variables. They can be calculated using any two numbers. However, for a ratio to be valid, a meaningful relationship must exist between the two variables being compared. In financial statement analysis, ratios are used to compare income statement and balance sheet accounts. For example, because the relationship between a company's sales and accounts receivable has meaning, the days accounts receivable ratio is important. The days accounts receivable ratio is a comparison of a company's net sales with its accounts receivable.

$$\text{Days accounts receivable} = \frac{365 \text{ days} \times \text{net sales}}{\text{Accounts receivable}}$$

A ratio of a company's inventory to its accrued expenses, however, would have no significance because no meaningful relationship exists between these two accounts.

The interrelationship of different ratios is also important to the analysis process. Ratios can have offsetting or balancing influences on each other. For example, high financial leverage, demonstrated by the debt-to-equity ratio, may be offset by a high debt-service-coverage-ratio that indicates a high level of cash flow.

When writing an analysis, a lender must interpret the ratio to understand what it says about the business at the moment and how it might affect the business in the future. It is incorrect merely to convert the number from a table of ratios to a sentence in prose, which is often called "elevator analysis." For example, a lender who states that the inventory increased from 34 to 56 days has presented an elevator analysis because he or she is merely stating that a ratio went up in a particular year. True analysis is stating the cause. In the above example, it would be better to say that inventory increased by 22 days due to the introduction of a new product line that is selling slower. A lender's responsibility is to understand individual ratios and relate the ratios to their possible causes. The purpose of understanding the cause is to raise more analytical questions to ask the prospective borrower. A lender needs to understand how the business operates, generates cash, and uses cash. A thorough understanding of those processes will lead to a correct borrowing structure.

Comparability

The quality of the numbers used to calculate a ratio also affects the importance of the ratio. Meaningful ratio analysis depends not only on the accuracy of the computations used in deriving a financial statement, but also on the consistency of the numbers. For example, any industry comparisons of ratios involving assets must consider the different valuation methods used.

- The valuation of inventory on the balance sheet may differ dramatically, depending on whether the company employs the first-in, first-out (FIFO) or the last-in, first-out (LIFO) method.

- The valuation of aged accounts receivable is affected by the company's debt policy—whether or not it has an allowance for bad debt or directly expenses bad debts to the income statement.

- The valuation of fixed assets is affected by the company's use of straight line or double-declining depreciation. In addition, some balance sheets may include significantly undervalued fixed assets (such as land and buildings) that have been held for a considerable length of time.

Management decisions that influence the valuation of a balance sheet item also affect the income statement. A lower valuation of inventory resulting from using LIFO in times of rising prices, establishing a larger allowance for bad debt, or using double-declining depreciation to rapidly write off depreciable assets all have the additional effect of reducing a company's net profit. This, in turn, affects the profit ratios, such as return on sales, the return on assets, or return on equity.

In a trend analysis that compares the ratios of a single company over time, the types of accounting policies used to prepare the statements are not significant as long as they are consistently applied. However, when making industry-wide comparisons, a lender should try to find companies that use the same accounting procedures and apply them consistently. Even if this cannot be done, industry comparisons have some validity, since ratios are not intended to be absolute indicators but, rather, relative indicators that may point to areas for further study or inquiry.

Industry Sources and Limitations

Useful sources of industry information include:

- The Risk Management Association (RMA) Annual Statement Studies
  (http://www.rmahq.org/)
- Dun & Bradstreet (D&B) Key Business Ratios
  (http://www.zapdata.com/)
- Standard and Poor's Industry Surveys
  (http://www.standardandpoors.com/)
- The Combined Financial and Merchandising and Operating Results
  for Retail Stores
  (http://www.cba.ua.edu/bruno/resources/guides/sguide6.htm)
- NWDA Industry Performance Report for Drug Stores
  (http://www.library.hbs.edu/industry/biotech-statistics.htm)

Care must be taken when using such sources, however, since the industry figures available for comparison typically will be a year behind the statements for the company being analyzed. When dealing with particular industries and some undiversified geographic regions subject to economic swings, it may be difficult to draw meaningful comparisons using year-old data. Also, when using industry comparisons, it is important to remember that the calculations are not always the same. For example, average or actual numbers, pre- or post-tax profits, and other variations of the financial statements may be used. Another drawback to using industry comparisons is that some diversified companies consolidate their various lines of business into a single financial statement, making accurate comparisons difficult. No single financial technique yields a complete financial picture of a company. This is especially true of ratios, which are relative measures that have significance only in relation to other reference points or benchmarks.

Selection and Interpretation of Ratios

For analytical purposes, ratios are grouped into four main categories, each of which represents an aspect of a company's financial well-being: liquidity, financial leverage, coverage, and profit (or operating). In practice, lenders do not calculate every ratio. They select one or two ratios from each category to begin a review and then select additional ratios appropriate to help interpret and complete the analytical picture. Experienced loan officers may use additional ratios not included in this module.

Each of the ratio categories is discussed in the following sections. In the examples, the calculation of ratios is based on common-sized financial statements for Turner Electronic Corporation. These statements are found in the *Master Case Book*.

LIQUIDITY RATIOS

In finance, **liquidity** means the ability to convert an asset into cash in a timely manner without the loss of market value. The assets must be converted in time to meet debt obligations as they come due. A company with high liquidity must maintain a good balance between the conversion of current assets and the maturity of current liabilities. Because maturing obligations must be paid in cash, the analysis of liquidity focuses on the availability of cash or the company's ability to generate it by converting its assets into cash without a significant loss in value in the event of liquidation.

Liquidation refers to lenders forcing a company to sell its assets to repay debt. Often, liquidation results in assets being auctioned at less than fair market value because of the urgency in the recovery process and the involuntary aspect of the sale for the owner. Ratios generally associated with liquidation are balance-sheet oriented and do not look at the dynamic quality of the income statement or statement of cash flows. The assumption is that the company has failed and liquidation is the only alternative left to the lender.

When calculating liquidity ratios, lenders often follow the rule of thumb that, in liquidation, the auction or fast-sale value is likely to be half the market value or less. On average, most lenders receive 50 percent or less of market or book values. In any given situation, the 50-percent rules of thumb may or may not be correct. Actual liquidation values are a result of the type of industry, the state of the economy, and the skill of managers in valuing their inventories and other assets.

Legitimate levels of current assets are required to meet short-term obligations and are related directly to the risk and fluctuations involved in a company's short-term cash flow. For example, a manufacturer with sales that cannot be predicted with reasonable accuracy needs a higher turnover of current assets to ensure the company's ability to meet its obligations. On the other hand, a utility company that can accurately forecast the demand for power and has a steady and predictable level of operating cash inflow from monthly billings needs a lower level of current assets.

A company's need for financial flexibility also affects its desired level of liquidity. For example, both a wholesaler that wants to deliver inventory rapidly when customers make large purchases and a retailer that wants to increase advertising outlays quickly to respond to competitive demands need higher liquidity. The amount of prearranged outside funding made available to a company on demand, such as a line of credit or revolving credit, also can affect the company's need for liquidity.

A company is illiquid if it is in danger of being unable to meet its current financial obligations. This may be a temporary, self-correcting problem, or it may be a symptom of more serious and permanent problems in a company's operation. Illiquidity typically results from a combination of several situations.

First, the company might have its funds tied up in illiquid assets—assets that the company cannot convert to cash in a timely manner. A women's clothing retailer that invests its money in new leasehold improvements is neither able to nor intends to liquidate those improvements to obtain cash if retail sales do not generate sufficient cash. There is also less cash to purchase sufficient inventory to generate more sales.

Second, the company may have funded its operation improperly. It may have taken on too much debt given its ability to generate cash and pay interest and principal, or the schedule for repaying its financial obligations may not match the timing of its cash generation.

Third, the company might be losing money on its operation. In other words, a business that spends more money than it takes in cannot generate sufficient cash to meet its obligations. This situation often occurs when the company is growing.

Depending on the reasons for and the magnitude of a company's illiquidity, the results can range from simple inconvenience to impending disaster. Illiquidity might

- result in merely having to forgo discounts offered by creditors for exceptionally prompt payment,
- result in a need to borrow short-term money from the bank,
- damage a company's credit rating, or
- force a company to pass up additional business because of its inability to handle its existing financial obligations.

In the most serious situation, the company may have to liquidate its operating assets, which can impair its future ability to generate cash through operations. Liquidity ratios show the margin of current assets to current liabilities that should result from a total liquidation of the company's accounts. Liquidity measures include working capital and working investment. Liquidity ratios are the current, quick, days receivable, days inventory, and days payable ratios.

Working Capital

Although it is not a ratio, working capital does indicate a company's liquidity. **Gross working capital** is the investment in the operating cycle of a business. **Net working capital** can be defined using the accounting definition—current assets minus current liabilities. In this module, the term **working capital** will mean net working capital.

Net working capital can be considered the owner's and long-term debt holders' investments in the current assets of the business. As such, net working capital is a long-term concept. Increasing current assets with financing provided by short-term debt does not change working capital. For example, a retailer purchases $100,000 of seasonal inventory and finances it with accounts payable. The calculation of net working capital being current assets (inventory, $100,000) minus current liabilities (accounts payable, $100,000) equals zero. Therefore, working capital did not change. However, if the inventory were financed with a long-term note payable to the bank, working capital would have changed. Considering that the purpose of the loan is to finance seasonal inventory, a long-term debt structure would be incorrect.

The amount of working capital needed is affected by

- the market in which the borrower operates,
- the borrower's ability to operate profitably,
- management's risk-taking philosophy,
- the stability of cash flow, and
- the company's ability to meet current liabilities as they come due.

Although working capital is considered a liquidity concept, current assets generally do not provide sufficient liquidity because they constantly turn over and are replaced in the operating cycle. The classic example is the company with plenty of working capital but no cash and, therefore, no ability to repay its short-term debt. The calculation for Turner Electronic Corporation's working capital in 20x1 is:

Current assets	$2,936
– current liabilities	$1,374
= working capital	$1,562

Turner Electronic Corporation's working capital may or may not be sufficient. The amount of working capital needed for a manufacturer depends on the length of the operating cycle, the company credit and collection policies, and the company's management of inventory.

Working Investment

A company's **working investment** is the difference between its working assets and working liabilities. It is calculated as:

$$\text{Working assets} = \text{Net accounts receivable} + \text{Inventory}$$

$$\text{Working liabilities} = \text{Accounts payable} + \text{Accruals}$$

$$\text{Working investment} = \text{Working assets} - \text{Working liabilities}$$

The **working investment ratio** is calculated by dividing the company's working investment by net sales.

$$\frac{\text{Working investment}}{\text{Net sales}} = \text{Working investment ratio}$$

For example, if a company's abbreviated balance sheet appeared as:

Assets		Liabilities	
Cash	$100	Notes payable—bank	$200
Net accounts receivable—net	$400	Accounts payable	$300
Inventory	$200	Accrued expenses	$100
Total current assets	$700	Total current liabilities	$600

The company's working investment would be:

Net accounts receivable	$400
+ inventory	$200
= working assets	$600
Accounts payable	$300
+ accrued expenses	$100
= working liabilities	$400
Working assets	$600
– working liabilities	$400
= working investment	$200

If the company had net sales of $1,000 per year, the working investment ratio would be calculated:

$$\frac{\$200}{\$1,000} = 0.20*$$

* This is sometimes referred to as the "working investment factor."

Assuming that the relationship between sales and accounts receivable and the relationship between inventory and accounts payable remain fairly stable, the working investment ratio can be used to estimate the amount of equity and financing needed to complete the operating cycle if sales increase.

If the company anticipates a sales increase of 15 percent in the next fiscal year (current sales of $1,000 with projected sales of $1,150), the level of working investment needed could be calculated as:

(Projected sales × working investment ratio)
– working investment

= additional working investment

($1,150 × 0.20) – $200 = $30

If the company already has a $200 working investment, it will need an additional $30 for its projected 15 percent sales increase. This quick calculation of the working investment (needed to support projected sales increases) helps the lender compare the company's borrowing requirements with available financing alternatives. Financing alternatives might include increasing bank debt, additional equity, increasing accounts payable, decreasing accounts receivable or inventory, reducing dividends, decreasing owners' salaries or other benefits, or improving profits. In the above example, if the company normally experiences a 2 percent profit margin, then 2 percent of $1,150 in sales would produce profits of $23. It would therefore have a $7 ($30 – $23) financing requirement to support the sales growth.

To determine the effects of different scenarios, the lender can vary any of the assumptions used. Although working investment analysis cannot replace forecast statements and cash budgets, it does provide a fast and relatively simple estimate of the cash needed to finance sales growth.

As a company's sales increase, the base level of its working assets grows proportionately. Accounts payable and accruals, which provide the basic financing for the growing accounts receivable and inventory, also increase because it is difficult to have sales growth without growth in accounts receivable and inventory. This growth is often referred to as "spontaneous growth of current assets."

Accounts payable and accruals often grow as fast as inventory and receivables. But, because they are smaller in dollars than inventory and receivables, accounts payable and accruals alone cannot support the growth in current assets. The portion of working assets that is not supported by the company's accounts payable and accruals must be financed by debt or equity. Therefore, working investment is not a pure liquidity measure. It does, however, address financing needs in order to maintain present liquidity.

Working Investment Application for Turner

If Turner Electronic Corporation's working investment for 20x1 were calculated as:

Net accounts receivable	$ 905
+ inventory	$1,980
= working assets	$2,885
Accounts payable	$ 507
+ accrued expenses	$ 163
= working liabilities	$ 670
Working assets	$2,885
– working liabilities	$ 670
= working investment	$2,215

Turner Electronic Corporation's working investment ratio would be:

$$\frac{\$2,215}{\$7,482} = 0.30$$

If Turner's sales were to increase 5 percent, or $374 ($7,482 × 0.05), it would need $112 in financing ($374 × 0.30). The lender should be prepared to discuss the source of the financing and the impact on the company's cash flow. However, Turner showed a 4.6 percent after tax net profit margin in 20x1. If it maintains a similar margin in the projected year, Turner might not need additional financing. In this case, the calculation would be:

$$(\text{Projected sales} \times \text{Net profit}) - \text{Financing required} = \text{Excess Available}$$

$$(\$7,482 + \$374)\ 0.046 - \$112 = \$249$$

Current Ratio

Ratios commonly used to get a rough indication of liquidity are the current, quick, days accounts receivable, days inventory, and days payable ratios. Some lenders may refer to the three days ratios as activity ratios.

The current ratio compares the absolute quantity of the company's current assets to its current liabilities at a certain point in time. In other words, it shows the amount of cushion provided by a company's current assets relative to its current liabilities.

Historically, a ratio of 2 to 1 (2:1) of current assets to current liabilities has been the accepted standard for the current ratio. This is partly based on the 50-percent rule of thumb of liquidation mentioned earlier. That is, if assets fall in value by 50 percent, then the remaining value will be sufficient to repay current liabilities—assuming the ratio was 2 to 1 before the liquidation.

The need for a high liquidity cushion and, thus, a high current ratio varies among industries and depends on such factors as the composition and quality of the company's current assets. The most important factors are the amount of available cash, the quality of the receivables, and the near-term maturity of the current liabilities. For example, consider a garden shop retailer who borrows money in the spring to pay for shrubs and flowers with the intention of repaying the loan after the summer or fall season. Reviewing the May financial statement without this knowledge of repayment would show a poor current ratio, but since the maturity of the current liability is after fall sales, the current ratio should not be alarming. Generally, the higher the current ratio, the more comfortable the cushion against the effects of reduced inventory values, uncollected receivables, and unanticipated cash needs. However, a large current ratio may signify idle cash, too much inventory, or a slow collection of accounts receivable.

Increasing current assets or decreasing current liabilities can improve a current ratio. This is accomplished by

- paying down current liabilities from profits or conversion to a long-term loan,
- acquiring a long-term loan to fund permanent increases in current assets,
- selling a fixed asset for more than book value and retaining the excess cash, or
- putting profits back into the business to fund current assets.

The current ratio is calculated using the following formula:

$$\frac{\text{Current assets}}{\text{Current liabilities}} = \text{Current ratio}$$

A look at the 20x1 figures on Turner Electronic Corporation's common-sized balance sheet located in the *Master Case Book* shows the company's current assets at $2,936 and its current liabilities at $1,374. Dollar amounts in this module are in thousands of dollars, corresponding with the amounts in the common-sized financial statements located in the *Master Case Book*. Using the formula above, Turner Electronic Corporation's current ratio can be calculated as:

$$\frac{\$2,936}{\$1,374} = 2.14$$

A current ratio of 2.14:1 means that, for every dollar of current debt, Turner Electronic Corporation has $2.14 of current assets. The value of Turner Electronic Corporation's current assets could shrink by more than half without significantly impairing the company's ability to pay its creditors through the liquidation of its current assets.

The current ratio is not an absolute measure of debt-paying ability because a company will never fully liquidate its current assets during its normal course of business. Moreover, the current ratio does not measure the quality of the current assets, but only their existence. For example, Turner Electronic Corporation's 20x1 current assets comprise $51 in cash, $905 in accounts receivable, and $1,980 in inventory. The ability of the company to pay its current liabilities relies on the sale of inventory on credit, which creates accounts receivable that need to be collected. The ratio does not tell the lender if this sale of inventory and collection of accounts receivable can be done in time to pay the current liabilities, nor does it tell the lender the aging of the accounts receivable, the validity of the accounts receivable, the quality of the inventory, or if the inventory can be sold. Also, the ratio does not reflect the timing of the current liability payments. For example, Turner Electronic Corporation's current liabilities include a $634 note payable to the bank. The ratio does not tell the lender if the note is due in 1 day or 180 days. If the note is due in 1 day, it is unlikely Turner will collect sufficient accounts receivable or sell sufficient inventory for cash to repay the debt.

Quick Ratio

The **quick ratio** (also called the **acid-test ratio**) is a more stringent measure of liquidity than the current ratio because it includes only the most theoretically liquid current assets. The company's inventory and other current assets are eliminated from current assets for this calculation, leaving only cash, marketable securities, and accounts receivable—those assets that a company should be able to convert to cash quickly to pay obligations. The quick ratio is calculated using the following formula:

$$\frac{\text{Cash + Marketable securities + Net accounts receivable}}{\text{Current liabilities}} = \text{Quick ratio}$$

Turner Electronic Corporation's 20x1 balance sheet shows the company's cash at $51, its net accounts receivable at $905, and its current liabilities (the same figure used in the current ratio) at $1,374. Using the formula above, Turner Electronic Corporation's quick ratio can be calculated as:

$$\frac{(\$51 + \$905)}{\$1,374} = 0.70$$

Historically, a quick ratio of 1:1 has been regarded as an indication of good liquidity. Turner Electronic Corporation's quick ratio of 0.70 means the company has 70 cents of liquid assets (accounts receivable and cash) available for each $1 of current debt. Because the ratio is less than 1:1, the ratio affirms the company's dependency on the sale of inventory. Again, the ratio does not tell the lender if the cash is available, the accounts receivable are collectable, and the accounts receivable are valid, or when the current liabilities need to be paid.

Days Ratios

Unlike the current and quick ratios, which use elements only from the balance sheet, the days ratios use a mix of income statement and balance sheet variables. These ratios also are indicators of liquidity because they attempt to ascertain the quality of the underlying asset and the timing of the debt. The faster a business can sell its inventory and collect accounts receivable, the higher that asset is in quality and the quicker it may repay its short-term bank or trade debt.

The days ratios provide further insights into how efficiently a company manages its current assets and current liabilities. Generally, these ratios compare the company's sales with three balance sheet accounts: accounts receivable, inventory, and accounts payable. The ratios measure how frequently the company turns over these accounts— that is, how long it takes for accounts receivable to be collected, inventory to be sold, and accounts payable to be paid. These ratios also have been called turnover ratios. As part of the calculation, the lender can determine how often the accounts receivable, inventory, and accounts payable turn.

Days Accounts Receivable Ratio

The relationship between accounts receivable and sales can be expressed in two ways. The first gives the number of times during the year that the average accounts receivable is collected. Often, customers use the word *turns* when referring to how often the accounts receivable is collected and the inventory is sold. The accounts receivable turns are calculated:

$$\frac{\text{Net sales}}{\text{Accounts receivable}} = \text{Accounts receivable turns}$$

The days accounts receivable ratio is calculated:

$$\frac{365 \text{ days} \times \text{net sales}}{\text{Accounts receivable}} = \text{Days accounts receivable ratio}$$

Some lenders use 360 days as the numerator on the basis that it is easier to calculate and is typical of most selling terms (30-day terms × 12 months = 360). The five-day difference has little effect on the result. The important issue is to be consistent and use 360 or 365 days for all ratio calculations. In this module, we will use 365 days. The **days accounts receivable ratio** gives the average number of days it takes to collect on the accounts receivable.

The additional work required to convert accounts-receivable-turns into days is outweighed by the added meaning that expressing the relationship in this way provides. For example, a slowing in a company's average collection period from 37 days to 44 is much easier to grasp than a decline in receivables turnover from 9.9 to 8.3 times per year. The conversion to days also makes it easier to compare a company's average accounts receivable with the credit terms it offers.

The days accounts receivable shows the average number of days it takes a company to collect credit sales from its customers. Because this factor will vary for different types of companies, it is important to make comparisons between similar companies or to look at trends over time. Ideally, this ratio is calculated using the average of monthly or quarterly credit sales that gave rise to the level of receivables shown on the balance sheet. Because most corporate financial statements do not distinguish between the company's credit sales and cash sales, and because cash sales often are insignificant amounts, lenders typically calculate the ratio using net sales.

Lenders should make every effort to obtain the monthly or quarterly net sales and receivables levels to confirm that the cash sales are, indeed, minimal. If such detailed information is not available, then information about the seasonality of the company needs to be obtained. Otherwise, the year-end balance sheet may not be at all representative of the average year. In the absence of any of this information, the days accounts receivable ratio can be calculated by using the average of the beginning and ending receivables and the aggregate sales level for the entire period, or only the ending accounts receivable.

If any significant deviation in the collection period shows up from the trend or comparative analysis, the lender should meet with the company's management to determine the cause. Also, the lender should compare the company's average collection period with the collection terms allowed by the company to determine if the collection of receivables is in line with the company's credit policy.

Turner Electronic Corporation's balance sheet shows accounts receivables for fiscal year-end 20x1 at $905. Since credit sales are not shown separately, the company's net sales for 20x1 ($7,482) is used.

The resulting calculation is:

$$\frac{365 \times \$905}{\$7,482} = 44 \text{ days}$$

Turner Electronic Corporation's days accounts receivable ratio is 44 days. The company does an adequate job collecting its accounts and approving credit policy within the company's terms of net 30 days. The ratio indicates the quality of the company's customers and, thus, the quality of the accounts receivable.

Of course, the days accounts receivable ratio does not tell a lender if it comprises two accounts receivable—one current, and the other past due 88 days for an average of 44 days. The ratio also fails to indicate the mix, concentration, or validity of the accounts receivable. An accounts receivable aging is needed in order to review these details and make a full analysis.

Days Inventory Ratio

The **days inventory ratio** shows how often the inventory is turned or sold to generate the current sales volume. Inventory turnover measures the company's purchasing, selling, and manufacturing efficiency, but it is meaningful only in relation to the company's past performance and to the performance of similar companies in the same industry. A change in this ratio results from a change in sales, selling time, or cost of goods sold. The lender should consider the components of cost of goods sold to determine how they are affecting the ratio. For example, if inventory purchase prices increase, they could affect the days inventory ratio.

Because they include the profit margin needed to support other expenses and provide a net profit to the company, sales figures are not used as the numerator. Cost of goods sold is used because it represents the true relationship to inventory and the cost of inventory sold during the year. For a manufacturer, cost of goods sold includes overhead and manufacturing costs. It is desirable that these costs (rather than just purchases) be included because the processing time and costs (adding value) are parts of the item the lender is trying to identify. Cost of goods for a manufacturer is calculated as:

Beginning inventory
+ raw materials used
+ labor expense
+ manufacturing overhead
− work-in-process
− ending inventory
──────────────
= cost of goods sold

The cost of goods sold for a wholesaler or retailer includes the net cost of inventory purchases and is calculated as:

$$
\begin{array}{l}
\text{Beginning inventory} \\
\text{+ net cost of purchases} \\
\underline{\text{– less ending inventory}} \\
\text{= cost of goods sold}
\end{array}
$$

The accuracy of the calculation is affected by differences in the numbers that make up the denominator. For example, whether LIFO or FIFO is used in valuing inventory affects the result of the calculation and may mean that days in inventory are not comparable among companies. A change in the days inventory ratio, although not conclusive in itself, may raise questions that will lead to a better understanding of a company's inventory strategy or problems. For example, a trend of increasing days in inventory may indicate obsolescence of inventory or a stockpiling of inventory to take advantage of pricing from a supplier or the need to fill a large special sales order. Although the ratio itself does not tell a lender if the mix of the inventory has changed or if any inventory is obsolete, it may signal a lender to ask these questions.

The days inventory looks like the days accounts receivable ratio and is calculated:

$$
\frac{365 \text{ days} \times \text{inventory}}{\text{Cost of goods sold}} = \text{Days inventory ratio}
$$

In the *Master Case Book,* Turner Electronic Corporation's balance sheet shows inventory for fiscal year-end 20x1 as $1,980, and its common-sized income statement shows the total cost of goods sold as $4,660.

Cost of goods sold	$ 4,377
+ rent	$ 202
+ depreciation in cost of goods sold	$ 81
= Total cost of goods sold	$ 4,660

Turner Electronic Corporation's 20x1 days inventory is calculated as:

$$
\frac{365 \times \$1,980}{\$4660} = 155 \text{ days}
$$

Turner Electronic Corporation's days inventory ratio during 20x1 was approximately 155 days. This means that if sales were to continue at the current level, theoretically the company could liquidate its entire inventory in 155 days. Because detailed inventory information is rarely available and a company may stock various types of inventory at widely varying levels, this ratio is only an approximation.

Turner Electronic Corporation's ratio of 155 days is of concern. Based on the current sales level, it would take more than five months to sell the inventory. A lender will want to determine the mix of raw material, work-in-process, and finished goods. If the raw materials are for finished products no longer being sold or selling slowly, a lender should be concerned about the company's ability to sell the inventory. The work-in-process and finished goods are matched to product orders and previous sales. This analysis tells the lender the probability and timing of finished product sales. Finished products are compared to the current sales orders and volumes by type of product.

Days Accounts Payable Ratio

The **days accounts payable ratio** measures how promptly the company pays its trade accounts. Because standard credit terms differ, this ratio varies significantly for different industries. Lenders should be alert to any significant changes in this ratio. A notable decrease could mean simply that the company is taking advantage of discounts offered for early payment, but it also could indicate that suppliers are withdrawing trade credit. A significant lengthening of the days payables could mean that suppliers have granted the company additional trade credit or longer terms, or it could mean cash flow problems are delaying payments to suppliers.

This ratio also is subject to inaccuracies. Although it should relate purchases to accounts payable, purchase figures frequently are unavailable. Consequently, the cost of goods sold is substituted for purchases even though, for a manufacturer, this includes certain overhead accounts as well as direct labor. For this reason, the ratio is best used as an approximation in comparing similar companies or in trend analysis.

It is possible to calculate purchases by taking current year cost of goods sold, adding this year's ending inventory (from the balance sheet), and subtracting last year's ending inventory (from last year's balance sheet), which was really this year's beginning inventory. The result will give the lender the purchases for a retail or wholesale business.

The days accounts payable ratio formula is similar to those previously used:

$$\frac{365 \text{ days} \times \text{accounts payable}}{\text{Cost of goods sold}} = \text{Days payable ratio}$$

Turner Electronic Corporation's balance sheet (in the *Master Case Book*) shows accounts payable to be $507 as of 20x1, and its income statement shows the cost of goods sold as $4,660.

The company's 20x1 days payable ratio is calculated as:

$$\frac{365 \times \$507}{\$4,660} = 40 \text{ days}$$

The days accounts payable ratio shows that Turner Electronic Corporation pays its creditors in 40 days on average. This is not accurate since, as a manufacturer, Turner Electronic Corporation's cost of goods includes other costs and expenses in addition to purchases. If greater accuracy is desired, especially for a manufacturer, a lender can request an aging of accounts payable from management.

Dollar Impact on Financing from Liquidity Ratios

In addition to reviewing the number of times per year and the days of the current asset and liability accounts, a lender also examines the dollar changes taking place. Because they lend money, bankers must know how much is represented in dollars to measure the amount of credit needed. This concept is related to the operating cycle of the company—processing raw materials or purchased goods, adding value for resale, and collecting the cash from the sales.

The length of the operating cycle directly influences a company's financing needs if sales grow in the future. Turner Electronic Corporation's accounts receivable increased from 38 days in 20x0 to 44 in 20x1. The company's cash cycle is delayed not just by six days, but also by six days times the dollar sales per day. In Turner Electronic Corporation's case, annual net sales for 20x1 are $7,482. Daily sales are that amount divided by 365 ($7,482/365 = $20). This means that the company will have a daily dollar delay of $20 times six days, or $120 in cash shortage or delay. If assets increase by this amount, so must debt or equity increase for the balance sheet to be in balance. The numbers above are from the common-size statements that have 000s omitted. The cash shortage is $120,000. A significant amount of new financing is needed to fund the slower accounts receivable.

FINANCIAL LEVERAGE RATIOS

Financial leverage in financial statement analysis measures the relative levels of financial risk borne by the creditors and the shareholders of a business. Because assets must be financed either by owners' equity (net worth) or creditors' liabilities (debt), **financial leverage ratios** show how much protection a company's total assets provide for a creditor's debt.

Like liquidity ratios, leverage ratios show the hypothetical margin of protection provided by assets relative to a corresponding group of liabilities if the company is liquidated. The higher the proportion of borrowed funds to owner-contributed funds, the greater the assumed risk to lenders. These ratios also could be interpreted to show how much the assets could contract, should liquidation occur, without harming the creditor. Two common leverage ratios are the debt-to-worth ratio and the debt-to-capitalization ratio.

A possible issue here is the definition of net worth. The lender must carefully evaluate the intangible and the tangible assets and use the most reliable data available to derive the tangible net worth of a company. Intangibles generally include patents, trademarks, goodwill, notes receivable officers, and, on occasion, leasehold improvements.

Debt-to-Worth Ratio

The **debt-to-worth** (or debt-to-equity) **ratio** indicates how well the share-holders' investment in the company provides a cushion for asset shrinkage. It also attempts to measure how much shareholders have at risk versus how much creditors have at risk and, thus, examines a company's capital structure. Like the current ratio, the debt-to-worth ratio measures a company's ability to liquidate its assets to satisfy debt. This ratio enables a lender to gauge how much a company can reduce the valuation of its assets before its creditors sustain a loss. If the asset values decrease below the value of liabilities as a result of reevaluation (true value versus book value), a company is considered to be insolvent.

Debt-to-worth ratios vary greatly for different industries. For example, the RMA average debt-to-worth ratio for a concrete construction company is 1.7 to 1; for a wholesaler of office supplies it is 5 to 1; for a movie theater, it is as high as 31 to 1. The debt-to-worth ratio is calculated using the following formula:

$$\frac{\text{Total liabilities}}{\text{Tangible net worth}} = \text{Debt-to-worth ratio}$$

Turner Electronic Corporation's balance sheet shows its total debt at $1,498 (as of year-end 20x1) and its net worth at $1,746. Since the presentation does not include any intangibles, Turner Electronic Corporation's 20x1 debt-to-worth ratio would be easily calculated as:

$$\frac{\$1,498}{\$1,746} = 0.86$$

Turner Electronic Corporation's debt-to-worth ratio of 0.86:1 indicates that creditors have invested 86 cents in the company for every $1 shareholders have invested. The relative value of the shareholders' and creditors' risks could be different from what the debt-to-worth ratio shows if the market, or liquidation, value of the assets differs significantly from their book value. Turner Electronic Corporation's debt-to-worth ratio appears to be low for a manufacturer. Most manufacturers depend heavily on financing fixed assets, resulting in a higher debt-to-worth ratio.

Debt-to-Capitalization Ratio (Sometimes Called Funded Debt-to-Net Worth)

The debt-to-capitalization ratio is calculated as:

$$\frac{\text{Long-term debt}}{\text{Long-term debt + net worth}} = \text{Debt-to-capitalization ratio}$$

If a company has on its balance sheet capitalized lease obligations that are not already included as part of its long-term debt, these obligations are added to long-term debt, both in the numerator and the denominator of this equation.

Turner Electronic Corporation's 20x1 balance sheet shows long-term debt at $124 and net worth at $1,746. Thus, the company's 20x1 debt-to-capitalization ratio is:

$$\frac{\$124}{\$124 + \$1,746} = 0.06$$

Turner Electronic Corporation's debt-to-capitalization ratio of 0.06:1 indicates that the company's long-term creditors supply just a small percentage of its permanent capital.

COVERAGE RATIOS

Coverage ratios measure the extent to which debt obligations are met or exceeded by the cash flow from the company's operations. A company's ability to cover principal and interest payments is a key indicator of financial health, which is of crucial concern to lenders.

Although a detailed examination of cash flows requires preparing a statement of cash flows, coverage ratios are most frequently calculated using traditional cash flow. Traditional cash flow from operations is cash flow before changes in current accounts have been considered. Basically, traditional cash flow from operations is net profit plus any noncash charges, such as depreciation and amortization. Coverage ratios may be calculated by using Statement of Financial Accounting Standards (SFAS) No. 95's net cash flow from operations, exclusive of current asset and current liability activity, as long as it is used consistently in trend and comparative analysis. In contrast to financial leverage ratios, which assess a lender's margin of comfort in the event of liquidation, coverage ratios indicate the traditional cash flow margin while the company is a going concern. Common coverage ratios are traditional cash flow to current maturities, times interest earned, and dividend payout.

Debt Service Coverage Ratio

The debt service coverage ratio shows the proportion of a company's net profit and noncash expenses that will be needed to pay the principal due on long-term debt in the coming year. This ratio serves as a fairly reliable indicator of a company's future

---

DEBT-TO-CAPITALIZATION RATIO

Used primarily by bond rating agencies like Standard & Poor's, the debt-to-capitalization ratio is based on an assessment of the permanent capital of a company. Permanent capital for this ratio is considered to be long-term debt and net worth. This ratio shows what percentage of the company's permanent capital is financed with debt as opposed to shareholders' investments. Because this ratio is used primarily by bond rating agencies, lenders typically use it when analyzing publicly held companies. Therefore, smaller community banks generally would not use this ratio.

The debt-to-capitalization ratio ignores short-term debt that is tied to the financing of inventories and accounts receivable, which is seasonal or of short duration and, conceptually, is repaid by current asset turnover or a seasonal decrease in business activity. This ratio suggests the extent to which the company is relying on long-term debt and lease obligations for financing assets and, consequently, needs profitable operations to support this leverage.

performance, provided that profit and noncash expenses are expected to remain the same or increase and that current asset growth will be funded by debt. The lower the ratio, the smaller the margin of safety becomes. Clearly, if its debt service coverage ratio falls below 1:1, a company is not generating enough cash to repay its fixed obligations and will have to borrow in the coming year to meet these obligations. Most lenders look for a debt service coverage ratio of 1.25 or greater.

Current generally accepted accounting principles (GAAP) add the current amount of any capitalized lease obligations to current maturities. Some lenders are concerned with recurring dividend payouts to owners of small businesses, particularly S corporations. These lenders would subtract dividends from the numerator. Because dividends are normally a discretionary outflow, a lender will restrict dividend payouts in earnings periods. The debt service coverage ratio is calculated as:

$$\frac{\text{(Net profit after tax + depreciation + other noncash charges − dividends)}}{\text{Current maturities of long-term debt}} = \text{Debt service coverage ratio}$$

Turner Electronic Corporation's income statement shows that for 20x1 net after-tax profits and depreciation were $347 and depreciation was $81. No noncash expense, other than depreciation, is shown. Turner Electronic Corporation's balance sheet shows current maturities of long-term debt at $70 for 20x1. Also, the company paid no dividends.

The company's 20x1 debt service coverage ratio is calculated as:

$$\frac{\$347 + \$81}{\$70} = 6.11$$

The company's ratio of more than 6:1 indicates that profits and noncash expenses could decrease significantly while still allowing the business to pay its current maturities.

An argument can be made that this calculation is misleading because debt service coverage ignores the changes in the current accounts. The calculation does not address the cash required to fund the increased accounts receivable and inventory associated with growth in sales. The counter argument is that company management can change or control working capital policy in tight times.

When full-year figures are used, the debt service coverage ratio does not consider the timing of a company's cash flow, which could affect the company's ability to repay debt as it comes due. Although a cash budget shows this timing, the debt service coverage ratio still is a good general measure to use. The ratio is especially good for doing a trend analysis of a company's earnings over several years. Cash budgets provide an estimate of a company's future cash position and borrowing requirements. Lenders use cash budgets to review the periods between the origination and repayment of loans to determine if a company can repay short-term debt. Companies develop cash budgets to control their monthly, weekly, or daily cash requirements.

Times-Interest-Earned and Dividend Payout Ratios

The **times-interest-earned ratio** provides a valuable picture of the potential impact of an increase in interest rates on the company's cash flow and the extent to which earnings are penalized to pay the financing costs of the company. A ratio of greater than one is almost mandatory, because a lower ratio would indicate that a company's earnings are insufficient to cover the interest on its debt.

The times-interest-earned ratio is calculated as:

$$\frac{\text{Profit before taxes + interest expense}}{\text{Interest expense}} = \text{Times-interest-earned ratio}$$

Turner Electronic Corporation's 20x1 income statement shows profits before taxes at $468 and interest expense at $86. Thus, the 20x1 times-interest-earned ratio for Turner Electronic Corporation is calculated as:

$$\frac{\$468 + \$86}{\$86} = 6.44$$

With a times-interest-earned ratio of 6.44:1, Turner Electronic Corporation's interest expense could increase significantly before the company (at its current level of earnings) would be unable to pay its interest from profits.

The **dividend payout ratio** shows the percentage of after tax profit a company pays to shareholders in the form of dividends. These funds thereby become unavailable for other uses, such as supporting asset growth and funding current maturities of long-term debt. The dividend payout ratio, which can help explain trends in equity growth and leverage, is calculated as:

$$\frac{\text{Cash dividends paid}}{\text{Net profit after tax}} = \text{Dividend payout ratio}$$

Turner Electronic Corporation paid no dividends in the last three years.

PROFIT OR OPERATING RATIOS

Profit ratios are also called operating ratios because they reflect how the owners or managers have performed the day-to-day operations. Profit implies that a company has long-term viability, but it does not imply the ability to repay debt. A lender examining a company's profits usually relates the company's profits to sales, assets, and equity. The sales-to-asset ratio indicates how well the owners have managed the company assets in relation to sales. Taken together, profit ratios give a good indication of a company's viability and its ability to survive and attract new equity or debt funding in the future.

The net profit margin, also called return on sales, is the most frequently used measure of profit. Other measures of profit assess the efficient use of assets and the return on the shareholders' equity. These profit ratios measure the amount of assets and equity required to support a given level of sales.

Consider, for example, Company X and Company Y. On the same level of sales, Company X makes $50,000 profit, whereas Company Y makes $100,000 profit. On the surface, it would appear that Company Y is more profitable. But suppose that Company Y required $500,000 in assets to support its sales, whereas Company X required only $150,000 in assets to support the same level of sales. Company X, then, made more profits per dollar of assets employed than did Company Y. Company X makes more efficient use of assets. However, if Company X offers no credit terms and carries limited inventory, and if its fixed assets are older and depreciated, then the ratio will be distorted. Lenders must consider all the variables when assessing a company's profit.

Return-on-Sales Ratio (Sometimes Called Net Profit Margin)

The **return-on-sales ratio** (ROS) (or net profit margin) simply measures the number of pennies a company earns for each dollar of sales. There is no benchmark figure that a lender looks for because return on sales will vary greatly with the industry and by the legal structure of the company. A company with highly volatile sales should have a higher return on sales than a company with predictable profits over the years. The return-on-sales ratio is useful in comparing companies within the same industry and analyzing the trend in the relationship between a company's profits and sales throughout several years.

The return-on-sales ratio, or net margin, is calculated as:

$$\frac{\text{Net profit before tax}}{\text{Net sales}} = \text{Return-on-sales ratio}$$

The return-on-sales ratio is often expressed as a percentage. This is accomplished by multiplying the ratio times 100. Lenders calculate the ratio using net profit before tax to eliminate variations in tax positions that comparable companies have as a result of using different accounting alternatives.

Turner Electronic Corporation's income statement shows net profit before tax at $468 and net sales at $7,482 for 20x1. The company's return-on-sales ratio for 20x1 is calculated as:

$$\frac{\$468}{\$7,482} \times 100 = 6.3\%$$

This return-on-sales ratio shows that the company earned 6.3 cents on each sales dollar after accounting for all expenses. The ratio also indicates how much cost of goods sold and operating expenses can change without adversely affecting profits. The 20x1 net profit margin for Turner Electronic Corporation is good. The company could fund some increases in expenses that are not passed on to customers and still remain profitable.

Return-on-Assets Ratio

The **return-on-assets ratio (ROA)** measures the profit of a company in terms of how efficiently it uses its assets. It is basically a comparison of net profit before tax to total assets. This ratio can be misleading if the company has significant fixed assets (such as buildings, land, or equipment) that are undervalued on the balance sheet. Another problem can occur when the income information is generated from a period that spans two or more points-in-time of asset value. An imbalance can occur due to timing differences. For example, if a manufacturing company spent much of the year installing a new piece of equipment that did not begin production until the end of the year, the equipment's impact as an asset in the denominator of the ratio will be far greater than its profit-generating impact in the numerator. The number can also be misleading if the company's accounts receivable are inflated due to a one-time large sale or the inventory is high due to the temporary stockpiling of product for sale.

The return-on-assets ratio is calculated as:

$$\frac{\text{Net profit before tax}}{\text{Total assets}} = \text{Return-on-assets ratio}$$

> ### NET PROFIT MARGINS
> Publicly held corporations will want to show a greater net profit margin to enhance stock value. Privately held companies with sales over $10 to $15 million and borrowing levels over $5 million tend to focus on company value rather than on owners' salary, which results in a larger net profit margin. Privately held companies with sales less than $5 million tend to have lower net profit margins because the owners "manage" the bottom line. The bottom line is managed by the amount of salary, benefits (vehicles, entertainment, and insurance are examples), and bonuses paid to the owners.

Turner Electronic Corporation's income statement shows net profit before tax of $468 for 20x1. The total assets as of the end of the 20x1 fiscal year are listed as $3,244. Turner Electronic Corporation's 20x1 return-on-assets ratio is calculated as:

$$\frac{\$468}{\$3,244} \times 100 = 14.4\%$$

Turner Electronic Corporation's return on assets is 14.4 percent, or about fourteen cents on every dollar of sales. This number is meaningful only when it is compared to the ROA of previous years or to other companies in the industry.

Net Sales to Assets Ratio

The **net sales to assets ratio** measures how efficiently a company uses its assets by showing how many dollars of sales are generated by each dollar of assets. When analyzing the net sales to assets ratios of various companies, a lender must remember that the ratio is calculated using the book value of assets (which may not reflect the "true" value of assets). For example:

- Accounts receivable may include accounts that may need to be discounted or cannot be collected.
- Inventory may appear large due to seasonal timing that slows the net sales to assets ratio.
- Inventory may be obsolete.
- A fully depreciated piece of equipment may produce as much as a new piece of equipment. Yet its effect will be to increase the company's net sales to assets ratio due to the decreased book value of the assets used in the calculation. This means that the net sales to assets ratio for companies with older equipment will tend to be higher than for companies with newer equipment.

The net sales to asset ratio is calculated as:

$$\frac{\text{Net sales}}{\text{Total assets}} = \text{Sales to asset ratio}$$

Turner Electronic Corporation's 20x1 income statement shows net sales of $7,482. Its assets as of fiscal year-end 20x1 are $3,244 on the balance sheet. Turner Electronic Corporation's asset turnover ratio for 20x1 is calculated as:

$$\frac{\$7,482}{\$3,244} = 2.31$$

The asset turnover ratio shows that Turner Electronic Corporation generates $2.31 of revenues for every $1 of assets employed. Again, this ratio is used primarily to compare a company to its industry peers. The ratio may appear higher due to the largely depreciated equipment.

A variation of the net sales to assets ratio is to calculate net sales to net fixed assets. This results in a much greater ratio than does using total assets. The **net sales to net fixed assets ratio** points out the effectiveness of using fixed assets. A very high ratio may indicate that the fixed assets are old or that the company is nearing its capacity. A very low ratio may indicate that the company has excess capacity. The net sales to net fixed assets ratio is meaningful when analyzing companies whose primary assets are equipment, vehicles, or other fixed assets. Examples of companies with fixed asset dependency are manufacturers, trucking, delivery, and warehousing.

Turner Electronic Corporation's 20x1 sales to net fixed assets ratio is:

$$\frac{\$7,482}{\$237} = 31.57$$

The company is generating $31.57 of net sales for each dollar of net fixed assets. The lender will want to determine the sales capacity and age of the fixed assets. A low number may indicate that the company has recently purchased fixed assets that are not yet generating sales or that the company has excess capacity. A high number may indicate that the company has reached capacity and may need additional fixed asset financing soon or that the company has largely depreciated its fixed assets. Again, this number is meaningful when compared to others in the same industry.

Return-on-Equity Ratio

Another measure of profit, the **return-on-equity ratio** (ROE), measures the efficiency with which a company uses its stockholders' equity. The amount of equity left in a company varies by management. Earlier it was discussed how publicly held and large privately held companies manage the return on sales. The net profit after tax directly affects the return on equity because the net profit after tax is the primary source of equity for existing companies.

If management is using the company's assets efficiently, and if the company has an adequate return on assets, a low return-on-equity ratio may result from excessive equity, which is relative to debt. From a shareholder's point of view, this suggests inefficient use of equity or insufficient financial leverage. A high return-on-equity ratio could indicate too little equity, which is usually associated with high financial leverage.

The return-on-equity ratio is calculated as:

$$\frac{\text{Net profit before tax}}{\text{Net worth}} = \text{Return-on-equity ratio}$$

Lenders calculate the ratio using before-tax net profit as a way to eliminate variations in accounting alternatives and tax variations. This ratio also provides a more consistent basis for comparison. However, for investor purposes, when measuring true return on equity, net profit after tax is used as the numerator.

Turner Electronic Corporation's 20x1 income statement shows a net profit before tax of $468, whereas the balance sheet lists the company's equity for fiscal year-end 20x1 as $1,746. The company's return-on-equity ratio is calculated as:

$$\frac{\$468}{\$1,746} \times 100 = 26.8\%$$

Turner Electronic Corporation's return-on-equity ratio is 26.8 percent. Depending on the alternative investments available, this return appears excellent. However, a one-year return on equity of 26.8 percent may not be indicative of return on equity in future years.

TECHNOLOGY RATIOS

Over the last decade, technology has been the most rapidly growing industry sector. The earlier ratios, common for analyzing commercial loans, need to be supplemented for high-tech companies. Some new ratios that have been developed for technology companies are:

$$\text{Adjusted net revenues} = \frac{\text{Sales per employee}}{\text{Equivalent full-time employees}}$$

$$\text{Total personnel costs} = \frac{\text{Personnel cost ratio}}{\text{Adjusted net revenues}}$$

$$\text{Software revenues} = \frac{\text{Software revenue ratio}}{\text{Adjusted net revenues}}$$

$$\text{Hours billed} = \frac{\text{Staff utilization rate}}{\text{Hours available}}$$

Adjusted net revenues are sales from software and services plus net hardware sales. Net hardware sales are the gross margin from hardware sales. Personnel costs are the payroll, payroll taxes, health insurance, and direct employee costs of the company. Additional key financial ratios for evaluating technology firms may be found on The Chalfin Group, Inc. web site: *http://www.chalfin.com/key_financial_ratios.htm.* These ratios tend to focus on costs per employee, revenue per employee, and expenses. This focus is needed because the technology industry generally has high fixed costs to develop products or to provide a service. Other industries tend to sell a "hard" asset, such as inventory, which creates accounts receivable. The accounts receivable in a tech company is partially or totally from providing consulting or software, neither of which is a "hard" asset.

Z-SCORE

The Z-Score, which is more complicated to calculate, is a very accurate guide to a company's financial solvency. In return for doing a little more arithmetic, a lender can determine a company's Z-Score. If it scores 1.81 or below, a company may be headed for bankruptcy; a score of 2.99 means a company is generally sound.

Edward I. Altman, a professor at the Leonard N. Stern School of Business at New York University, developed the Z-Score. Dr. Altman researched dozens of companies that had gone bankrupt and others that were doing well. He eventually concentrated on five key balance sheet ratios. He assigned a weight to each of the five, and then multiplied each ratio by a number he derived from his research to indicate its relative importance. The sum of the weighted ratios is the Z-Score.

Calculating the Z-Score

Ratio	Formula	Weighting Factor	Weighted Ratio
Return on total assets	$\dfrac{\text{Earnings before interest and taxes}}{\text{Total assets}}$	× 3.3	
Sales to total assets	$\dfrac{\text{Net sales}}{\text{Total assets}}$	× 0.999	
Equity to debt	$\dfrac{\text{Market value of equity}}{\text{Total liabilities}}$	× 0.6	
Working capital to total assets	$\dfrac{\text{Working capital}}{\text{Total assets}}$	× 1.2	
Retained earnings to total assets	$\dfrac{\text{Retained earnings}}{\text{Total assets}}$	× 1.4	

Total of all weighted rations = Z-Score

Like many other ratios, the Z-Score can be used both to see how a company is doing on its own and how it compares to others in the industry.

RATIO DEFINITIONS

A lender must understand how to calculate each ratio and how to interpret the result. The ratios must then be used with other information to perform a complete analysis. A summary of the calculations, definitions, and interpretations of each ratio is found in the *Master Case Book*.

THE RISK MANAGEMENT ASSOCIATION
ANNUAL STATEMENT STUDIES

The Risk Management Association (RMA) is the national association for bank loan and credit officers. It has more than 15,000 associate members. Each year RMA requests that members complete a limited-detail statement spreadsheet that uses Standard Industrial Classification (SIC) code, sales, and asset sizes for companies to which the member banks lend. RMA then common-sizes the financial statements for each company (more than 100,000) and calculates the averages by asset and sales sizes for six different sizes of companies, as shown in exhibit 5.1.

RMA Ratio Categories

Exhibit 5.2 is part of the RMA statement for the asset-size categories of Manufacturers—Household Audio & Video equipment, SIC No. 3651. Turner Electronic Corporation falls into this category. The following analysis uses information from the exhibit, which shows only the middle four asset and sales categories. These calculations are not a standard or benchmark, but a guideline average.

As the notes to exhibit 5.2 show, RMA occasionally does not get data from a sufficient number of companies (more than ten) to produce statistically significant averages. Therefore, cells for those companies are left blank, although the companies are included in the comparative historical data columns, which are not shown in this exhibit.

The comparative historical data columns present five-year historical comparisons. Because they contain unweighted averages of all financial statements' results, the numbers in these columns are not particularly reliable for inter-company comparisons. For instance, the net sales and total assets in the largest two categories often are many times the total sales of the firms in the smallest category. Because the comparative historical data columns average all firms together, the number of firms is what matters. The smaller categories may have more entries than larger categories. The smaller categories of firms contribute much more to the average than do the larger firms, making comparison of any single firm with the "all" column less useful. Therefore, these columns should be avoided for comparing individual firms. Instead, the comparative history

---

Exhibit 5.1 RMA Ratio Categories

Asset Categories	Sales Categories
0 to 500,000	0 to 1,000,000
500,000 to 2,000,000	1,000,000 to 3,000,000
2,000,000 to 10,000,000	3,000,000 to 5,000,000
10,000,000 to 50,000,000	5,000,000 to 10,000,000
50,000,000 to 100,000,000	10,000,000 to 25,000,000
100,000,000 to 250,000,000	25,000,000 and over

Exhibit 5.2 Manufacturers—Household Audio & Video Equipment

Current Data Sorted by Assets

						Type of statement
		6	5	1	2	Unqualified
	1	4	2	1		Reviewed
1		4	1	1		Complied
						Tax returns
	3	6	8	4		Other
	9 (4/1— 9/30/01)		42 (10/1/01—3/31/02)			
0—500M	500M—2MM	2—10MM	10—50MM	50—100MM	100—250MM	
2	4	20	16	7	2	NUMBER OF STATEMENTS
%	%	%	%	%	%	ASSETS
		10.5	10.0			Cash & equivalents
		30	32.5			Net trade receivables
		36.2	36.0			Inventory
		5.2	1.8			All other current
		81.9	80.4			Total current
		11.7	14.5			Net fixed assets
		2.4	2.1			Net intangibles
		4.0	3.1			All other non current
		100.0	100.0			Total
						LIABILITIES
		18.1	12.9			Notes payable—short term
		1.5	1.2			Cur. Mat. - LTD
		11.7	11.2			Trade payables
		0.5	0.2			Income taxes payable
		10.3	7.9			All other current
		42.2	33.3			Total current
		7.3	4.0			Long-term debt
		0.1	0.3			Deferred taxes
		3.6	2.1			All other non current
		46.9	60.3			Net worth
		100.0	100.0			Total liabilities & net worth
						INCOME DATA
		100.0	100.0			Net sales
		37.9	34.5			Gross profit
		33.8	27.2			Operating expenses
		4.1	7.3			Operating profit
		0.7	-0.1			Net all other expenses
		3.3	7.4			Profit before taxes

Exhibit 5.2 (Continued)

0—500M	500M—2MM	2—10MM		10—50MM		50—100MM	100—250MM	
9 (4/1— 9/30/01)				**42 (10/1/01—3/31/02)**				
2	4	20		16		7	2	NUMBER OF STATEMENTS
%	%		%		%	%	%	RATIOS
			3.8		5.9			
			1.8		3.3			Current
			1.3		1.5			
			1.8		3.0			
			0.8		1.3			Quick
			0.6		0.8			
		32	11.3	45	8.1			
		45	8.1	55	6.6			Sales/receivables
		66	5.5	60	6.0			
		50	7.3	62	5.9			Cost of
		88	4.1	101	3.6			sales/inventory
		146	2.5	135	2.7			
		17	21.7	11	33.0			Cost of
		26	14.0-	33	11.1			sales/payables
		47	7.8	41	8.9			
			2.9		3.1			Sales/working
			6.7		4.5			capital
			13.5		7.5			
			9.7		168.5			
	(18)		2.5		10.0			EBIT/interest
			-2.2		2.9			
								Net profit + dept., dep., amort./cur. mat. LTD
			0.1		0.1			
			0.3		0.2			Fixed/worth
			0.5		0.5			
			0.6		0.2			
			1.5		0.5			Debt/worth
			2.4		2.3			
			53.4		48.9			% profit before
	(19)		13.2		22.8			Taxes/tangible
			-4.9		15.5			Net worth

Exhibit 5.2 *(Continued)*

		9(4/1—9/30/01)		42 (10/1/01—3/31/02)			
0—500M	500M—2MM	2—10MM		10—50MM	50—100MM	100—250MM	
2	4	20		16	7	2	
%	%	%		%	%	%	
		19.6		20.8			% profit before taxes/total assets
		4.1		12.3			
		-3.8		5.0			
		46.9		34.2			Sales/net fixed assets
		24.1		15.9			
		11.0		10.9			
		2.9		2.9			Sales/total assets
		2.2		1.9			
		1.5		1.7			
		0.5		0.9			% dept., dep., amort./sales
	(16)	1.0	(15)	1.6			
		1.8		2.5			% officers', directors', owners', comp/sales
5502M	16399M	194152M		662820M	713217M	316909M	Net sales ($)
677M	5533M	92098M		300727M	467761M	261594M	Total assets ($)
							M = $ thousand MM = million

data columns should be used only to look at trends within the industry as a whole, not to identify specific comparison data.

The Risk Management Association Common-Sizes

The top-most portion of the RMA statement lists the type and number of statements incorporated into each category. The next portion is a straightforward common-size analysis of the balance sheet. Assets are listed as a percentage of total assets; liabilities and net worth are listed as a percentage of total liabilities and net worth. Users select the relationships they wish to scrutinize. The account breakdown of the RMA spread is abbreviated compared to the usual multiple page spreadsheet used by lenders. Lenders may have to re-spread the company's financials to make an item-by-item comparison.

By comparing the individual companies being analyzed with the specific sheet in the RMA Annual Statement Studies book, a lender easily can detect which balance sheet or income statement items are out of line.

RMA Ratios

The bottom two-thirds of the RMA statement consists of a list of ratios. Three values are presented for each ratio. The middle number is the median (middle) score of all companies individually. The top number is the median score for the better half of all companies. The lower number is the median for the worse half. These three medians give rise to four quartiles, which are used to calculate the three ratios in each category. Ratios for the first quartile of companies appear entirely above the top number. Ratios for companies in the second quartile appear between the top and middle number. Ratios of companies in the third quartile appear between the middle and lower number. Fourth-quartile company ratios appear below the lowest number. This means that only 50 percent of the companies have ratios between the top and bottom numbers. As exhibit 5.3 shows, many lenders refer to the quartile position of the company in their credit analysis.

RMA arranges all ratio calculations so that the quartiles accurately position the best companies in the top quartile and vice versa. Therefore, the best-ranked values are the top numbers. Analysis of some of the key ratios using RMA data follows.

Liquidity and Activity Ratios

In exhibit 5.2, current and quick ratios are followed by activity-focused ratios of receivables, inventory, and payables turnovers. Turnovers ratios in the exhibit have two columns of ratios: the column to the left lists the average number of days per year, and the other column lists the average turns per year.

Financial Leverage Ratios

The fixed assets-to-worth and debt-to-worth ratios are shown in exhibit 5.2 as examples of the leverage ratios. The fixed assets-to-worth ratio is useful in reviewing manufacturing industries, which are heavily invested in fixed assets. These ratios indicate the amount of equity investment needed for the assets. The debt-to-worth ratio was discussed earlier. The interest coverage ratio is particularly important when reviewing companies with long-term debt and those with little amortizing debt.

Profit Ratios

The return on net worth ratio in exhibit 5.2 is calculated by taking profits before taxes and dividing by tangible net worth. The tangible net worth may need further individual investigation because some companies have undervalued assets. Because tangible net worth is smaller than total assets less liabilities, the return on net worth percentage will appear to be better than if intangibles are included.

The next ratio listed in exhibit 5.2 is profit before taxes to total assets. Although accurate for comparable calculations, this ratio is not an accurate calculation of return

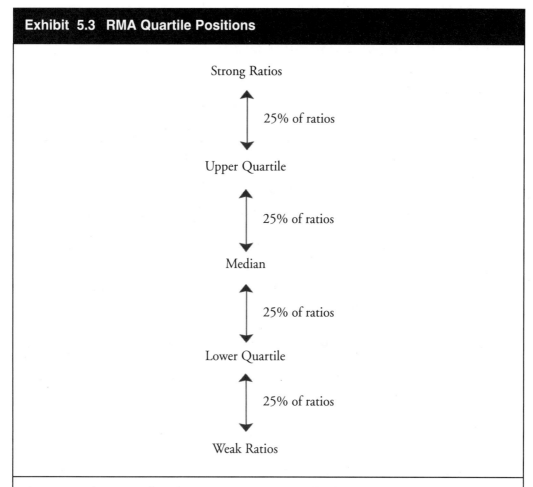

Strong Ratios

↕ 25% of ratios

Upper Quartile

↕ 25% of ratios

Median

↕ 25% of ratios

Lower Quartile

↕ 25% of ratios

Weak Ratios

on assets. As discussed, this formulation of ROA sharply penalizes companies that have significant debt in their capital structures.

Example of Ratio Analysis

Turner Electronic Corporation ratios will first be compared with ratios calculated for the industry, as shown in The Risk Management Association Annual Statement Studies discussed in the section above on comparative analysis. Because Turner Electronic Corporation's total assets in the latest year are between $2 and $10 million, industry comparisons will come from the third column of the RMA statement, as shown in exhibit 5.2. Ratios provided by RMA but not developed in this book will not be discussed.

Next, Turner Electronic Corporation's own ratios will be compared with its own showing in previous years. Comparing multiple years of a company's own ratios is called **trend analysis**. With regard to the trend anaysis, all ratios will be compared, but those that appear to be significant for the Turner Electronic Corporation will be emphasized.

DuPont Ratios

The last two performance ratios in exhibit 5.2 are sales to net fixed assets (fixed asset turnover) and sales to total assets (total asset turnover). Used by the treasury division of E.I. DuPont de Nemours & Co., Inc., for interdivisional analysis, these ratios have earned a reputation for being good industry comparisons. If a company is significantly above or below industry averages in these ratios, it may be evidence of either strikingly superior management or serious problems ahead. These ratios are typically used for publicly held companies or privately held companies with sales over $10 to $15 million.

Liquidity and Current Asset Management Analysis

Liquidity will be analyzed using the current and quick ratios. These ratios also reflect how the company is managing current assets.

Comparative Analysis

Ratio	Turner 20x1	Higher	Median	Lower
Current	2.13	3.8	1.8	1.3
Quick	0.70	1.8	0.8	0.6

Turner Electronic Corporation's current ratio appears in the second quartile, between the median and the higher quartile. The ratio of 2.13 times suggests that, in liquidation, Turner Electronic Corporation's current assets possibly will be enough to pay its current liabilities. Moreover, its quick ratio is in the third quartile. An experienced lender would recognize that the median of Turner Electronic Corporation's quick ratio is low.

A lender could conclude that Turner Electronic Corporation's current position is in line with that of other companies in the industry. Because of the lower quick ratio, a lender will want to review the company's inventory list to determine if any products or parts are obsolete.

It is difficult to be conclusive about any ratio, since the primary purpose of a ratio is to reflect trends. This uncertainty is a clear example of the need to understand the business and its industry. Contrary opinions could be expressed about the same set of figures.

Trend Analysis

Turner Ratio	20x0	20x1
Current ratio	2.09	2.13
Quick ratio	0.55	0.70

Turner Electronic Corporation's current ratio increased to 2.13 in 20x1. An examination of Turner Electronic Corporation's balance sheets shows that accounts receivable and inventory increased by approximately $450,000 during fiscal 20x1. These changes increased the company's need for short-term borrowings to support its asset base, thus increasing its current ratio for 20x1.

From fiscal year-end 20x0 to 20x1, Turner Electronic Company's quick ratio improved from 0.55 to 0.70. This improvement was due to the increased cash and accounts receivable without a corresponding increase in current liabilities.

Leverage and Debt Management Analysis

For comparison, the debt-to-worth and times-interest-earned ratios are provided by RMA. Trend analysis will be examined using the debt-to-worth, debt-to-capitalization, times-interest-earned, and debt service coverage ratios. These ratios indicate how the company is managing its leverage and debt.

COMPARATIVE ANALYSIS

Ratio	Turner 20x1	Higher	Median	Lower
Debt-to-worth	0.86	0.6	1.5	2.4
Times-interest-earned	6.44	9.7	2.5	−2.2

Turner Electronic Corporation's debt-to-worth ratio of 0.86:1 in 20x1 indicates that in a liquidation, where 50-percent markdowns are the rule of thumb, the assets may be sufficient to repay creditors. Moreover, the ratio is higher than the median for its industry, which means the company has less financial leverage than comparable companies.

Turning to the coverage ratio, an examination of the times-interest-earned ratio for the industry shows that Turner Electronic Corporation is higher than the median position. This may indicate that the company is less leveraged or more profitable or pays higher interest rates than other companies.

Trend Analysis

Calculations of the debt-to-worth, debt-to-capitalization, times-interest-earned, and debt service coverage ratios of Turner Electronic Corporation for the period 20x0 to 20x1 yield the following results:

	20x0	20x1
Debt-to-worth	0.96:1	0.86:1
Debt-to-capitalization	0.10	0.06
Times-interest-earned	3.12	6.44
Debt service coverage	1.9	6.11

The decreasing debt-to-worth ratio suggests that Turner Electronic Corporation's retained earnings are sufficient to fund its balance-sheet growth in the same proportions as it had in former years. This situation could have resulted from a conscious managerial decision to use the company's leverage less aggressively. A review of Turner Electronic Corporation's after-tax profits for fiscal years 20x0 and 20x1 ($21,000 and $347,000), and its dividend policy (a dividend payout ratio of zero), appears to support this conclusion.

To continue its present debt-to-worth ratio, Turner Electronic Corporation could either slow its asset growth relative to its equity growth or increase its equity more rapidly relative to its asset growth. The company could control its asset growth through either more efficient use of assets or slower growth in revenues and number of products, thus reducing the need for operating assets. The company also could increase its equity growth through higher earnings or additional equity contributions. Any of these solutions may be acceptable to the lender as long as the result is leverage and coverage ratios that are comparable to the industry standard.

The change in Turner Electronic Corporation's debt-to-capitalization ratio from 0.10 to 0.06 is not large enough to be considered significant.

For the last three years, Turner Electronic Corporation has experienced an improvement in its coverage ratios. The company's 20x1 times-interest-earned ratio of 6.44 remains in the acceptable range.

Profit Analysis

For comparison, RMA provides the return on sales and return on assets ratios. Trend analysis will be done using these ratios and the return on equity ratio.

Comparative Analysis

Ratio	Turner 20x1	Higher	Median	Lower
Return on sales	6.3		3.3	
Return on assets	14.4	19.6	4.1	−3.8

The higher-than-median return on sales in 20x1 shows that Turner Electronic Corporation receives more profit for each dollar of sales than does the industry. Its above-median return on assets indicates that it uses its assets more efficiently than others in its industry to produce profits. Perhaps it collects the accounts receivable quicker, sells the inventory faster, or has older equipment than its competition. RMA does not provide the return on equity ratio.

Trend Analysis

A review of Turner Electronic Corporation's profit ratios shows an improvement in its operating performance.

Turner Ratio	20x0	20x1
Return on sales	0.56	6.3
Return on assets	1.1	14.4
Return on equity	2.2	26.8

From 20x0 to 20x1, Turner Electronic Corporation's profit improved from 0.56 percent to 6.3 percent; its return on assets improved from 1.1 percent to 14.4 percent; and its return on equity improved from 2.2 percent to 26.8 percent.

The return on sales may signify the lack of competition, improved sales mix, good expense control, or some combination of all three. The return on assets is again from a good sales-to-assets ratio (reflected in the activity ratios) and the high return on sales. However, in 20x1, all profit ratios improved significantly. The lender will want to understand what caused the improvement and evaluate whether it will continue.

SUMMARY

Although they are easy to calculate, by themselves, ratios are not meaningful and can lead to erroneous conclusions if they are not analyzed in a broad context. Ratio analysis is only one part of the total financial statement analysis of a company and should not lead to final lending decisions.

Ratios do, however, assist in converting a company's financial information into a meaningful analytical format. Ratios are particularly useful in facilitating comparisons of companies of varying size, particularly among companies in the same industry. They also facilitate trend analysis, which entails looking at a company's ratios over a period of two or more years. The most widely used ratios help in analyzing a company's liquidity, financial leverage, coverage, and profit.

The primary liquidity ratios are the current, quick, and days ratios. Based on the assumption that all assets will be sold in a forced sale and that all liabilities will be paid, these ratios provide a quantitative measure of a company's financial strength in the event of liquidation. Although they are not ratios, working capital and working investment also indicate a company's liquidity. The principal days ratios compare income-statement accounts (sales or cost of goods sold) with balance-sheet accounts to determine days accounts receivable, days inventory, and days accounts payable. These days ratios are often expressed as the average accounts receivable collection period, the average selling time of inventory, and the average payment time of accounts payable.

Financial leverage ratios—debt-to-worth and debt-to-capitalization—attempt to measure the equity cushion or risk shouldered by a company's creditors in the event of liquidation. Coverage ratios—times-interest-earned, cash flow to current maturities, and dividend payout—measure the ability of a company to meet its long-term debt obligations through the flow of funds (cash) from its operations.

Profit ratios of return on sales, return on assets, and return on equity examine the relationship between net profit and sales, assets, and equity, respectively. The sale-to-asset ratio also reflects a company's operating performance. For the technology industry, lenders are developing ratios that focus on productivity and cost management. Although it is not a ratio, the Z Score is an additional tool used by some lenders.

It is important to keep in mind that, although financial statements may reflect different accounting methods, corporate structures, and management policies, ratio comparison is rarely exact. Therefore, a lender should view any findings as general indicators of performance rather than as absolute predictors.

QUESTIONS FOR DISCUSSION

1. If a company's current ratio for the last three years is 1.2, 1.4, and 2.0, and its quick ratio is 0.8, 1.1, and 1.8, what might you conclude?
2. What doesn't the days receivable ratio tell you to do?
3. How do technology ratios defer from other ratios?
4. What ratio tells you about the earning power of a company's assets?
5. What is the difference between trend and comparative analysis?

Exercise

Using the information from the common-sized financial statements located in the *Master Case Book*, calculate the following ratios for Turner Electronic Corporation for 20x2.

- current ratio
- quick ratio
- days accounts receivable
- days inventory
- days accounts payable
- debt-to-worth
- times-interest-earned ratio
- return on sales
- return on assets
- return on equity

6

CALCULATING AND INTERPRETING CASH FLOW

LEARNING OBJECTIVES

After studying *Calculating and Interpreting Cash Flow*, you will be able to

- identify the questions a cash flow statement answers,
- explain operating, investing, and financing activities as defined on the SFAS No. 95 Statement of Cash Flows,
- calculate and interpret the SFAS No. 95 and lender-prepared direct method cash flow statements,
- use the abbreviated cash flow statement to understand sources and uses of cash,
- calculate and explain variations of traditional cash flow,
- use a cash flow statement in financial statement analysis, and
- define the key terms that appear in **bold** type in the text.

INTRODUCTION

Before GAAP endorsed a standardized form for the cash flow statement in November 1987, lenders had been using a similar statement known as the sources and uses of cash statement. Many lenders, particularly community banks, still use it. Some lenders, however, now use a variation— the abbreviated cash flow statement.

Today, accountants primarily use the GAAP-approved statement of cash flows. When a company seeks a loan, its accountant will submit to a lender a completed Statement of Financial Accounting Standards and its form No. 95 (SFAS). The SFAS No. 95 statement of cash flows is prepared using either the direct or indirect method. The **direct method SFAS N0. 95 (statement of cash flows)** begins with revenues from sales; breaks down activities into operating, investing, and financing; and balances to the change in cash. The **indirect method of SFAS No. 95** begins with net income and then considers changes in operating, investing, and financing activities.

Some companies submit financial statements that are compilations or reviews prepared by auditors. In these circumstances, the auditor may not prepare a statement of cash flows. In lieu of a statement of cash flows, a lender may have to create a statement of cash flows using two consecutive years of balance sheets and the current year's income statement.

Lenders may also calculate cash flow using the traditional method or several variations of it. Traditional cash flow is commonly used in community banks. Lenders calculate a variation of the traditional cash flow statement when the company owner also owns the real estate leased to the company. Another variation includes maintenance capital expenditures.

No matter what formula is used, the purpose of calculating a cash flow statement is to determine the company's capacity to generate internal cash and to repay debt.

In this module, the focus is on analyzing the accountant-prepared direct method SFAS No. 95 statement of cash flows, the lender-prepared direct method statement of cash flows, and various traditional methods lenders use to calculate cash flow.

SUMMARY AND PURPOSE OF THE CASH FLOW STATEMENT

The cash flow statement reflects all of the economic resources available to a company. It shows the flow of cash that results from the company's use of its economic resources during a given period of time, typically one year. Because it spans one year, the cash flow statement does not tell the lender the peak or low point of debt. But it does allow a lender to evaluate managerial decisions regarding cash. Similar to the way the income statement identifies the flow of revenues and expenses, the cash flow statement determines the total resources employed from the balance sheet and the income statement, how these resources became available, and how efficiently they were used. Cash flow statements can help a lender predict whether and why a company would seek a loan and whether it has the capacity to repay debt.

Borrowers, lenders, and accountants differ in how they look at loan repayment. Borrowers feel that loans are repaid from profit or collateral. Accountants look at the long-term profitability of the company when evaluating loan repayment. Lenders who know that cash, and only cash, repays loans focus on a company's ability to produce cash that is used to repay debt, invest in fixed assets, and support sales growth.

In addition to using them to appraise management decisions that are made over time, lenders use cash flow statements to

- evaluate the sources and uses of cash—where it came from and how it was used
- explain the disposition of profits
- evaluate the size, composition, and stability of operating cash flows
- determine how wisely and prudently the company manages its cash

One of the primary goals of a company is to maximize profits by increasing sales and reducing costs. Profits are generally the primary source of cash flow used to repay term debt. Profit, working capital, and cash have different functions in analyzing a company's operating cycle and cash flow.

Profit is recognized on the income statement when inventory is converted to a receivable. The income statement reports the affects of net profit on total assets, not the effect of cash on total assets; nor does it consider the timing of cash flows. As such, profit relates to past and present management decisions.

Working capital does not change in the operating cycle, except for the net profit margin added at sale. There is only a change in the *character* of working capital. The working capital requirement grows as sales grow or the operating cycle lengthens.

Cash flows occur when inventory is purchased or manufactured and when receivables are converted to cash. These events reflect current management decisions.

Bankers are primarily interested in the flow of cash, not working capital, because cash flow reflects financing requirements and the ability to repay loans. Some additional concepts to remember when analyzing the cash flow statement are:

- Accrual accounting recognizes a sale when products or services are provided in exchange for cash or increases in accounts receivable rather than only as cash received.

- Accrual accounting recognizes cash outlays for services with benefits anticipated in future periods as assets (prepaid expenses) on the balance sheet rather than as expenses on the income statement.

- Cash-basis accounting recognizes cash outlays for inventory and labor in the inventory account and cash outlays for plant and equipment in the fixed asset account. The income statement contains charges for expenses that do not incur any outlay of cash. These include

  - Depreciation—expensing a building and equipment throughout its useful life

  - Provision of taxes— depreciation alternatives for taxes versus book result in lower cash payments for taxes

  - Amortization—expensing capitalized assets that incurred cash outlays in the past (goodwill, leasehold improvements, patents, and copyrights)

Sources and Uses of Cash

Managers of companies must oversee the administration of sales, expense control, accounts receivable, inventory, accounts payable, and sources of financing— all of which affect cash flow. Here are some examples of management decisions that affect cash flow.

Sales Expansion or Contraction

Management may choose to expand temporarily by bidding low for a one-time sale. When sales increase, accounts receivable and inventory increase. This temporary increase in current assets is a use of cash and should be financed short term. Conversely, management may permanently expand sales by introducing new products, expanding the customer base, or adding a location. A permanent increase in sales results in a permanent increase in accounts receivable and inventory. This increase in current assets needs to be funded by a permanent increase in debt to be repaid over a longer period.

Credit or Collection Policies That Result in Accounts Receivable Changes

If a company chooses to loosen its credit or collection policies, accounts receivable usually increase. This increase results in a use of cash. However, if a company decides to tighten its credit and collection policy, this results in a source of cash. In either case, the change in cash primarily alters cash flow for the next year only and then remains the same unless other changes are made.

The Amount of Inventory Kept on Hand

Management controls the inventory on hand by the size and frequency of purchases. If management decides to purchase inventory in greater quantities, this increase in inventory is a use of cash. Conversely, if management decides to drop a product line, which decreases inventory, this results in a source of cash. Also, the amount of inventory kept on hand is directly related to the increase or decrease in sales levels discussed above.

Accounts Payable Policies That Affect Supplier Relations and Cash Requirements

Inventory purchases are generally made on credit. Many companies offer a discount for paying for inventory early or at the time of purchase. This early repayment is a use of cash. A company may choose to extend payment due to suppliers, which results in a source of cash.

Fixed Asset Additions That Increase Capacity; Replacements That Improve Operations

Capital expenditures are usually financed with term debt. However, some lenders require a cash down payment for fixed asset purchases, which is a use of cash. If a company expands its fixed assets or replaces fixed assets with more efficient models, sales generally increase. This increase in sales results in more accounts receivable and inventory. Therefore, purchasing fixed assets may result in three potential users of cash: the fixed asset being purchased, the accounts receivable that increases because of increased sales, and the increases in inventory needed to support the increased sales.

Debt Structure—Aggressive Repayment versus the Life of the Fixed Asset

Prepayment of a loan results in a use of cash. If the asset has a long useful life, the fixed asset will generate cash after being depreciated.

Dividend Policy—Excessive Dividends to Support an Owner's Lifestyle

Dividends paid to owners are a use of cash. If the owner has a lifestyle that needs to be supported continually, then this use of cash will be permanent and ongoing.

When analyzing the statement of cash flows (whether SFAS No. 95 or lender-prepared statements), a lender must remember that an increase in assets constitutes a use of cash, and a decrease in assets constitutes a source of cash. Similarly, any increase in liabilities constitutes a source of cash, while a decrease in liabilities constitutes a use of cash. For example, borrowing more debt increases liabilities and provides a source of cash to the company. Similarly, an increase in equity constitutes a source of cash, while a decrease in equity constitutes a use of cash. Exhibit 6.1 illustrates this concept.

SFAS NO. 95 STATEMENT OF CASH FLOWS—DIRECT METHOD

The three subdivisions for this statement of cash flows are operating, investment, and financing.

Operating activities measure the cash generated by the current operating cycle and short-term changes in current accounts requiring cash. Investment activities measure long-term increases in fixed assets, other long-term investments, and proceeds from disposing of these assets. Financing activities measure cash flows from debt, debt payments, and proceeds from and payments to shareholders.

The calculation results of the direct method SFAS No. 95 Statement of Cash Flow accounts for and balances to the change in the cash position from one year to the next. Exhibit 6.2 on the following page illustrates the direct method SFAS No. 95 cash flow statement form prepared by accountants. Exhibit 6.3 on page 179 illustrates the direct method SFAS No. 95 form an accountant prepared for Turner Electronic Corporation.

Cash Flow from Operating Activities

Cash flow from operating activities is the first category on the direct method SFAS No. 95 cash flow statement. This portion of the statement first examines the cash coming into the company through sales and receivables. Next, it presents cash paid to accounts payable (suppliers) and employees. Finally, this section totals net cash provided by

Exhibit 6.1 Balance Sheet Sources and Uses	
Sources of Cash	*Uses of Cash*
Decrease in assets	Increase in assets
Increase in liabilities	Decrease in liabilities
Increase in equity	Decrease in equity

Exhibit 6.2 Accountant's Presentation—Direct Method

Years Ended Dec 31, 20___ and 20___

Statement of Cash Flows	20___	20___
Cash Flows from Operating Activities:		
Cash received from customers	$ 000	$ 000
Cash paid to suppliers and employees	(000)	(000)
Dividend received from affiliate	000	000
Interest received	000	000
Interest paid (net of amount capitalized)	(000)	(000)
Income taxes paid	(000)	(000)
Insurance proceeds received	000	000
Net cash provided by operating activities	000	000
Cash Flows from Investing Activities:		
Proceeds from sale of equipment	000	000
Payment received on note for sale of plant	000	000
Capital expenditures	(000)	(000)
Net cash used in investing activities	(000)	(000)
Cash Flows from Financing Activities:		
Proceeds from sale of stock	000	000
Proceeds from notes payable short-term debt	000	000
Proceeds from long-term debt	000	000
Repayment of debt	(000)	(000)
Payment under capital lease obligation	(000)	(000)
Dividends paid	(000)	(000)
Net cash provided by financing activities	000	000
Net increase in cash and equivalents	000	000
Cash and equivalents at beginning of year	000	000
Cash and equivalents at end of year	000	000
Reconciliation of Net Income to Net		
Cash Provided by Operating Activities:		
Net income	000	000
Adjustments:		
Depreciation and amortization	000	000
Provision for losses on accounts receivable	000	000
Gain on sale of equipment	(000)	(000)
Undistributed earnings of affiliate	(000)	(000)
Increase/decrease in current assets:		
Accounts receivable	(000)	(000)
Inventory	000	000
Prepaid expenses	(000)	(000)
Increase/decrease in current liabilities:		
Accounts payable and accrued expenses	(000)	(000)
Interest and income taxes payable	000	000
Deferred taxes	000	000
Net cash provided by operating activities	000	000
Schedule of Noncash Investing		
and Financing Activities:		
	Assets	*Liabilities*
Property acquired under capital lease	000	000

Note: The Notes to Financial Statements are an integral part of these statements.

Exhibit 6.3 Statement of Cash Flows—Turner Electronic Corporation

| Years Ended Dec 31, 20x0, 20x1, and 20x2 | | (000s omitted) | |
Statements of Cash Flows	20x0	20x1	20x2
Cash Flows from Operating Activities:			
Cash received from customers	$6,079	$7,227	$7,403
Cash paid to suppliers and employees	(6,086)	(6,888)	(7,021)
Dividend received from affiliate	0	0	0
Interest received	0	0	0
Interest paid (net of amount capitalized)	(66)	(86)	(109)
Income taxes paid	(7)	(121)	(17)
Insurance proceeds received	0	0	0
Net cash provided by operating activities	(80)	132	256
Cash Flows from Investing Activities:			
Proceeds from sale of equipment	3	0	0
Payment received on note from sale of plant	0	0	0
Capital expenditures	(76)	(82)	(50)
Net cash used in investing activities	(73)	(82)	(50)
Cash Flows from Financing Activities:			
Proceeds from sale of stock	0	0	0
Proceeds from notes payable short-term debt	97	(13)	(126)
Proceeds from long-term debt	47	37	13
Repayment of debt	(44)	(60)	(70)
Payment under capital lease obligation	0	0	0
Dividends paid	0	0	0
Net cash provided (used) by financing activities	100	(36)	(183)
Net increase in cash and equivalents	(53)	14	23
Cash and equivalents at beginning of year	90	37	51
Cash and equivalents at end of year	37	51	74
Reconciliation of Net Income to Net			
Cash Provided by Operating Activities:			
Net income	21	347	34
Adjustments:			
Depreciation and amortization	93	81	72
Provision for losses on accounts receivable	0	0	0
Gain on sale of assets	3	0	
Undistributed earnings of affiliate	0	0	0
Increase/decrease in current assets:			
Accounts receivable	(181)	(255)	133
Inventories	(91)	(193)	(412)
Prepaid expenses	46	(44)	(31)
Decrease/increase in current liabilities:			
Accounts payable	102	150	462
Accrued liabilities	(73)	46	(2)
Net cash provided by operating activities	(80)	132	256
Property acquired under capital lease	0	0	0

operating activities, which theoretically represents the sum that management could use for the next two sections—investing and financing activities.

SFAS No. 95 cash flow from **operating activities** includes activities "normally involved in producing and delivering goods and services," such as

- collecting accounts receivable and short- and long-term notes receivable from customers;
- cash expenditures for acquiring materials and making payments to vendors and employees for services, including net payments to accounts payable;
- interest expense (in contrast with the income statement presentation, which shows interest expense as a nonoperating expense); and
- extraordinary items, including lawsuit settlements and insurance claims (a lender should recognize that lawsuits and insurance claims usually are one-time events and are not related to the operation of the business).

Key questions to ask regarding operating activities are:

- How is the company's sales growth or sales decrease affecting its operating cash needs?
- Are accounts receivable and inventory being used to fund long-term assets or payments of long-term debt?
- Are the changes in accounts receivable and inventory permanent or temporary?
- Has the company changed its credit or collection policies?
- Has the company added or deleted products that affect inventory?
- How did the changes in cost of goods sold and operating expenses alter cash flow?
- What is causing the change in interest income and interest expense?
- Were there any one-time insurance claims or lawsuits that need further research?

Calculating Cash Flows from Operating Activities

The calculations of cash flows from operating activities are as follows:

Cash Received from Customers

This line is calculated:

Net sales + or − net change in accounts receivable = cash received from customers

The 20x2 calculation for Turner Electronic Corporation is

Net Sales		$7,270
Change in accounts receivable		
20x1 net accounts receivable	$905	
− 20x2 net accounts receivable	772	
= net change in accounts receivable (decrease)		133
Total cash received from customers		7,403

A decrease in accounts receivable is a source of cash. Therefore, the change from 20x1 to 20x2 is a positive number. If the accounts receivable had grown in 20x2, the change would have been a use of cash and, therefore, a negative number. The total cash received from customers is calculated:

$$(\$7,270 + \$133 = \$7,403)$$

Cash Paid to Suppliers and Employees

This line is calculated: cost of goods sold and selling, general and administrative expenses (both net of depreciation), plus or minus the changes in inventory, accounts payable, prepaid expenses, and accrued expenses.

Cost of goods sold (net of depreciation)		$ (4,676)
Selling, general and administrative expenses (net of depreciation)		(2,362)
Change in Inventory Calculation		
20x1 inventory	$1,980	
− 20x2 inventory	2,392	
Change in inventory		(412)
Change in Accounts Payable Calculation		
20x1 accounts payable	507	
− 20x2 accounts payable	969	
Change in accounts payable		462
Change in Prepaid Expenses		
20x1 prepaid expenses	71	
− 20x2 prepaid expenses	102	
Change in prepaid expenses		(31)
Change in Accrued Expenses		
20x1 accrued expenses	163	
− 20x2 accrued expenses	161	
Change in accrued expenses		(2)
Total cash paid to suppliers and employees		(7,021)
Interest paid		
Actual expense from 20x2 income statement		(109)
Income taxes paid		
Actual expense from 20x2 income statement ± any changes in accrued taxes. There were no accrued taxes for Turner Electronic Corporation		(17)
Net cash provided by operating activities		256

Because they are expenses from the income statement, the cost of goods sold and the selling, general, and administrative expenses are always a negative number (net of depreciation). The $412 increase in inventory is a use of cash and therefore a negative number. The $462 increase in accounts payable is a source of cash and therefore a positive number. The $31 increase in prepaid expenses is a use of cash and therefore a negative number. The $2 decrease in accrued expenses is a use of cash and therefore a negative number. Interest expense is always the actual figure from the income statement and a negative number. Taxes may be a positive or negative number depending on the changes in deferred taxes and accrued income taxes. Because Turner had no deferred or accrued taxes, the actual tax expenses are used from the income statement ($17), a negative number.

The net cash provided by operating activities is therefore calculated:

Total cash received from customers		$7,403
Cost of goods sold (net of depreciation)	(4,676)	
Selling, general, and administrative expenses		
(net of depreciation)	(2,362)	
Change in inventory	(412)	
Change in accounts payable	462	
Change in prepaid expenses	(31)	
Changed in accrued expenses	(2)	
Cash paid to suppliers and employees		(7,021)
Interest paid		(109)
Income taxes paid		(17)
Net cash provided by operating activities		256

Exhibit 6.4 illustrates Turner Electronic Corporation's cash flows from operating activities for three years.

Cash received from customers has grown each year from increased sales. The cause of the increase and whether it will continue should be determined. A lender will want to note that in 20x0 the cash paid to suppliers and employees exceeded the cash received from customers for sales. This is unusual, and a lender will want to understand what caused this event. A detailed analysis of accounts receivable and accounts payable will reveal the nature of this unusual event. This analysis also could further clarify the reasoning behind management's decisions leading to this event. The interest expense

Exhibit 6.4   Operating Activities—Turner Electronic Corporation

	(000s omitted)		
Cash Flows from Operating Activities	*20x0*	*20x1*	*20x2*
Cash received from customers	$6,079	$7,227	$7,403
Cash paid to suppliers and employees	(6,086)	(6,888)	(7,021)
Interest paid	(66)	(86)	(109)
Income taxes paid	(7)	(121)	(17)
Net cash provided by operating activities	(80)	132	256

increased each year. A lender will want to know if this is from short- or long-term financing, what was financed, and how the debt will be repaid. The income taxes paid have varied depending on the company's net profit before tax. In the last two years, the net cash provided by operating activities increased, leaving extra cash for other activities.

Cash Flows from Investing Activities

The second section of the cash flow statement summarizes the purchase and sale of fixed assets. **Investing activities** are considered to be more discretionary than operating activities because they can be delayed and are controlled more closely by management.

When analyzing investing activities, a lender should consider the following questions:

- Will new equipment purchases increase the company's asset-use efficiency?
- Has the company reached its operating capacity?
- What is the amount of revenue produced for each major fixed asset?
- Were assets that were disposed of critical to the company?
- Was the disposition of assets a one-time event?
- What assets need to be replaced in the future?
- Has the company chosen the correct debt structure to pay for the assets?

Calculating Cash Flows from Investing Activities

The capital expenditures are calculated using the change in net fixed assets plus depreciation expense. Depreciation expense is a noncash charge, and a lender is concerned with cash flow.

The calculation for Turner Electronic Corporation for 20x2 is

20x1 net fixed assets	$237
− 20x2 net fixed assets	215
= 20x2 adjusted fixed assets	22
− depreciation expense	(72)
= net change in fixed assets	(50)

The net fixed assets increase by $50 and are considered a use of cash. Because fixed assets were a use of cash, the increase is shown as a negative number. The depreciation expense is the actual expense from the common-sized income statement in the *Master Case Book*. Any proceeds from the sale of equipment should be noted as gains or losses in the income statement. The lender should research the type of fixed assets purchased, their useful life, and if they were additions or replacements; he or she also should request a list of future needs for fixed assets.

Exhibit 6.5 illustrates cash flows from investing activities for the last three years for Turner Electronic Corporation. Turner Electronic Corporation is replacing fixed assets each year and has had nominal proceeds ($3,250 in 20x0) from the sale of equipment. A lender will want to know the remaining life of the equipment currently being used. Keeping in mind that technology is changing rapidly in the electronics industry, a lender will want to know if the current equipment is up to date and what the cost will be to update the plant with new equipment.

Exhibit 6.5   Investing Activities—Turner Electronic Corporation

	(000s omitted)		
Cash Flows from Investing Activities	20x0	20x1	20x2
Purchases of equipment	$ (76)	$ (82)	$ (50)
Proceeds from sale of equipment	3	0	0
Net cash used by investing activities	(73)	(82)	(50)

Cash Flows from Financing Activities

This final category on the cash flow statement includes cash flows that directly relate to the external financing of the business. These involve either debt or equity. For example, an increase in a company's common stock and paid-in capital accounts is a positive sign because it generally lowers the company's financial leverage, which may reduce the risk to the lender. The retention of profits is the primary source of equity growth and cash flow to repay debt.

The company's dividend policy is important to examine because dividends diminish the amount of cash available to repay loans; they also fund growth and reduce the amount of cash available for equity. The amount of the dividend is compared to the operating cash flows and debt requirements. Sub S corporations pay dividends to fund the personal tax liability of the owners. The amount of the dividend is compared to the actual tax liability.

Key questions to ask regarding financing activities are:

- How fast can the company grow from internally generated cash?
- What are the company's future borrowing needs?
- Is the debt structured correctly?
- What has been the trend in dividends?
- What outside sources of equity are available?

Calculating Cash Flows from Financing Activities

The cash flows from **financing activities** are the net changes to notes payable bank, long-term debt, current maturities of long-term debt, and any dividends paid to stockholders. The calculation for 20x2 for Turner Electronic Corporation would be as follows:

	$	$
Increase in notes payable short term—bank		
20x1 notes payable—bank	634	
– 20x2 notes payable—bank	508	
= changes in notes payable—bank		(126)
Proceeds from long-term debt		
20x1 long-term debt	59	
+ current maturities 20x2	78	
– 20x1 long-term debt	124	
= net change in long-term debt		13
Repayment of long-term debt		(70)

The notes payable bank is the amount of short-term debt due in one year or less. The decrease of $126 represents a use of cash and therefore is a negative number. The company reduced its short-term bank debt while sales were flat. This is unusual, and the lender will want to determine how the increased accounts receivable and inventory associated with sales growth were funded. Current maturities of long-term debt are the principal amounts due in the coming year. Therefore, 20x1 current maturities are due in 20x2; 20x2 current maturities are due in 20x3; and so forth. Because a lender is concerned with cash flow, the current cash paid out for 20x2 is the current maturities from the 20x1 balance sheet or $70,000. Therefore, the calculation for long-term debt is:

> The most recent year current maturities long-term debt
> + most recent year long-term debt
> _____
> – previous year's long-term debt
>
> = the change in long-term debt

Distributions to Stockholders

Distributions to stockholders mean the amount of dividends paid to stockholders. It is calculated as:

Previous year's retained earnings	$ 1,141
+ current year earnings or	34
– current year loss	0
– current year's retained earnings	1,175
= distributions to stockholders	0

Turner Electronic Corporation has not paid out dividends to the owners for three years. The company does not pay dividends but rather manages the net profit by the amount of salary and other benefits it pays the owner. Exhibit 6.6 illustrates Turner Electronic Corporation's cash flows from financing activities for the last three years.

Turner Electronic Corporation reduced its credit line by $126 in 20x2. However, the accounts payable shown in the operating activities is increasing to fund this payment. A lender will want to determine how the company will be able to repay the trade suppliers. Moreover, a lender should note from the investing activities section that the company purchased $73 worth of equipment in 20x0 and financed $47; purchased $82 in 20x1 and financed $37; and, in 20x2, purchased $50 and financed $13. All the fixed asset purchases were financed long term.

The company purchased equipment, and the bank financed a portion of the purchase with a long-term loan. This should be expected because most banks require some down payment on equipment purchases. The source of the down payment came from profits retained in the business.

SFAS NO. 95 STATEMENT OF CASH FLOWS—INDIRECT METHOD

The indirect method starts with net income and makes the necessary noncash adjustments. The indirect cash flow then continues with operating, investing, and financing activities and balances to the change in cash. Exhibit 6.7 illustrates the indirect method form used by accountants.

LENDER-PREPARED DIRECT METHOD CASH FLOW ANALYSIS

Many bankers use the lender-prepared direct method of cash flow analysis. In some states, it is known as the Uniform Cash Analysis, or UCA. This direct method approach is designed to meet the needs of bankers who focus on the borrower's ability to generate sufficient operating cash flow to pay the costs of operation, interest, scheduled principal, and growth. The order of presentation reflects the priorities of claims on operating cash flow with later items being more discretionary. To calculate

Exhibit 6.6 Financing Activities—Turner Electronic Corporation			
	(000s omitted)		
Cash Flows from Financing Activities	20x0	20x1	20x2
Increase in notes payable—bank	$ 97	$ (13)	$ (126)
Proceeds from long-term debt	47	37	13
Repayment of long-term debt	(44)	(60)	(70)
Distribution to stock holders	0	0	0
Net cash provided (used) by financing activities	100	(36)	(183)

Exhibit 6.7 Accountant's Presentation—Indirect Method

Years Ended Dec 31, 20___ and 20___

Statements of Cash Flows	20___	20___
Cash Flows from Operating Activities:		
Net income	$ 000	$ 000
Adjustments:		
Depreciation and amortization	000	000
Provision for losses on accounts receivable	000	000
Gain on sales of equipment	(000)	(000)
Undistributed earnings of affiliate	(000)	(000)
Changes in assets and liabilities:		
Increase in accounts receivable	(000)	(000)
Decrease in inventory	000	000
Increase in prepaid expenses	(000)	(000)
Decrease in accounts payable and accrued expenses	(000)	(000)
Increase in interest and income taxes payable	000	000
Increase in deferred taxes	000	000
Net cash provided by operating activities	000	000
Cash Flows from Investing Activities:		
Proceeds from sale of equipment	000	000
Payment received on note for sale of plant	000	000
Capital expenditures	(000)	(000)
Net cash used in investing activities	(000)	(000)
Cash Flows from Financing Activities:		
Proceeds from sale of stock	000	000
Proceeds from long-term debt	000	000
Repayment of debt	(000)	(000)
Payment under capital lease obligation	(000)	(000)
Dividends paid	(000)	(000)
Net cash provided by financing activities	000	000
Net increase in cash and equivalents	000	000
Cash and equivalents at beginning of year	000	000
Cash and equivalents at end of year	000	000
Supplemental Disclosure of		
Cash Flow Information:		
Cash paid during the year for:		
Interest (net of amount capitalized)	000	000
Income taxes	000	000

Supplemental Schedule of Noncash Investing and Financing Activities:	*Assets*	*Liabilities*
Property acquired under capital lease	000	000

Note: The Notes to Financial Statements are an integral part of these statements.

the lender-prepared direct method, a lender uses actual dollar amounts from the income statement and changes in the balance sheet. Therefore, to calculate the direct method cash flow, a lender needs two years of financial statements. A blank form of the direct method is located in the *Master Case Book*. Exhibit 6.8 illustrates a lender prepared form of Turner Electronic Corporation's cash flow using the direct method.

Cash from Sales

The actual amount of net sales from income statement is filled in first. Next, the change in accounts receivable is calculated. Increases are a use of cash and, therefore, a negative number. Decreases are a source of cash and, therefore, a positive number. The cash from sales is the sum of net sales plus or minus the change in accounts receivable.

Net sales		$ 7,270
Accounts receivable—20x1	$ 915	
− accounts receivable—20x2	782	
= change in accounts receivable		133
Cash from sales		7,403

Gross Cash Profits

The cost of goods sold is always a negative number, and the actual number from the income statement, less depreciation, is a noncash expense. The changes in inventory and accounts payable are from the balance sheet. Increases in assets (inventory) are a use of cash and, therefore, a negative number. Decreases in assets (inventory) are a source of cash and, therefore, a positive number. Accounts payable are the changes in amounts due to the trade. Increases are a source of cash and, therefore, a positive number. Decreases are a use of cash and, therefore, a negative number. Cash production costs are the sum of cost of goods sold, inventory, and accounts payable. Gross cash profits are the difference between cash from sales and cash production costs.

Cash from sales		$ 7,403
(Cost of goods sold) 20x2		$ (4,676)
Inventory 20x1	$ 1,980	
− inventory 20x2	2,392	
= change in inventory		(412)
Accounts payable 20x1	507	
− accounts payable 20x2	969	
= change in accounts payable		462
Cash production costs		(4,626)
Gross cash profits		2,777

Exhibit 6.8   Lender-Prepared Direct Method—Turner Electronic Corporation

Cash Flow	20x0	20x1	20x2
Net sales	$ 6,260	$ 7,482	$ 7,270
(Increase) decrease in receivables	(181)	(255)	133
Cash from sales	6,079	7,227	7,403
(Cost of goods sold)[1]	(3,896)	(4,579)	(4,676)
(Increase) decrease in inventories	(91)	(193)	(412)
Increase (decrease) in payables	102	150	462
Cash production costs	(3,885)	(4,622)	(4,626)
Gross cash profits	2,194	2,605	2,777
(Selling, general and administrative expense)[1]	(2,174)	(2,268)	(2,362)
(Increase) decrease in prepaid expense	46	(44)	(31)
Increase (decrease) accrued expenses	(73)	46	(2)
Cash operating expense	(2,201)	(2,266)	(2,395)
Cash after operations	(7)	339	382
Miscellaneous cash income[2]	0	0	0
Income taxes paid[3]	(7)	(121)	(17)
Net cash after operations	(14)	218	365
(Interest expense)	(66)	(86)	(109)
(Dividends paid)	0	0	0
Financing costs	(66)	(86)	(109)
Net cash income	(80)	132	256
(Current portion long-term debt)[4]	(44)	(60)	(70)
Cash after debt amortization	(124)	72	186
Capital expenditures[5]	(73)	(82)	(50)
Long-term investments/intangibles	0	0	0
Financing surplus (requirements)	(197)	(10)	136
Increase (decrease) short-term debt	97	(13)	(126)
Increase (decrease) in long-term debt[6]	47	37	13
Increase (decrease) equity[7]	0	0	0
Total external financing	144	24	(113)
Cash after financing	(53)	14	23
Actual change in cash	(53)	14	23

( ) Indicates decline in cash; Inc = Increase; Dec = Decrease
1. Net of depreciation
2. Other income: other expense ± change or other current assets/liabilities
3. Tax provision ± change in deferred tax asset, accrued income taxes payable, and deferred taxes payable
4. Previous year's current maturities long-term debt
5. Change in net fixed assets plus depreciation
6. Change in long-term debt plus this year's current maturities
7. Common, preferred, treasury stock only

Cash after Operations

Selling, general, and administrative expenses are always a negative number. The actual amounts from the income statement, net of depreciation, are a noncash expense. Prepaid expenses and accrued expenses are the changes in the balance sheet. Increases in prepaid expenses are a use of cash and, therefore, a negative number. Decreases in prepaid expenses are a source of cash and, therefore, a positive number. Increases in accrued expenses are a source of cash and, therefore, a positive number. Decreases in accrued expenses are a use of cash and, therefore, a negative number. Cash operating expense is the sum of selling, general, and administrative expense plus or minus the changes in prepaid expense and accrued expense. Gross cash profits minus cash operating expenses equal cash after operations.

Gross cash profits		$ 2,777
(selling, general, and administrative expense)		$ (2,362)
Prepaid expense 20x1	$ 71	
– prepaid expense 20x2	102	
= change in prepaid expense		(31)
Accrued expense 20x1	163	
– accrued expense 20x2	161	
= change in accrued expense		(2)
Cash operating expense		(2,395)
Cash after operations		382

Net Cash after Operations

Cash after operations minus miscellaneous cash income and income taxes paid equals net cash after operations. Miscellaneous income is the sum of other income–other expense plus or minus the change in other current assets plus or minus the change in other current liabilities. There were no miscellaneous changes the last three years. Income taxes paid equals the tax provision plus or minus the changes in deferred tax asset, accrued income tax, and deferred taxes payable.

Cash after operations	382
Miscellaneous cash income	0
Income taxes paid from 20x2 income statement	(17)
Net cash after operations	365

Analysis of Net Cash after Operations

Net cash after operations, purpose of short-term debt, and purpose of long-term debt are analyzed in the lender-prepared direct method cash flow statement.

If net cash flow after operations is negative, there will not be sufficient cash to pay long-term debt, interest, and dividends or to invest in fixed assets.

The following factors contribute to negative net cash after operations:

- operating losses due to insufficient sales volume, poor pricing of product or service, or poor cost controls
- poor control of accounts receivable, inventory, and accounts payable
- growth in accounts receivable, inventory, and sales

Turner Electronic Corporation's Net Cash after Operations

Turner Electronic Corporation's net cash flow after operations for the last three years is:

	20x0	20x1	20x2
Net sales	$ 6,260	$ 7,482	$ 7,270
Change in receivables	(181)	(255)	133
Cash from sales	6,079	7,227	7,403
Cost of goods sold	(3,896)	(4,579)	(4,676)
Change in inventories	(91)	(193)	(412)
Change in payables	102	150	462
Cash productions costs	(3,885)	(4,622)	(4,626)
Gross cash profits	2,194	2,605	2,777
Selling, general, and administrative expenses	(2,174)	(2,268)	(2,362)
Change in prepaid expenses	46	(44)	(31)
Change in accrued expenses	(73)	46	(2)
Cash operating expense	(2,201)	(2,266)	(2,395)
Cash after operations	(7)	339	382
Income taxes paid	(7)	(121)	(17)
Net cash after operations	(14)	218	365

The net cash after operations was negative in 20x0 due to the rapid growth in accounts receivable ($181) and inventory ($91). This growth was partially funded by accounts payable ($102). In 20x1, current asset growth, namely accounts receivable ($255) and inventory ($193), needed to be funded due to the sales growth. The company cost of goods sold increased to 3 percent of sales (20x2), which decreased cash flow by $218 (annual sales $7,270 × 0.03).

Also, the operating expenses for 20x2 increased by 2 percent, which further decreased cash flow by $145 ($7,270 × 0.02). These two changes caused company net profits to decrease from $347 in 20x1 to $34 in 20x2. The company was able to repay short-term debt by collecting accounts receivable ($133). The company has had positive cash flow from operations for the last two years. The lender will want to monitor net cash after operations to be sure it is positive.

Management of Accounts Receivable, Inventory, and Accounts Payable

When a statement of cash flows reveals that accounts receivable or inventory has grown (a use of cash), lenders investigate whether or not this growth is in proportion to the growth of sales or if it suggests a managerial problem or a change in strategy. If the company's accounts receivable or inventory has decreased (a source of cash), lenders determine whether that decrease reflects a decrease in sales, is a conscious management decision to change the way the company manages that asset category, or the company is using short-term assets to fund operating losses.

In addition, lenders must address whether or not these changes are permanent or temporary. Permanent changes are caused by a permanent increase or decrease in sales. Sales can permanently change due to products, prices, or markets. Temporary changes usually relate to one-time sales increases.

If the statement of cash flows shows that accounts payable or other accruals have grown (a source of cash), lenders determine whether that growth is in response to increased sales or whether the company has been slow in paying the accounts payable due to cash shortages. If the trade payment is slowing, the company could face a cash need later in order to bring the accounts payable current. Accounts payable changes in relation to sales, accounts receivable, and inventory.

Turner Electronic Corporation Accounts Receivable, Inventory, and Accounts Payable Analysis

Turner Electronic Corporation's short-term assets and debt have changed in the last two years, as shown here:

	20x1	*20x2*
Accounts receivable	(255)	133
Inventory	(193)	(412)
Accounts payable	150	462
Short-term bank debt	(13)	(126)

In 20x1, the company increased its accounts receivable by $255,000 and financed $150,000 of the inventory growth with accounts payable. The company used its net profit of $347,000 to fund the growth in accounts receivable and the balance of the inventory. This appears to be a good use of the company's profits. In 20x2, accounts receivable declined by $133,000. This decline was a source of cash. The cash collected from the accounts receivable repaid the short-term debt of $126,000. However, the inventory increased by $412,000 and was entirely funded by the accounts payable trade. A lender will want to check trade references to determine whether the company is paying its trade payments in a timely manner.

Net Cash Income

Interest expense plus dividends paid equals financing costs. Interest expense is the actual expense from the income statement. Dividends are calculated:

Previous years retained earnings
+ current years net income after tax
– current years retained earnings
_____

= dividends paid

Net cash after operations
– financing costs
_____

= net cash income

Net cash after operations	365
(Interest expense) from 20x2 income statement	(109)
– (dividends paid)	0
= financing costs	(109)
Net cash income	256

Cash after Debt Amortization

Current portion long-term debt is the current maturities listed in the previous year and is always a negative number.

Net cash income
– current portion long-term debt
_____

= cash after debt amortization

Net cash income	256
(Current portion long-term debt from 20x1 balance sheet)	(70)
Cash after debt amortization	186

Financing Surplus (Requirements)

Capital expenditures are the change in net fixed assets plus depreciation. Long-term investments and intangibles are the changes in these accounts from the balance sheet. There have been no long-term investments or intangible changes the last three years. Cash after debt amortization plus or minus the changes in capital expenditures and long-term investments and intangibles equals a financing surplus or requirement.

Cash after debt amoritization		186
Net fixed assets 20x1	237	
– net fixed assets 20x2	215	
+ depreciation expense	(72)	
= capital expenditures		(50)
– long-term investments/intangibles		0
= financing surplus (requirements)		136

Total External Financing

The change in notes payable short term is listed as an increase or decrease in short-term debt. Long-term debt is the change in long-term debt plus this year's current maturities. The change in equity is the change in stock. There have been no changes in stock the last three years. The sum of the changes in short-term debt, long-term debt, and equity equals total external financing.

Financing surplus		136
Notes payable short-term 20x1	634	
− notes payable short-term 20x2	508	
= change in short-term debt	(126)	
Current maturities long-term debt 20x2	78	
+ long-term debt 20x2	59	
− long-term debt 20x1	124	
= change in long-term debt	13	
Total external financing		(113)
Cash after financing		23

Cash after Financing

The financing surplus or requirement plus or minus the total external financing equals the cash after financing. The cash after financing equals the actual change in cash. If the statement does not balance, an error was made in one of the calculations.

Cash after financing		23
Cash 20x1	51	
− cash 20x2	74	
= actual change in cash		23

Long-term Debt and Fixed Asset Expenditures

The purchase of fixed assets is considered discretionary because a company's management can postpone or cancel fixed asset purchases or investments. Fixed assets also could decrease due to the accounting for depreciation or as the result of no new assets being purchased or replaced. Lenders consider the following questions if fixed assets have decreased:

- Is the existing equipment reaching capacity?
- If the equipment is old, is its age affecting its use?

For the last three years, Turner Electronic Corporation's capital expenditures and long-term debt increases have been:

	20x0	20x1	20x2
Capital expenditure increases	73	82	50
Long-term debt increases	47	37	13

It appears that Turner is funding the down payments for capital expenditures from profit or other short-term liabilities.

ABBREVIATED CASH FLOW STATEMENT

The lender-prepared direct method cash flow statement calculates all the changes between two balance sheets and then uses the actual income statement numbers. This method generally is not used for smaller loan requests. For loan requests under $500,000, many banks use an abbreviated cash flow statement. The abbreviated cash flow statement summarizes the sources and uses of cash flow. The statement is completed using two consecutive fiscal years of balance sheets and the current-year income statement. By completing this form, a lender can determine how the company used its profits, how it structured its debt, and what questions to ask the company. A blank abbreviated cash flow statement form is located in the *Master Case Book*. Exhibit 6.9 illustrates a completed abbreviated cash flow statement for Turner Electronic Corporation for fiscal year 20x2.

Exhibit 6.9 Abbreviated Cash Flow Statement Form—Turner Electronic Corporation—Year 20x2

Cash Sources—"Inflows"			Cash Uses—"Outflows"	
Cash profit (net income plus depreciation expense)	106	OR	Cash loss (net loss, offset by depreciation expense)	0
Decrease in accounts receivable	133	OR	Increase in accounts receivable	0
Decrease in inventories	0	OR	Increase in inventories	412
Increase in accounts payable	462	OR	Decrease in accounts payable	0
Increase in short-term debt	0	OR	Decrease in short-term debt	126
			Cash dividends	0
Disposals of fixed assets	0	OR	Fixed asset additions	50
New long-term debt	13		Long-term loan payments	70
New capital stock issued	0		Increase in Treasury stock	0
Decrease in cash balance	0	OR	Increase in cash balance	23
Decrease in all other assets	0		Increase in all other assets	31

The calculations for the abbreviated cash flow are:

1. Cash profit

net income	34
plus depreciation	72
cash profit	106

2. Decrease in accounts receivable

20x1 accounts receivable	905
20x2 accounts receivable	772
decrease in accounts receivable	133

3. Increase in inventory

20x1 inventory	1980
20x2 inventory	2392
increase in inventory	412

4. Increase in accounts payable

20x1 accounts payable	507
20x2 accounts payable	969
increase in account payable	462

5. Decrease in short-term debt

20x1 notes payable bank	634
20x2 notes payable bank	508
decrease in short-term debt	126

6. Fixed asset addition

20x1 net fixed assets	237
20x2 net fixed assets	215
	22
depreciation expense	(72)
net change fixed assets	(50)

7. New long-term debt

20x2 current maturities	78
plus 20x2 long-term debt	59
minus 20x1 long-termdebt	124
new long-term debt	13

8. Long-term loan payments are the 20x1 current maturities

9. Increase in cash balance

20x1 cash	51
20x2 cash	74
Increase in cash balance	23

10. Increase in other assets

20x1 prepaid expense	71
20x2 prepaid expense	102
	31

The abbreviated cash flow is summarized by circling the four largest inflows and outflows of cash. For Turner Electronic Corporation those were:

Inflows		Outflows	
Net income plus depreciation	106	Increase in inventory	412
Decrease in accounts receivable	133	Fixed asset additions	50
Increase in accounts payable	462	Long-term debt payments	70
New long-term debt	13	Decrease in short term debt	126
Total	714	Total	668

The abbreviated form affirms earlier cash flow statements. The company funded an increase in inventory with accounts payable. Collections of accounts receivable were used to repay short-term debt. Profits were used to fund fixed asset purchases and repay existing long-term debt.

By using a completed abbreviated cash flow statement, the lender can quickly answer the following cash flow questions:

- What is causing more cash to go out than to come in?
  (The purpose of the loan.)
- What has changed in the company's business operations?
  (The repayment sources.)
- What is the possibility that these changes will continue in the future?
  (The risk of nonpayment.)
- What is the proper loan structure?
  (The term of the loan.)

TRADITIONAL CASH FLOW

Many bankers use traditional cash flow for loan agreements because the calculation is simpler to understand and explain in a loan agreement. It is calculated:

$$\frac{\text{(Net profit after tax + depreciation + amortization − dividends)}}{\text{Current maturities long-term debt}} = \text{Traditional cash flow}$$

Some lenders add interest expense to each side of the equation. The current year interest expense would be added to the net profit side and the projected interest expense to the debt side. The traditional cash flow method generally is used for stable, mature borrowers. For such borrowers, the balance sheet usually is seasoned with only a few changes to the accounts receivable, inventory, and accounts payable. The cost of goods sold and operating expenses normally do not change by large percentages from year to year. Of course, many mature borrowers whose financial statements demonstrate these characteristics need as much financing as a growth company does. Growth companies tend to have larger increases in accounts receivable and inventory that need to be funded. However, the traditional cash flow model does not consider changes in current assets.

A variation of the traditional cash flow is called EBITDA to Funded Debt. EBITDA stands for:

E earnings after taxes
B before
I interest
T taxes
D depreciation
A amortization

Funded debt is considered to be existing long-term debt plus interest expense. EBITDA is similar to traditional cash flow as explained by the following:

E earnings after taxes
D depreciation
A amortization
_____
TCF traditional cash flow
+ taxes
+ interest expense
_____
EBITDA earnings before interest, taxes, depreciation, and amortization

---

EBITDA to Funded Debt

This variation to traditional cash flow became popular when large banks funded highly leveraged companies. It is more commonly used when analyzing loan requests greater than $5 million and loan requests from companies doing leverage buyouts. For loans under $5 million, traditional cash flow is generally used. It has been found that EBITDA is a better measure for companies whose assets have longer lives, but it is not necessarily good for companies whose assets are short term in nature. The analytical problems of EBITDA are:

1. It ignores a company's tax obligation. In early years, highly leveraged companies may not pay taxes, but EBITDA does not consider the cash flow needed to pay taxes later.
2. It assumes that fixed assets do not need to be replaced.
3. It does not consider the financing needs for current assets to support sales growth.
4. Publicly held companies need to be committed to paying dividends. Dividends are not considered in the EBITDA cash flow calculation.

Turner Electronic Corporation Traditional Cash Flow Analysis

The traditional cash flow for Turner Electronic Corporation for the years 20x1 and 20x2 would be calculated:

20x1

$$\frac{347 + 81 + 0}{70} = 6.1$$

20x2

$$\frac{34 + 72 + 0}{78} = 1.36$$

Turner's traditional cash flow for 20x1 is over 6 times the needed debt service, which means it should be more than able to pay its debt. The decrease in 20x2 is caused by the large decline in net profit after tax. However, most lenders consider traditional cash flow coverage of 1.25 to be adequate. Turner paid no dividends in either year.

Traditional Cash Flow with Rent

There are several variations of the traditional cash flow. Turner Electronic Corporation rents its building from the primary shareholder. For this situation, some lenders calculate traditional cash flow by adding the rent and the building's debt to the equation.

$$\frac{\text{(Net profit + depreciation + amortization + rent)}}{\text{(Current maturities long-term debt + building debt*)}} = \text{Traditional cash flow}$$

* (from owner's personal financial statement)

For Turner Electronic Corporation, the amended traditional cash flow would be:

20x1

$$\frac{347 + 81 + 0 + 280}{70 + 181} = 2.82$$

20x2

$$\frac{34 + 72 + 0 + 280}{78 + 181} = 1.49$$

The rent of $280 was obtained from the footnotes for Turner Electronic Corporation located in the *Master Case Book* ($23,340 × 12). The rent for the Florida location and airplane is not used because the owner's debt and lease payments are the same as the amounts paid by the company. The lender determined the mortgage payment from the owner's personal financial statement. The traditional cash flow coverage with rent was less in 20x1 but improved for 20x2. The improvement in 20x2 is because the rent paid by the company to the owner, which exceeds the mortgage payment, had a greater effect in 20x2.

Traditional Cash Flow with Maintenance Cap Ex

For companies that are fixed-asset dependent, such as manufacturers and certain service companies, some banks use a variation of traditional cash flow that adds the maintenance cap ex (capital expenditures) component. Maintenance cap ex are those capital expenditures needed to maintain the current level of sales and net profit. The analytical argument for using maintenance cap ex is that the current sales and net profit margins need to be maintained to produce the cash flow needed to service the existing debt. Some lenders feel all capital expenditures may be financed with long-term debt. Others feel the maintenance cap ex should be financed by internally generated cash flow.

Turner Electronic Corporation has had the following levels of sales and capital expenditure purchases for the last three years:

	20x0	20x1	20x2
Sales	$ 6,260	$ 7,480	$7,270
Capital expenditures	73	82	50

As its annual expenses indicate, the company needs to purchase about $75 of capital expenditures each year to maintain its current level of sales. The traditional cash flow calculation now would be amended to be:

$$\frac{\text{(Net profit + depreciation + amortization)}}{\text{(Current maturities long-term debt + maintenance cap ex)}} = \text{Traditional cash flow}$$

For Turner Electronic Corporation the traditional cash flow including maintenance cap ex would be:

20x1

$$\frac{347 + 81 + 0}{70 + 75} = 2.95$$

20x2

$$\frac{34 + 72 + 0}{78 + 75} = 0.69$$

For year 20x2, Turner Electronic Corporation did not generate sufficient traditional cash flow to fund maintenance cap ex. The company could finance these expenditures using long-term debt. However, the lender will then need to consider the impact of the new debt on future cash flow.

SUMMARY

The direct method SFAS No. 95 Statement of Cash Flows is an important analytical tool that enables the lender to determine how a company obtains and uses its economic resources. By creating a structured report that shows the inflows and outflows of cash associated with the operating, investing, and financing activities of a company, the lender can understand management's decisions over time. Besides changes in balance sheet accounts, actual cash flow information is taken from the current income statement. Analysis of a company's cash flow statement focuses on the adequacy of the company's operating cash flow, the appropriateness of its investment cash flows, and the proper structuring of the financing cash flows.

The lender-prepared direct method cash flow statement is used by many banks. The statement allows the lender to focus on net cash after operations. Net cash after operations must be positive to repay bank debt, fund fixed asset purchases, and repay debt. This method also allows the lender to analyze accounts receivable, inventory, and accounts payable issues. Some banks also use an abbreviated form of cash flow to perform a quick analysis.

Many banks use the traditional cash flow method because it is easily used in loan agreements. Variations of traditional cash flow include methods using rent and maintenance cap ex. Whichever method is used, lenders need to remember that cash and only cash repays loans.

QUESTIONS FOR DISCUSSION

1. In which cash flow activity would you expect the following to be found?

   a. sale of land
   b. purchase of finished products on credit
   c. a quarterly tax payment
   d. new long-term debt
   e. interest payment on a revolving line of credit
   f. purchase of a new telephone system
   g. dividends to the company owners

2. What types of financial information are needed to construct an abbreviated cash flow statement?
3. List five questions that the lender-prepared direct method Statement of Cash Flows answers.
4. What causes negative cash flow from operations?
5. Explain the calculation of traditional cash flow when the owner of the business personally owns a building rented to a company.

Exercise

Prepare a direct-method cash flow statement for one year using the information and forms that follow.

Balance Sheet Spreadsheet (000s omitted)

Income Statement	20x1 Amount	20x2 Amount
Net sales	$ 5,015	$ 7,296
Cost of goods sold	3,527	5,163
Gross profit	1,488	2,133
Operating expenses*	1,456	1,770
Operating profit (loss)	32	363
Other income	135	63
Interest expense	8	7
Net profit before tax	159	419
Taxes	0	0
Net profit after tax	159	419

Balance Sheet		

Assets	20x1 Amount	20x2 Amount
Cash	$ 318	$ 668
Accounts receivable	381	758
Inventory	412	166
Total current assets	1,111	1,592
Equipment	1,157	1,406
Other fixed assets		
Depreciation	814	973
Net fixed assets	343	433
Prepaid expenses	28	36
Other noncurrent assets	28	60
Total assets	1,510	2,121

Liabilities	20x1 Amount	20x2 Amount
Notes payable bank short term	$ 32	$ 1
Accounts payable-trade	318	429
Accrued expenses	155	267
Total liabilities	505	697

Net Worth	20x1 Amount	20x2 Amount
Common stock	$ 40	$ 40
Retained earnings	965	1,384
Total net worth	1,005	1,424

* Operating expenses include $159 of depreciation in the second year.

Cash Flow—Lender-Prepared Direct Method

Cash Flow		20x2
Net sales		
(Increase) decrease in receivables		
Cash from sales		
(Cost of goods sold)[1]		
(Increase) decrease in inventories		
Increase (decrease) in payables		
Cash production costs		
Gross cash profits		
(Selling, general and administrative expense)[1]		
(Increase) decrease in prepaid expense		
Increase (decrease) in accrued expenses		
Cash operating expense		
Cash after operations		
Miscellaneous cash income[2]		
Income taxes paid[3]		
Net cash after operations		
(Interest expense)		
(Dividends paid)		
Financing costs		
Net cash income		
(Current portion long-term debt)[4]		
Cash after debt amortization		
Capital expenditures[5]		
Long-term investments/intangibles		
Financing surplus (requirements)		
Increase (decrease) short-term debt		
Increase (decrease) in long-term debt[6]		
Increase (decrease) equity[7]		
Total external financing		
Cash after financing		
Actual change in cash		

  ( ) Indicates decline in cash
  [1] Net of depreciation
  [2] Other income – other expense ± change or other current assets/liabilities
  [3] Tax provision ± change in deferred tax asset, accrued income taxes payable, and deferred taxes payable
  [4] Previous year's current maturities long-term debt
  [5] Change in net fixed assets plus depreciation
  [6] Change in long-term debt plus this year's current maturities
  [7] Common, preferred, treasury stock only

7

ANALYZING PERSONAL FINANCIAL STATEMENTS AND CASH FLOW

LEARNING OBJECTIVES

After studying *Analyzing Personal Financial Statements and Cash Flow,* you will be able to

- evaluate a personal financial statement,
- calculate adjusted personal net worth,
- calculate and interpret net personal cash flow,
- understand how to interpret a U.S. Individual Tax Return Form 1040 and the related schedules, and
- define key terms that appear in **bold** type in the text.

INTRODUCTION

A **personal financial statement** is a summary of personal assets, liabilities, and net worth. It provides information on income, expenditures, contingent liabilities, asset ownership and value, liabilities owed, and representations and warranties.

In the case of a small business owner, the assets and income of the borrower and the business are often combined and analyzed together. The criteria for preparing personal financial statements have been defined by the American Institute of Certified Public Accountants (AICPA) in Statement of Position No. 82-1, *Accounting and Financial Reporting for Personal Financial Statements*. These criteria are used when an independent accountant prepares personal financial statements. However, the borrower prepares most personal financial statements. Generally, borrower-prepared personal financial statements are presented on a form provided by the bank or on a computer-generated form. Using a standard form helps ensure consistency in presentation. Many borrowers need assistance in filling out a personal financial statement form. A lender may need to explain the form to the borrower in order to have it completed properly. In order to analyze the information properly, a lender will need to understand how the form was prepared.

When borrowers prepare personal financial statements using a computer-generated form, they also should partially complete a bank form. The applicant would use the bank form to address the statement to the bank; answer questions on income, expenditures, and contingent liabilities; sign and date the form; indicate "see attached" on the asset and liability section; and attach the computer-generated statement.

With two completed personal financial statements and a current year personal tax return, a lender can calculate personal cash flow. Also, a lender can calculate the debt-to-income ratio to determine if personal debt levels are excessive. The personal tax return should include Individual Form 1040 and Schedules A, B, C, D, and E. If the individual owns a partnership or S Corporation, the company tax returns with supporting K-1's will also be needed to calculate personal cash flow. For small businesses, some banks calculate global personal cash flow. Global personal cash flow includes all personal and company income and the related debt.

Throughout this module, a fictitious couple named Edward G. and Linda C. Dezine demonstrate how to analyze personal financial statements and interpret personal tax returns. Designs by Dezine, Inc., an S corporation owned by Linda C. Dezine, is used to demonstrate how ownership of an S corporation affects personal cash flow. Additional background information, a blank personal financial statement form, and a personal cash flow form are located in the *Master Case Book*.

PERSONAL FINANCIAL STATEMENT OVERVIEW

A blank four-page personal financial statement form is located in the *Master Case Book*. The personal financial statement form used by banks varies. The first page of the form requires the following information: the name of the person to whom the information is submitted, and such personal information on the applicant and co-applicant as address, telephone number, and the names of employers. The second and third pages summarize the balance sheet and contingent liabilities and provide schedules for certain assets and liabilities. The last page asks questions of the applicant and co-applicant, states the representations and warranties, and provides space for the date and signature.

Regardless of the form used, the following information is reviewed and verified prior to analyzing the personal financial statement:

- The financial statement is addressed to the lending bank. If the financial statement is not addressed to the lending bank, it is the policy of some financial institutions to have the statement readdressed to them. This ensures that the information provided was given to the named bank in order to receive an extension of credit.

- The form and all supporting schedules are completed. Before a credit decision is made, the borrower must fill in all lines on the form.

- The form contains no math errors. The statement is checked for accurate addition and subtraction of assets and liabilities. Schedules must match the assets and liabilities listed.

- All contingent liabilities are itemized.

- A paragraph stating that the applicant represents and warrants the information to be true and correct.

- The statement is signed and dated by the borrower and his or her spouse if assets are owned jointly. The statement is dated prior to the loan date.

The lender verifies the methodology used to value assets, and may need to obtain supporting documents. For example, the lender may request a copy of a broker's statement to verify the value of marketable securities. As part of the review, the lender requires the applicant to supply any incomplete information.

PERSONAL FINANCIAL STATEMENT ANALYSIS

Edward G. Dezine and Linda C. Dezine have provided personal financial statements annually to the bank. Their personal financial statement dated June 7, 2002, is shown in exhibit 7.1. The form, from The Risk Management Association, is commonly used by banks.

Personal Information

The first page of this personal financial statement form begins with the applicant's name, address, occupation, and telephone number. If the applicant is new to the bank, the lender obtains identification to verify that the individual presenting the statement and the name on the financial statement are the same. Acceptable identification includes: drivers license, social security card, or temporary residence card.

Exhibit 7.1   Personal Financial Statement as of June 7, 2002

Personal Financial Statement

CONTACT YOUR REPRESENTATIVE AT THE BANK
IF YOU HAVE ANY QUESTIONS REGARDING THE
COMPLETION OF THIS FORM

YOU MAY APPLY FOR A CREDIT EXTENSION OR FINANCIAL ACCOMMODATION INDIVIDUALLY OR JOINTLY WITH A CO-APPLICANT. THIS STATEMENT AND ANY APPLICABLE SUPPORTING SCHEDULES MAY BE COMPLETED JOINTLY BY BOTH MARRIED AND UNMARRIED CO-APPLICANTS IF THEIR ASSETS AND LIABILITIES ARE SUFFICIENTLY JOINED SO THAT THE STATEMENT CAN BE MEANINGFULLY AND FAIRLY PRESENTED ON A COMBINED BASIS; OTHERWISE SEPARATE STATEMENTS AND SCHEDULES ARE REQUIRED.

APPLICANT

NAME   Linda C. Dezine   Social Security #   123-45-6789

ADDRESS   9425 Norwood Avenue, Hometown, MN

TELEPHONE NUMBER   617-9526   DATE OF BIRTH   3/7/48

PRESENT EMPLOYER   Designs by Dezine, Inc   POSITION   President

ADDRESS   9425 Norwood Avenue, Hometown, MN

CO-APPLICANT

NAME   Edward G. Dezine   Social Security #   234-56-7890

ADDRESS   9425 Norwood Avenue, Hometown, MN

TELEPHONE NUMBER   387-1301   DATE OF BIRTH   9/14/48

PRESENT EMPLOYER   Structured Engineering, Inc   POSITION   VP Engineering

ADDRESS   301 3rd Street, Hometown, MN

DATE OF VALUATION 6/7/02 _____

- Round all amounts to the nearest $100
- Attach separate sheet if you need more space to complete detail schedule

ASSETS	AMOUNT	LIABILITIES	AMOUNT
Cash in this Bank	45,000	Notes Payable Banks (Schedule 7)	
Cash in Other Banks (Detail)		Notes Payable Others (Schedule 7)	
IRA, Keogh, Retirement	440,000	Installment Contracts Payable (Schedule 7)	11,000
		Due Dept. Stores, Credit Cards & Others	3,000
		Margin Account	
Due from Friends, Relatives & Others (Sched. 1)	46,000	Income Taxes Payable	
Mortgage & Contracts for Deed Owned (Sched. 2)		Other Taxes Payable	
Securities Owned (Schedule 3)	132,000		
Cash Surrender Value of Life Insur. (Sched. 4)	20,000	Loans on Life Insurance (Schedule 4)	
Homestead (Schedule 5)	700,000		
Other Real Estate Owned (Schedule 5)		Mortgage on Homestead (Schedule 6)	410,000
Automobiles		Mortgage or Liens on Other Real Estate	
Partnerships		Owned (Schedule 6)	
Deferred Income			
Personal Property	85,000	Other Liabilities (Detail)	
Other Assets (Detail) Antiques	35,000		
		TOTAL LIABILITIES	424,000
		Net Worth (Total Assets Less Total Liabilities)	1,079,000
TOTAL	1,503,000	TOTAL	1,503,000

ANNUAL INCOME	APPLICANT	CO-APPLICANT	CONTINGENT LIABILITIES	
Salary	42,700	80,000	As Endorser	
Commissions			As Guarantor	40,000
Dividends			Lawsuits	
Interest	2,400		For Taxes	
Rentals			Other (Detail)	
Alimony, child support or maintenance (you need not show this unless you wish us to consider it).				
Other	40,000		☐ Check here if "None"	
TOTAL INCOME	85,100	80,000	TOTAL CONTINGENT LIABILITIES	40,000

SCHEDULE 1 DUE FROM FRIENDS, RELATIVES & OTHERS

Name of Debtor	Owed To	Collateral	How Payable		Maturity Date	Unpaid Balance
Designs by Dezine	Linda C.	Unsecured	$ 0	per mo.	20x5	46,000
			$	per		
			$	per		
					TOTAL	

SCHEDULE 2 MORTGAGE AND CONTRACTS FOR DEED OWNED

Name of Debtor	Type of Property	1st or 2nd Lien	Owed To	How Payable		Unpaid Balance
				$	per	
				$	per	
				$	per	
				$	per	
					TOTAL	

SCHEDULE 3 SECURITIES OWNED

No. Shares or Bond Amount	Description	In Whose Name(s) Registered	Cost	Present Market Value	L-listed U-unlisted
100	National Fund	Linda C. & Edward G.	45,000	32,000	L
1000	Designs by Dezine	Linda C.	1,000	100,000	U
		TOTAL	46,000	132,000	

SCHEDULE 4 LIFE INSURANCE

Insured	Insurance Company	Beneficiary	Face Value of Policy	Cash Value	Loans
Linda C.	Mutual Co.	Edward G.	200,000	10,000	0
Edward G.	Mutual Co.	Linda C.	200,000	10,000	0
		TOTAL			

SCHEDULE 5 REAL ESTATE

Address and Type of Property	Title in Name(s) of	Monthly Income	Cost / Year Acquired	Present Market Value	Amount of Insurance
Homestead	Edward G & Linda C. Dezine		$ 600,000 Year 2000	700,000	700,000
			$ ____ Year		
			$ ____ Year		
			$ ____ Year		
			$ ____ Year		

SCHEDULE 6 MORTGAGES OR LIENS ON REAL ESTATE

To Whom Payable	How Payable	Interest Rate	Maturity Date	Unpaid Balance
Homestead	$ 3800 per mo.	7%	2030	410,000
	$ per			
	$ per			
	$ per			
	$ per			

SCHEDULE 7 NOTES PAYABLE BANKS & OTHERS AND INSTALLMENT CONTRACTS PAYABLE

To Whom Payable	Address	Collateral or Unsecured	How Payable	Unpaid Balance
Car Co.		Auto	$ 333 per mo.	11,000
			$ per	
			$ per	
			$ per	
			$ per	
			$ per	
			$ per	
			$ per	

	APPLICANT		CO-APPLICANT	
Have you ever gone through bankruptcy or had a judgment against you?	☐ Yes	☒ No	☐ Yes	☒ No
Are any assets pledged or debts secured except as shown?	☐ Yes	☐ No	☐ Yes	☐ No
Have you made a will?	☐ Yes	☒ No	☐ Yes	☒ No
Number of Dependents (If "None" check None)	_____	☐ None	_____	☐ None

Marital Status (answer only if this financial statement is provided in connection with a request for secured credit or applicant is seeking a joint account with spouse.)

APPLICANT	CO-APPLICANT
☒ Married	☒ Married
☐ Separated	☐ Separated
☐ Unmarried	☐ Unmarried

(Unmarried includes single, divorced, widowed)

The foregoing statement, submitted for the purpose of obtaining credit, is true and correct in every detail and fairly shows my/our financial condition at the time indicated. I/we will give you prompt written notice of any subsequent substantial change in such financial condition occurring before discharge of my/our obligations to you. I/we understand that you will retain this personal financial statement whether or not you approve the credit in connection with which it is submitted. You are authorized to check my/our credit and employment history or any other information contained herein.

THE UNDERSIGNED CERTIFY THAT THE INFORMATION CONTAINED ON THIS FORM HAS BEEN CAREFULLY REVIEWED AND THAT IT IS TRUE AND CORRECT IN ALL RESPECTS.

_6/7/02_
Date

x _Linda C. D'ozine_
Your Signature

_6/7/02_
Date

Edward L. D'ozine
Co-Applicant Signature (if you are requesting the financial accommodation jointly)

Income Analysis

The second page of the personal financial statement summarizes the balance sheet, income information, contingent liabilities, and schedules 1 and 2. The loan officer must verify the annual income information. Salaries and bonuses can be verified using pay stubs, W-2s, or the Federal Individual Form 1040. Other sources of income, such as rental, interest, dividend, capital gains, partnership, other investment, and other income, also can be verified from the personal tax return schedules.

When analyzing income, the lender addresses the following issues:

- What are the probabilities the salary will continue? Is the reported salary information reliable? Are the liquid assets reported on the financial statement sufficient in relation to the salary level listed? If the borrower has a large income and no cash on hand, this may indicate the borrower has excessive spending or investing habits.
- Bonuses and commissions may be tied to certain performance objectives and may or may not recur.
- Use assets owned to validate rental income, interest, dividends, capital gains, and partnership income received.
- Obtain a signed Form 8821 from the Internal Revenue Service (IRS) and submit the form to the IRS to obtain a copy of the most recent tax return.
- Is the income material? Does the income represent a significant portion of the borrower's total income? If the income is not reliable and is material, it can have an adverse impact on the borrower if the income does not continue.

The Dezines report an income of $165,100 per year on their personal financial statement. This comprises Linda's income of $42,700 from Designs by Dezine, Inc., $2,400 of interest income, and Linda's consulting/teaching income of $40,000 per year. Edward earns $80,000 per year employed as an engineer at Structured Engineering, Inc. This income will be verified later when the personal tax returns are reviewed and personal cash flow is calculated.

When analyzing income for a business owner, the lender should consider expenses that may be paid for by the business and will not need to be paid from the owner's personal income. These expenses include:

- Travel expenses—What amount is paid for by the business when personal time is added to the expense? For example, a company convention may include additional personal vacation time, yet the company pays the travel expenses during the business portion of the trip.
- Auto expenses—What type of auto, how old, and how much is it used for personal use?
- Office expenses—Are there any personal expenses for telephones, correspondence, and so forth included?
- Insurance—What type of insurance is carried, who is insured, and who are the beneficiaries?

- Pension—How is it determined, what is the age of the borrower, when can payments begin?
- Profit sharing—What is the formula, is the owner vested in the plan, when is it available as income?
- Rent—Is rent paid to the owner for equipment or buildings, is it excessive, and what are the market amounts? If the amount is excessive, there may be excess cash flow available for personal use.
- Leasing—Are there any leases from the owner, what are the purposes, what are the terms, and are the amounts excessive?

Annual Expenditures Analysis

Personal expenses to be examined and questions to be asked include:

- Taxes—federal and state. What amounts are due? Are estimates needed? Are taxes current?
- Rental payments—What are the terms of lease? Are there any pending special assessments to the tenants?
- Mortgage payments—What are the terms of the mortgage? Is there a long-term maturity or a balloon payment coming due? Does the payment include principal, interest, taxes, insurance, and association fees if any? How does the amount of debt relate to the current asset value and original cost?
- Real estate taxes—When are the taxes payable? What has been the trend in the tax amount due? Have all tax payments been paid?
- Interest and principal payments—When are the payments due and to whom? If this is an existing bank customer, do the bank's records agree with the amount reported?
- Insurance—What is the annual expense and what type of insurance is being purchased?
- Investments—What is the frequency of this activity and the reason?
- Alimony/child support—what are the terms of the divorce decree? How long will the payments continue?
- Tuition—How much longer will it need to be paid? When are the payments due?
- Medical expenses—What is the cause? What type of medical insurance is carried? Will the expenses be recurring? Who pays the premium?
- Other expenses—What are these expenses? Will they be recurring?

The total expenses are compared to the total income. If the total expenses were too high in relation to the income, the individuals' ability to repay the debt would be affected. The owners may need to take out excessive salaries and dividends from their company to pay for their personal lifestyles. The calculation for personal cash flow using income and expense will be demonstrated later in the module.

Most banks have a maximum personal debt-to-income ratio. The debt-to-income ratio is calculated by dividing the total monthly debt by the total monthly gross income. For example, if the total monthly debt payments are $500 and the total monthly gross income is $2,000, the debt-to-income ratio is 25 percent (500/2,000). Most banks consider a maximum debt-to-income ratio of 40 percent. Total monthly debt includes monthly mortgage or rent payments, monthly payments for bank loans, credit card payments, and any other personal monthly payments. Total income is the gross monthly income earned from employers, interest income, and other forms of regular monthly income. Based on the personal financial statement information, the debt-to-income for the Dezines would be calculated as illustrated in exhibit 7.2.

The maximum amount the Dezines should be paying for all debt (including principal and interest) is $5,503 per month. The Dezines debt-to-income ratio is 31.6 percent ($4,350/13,758 = 31.6%), well below the industry standard of 40 percent. However, the lender will want to consider the loan applicant's personal life style to determine if the amount is low. For example, if the Dezines typically take three vacations per year, each costing $15,000, it is possible that their debt-to-income ratio is not low.

Balance Sheet and Contingent Liabilities

The balance sheet is dated, usually with the same date given on the personal financial statement.

The analysis of the borrower's assets is based on **liquidity, solvency,** and **marketability.** Liquidity answers the question: Can the borrower generate enough cash to pay

---

Exhibit 7.2   Debt-to-Income Calculation

The Dezines' maximum monthly debt payments are calculated as follows:

Total gross income	$ 165,100
Monthly income	13,758
× allowable maximum percentage	0.40
= maximum monthly debt payment	5,503

The Dezines' debt is calculated as follows:

Residence mortgage payments	$ 45,600
+ auto loans	4,800
+ credit cards (5% of amount owed)	1,800
= total annual payments	52,200
Monthly payments	4,350

The Dezines' monthly debt-to income is calculated as follows:

$$\frac{\text{Total monthly debt payments } \$4{,}350}{\text{Total monthly income payments } 13{,}758} \times 100 = 31.6\%$$

---

personal living expenses? Assets on the personal balance sheet are listed in order of liquidity, as they are on a business financial statement. Personal assets are listed at the current market value and not at net book value. Therefore, the lender must consider how solvent the individual is. A solvent borrower can sell assets for sufficient cash to repay all debt. The ability to sell assets depends on the market. Does a market exist in which to sell the assets and at what price? Not all assets have a ready market. For example, investments in partnerships may be marketable to the other partners only. They determine a price based on the limited market.

Proprietorships often mix personal and business assets and liabilities on a financial statement. Like those on a business balance sheet, current assets are expected to convert to cash in 12 months or less. Noncurrent assets are not expected to convert to cash within one year. Current liabilities are debts due in one year or less, and noncurrent liabilities are due in more than one year. Therefore, the lender needs to determine which liabilities are current and which are noncurrent. Exhibit 7.3 on the following page summarizes current and noncurrent personal and business accounts.

Assets

Cash, the most liquid asset, is listed first on the personal balance sheet. A lender must know where the cash is on deposit, in what type of account, and the amount. Remember, a balance sheet lists the amount of cash on hand that day, not necessarily the amount of cash always on deposit. Cash is compared to the amount of income earned. The lower the income, the fewer reserves the applicant usually has available. The greater the income, the greater amount of liquid cash a borrower has on hand. The amount of cash also varies depending on the lifestyle of the applicant. The Dezines list $45,000 in cash on deposit with the bank the statement is addressed to. The amount seems reasonable compared to their stated income and other assets.

Due from friends, relatives, and others are amounts owed to the applicant from other individuals or businesses and are summarized in schedule 1 (exhibit 7.1). A lender will want to know when such loans originated, the terms of repayment, the collateral, and the ability of the individual or company to repay the debt. Often the amounts of accounts receivable listed on the personal balance sheet are notes receivable from a privately held company owned by the applicant. Notes receivable is created when the owners of the company lend part of their salary or dividends back to the company. It is deducted from the net worth when the lender determines that the note cannot be repaid. The Dezines list notes receivable of $46,000 from Designs by Dezine, Inc. Linda Dezine loaned this to her company to fund beginning operating expenses.

Securities owned are listed on schedule 3 (exhibit 7.1). Included here are the number of shares, a description, who the owner is, where securities are held, their original cost, current market value, and whether securities are pledged as collateral. The sum of schedule 3 should equal the amount of readily and non-readily marketable securities listed on the balance sheet. Readily marketable securities are stocks listed on a major stock exchange and can be traded daily or the value of a mutual fund. If the security is a publicly traded stock, the lender needs to know the high and low value per share in the last year. This information tells the lender how much the value may vary. The number of shares traded daily also is determined. If the customer owns a large number of shares, the stock may not be liquid. For example, if the borrower lists 50,000 shares

Exhibit 7.3 Personal and Business Statement Classifications

Asset Classifications	Current*	Noncurrent
Accounts receivable—business	X	
Accounts receivable—relatives, friends		X
Annuities		X
Automobiles		X
Boats		X
Cash	X	
Cash value life insurance	X	
Certificates of deposit	X	
Collectibles (artwork, coins)		X
Deferred compensation		X
Deferred taxes (asset)		X
Due from affiliates		X
Due from officers, partners		X
Equipment		X
Face value of life insurance		X
Finished goods		X
General partnerships		X
Goodwill		X
Income tax refund	X	
Inventory		X
Investment in affiliates		X
Investment in real estate		X
Land		X
Leasehold improvements		X
Limited partnerships		X
Marketable securities	X	
Money market accounts	X	
Non-readily marketable securities		X
Notes receivable		X
Operating rights		X
Personal property		X
Pension funds		X
Prepaid expenses		X
Residential real estate		X
Retirement accounts (401ks, IRAs)		X
Securities (privately held)		X
Trademarks		X
Trusts		X
Work -in-process		X

Liabilities and Equity Classifications	Current*	Noncurrent
Accrued expenses	X	
Cash value life insurance loans	X	
Common stock		X
Credit cards	X	
Current maturities long-term debt	X	
Home equity lines	X	
Home equity loans		X
Income taxes	X	
Long-term debt		X
Margin account loans	X	
Mortgages		X
Notes payable—bank	X	
Paid-in-capital		X
Partnership contributions (due in next year)	X	
Partnership contributions (due over one year)		X
Retained earnings		X
Subordinated debt		X

* To be considered current, the lender must determine whether liabilities and/or equity are expected to be converted to cash in less than 12 months.

of stock in ABC Inc., and the number of shares traded daily is 1,000, the customer cannot readily liquidate the shares. In fact, selling excessive shares in a short period of time could drive down the value of the stock. Unlike a business entity that invests in marketable securities to employ excess funds until they are needed in the business, individuals invest in order to gain wealth or additional income. Mutual funds, typically invested in a variety of stocks, also change in value daily. The Dezines list the current market value of their mutual fund at $32,000. The original investment was $45,000. The lender will want to determine the current value of the fund by obtaining a copy of the most recent statement from the mutual fund.

Securities owned by the applicant and held by brokers in margin accounts are also readily marketable. Usually, they are pledged on margin loans through the broker. Amounts owed on securities are listed on the balance sheet as liabilities due to brokers. Restricted securities are owned by the applicant but have prior restrictions, for example, stock options that cannot be exercised until a later date.

Non-readily marketable securities are common stock held in privately held companies. Most privately held business owners list the value of the business here. The methods used to value privately held companies vary greatly. A company's value can be based on sales volume, as a multiple of net profit, as a combination of the two, or as a multiple of the company's tangible net worth. Non-readily marketable securities usually are deducted from the net worth to determine a tangible net worth.

The Dezines value Designs by Dezine, Inc. at $100,000. This amount seems high, considering the earnings performance of the company. The value of the company's stock on the personal financial statement should approximate the total equity of the company, multiplied by the percentage of ownership. The equity should be adjusted to represent the "true" value of the assets, which would usually increase the equity. Linda Dezine owns 100 percent of Designs by Dezine, Inc. The value listed for the company should be zero because the company has a negative net worth. The net worth will need to be adjusted for this change to calculate adjusted net worth.

Life insurance is summarized in schedule 4 (exhibit 7.1). The **net cash value**—the amount of cash the insurance policy is currently worth—is listed on the personal balance sheet as an asset. The **face value** of life insurance is the amount payable upon death. Schedule 4 summarizes the insurance company, face amount of the policy, type of policy, beneficiary, cash surrender value, amount borrowed against the policy (if any), and the owner. A lender estimates whether the insurance policy is sufficient to pay estate taxes upon the death of the business owner. In a privately held business, estate planning can be complicated. Usually, a customer's personal attorney can verify the estimate of estate taxes. A lender asks the customer for permission to contact the attorney. In some cases, a letter from the attorney is sufficient. If the life insurance were insufficient, the company or other assets would have to be liquidated or sold to pay the estate taxes.

The amount of disability insurance also is determined. A lender calculates whether the amount of the monthly disability payments to be received if the owner becomes disabled will be sufficient to pay the loan applicants' current obligations. The Dezines indicate each of them has a $200,000 face value life insurance policy with cash value of $10,000. This amount may or may not be sufficient to pay estate taxes. The amount of estate taxes will depend on the value of the assets at the time of the Dezine's death.

Real estate is listed on schedule 5 (exhibit 7.1). Residential real estate includes the applicants' personal residence and secondary personal residences. Investment property includes real estate, such as apartment buildings and commercial buildings owned for business purposes. A completed schedule shows the property address, legal owner, purchase year and price, market value, present loan balance, interest rate, loan maturity date, monthly payment, and name of the lender. The lender compares the names of the legal owner with the names of the people providing the financial statement. If the financial statement is submitted by one individual and the property is owned by two individuals, the asset and the equity in the property is deducted from the net worth because the individual cannot convert the asset to cash without the permission of the other owner. If the second owner is a joint borrower, the asset and equity in the property are considered.

The year and purchase price are important because real estate values vary over time. Real estate usually increases in value, but it can decrease in value. If the owner purchased the real estate in a high market, the property could be worth less than the purchase price. In most cases, real estate is a source of equity available to the borrower. However, it is not very liquid to the lender, due to the amount of time it would take to foreclose and liquidate. When analyzing investment property, a lender needs to consider the amount of rental income, the expenses to maintain the property, and the debt service requirements. The expense for investment property is compared to the rental payments and other expenses on page one of the financial statement.

The Dezines' personal financial statement reports real estate valued at $700,000, which is higher than the original cost. Because the Dezines did not submit a new appraisal to support the stated value of their home, the lender needs to determine the method and source of the valuations. In a discussion with the Dezines, the lender learned that the couple increased the value after a $100,000 remodeling project. The lender must determine whether the remodeling really added value to the home or if the home is now overvalued. Also, some properties can be overimproved. This means that a property worth more than other properties in a neighborhood may not receive its stated value when sold.

The partnerships' section of the personal financial statement refers to the amount of equity the applicant holds in businesses, tax shelters, and other investments. The lender has to determine the type of investment, date of initial investment, cost, percent owned, current market value, balance due on partnership notes, and future contributions due. From the loan applicant, the lender obtains a copy of the partnership financial statement and tax return. General partnerships carry contingent liability, and the total amount of that liability must be determined. Partnerships in tax shelters require future payments that can affect the liquidity of the borrower. The amount, timing, and source of funding are discussed with the borrower. If it is a limited partnership, the limited partner does not incur personal liability. Because there usually is not a market for partnership investments, they are not liquid. The amount listed as an asset in partnerships is deducted from the net worth. The Dezines list no partnerships owned.

The current values of **IRA, Keogh, 401(k)**, profit sharing, and other retirement accounts are considered other noncurrent assets. The lender will want to verify the current value, determine future contributions, when distributions can begin, what type of account the funds are held in, and if any vesting is required. Retirement accounts are not liquid if the owner is not near retirement age. The penalties for early withdrawal of IRA, Keogh, or 401(k) funds are severe, and the tax consequences are significant. The Dezines list $440,000 in IRA and 401k accounts.

Deferred income is the amount of income the borrower has postponed from the employer. Individuals may choose to delay income due to their tax status. Applicants in a high tax bracket, for example, may defer income until they are in a lower tax bracket. Lenders usually deduct deferred income from the net worth because it is not liquid or marketable unless it is paid within 12 months of the date of the statement. The Dezines list no deferred income.

Personal property is the value of household furnishings, automobiles, and other personal items, such as boats, recreational vehicles, art, and collectibles. This amount is usually deducted from the net worth because it is difficult to determine the real value. Used household furnishings are more valuable to the owner than they are at an auction. If the applicant is married, most personal property is considered jointly owned. The Dezines report $50,000 worth of personal property and $35,000 worth of automobiles.

Other assets include antiques and collectibles not listed in personal property. Copies of appraisals or valuation methods are obtained to verify the ownership and value. If appraisals are not obtained, assets are treated as personal assets and the value deducted from the net worth. The Dezines list $35,000 of antiques owned.

Assets are then totaled and balanced to the liabilities and net worth.

Liabilities

Liabilities are amounts owed by the applicant. Loans owed to the bank to which the statement is addressed are listed first. Loans may be secured or unsecured. Secured loans have collateral pledged to the note. Personal collateral includes cash, marketable securities, residence, cash-value life insurance, autos, boats, and motorcycles. Unsecured notes are used for a short period of less than one year. Other unsecured debt, including credit cards, is listed as accounts payable. The lender needs to know the amount of credit available and the amount not used. The interest rates for credit cards may be high compared to those for bank financing, so significant amounts owed on credit cards have an adverse impact on the borrower. A lender obtains a personal credit report and then compares the liabilities listed to those listed on the credit report. Any discrepancies must be discussed with the loan applicant.

Loans payable to banks and others are listed on schedule 7 (exhibit 7.1). This schedule indicates to whom the loan is owed, the name of the financial services company, the amount of the line of credit, whether the loan is secured or unsecured, the collateral, the interest rate, the maturity date of the loan, and the unpaid balance. It is important to know the terms and conditions under which the maturity of the loans would be accelerated. The lender compares the monthly amount due with the income available to repay the debt. Lenders consider their applicant's loans from others as potential sales opportunities. Often, the lender can show the applicant that it is to his or her advantage to refinance the debt by borrowing an amount large enough to pay off all other loans and have a single, smaller, monthly payment. The Dezines owe $11,000 on autos and $3,000 on credit cards.

A **margin account** is an investor's credit account with a broker or dealer, which permits the investor to pay only part of the purchase price and borrow the rest from the broker. The part paid initially—the margin—is a percentage of the total price. This percentage is called the margin requirement. An applicant may appear to have high liquidity but may have large amounts owed on margin. If the price of the stocks drops in value, the applicant may have to come up with cash quickly to pay the amount owed on the margin account or sell the securities to maintain the margin. The Dezines owe no money on margin accounts.

Taxes payable are the amount owed to the IRS and state and local taxing authorities based on current income. Any amount listed here should be for the current year only. Any amounts owed for prior years are a warning sign to the lender that the applicant has problems with illiquidity or disagreements with the IRS. In either case, the reasons for the delinquent payments should be clearly understood, and the lender should proceed only with caution. Another tax issue for the lender to consider is capital gains tax. If the loan applicant has owned real estate or securities that have increased in value, there may be capital gains taxes to pay if these assets were sold.

Life insurance loans, amounts borrowed on life insurance policies, are summarized in schedule 4. These loans are usually at a low interest rate and have no scheduled principal payment due. The Dezines do not owe on their life insurance policies.

Schedule 6 lists mortgages payable. The amount of the mortgages are compared with the original cost of the property. Amounts owed beyond the original cost indicate that the property has been refinanced since it was purchased and that loans against the increased equity have been obtained. The lender should understand the reason for the refinancing. The lender also verifies that real estate taxes are current and that the insurance is for at least the amount of the debt or replacement value of the property. The Dezines owe $410,000 on their residence.

The lender compares the mix of liabilities with the mix of assets. The terms of the liabilities are compared with the life of the asset. For example, residential real estate has a long life, and therefore the term of the liability is expected to be longer than the term of a credit card account. The difference between the assets and liabilities is the applicant's net worth. The Dezines stated net worth is $1,079,000.

Adjusted Net Worth

The borrower's personal financial statement must be adjusted for any overstated valuation of an asset and any understated liabilities. To construct an adjusted personal net worth statement, take the following steps:

- Verify that all assets are owned and all liabilities are owed by the individual(s) presenting the statement.
- Compare reported values of marketable securities to the most recently quoted prices.
- Be sure all marketable securities are properly identified as to where they were traded, the type of security, and how they were valued.
- Compare liabilities to a recent personal credit report.
- Compare the cost of real estate and the date it was acquired against current market value and test the value for reasonableness.
- Verify cash balances and where they are held.
- Verify that the borrower has properly distinguished between the face value and the cash value of any insurance policies owned.
- Verify that all loans are listed and have not been netted (netted amounts are where the applicant lists only the net value of the asset after subtracting the liability).

To calculate the adjusted net worth (illustrated in exhibit 7.4 on the next page), the following deductions are taken from the net worth indicated:

- properties held in names other than the applicant's,
- personal property,
- excessive values of privately held businesses,
- amounts due from relatives, friends, and privately held companies,
- values of IRAs, Keoghs, and other retirement accounts,
- cash value life insurance that is pledged as collateral,
- fractional ownership interests in investments, and
- unlisted securities not supported with financial statements.

The Dezines' adjusted net worth is $408,000, compared to their stated net worth $1,079,000. The adjusted net worth consists primarily of equity in their homestead. The "true" value of the assets cannot be determined until the Dezines sell the assets or the bank liquidates the assets. If liquidated, rarely would a bank recover the stated or adjusted net worth of a company. Therefore, from a lender's assessment, the Dezines' net worth is not liquid, but it also is not atypical for the owner of a privately held business or individuals with large amounts of retirement assets.

Exhibit 7.4 Adjusted Net Worth for Edward G. and Linda C. Dezine	
	(000s omitted)
Stated net worth	$ 1,079
− note receivable Designs by Dezine, Inc	46
− value of Designs by Dezine, Inc	100
− value of personal property/antiques	85
− value of IRAs and 401(k)	440
= adjusted net worth	408

Contingent Liabilities

Contingent liabilities—amounts for which the loan applicant is not directly liable—will need to be repaid at some time in the future. Contingent liabilities include loans guaranteed, outstanding letters of credit, legal actions pending, past-due tax obligations, and future tax liabilities based on the gain in value of the assets. For example, the Dezines may guarantee debt for the company. The amount of the guaranty is listed as a contingent liability. The amounts listed are compared to the annual income to determine the applicant's ability to repay the debt if needed. The Dezines list their personal guaranty of Designs by Dezine, Inc., as their only contingent liability.

Questions, Representations, and Warranties

On the final page of the personal financial statement, the borrower is asked to answer questions about his or her personal finances including whether

- bankruptcy has ever been declared,
- a will has been drawn, and
- any assets have been pledged or debts served except as shown.

The borrower also is asked to list the number of dependents.

A statement of representations and warranties is summarized on the back page before the applicant's signature line. The applicant warrants the information to be true and correct. Representations include the applicant acknowledging that he or she is providing the information needed by the lender to grant a credit request, authorizing the bank to make credit inquiries, and agreeing to supply annual financial statements upon request. The applicant then dates and signs the financial statement. A borrower can be criminally prosecuted for knowingly submitting a fraudulent financial statement to a federally insured financial institution to obtain credit. This is another reason why the financial statement is addressed to the lending bank. Also, it is important to know that debts incurred fraudulently are not dischargeable in bankruptcy.

PERSONAL TAX RETURNS

Federal tax returns are used to verify income and ownership of assets and provide information needed to construct a personal cash flow for a loan applicant. Reported income also is used to test the reasonableness of values assigned to assets.

The personal tax return is a hybrid form of cash accounting. Most personal returns are prepared on a cash basis, except for depreciation. The tax return details the major sources of income net of expenses, which are detailed in supporting schedules. It is important that the borrower supply the total tax return and all supporting schedules. The adjusted gross income on Form 1040 is not the actual amount of income received, nor is it cash. Some forms of income are exempt from taxes. Other types of income may be deferred. Income reported from the sale of assets is net of expenses incurred from the sale. Schedule E (income/loss) rarely bears any relationship to cash flow. Contributions, distributions, and repayments of debt to partners or shareholders of a partnership or S corporation are available only from schedule K-1 and are not reported anywhere in the tax return. Exhibit 7.5 lists a sample of the various tax returns and schedules the lender may need for a complete analysis of personal cash flow.

The U.S. Individual Income Tax Return Form 1040 is the most common form lenders receive. The personal tax return for the year 2001 for Edward G. and Linda C. Dezine (exhibit 7.6 to follow) will be used as an example. IRS publications *Starting a Business and Keeping Records, Publication 583* and *Tax Guide for Small Businesses, Publication 334* are excellent sources when examining personal tax returns for business income.

Initial Review

The lender must first ascertain whose return it is and whether the return is joint or individual. The name, address, and Social Security number should be corroborated with those on the personal financial statement and bank records. In the initial review, a lender verifies that all supporting schedules are included.

Exhibit 7.5 Tax Returns and Selected Schedules	
Form 1040	U.S. Individual Tax Return
Schedule A	Itemized Deductions
Schedule B	Interest and Dividend Income
Schedule C	Profit and Loss from Business
Schedule D	Capital Gains and Losses
Schedule E	Supplemental Income and Loss
Schedule F	Farm Income and Expenses
Form 1065	U.S. Partnership Return of Income
Schedule K-1 (Form 1065)	Partner's Share of Income, Credits, Etc.
Form 1020S	U.S. Income Tax Return for an S Corporation
Schedule K-1 (Form 1120S)	Shareholder's Share of Income, Credits, Etc.
Form 4562	Depreciation and Amortization
Form 4797	Sale of Business Property

Analysis of Income

Income received is listed on lines 7 through 21 of the tax return. The key questions on income are:

- Was it really cash received?
- What was the source?
- Will it recur?
- What amount is noncash income (depreciation)?
- What amount is available to the individual?

Line 7: Wages and Salaries

This line includes only wages paid by employers. Income from sole proprietorships or partnerships is not included, but salaries from employers or S corporations are reported on line 7. Use the W-2 form to verify wages. Reported income is net of pretax deductions, such as 401(k) contributions. Reported income can include noncash benefits, such as personal use of a company vehicle. A lender should verify the mix and amount of income for this line. In 2001, the Dezines reported wages of $159,588 from Designs by Dezine, Inc., Structured Engineering Corp., and Linda's previous employer, Interiors Inc. Compare the amount from Designs by Dezine, Inc. to the corporate tax return (exhibit 7.7 on page 238).

Line 8: Taxable Interest Income

The amount on line 8 is itemized on schedule B. Interest income includes taxable and tax-exempt interest earned on deposits, bonds, notes, mortgages, and accounts receivables. Compare the amounts reported on line 8 to the personal financial statement, to ensure that the income will continue. The Dezines received $2,428 in interest income, which is listed on schedule B. A lender verifies the current account balances and determines whether the deposits are expected to remain the same in the future. This will tell the lender if the income will recur in 2002. The lender also reviews predicted interest rates for the coming years. If rates are expected to fall, the interest income may decrease even if the deposits remain the same.

Line 9: Dividend Income

The amount of dividend income is itemized on schedule B. A distinction must be made between dividends and capital gains. Capital gains, but not dividends, are reported on schedule D. The Dezines own a mutual fund account that received $8 in dividends in 2001.

Line 10: State Income Tax Refunds

Verify the amount reported on line 10 with the previous year's state income tax return. Generally, amounts reported on line 10 are not recurring and are not considered as cash available to service future debt. The Dezines list no previous state income tax refunds.

Line 11: Alimony

Verify the terms of the alimony payments with the divorce decree. If the payment is to be discontinued in the near future, the lender needs to take that into account when assessing the ability to repay long-term loans. Review the divorce decree to determine if there are any escalation clauses in the payments.

Line 12: Business Income

Schedule C details all income and expenses from sole proprietorships. In schedule C, Linda Dezine indicates that she also owns a teaching and consulting company. This company provides seminars to contractor associations and consults with other contractors on remodeling projects. The company indicates gross receipts of $39,587 on schedule C. A net income of $39,518 is reported on line 12.

Line 13: Capital Gain and Loss

Gains and losses occur when assets are sold for more or less than their value. Determine from schedule D if cash was received and whether the gains are a continuing source of income. If they are not going to continue, gains are subtracted from the income when determining the ability to repay future loans. If the gain results from an installment sale, report the sale on schedule D and Form 6252. The Dezines are reporting a loss on sale of securities of $1,324 from their mutual fund.

Line 14: Other Gains and Losses

Amounts listed on line 14 are from miscellaneous income arising from the sale of business assets and are generally nonrecurring. Therefore, do not consider amounts on line 14 as sources of income to repay future debt.

Line 15a and 16a: IRA Distributions and Pensions and Annuities

This is the taxable portion of amounts disbursed to the individual. If the individual is not eligible for retirement, then amounts taken out early are subject to penalty. If the individual is retired, distributions should be received in the future. The amount to be received depends on the value of retirement accounts. Verify distributions with the amount listed on the personal financial statement.

Line 17: Rents, Royalties, Partnerships, Estates, and Trusts

Report the amount listed on line 17 on Schedule E. Reported income is not necessarily cash. Amounts reported are net of depreciation and amortization. For partnerships, use Form 1065, U.S. Partnership Income, Credits, Deductions and Schedule K-1. For S Corporations, use Form 1120 S U.S. Income Tax Return for an S Corporation and the corresponding Schedule K-1. These forms detail the amount of cash received or paid out by the individual. The Dezines report a net loss of $26,031 on Schedule E part II. This is the net amount of taxable loss from Designs by Dezine, Inc., after allowable deductions.

Line 18: Farm Income Schedule F

Line 18 lists net farm income after all expenses. A lender considers future crop prices, crops on hand, future prices of livestock, and other variables that affect agricultural income.

Lines 19-21: Unemployment, Social Security Benefits, and Other Income

Verify any amounts listed on these lines to determine if they would continue. Unemployment benefits, which carry a maximum payment time frame, are not considered a continuing source of income. Other income may not occur in the future, and the source should be verified. The Dezines report $8,900 of other income.

Line 22: Line Totals

Line 22 is the total of lines 7 through 21. For the Dezines, the total income listed is $183,087. A lender needs to determine how much of that was cash received and how much income was lowered due to noncash deductions for depreciation and amortization. Schedule E and Form 4562 summarize depreciation and amortization. The Dezines funded the loss of $26,031 on Form 1120S with a note payable to shareholder. This form will be discussed later when the 1120S and personal cash flow are reviewed.

Lines 23-30: Adjustments to Income

Usually, adjustments to income are not recurring, except for IRA and retirement contributions. The $800 the Dezines list on line 27 represents one-half of the self-employment tax due for the consulting/teaching business. Line 28 lists the deductible portion of the self-employed health insurance deduction.

Line 36: Itemized Deductions

Itemized deductions listed on schedule A include cash and noncash deductions. For example, a donation of a used vehicle to a charitable organization is a noncash deduction. After investigation, the lender determined that all the itemized deductions, with the exception of the $500 charitable contribution, were cash deductions. Medical expenses on line 1 rarely exceed the amount to be deducted, yet are a cash outlay. Compare the state taxes listed on line 5 to the W-2s. Use local county records to verify information on line 6. Check the home interest on line 10 with the information given on the personal financial statement. Discuss the contributions on lines 15 and 16 with the loan applicant to determine whether these commitments will continue in the future. The total on line 28, schedule A, does not add up because the IRS limits the amount. The amount is limited because the income reported on line 34 of form 1040 is over $132,950.

Line 58: Total Tax Due

The amount of taxes due is taken from one of the tax rate schedules and adjusted for credits (lines 43-50) and other taxes (lines 53-58). The lender compares this amount to total tax payments on line 58. Tax payments may be withheld, as indicated on a W-2, or estimated taxes may have been paid. To avoid a penalty, estimates must be within $500 of the total tax due. Total tax due can vary greatly with Sub S corporations because of the amount of income or loss reported by the corporation. The Dezines are receiving a large refund and should consider amending their estimated tax payments for 2002 if they do not expect major changes in income or deductions. If the Dezines amend their estimated tax payments, this would increase their monthly cash flow and their ability to repay their debt.

S CORPORATION TAX ANALYSIS

Exhibit 7.7 is the corporate tax return form 1120S for Designs by Dezine, Inc. This form summarizes the income statement and gives an abbreviated balance sheet. For the first eight months of operations, Designs by Dezine, Inc., had sales of $384,332 and showed a net loss of $26,031. Many newly started companies show an operating loss the first year of operations. The lender will want to understand what expenses were one-time expenses to begin the company and which expenses are fixed and ongoing. The major expenses were the cost of goods sold, which includes employee wages and materials for remodeling projects. Line 14a lists a noncash expense of $11,866 for depreciation.

The income from Designs by Dezine, Inc., does not flow to the Dezines. The income, or in this case loss, is only reported on the personal tax return. Schedule K1 shows the loss of $26,031, which is also reported on line 17 of the personal tax return. When the company is profitable, a dividend or distribution may be paid to the Dezines to pay income taxes due on the company profits.

The balance sheet on page 4 of 1120S indicates the company owns $60,822 in building and other depreciable assets. These depreciable assets are two company vehicles provided to employees. On line 18 of page 4 is the related debt for the company vehicles. The company also owes Linda Dezine $46,172, which is listed on her personal financial statement as a note receivable in the amount of $46,000. Many customers round personal financial statements to the nearest thousand, so this difference is not material. The personal cash flow is Linda's salary, which is listed as officer's compensation on line 7 of 1120S and included as W-2 wages on the personal tax return line 7 and the note receivable shareholder.

PERSONAL CASH FLOW ANALYSIS

The lender should perform a personal cash flow analysis using the applicant's individual tax return. To analyze personal cash flow, the lender requires two years of personal financial statements and the current year's individual tax return. The Dezines provided the bank with personal financial statements for each year. Exhibit 7.8 on page 244 summarizes the changes to their personal financial statement from 2000 to 2001. The personal financial statement analyzed earlier is as of June 2002, so the numbers listed in exhibit 7.8 do not match the earlier personal financial statement.

Exhibit 7.6   1040 U.S. Individual Income Tax Return

Form **1040**

Department of the Treasury—Internal Revenue Service
U.S. Individual Income Tax Return   2001   (99)   IRS Use Only—Do not write or staple in this space.

For the year Jan. 1–Dec. 31, 2001, or other tax year beginning , 2001, ending , 20   OMB No. 1545-0074

Label
(See instructions on page 19.)

Use the IRS label. Otherwise, please print or type.

Your first name and initial	Last name	Your social security number
Edward G.	Dezine	234 : 56 : 7890
If a joint return, spouse's first name and initial	Last name	Spouse's social security number
Linda C.	Dezine	123 : 45 : 6789

Home address (number and street). If you have a P.O. box, see page 19.   Apt. no.
9425 Norwood Avenue

City, town or post office, state, and ZIP code. If you have a foreign address, see page 19.
Hometown, MN 55378

▲ **Important!** ▲
You **must** enter your SSN(s) above.

Presidential Election Campaign
(See page 19.)

Note. Checking "Yes" will not change your tax or reduce your refund.
Do you, or your spouse if filing a joint return, want $3 to go to this fund? . . . ▶

You   Spouse
☐ Yes ☒ No   ☐ Yes ☒ No

Filing Status

Check only one box.

1 ☐ Single
2 ☒ Married filing joint return (even if only one had income)
3 ☐ Married filing separate return. Enter spouse's social security no. above and full name here. ▶ _____
4 ☐ Head of household (with qualifying person). (See page 19.) If the qualifying person is a child but not your dependent, enter this child's name here. ▶ _____
5 ☐ Qualifying widow(er) with dependent child (year spouse died ▶). (See page 19.)

Exemptions

6a ☒ **Yourself.** If your parent (or someone else) can claim you as a dependent on his or her tax return, **do not** check box 6a . . . .
b ☒ **Spouse** . . . .

If more than six dependents, see page 20.

c **Dependents:**

(1) First name Last name	(2) Dependent's social security number	(3) Dependent's relationship to you	(4) ✔ if qualifying child for child tax credit (see page 20)
Kathy Dezine	345 : 67 : 8901	Parent	☐
			☐
			☐
			☐
			☐
			☐

No. of boxes checked on 6a and 6b   **2**

No. of your children on 6c who:
• lived with you   **1**
• did not live with you due to divorce or separation (see page 20) ____
Dependents on 6c not entered above ____
Add numbers entered on lines above ▶   **3**

d Total number of exemptions claimed . . . .

Income

Attach Forms W-2 and W-2G here. Also attach Form(s) 1099-R if tax was withheld.

If you did not get a W-2, see page 21.

Enclose, but do not attach, any payment. Also, please use Form 1040-V.

7	Wages, salaries, tips, etc. Attach Form(s) W-2	7	159,588
8a	**Taxable interest.** Attach Schedule B if required	8a	2,428
b	**Tax-exempt** interest. **Do not** include on line 8a . . . 8b		
9	Ordinary dividends. Attach Schedule B if required	9	8
10	Taxable refunds, credits, or offsets of state and local income taxes (see page 22) . .	10	
11	Alimony received	11	
12	Business income or (loss). Attach Schedule C or C-EZ	12	39,518
13	Capital gain or (loss). Attach Schedule D if required. If not required, check here ▶ ☐	13	(1,324)
14	Other gains or (losses). Attach Form 4797	14	
15a	Total IRA distributions . 15a b Taxable amount (see page 23)	15b	
16a	Total pensions and annuities 16a b Taxable amount (see page 23)	16b	
17	Rental real estate, royalties, partnerships, S corporations, trusts, etc. Attach Schedule E	17	(26,031)
18	Farm income or (loss). Attach Schedule F	18	
19	Unemployment compensation	19	
20a	Social security benefits . 20a b Taxable amount (see page 25)	20b	
21	Other income. List type and amount (see page 27) _____	21	8,900
22	Add the amounts in the far right column for lines 7 through 21. This is your **total income** ▶	22	183,087

Adjusted Gross Income

23	IRA deduction (see page 27)	23	
24	Student loan interest deduction (see page 28)	24	
25	Archer MSA deduction. Attach Form 8853	25	
26	Moving expenses. Attach Form 3903	26	
27	One-half of self-employment tax. Attach Schedule SE .	27	800
28	Self-employed health insurance deduction (see page 30)	28	1,978
29	Self-employed SEP, SIMPLE, and qualified plans . .	29	
30	Penalty on early withdrawal of savings	30	
31a	Alimony paid b Recipient's SSN ▶ _____	31a	
32	Add lines 23 through 31a	32	2,778
33	Subtract line 32 from line 22. This is your **adjusted gross income** . . . . . ▶	33	180,309

For Disclosure, Privacy Act, and Paperwork Reduction Act Notice, see page 72.   Cat. No. 11320B   Form **1040** (2001)

Tax and Credits	34	Amount from line 33 (adjusted gross income)	**34** 180,309

Standard Deduction for—

- People who checked any box on line 35a or 35b **or** who can be claimed as a dependent, see page 31.
- All others:

Single, $4,550

Head of household, $6,650

Married filing jointly or Qualifying widow(er), $7,600

Married filing separately, $3,800

35a	Check if: ☐ **You** were 65 or older, ☐ Blind; ☐ **Spouse** was 65 or older, ☐ Blind. Add the number of boxes checked above and enter the total here . . . . ▶ **35a**	
b	If you are married filing separately and your spouse itemizes deductions, or you were a dual-status alien, see page 31 and check here . . . . . . ▶ **35b** ☐	
36	**Itemized deductions** (from Schedule A) **or** your **standard deduction** (see left margin) . .	**36** 71,294
37	Subtract line 36 from line 34	**37** 109,015
38	If line 34 is $99,725 or less, multiply $2,900 by the total number of exemptions claimed on line 6d. If line 34 is over $99,725, see the worksheet on page 32	**38** 8,700
39	**Taxable income.** Subtract line 38 from line 37. If line 38 is more than line 37, enter -0-	**39** 100,315
40	**Tax** (see page 33). Check if any tax is from **a** ☐ Form(s) 8814 **b** ☐ Form 4972 . .	**40** 21,937
41	**Alternative minimum tax** (see page 34). Attach Form 6251	**41**
42	Add lines 40 and 41 . . . . ▶	**42** 21,937
43	Foreign tax credit. Attach Form 1116 if required . . . **43**	
44	Credit for child and dependent care expenses. Attach Form 2441 **44**	
45	Credit for the elderly or the disabled. Attach Schedule R . . **45**	
46	Education credits. Attach Form 8863 . . . . **46**	
47	Rate reduction credit. See the worksheet on page 36 . . . **47**	
48	Child tax credit (see page 37) **48**	
49	Adoption credit. Attach Form 8839 . . . . **49**	
50	Other credits from: **a** ☐ Form 3800 **b** ☐ Form 8396 **c** ☐ Form 8801 **d** ☐ Form (specify) _____ **50**	
51	Add lines 43 through 50. These are your **total credits**	**51**
52	Subtract line 51 from line 42. If line 51 is more than line 42, enter -0- . . . . . . ▶	**52** 21,937

Other Taxes	53	Self-employment tax. Attach Schedule SE	**53** 1,600
	54	Social security and Medicare tax on tip income not reported to employer. Attach Form 4137	**54**
	55	Tax on qualified plans, including IRAs, and other tax-favored accounts. Attach Form 5329 if required .	**55**
	56	Advance earned income credit payments from Form(s) W-2	**56**
	57	Household employment taxes. Attach Schedule H	**57**
	58	Add lines 52 through 57. This is your **total tax** . . . . ▶	**58** 23,537

Payments	59	Federal income tax withheld from Forms W-2 and 1099 . . **59** 28,359	
	60	2001 estimated tax payments and amount applied from 2000 return . **60**	

If you have a qualifying child, attach Schedule EIC.

61a	**Earned income credit (EIC)** **61a**	
b	Nontaxable earned income . . **61b**	
62	Excess social security and RRTA tax withheld (see page 51) **62** 930	
63	Additional child tax credit. Attach Form 8812 . . . . **63**	
64	Amount paid with request for extension to file (see page 51) **64**	
65	Other payments. Check if from **a** ☐ Form 2439 **b** ☐ Form 4136 **65**	
66	Add lines 59, 60, 61a, and 62 through 65. These are your **total payments** . . . . ▶	**66** 29,289

Refund	67	If line 66 is more than line 58, subtract line 58 from line 66. This is the amount you **overpaid**	**67** 5,752

Direct deposit? See page 51 and fill in 68b, 68c, and 68d.

68a	Amount of line 67 you want **refunded to you** . . . . ▶	**68a**
▶ b	Routing number _____ ▶ c Type: ☐ Checking ☐ Savings	
▶ d	Account number _____	
69	Amount of line 67 you want **applied to your 2002 estimated tax** ▶ **69**	

Amount You Owe	70	**Amount you owe.** Subtract line 66 from line 58. For details on how to pay, see page 52 ▶	**70**
	71	Estimated tax penalty. Also include on line 70 . . . . . **71**	

Third Party Designee	Do you want to allow another person to discuss this return with the IRS (see page 53)? ☐ **Yes.** Complete the following. ☐ **No**	

Designee's name ▶   Phone no. ▶ ( )   Personal identification number (PIN) ▶

Sign Here

Under penalties of perjury, I declare that I have examined this return and accompanying schedules and statements, and to the best of my knowledge and belief, they are true, correct, and complete. Declaration of preparer (other than taxpayer) is based on all information of which preparer has any knowledge.

Joint return? See page 19. Keep a copy for your records.

Your signature	Date	Your occupation	Daytime phone number
Edward G. Dezine	4/15/02	Engineer	( )
Spouse's signature. If a joint return, **both** must sign.	Date	Spouse's occupation	
Linda C. Dezine	4/15/02	Self Employed	

Paid Preparer's Use Only

Preparer's signature ▶	Date	Check if self-employed ☐	Preparer's SSN or PTIN
Firm's name (or yours if self-employed), address, and ZIP code ▶		EIN	
		Phone no.	( )

Form **1040** (2001)

SCHEDULES A&B
(Form 1040)

Department of the Treasury
Internal Revenue Service (99)

Schedule A—Itemized Deductions

(Schedule B is on back)

► **Attach to Form 1040.** ► **See Instructions for Schedules A and B (Form 1040).**

OMB No. 1545-0074

20**01**

Attachment
Sequence No. **07**

Name(s) shown on Form 1040

Your social security number

Medical and Dental Expenses		**Caution.** Do not include expenses reimbursed or paid by others.				
	1	Medical and dental expenses (see page A-2)	1	1,318		
	2	Enter amount from Form 1040, line 34 . **2**				
	3	Multiply line 2 above by 7.5% (.075)	3	13,523		
	4	Subtract line 3 from line 1. If line 3 is more than line 1, enter -0-			4	0
Taxes You Paid (See page A-2.)	5	State and local income taxes	5	8,866		
	6	Real estate taxes (see page A-2)	6	3,221		
	7	Personal property taxes	7	188		
	8	Other taxes. List type and amount ►				
			8			
	9	Add lines 5 through 8			9	12,275
Interest You Paid (See page A-3.)	10	Home mortgage interest and points reported to you on Form 1098	10	29,410		
	11	Home mortgage interest not reported to you on Form 1098. If paid to the person from whom you bought the home, see page A-3 and show that person's name, identifying no., and address ►				
Note. Personal interest is not deductible.			11			
	12	Points not reported to you on Form 1098. See page A-3 for special rules	12			
	13	Investment interest. Attach Form 4952 if required. (See page A-3.)	13			
	14	Add lines 10 through 13			14	29,410
Gifts to Charity If you made a gift and got a benefit for it, see page A 4.	15	Gifts by cash or check. If you made any gift of $250 or more, see page A-4	15	30,530		
	16	Other than by cash or check. If any gift of $250 or more, see page A-4. You **must** attach Form 8283 if over $500	16	500		
	17	Carryover from prior year	17			
	18	Add lines 15 through 17			18	31,030
Casualty and Theft Losses	19	Casualty or theft loss(es). Attach Form 4684. (See page A-5.)			19	
Job Expenses and Most Other Miscellaneous Deductions (See page A-5 for expenses to deduct here.)	20	Unreimbursed employee expenses—job travel, union dues, job education, etc. You **must** attach Form 2106 or 2106-EZ if required. (See page A-5.) ►				
			20			
	21	Tax preparation fees	21	250		
	22	Other expenses—investment, safe deposit box, etc. List type and amount ►				
			22	105		
	23	Add lines 20 through 22	23	355		
	24	Enter amount from Form 1040, line 34 . **24**				
	25	Multiply line 24 above by 2% (.02)	25	3,606		
	26	Subtract line 25 from line 23. If line 25 is more than line 23, enter -0-			26	0
Other Miscellaneous Deductions	27	Other—from list on page A-6. List type and amount ►				
					27	71,294
Total Itemized Deductions	28	Is Form 1040, line 34, over $132,950 (over $66,475 if married filing separately)?				
		☐ **No.** Your deduction is not limited. Add the amounts in the far right column for lines 4 through 27. Also, enter this amount on Form 1040, line 36. ⎬ ►			28	
		☒ **Yes.** Your deduction may be limited. See page A-6 for the amount to enter.				

For Paperwork Reduction Act Notice, see Form 1040 instructions.   Cat. No. 11330X   **Schedule A (Form 1040) 2001**

Name(s) shown on Form 1040. Do not enter name and social security number if shown on other side.	**Your social security number**

Schedule B—Interest and Ordinary Dividends

Attachment Sequence No. **08**

		Amount
Part I **Interest** (See page B-1 and the instructions for Form 1040, line 8a.)	**1** List name of payer. If any interest is from a seller-financed mortgage and the buyer used the property as a personal residence, see page B-1 and list this interest first. Also, show that buyer's social security number and address ▶	
	Hometown Bank	2,428
Note. If you received a Form 1099-INT, Form 1099-OID, or substitute statement from a brokerage firm, list the firm's name as the payer and enter the total interest shown on that form.	**1**	

			Amount
2 Add the amounts on line 1	**2**	2,428
3 Excludable interest on series EE and I U.S. savings bonds issued after 1989 from Form 8815, line 14. You **must** attach Form 8815	**3**	
4 Subtract line 3 from line 2. Enter the result here and on Form 1040, line 8a ▶	**4**	2,428

Note. If line 4 is over $400, you must complete Part III.

			Amount
Part II **Ordinary** **Dividends** (See page B-1 and the instructions for Form 1040, line 9.)	**5** List name of payer. Include only ordinary dividends. If you received any capital gain distributions, see the instructions for Form 1040, line 13 ▶		
	National Fund. UC		8
Note. If you received a Form 1099-DIV or substitute statement from a brokerage firm, list the firm's name as the payer and enter the ordinary dividends shown on that form.		**5**	

			Amount
6 Add the amounts on line 5. Enter the total here and on Form 1040, line 9 . ▶		**6**	8

Note. If line 6 is over $400, you must complete Part III.

		Yes	No
Part III **Foreign** **Accounts** **and Trusts** (See page B-2.)	You must complete this part if you **(a)** had over $400 of taxable interest or ordinary dividends; **(b)** had a foreign account; or **(c)** received a distribution from, or were a grantor of, or a transferor to, a foreign trust.		
	7a At any time during 2001, did you have an interest in or a signature or other authority over a financial account in a foreign country, such as a bank account, securities account, or other financial account? See page B-2 for exceptions and filing requirements for Form TD F 90-22.1		X
	b If "Yes," enter the name of the foreign country ▶		
	8 During 2001, did you receive a distribution from, or were you the grantor of, or transferor to, a foreign trust? If "Yes," you may have to file Form 3520. See page B-2		X

For Paperwork Reduction Act Notice, see Form 1040 instructions.   Schedule B (Form 1040) 2001

SCHEDULE C
(Form 1040)

Department of the Treasury
Internal Revenue Service   (99)

Profit or Loss From Business

(Sole Proprietorship)

▶ **Partnerships, joint ventures, etc., must file Form 1065 or Form 1065-B.**

▶ **Attach to Form 1040 or Form 1041.**   ▶ **See Instructions for Schedule C (Form 1040).**

OMB No. 1545-0074

2001

Attachment
Sequence No. **09**

Name of proprietor	Social security number (SSN)
Linda C. Dezine	123 45 6789

A Principal business or profession, including product or service (see page C-1 of the instructions)
Service Teaching

B Enter code from pages C-7 & 8
▶ 6 1 1 0 0 0

C Business name. If no separate business name, leave blank.

D Employer ID number (EIN), if any

E Business address (including suite or room no.) ▶ 9425 Norwood Avenue
City, town or post office, state, and ZIP code   Hometown, MN 55378

F Accounting method: **(1)** ☐ Cash   **(2)** ☐ Accrual   **(3)** ☐ Other (specify) ▶ ....

G Did you "materially participate" in the operation of this business during 2001? If "No," see page C-2 for limit on losses   ☐ Yes ☐ No

H If you started or acquired this business during 2001, check here . . . . ▶ ☐

Part I   Income

1	Gross receipts or sales. **Caution.** If this income was reported to you on Form W-2 and the "Statutory employee" box on that form was checked, see page C-2 and check here . . . . . . ▶ ☐	**1**	39,587
2	Returns and allowances	**2**	
3	Subtract line 2 from line 1	**3**	39,587
4	Cost of goods sold (from line 42 on page 2)	**4**	
5	**Gross profit.** Subtract line 4 from line 3	**5**	39,587
6	Other income, including Federal and state gasoline or fuel tax credit or refund (see page C-3) . . .	**6**	
7	**Gross income.** Add lines 5 and 6 . . . . ▶	**7**	39,587

Part II   Expenses. Enter expenses for business use of your home **only** on line 30.

8	Advertising	**8**		19	Pension and profit-sharing plans	**19**	
9	Bad debts from sales or services (see page C-3) . .	**9**		20	Rent or lease (see page C-4):		
				a	Vehicles, machinery, and equipment .	**20a**	
10	Car and truck expenses (see page C-3)	**10**		**b**	Other business property . .	**20b**	
11	Commissions and fees . .	**11**		21	Repairs and maintenance . .	**21**	
12	Depletion	**12**		22	Supplies (not included in Part III) .	**22**	
13	Depreciation and section 179 expense deduction (not included in Part III) (see page C-3) . .	**13**		23	Taxes and licenses	**23**	
				24	Travel, meals, and entertainment:		
				a	Travel	**24a**	
14	Employee benefit programs (other than on line 19) . . .	**14**		**b**	Meals and entertainment		
15	Insurance (other than health) .	**15**		**c**	Enter nondeductible amount included on line 24b (see page C-5) .		
16	Interest:						
a	Mortgage (paid to banks, etc.) .	**16a**		**d**	Subtract line 24c from line 24b .	**24d**	
b	Other	**16b**		25	Utilities	**25**	
17	Legal and professional services	**17**		26	Wages (less employment credits) .	**26**	
				27	Other expenses (from line 48 on page 2)	**27**	
18	Office expense	**18**	69				

28	**Total expenses** before expenses for business use of home. Add lines 8 through 27 in columns . ▶	**28**	69
29	Tentative profit (loss). Subtract line 28 from line 7	**29**	39,518
30	Expenses for business use of your home. Attach **Form 8829**	**30**	
31	**Net profit or (loss).** Subtract line 30 from line 29. • If a profit, enter on **Form 1040, line 12,** and **also** on **Schedule SE, line 2** (statutory employees, see page C-5). Estates and trusts, enter on Form 1041, line 3. • If a loss, you **must** go to line 32.	**31**	39,518
32	If you have a loss, check the box that describes your investment in this activity (see page C-6). • If you checked 32a, enter the loss on **Form 1040, line 12,** and **also** on **Schedule SE, line 2** (statutory employees, see page C-5). Estates and trusts, enter on Form 1041, line 3. • If you checked 32b, you **must** attach **Form 6198.**	**32a** ☐ All investment is at risk. **32b** ☐ Some investment is not at risk.	

For Paperwork Reduction Act Notice, see Form 1040 instructions.   Cat. No. 11334P   Schedule C (Form 1040) 2001

Part III	**Cost of Goods Sold** (see page C-6)

33 Method(s) used to value closing inventory: **a** ☐ Cost   **b** ☐ Lower of cost or market   **c** ☐ Other (attach explanation)

34 Was there any change in determining quantities, costs, or valuations between opening and closing inventory? If "Yes," attach explanation . . . . ☐ **Yes**   ☐ **No**

35	Inventory at beginning of year. If different from last year's closing inventory, attach explanation . .	**35**
36	Purchases less cost of items withdrawn for personal use	**36**
37	Cost of labor. Do not include any amounts paid to yourself	**37**
38	Materials and supplies	**38**
39	Other costs	**39**
40	Add lines 35 through 39	**40**
41	Inventory at end of year	**41**
42	**Cost of goods sold.** Subtract line 41 from line 40. Enter the result here and on page 1, line 4 . .	**42**

Part IV	**Information on Your Vehicle.** Complete this part **only** if you are claiming car or truck expenses on line 10 and are not required to file Form 4562 for this business. See the instructions for line 13 on page C-3 to find out if you must file.

43 When did you place your vehicle in service for business purposes? (month, day, year) ▶ ..../........../...... .

44 Of the total number of miles you drove your vehicle during 2001, enter the number of miles you used your vehicle for:

a Business .... **b** Commuting .... **c** Other ....

45 Do you (or your spouse) have another vehicle available for personal use? . . . . ☐ **Yes**   ☐ **No**

46 Was your vehicle available for personal use during off-duty hours? . . . . ☐ **Yes**   ☐ **No**

47a Do you have evidence to support your deduction? . . . . ☐ **Yes**   ☐ **No**

   b If "Yes," is the evidence written? . . . . ☐ **Yes**   ☐ **No**

Part V	**Other Expenses.** List below business expenses not included on lines 8–26 or line 30.

....		
....		
....		
....		
....		
....		
....		
....		
....		
....		
48 Total other expenses. Enter here and on page 1, line 27	**48**	

Schedule C (Form 1040) 2001

SCHEDULE D
(Form 1040)

Department of the Treasury
Internal Revenue Service   (99)

Capital Gains and Losses

▶ Attach to Form 1040.   ▶ See Instructions for Schedule D (Form 1040).

▶ Use Schedule D-1 to list additional transactions for lines 1 and 8.

OMB No. 1545-0074

2001

Attachment
Sequence No. **12**

Name(s) shown on Form 1040

Edward G. and Linda C. Dezine

Your social security number

234 : 56 : 7890

Part I Short-Term Capital Gains and Losses—Assets Held One Year or Less

(a) Description of property (Example: 100 sh. XYZ Co.)	(b) Date acquired (Mo., day, yr.)	(c) Date sold (Mo., day, yr.)	(d) Sales price (see page D-5 of the instructions)	(e) Cost or other basis (see page D-5 of the instructions)	(f) Gain or (loss) Subtract (e) from (d)	
1 Mutual Fund	1-1-01	2-1-01	9,728	11,052	(1,324)	

2 Enter your short-term totals, if any, from Schedule D-1, line 2	**2**	
3 **Total short-term sales price amounts.** Add lines 1 and 2 in column (d)	**3**	9,728

4 Short-term gain from Form 6252 and short-term gain or (loss) from Forms 4684, 6781, and 8824	**4**	
5 Net short-term gain or (loss) from partnerships, S corporations, estates, and trusts from Schedule(s) K-1	**5**	
6 Short-term capital loss carryover. Enter the amount, if any, from line 8 of your 2000 Capital Loss Carryover Worksheet	**6**	( )
7 **Net short-term capital gain or (loss).** Combine lines 1 through 6 in column (f).	**7**	(1,324)

Part II Long-Term Capital Gains and Losses—Assets Held More Than One Year

(a) Description of property (Example: 100 sh. XYZ Co.)	(b) Date acquired (Mo., day, yr.)	(c) Date sold (Mo., day, yr.)	(d) Sales price (see page D-5 of the instructions)	(e) Cost or other basis (see page D-5 of the instructions)	(f) Gain or (loss) Subtract (e) from (d)	(g) 28% rate gain or (loss) * (see instr. below)
8						

9 Enter your long-term totals, if any, from Schedule D-1, line 9	**9**	
10 **Total long-term sales price amounts.** Add lines 8 and 9 in column (d)	**10**	

11 Gain from Form 4797, Part I; long-term gain from Forms 2439 and 6252; and long-term gain or (loss) from Forms 4684, 6781, and 8824	**11**	
12 Net long-term gain or (loss) from partnerships, S corporations, estates, and trusts from Schedule(s) K-1.	**12**	
13 Capital gain distributions. See page D-1 of the instructions	**13**	
14 Long-term capital loss carryover. Enter in both columns (f) and (g) the amount, if any, from line 13 of your 2000 Capital Loss Carryover Worksheet	**14**	( ) ( )
15 Combine lines 8 through 14 in column (g)	**15**	
16 **Net long-term capital gain or (loss).** Combine lines 8 through 14 in column (f) **Next:** Go to Part III on the back.	**16**	0

*
28% rate gain or loss includes **all** "collectibles gains and losses" (as defined on page D-6 of the instructions) and up to 50% of the eligible gain on qualified small business stock (see page D-4 of the instructions).

For Paperwork Reduction Act Notice, see Form 1040 instructions.   Cat. No. 11338H   Schedule D (Form 1040) 2001

Part III   **Taxable Gain or Deductible Loss**

17   Combine lines 7 and 16 and enter the result. If a loss, go to line 18. If a gain, enter the gain on Form 1040, line 13, and complete Form 1040 through line 39 . . . . | **17** |

    Next: • If both lines 16 and 17 are gains **and** Form 1040, line 39, is more than zero, complete Part IV below.

            • Otherwise, skip the rest of Schedule D and complete Form 1040.

18   If line 17 is a loss, enter here and on Form 1040, line 13, the **smaller** of **(a)** that loss or **(b)** ($3,000) (or, if married filing separately, ($1,500)). Then complete Form 1040 through line 37 | **18** | (   ) |

    Next: • If the loss on line 17 is more than the loss on line 18 **or** if Form 1040, line 37, is less than zero, skip **Part IV** below and complete the **Capital Loss Carryover Worksheet** on page D-6 of the instructions before completing the rest of Form 1040.

            • Otherwise, skip **Part IV** below and complete the rest of Form 1040.

Part IV   **Tax Computation Using Maximum Capital Gains Rates**

19   Enter your unrecaptured section 1250 gain, if any, from line 17 of the worksheet on page D-7 of the instructions . . . . . | **19** |

    If line 15 or line 19 is more than zero, complete the worksheet on page D-9 of the instructions to figure the amount to enter on lines 22, 29, and 40 below, and skip all other lines below. Otherwise, go to line 20.

20   Enter your taxable income from Form 1040, line 39 . . . . . . | **20** |

21   Enter the **smaller** of line 16 or line 17 of Schedule D . . . . | **21** |

22   If you are deducting investment interest expense on Form 4952, enter the amount from Form 4952, line 4e. Otherwise, enter -0- | **22** |

23   Subtract line 22 from line 21. If zero or less, enter -0- . . . . . | **23** |

24   Subtract line 23 from line 20. If zero or less, enter -0- . . . . . | **24** |

25   Figure the tax on the amount on line 24. Use the Tax Table or Tax Rate Schedules, whichever applies | **25** |

26   Enter the **smaller** of:

     • The amount on line 20 **or**

     • $45,200 if married filing jointly or qualifying widow(er);

       $27,050 if single;

       $36,250 if head of household; or

       $22,600 if married filing separately   . . . | **26** |

    If line 26 is greater than line 24, go to line 27. Otherwise, skip lines 27 through 33 and go to line 34.

27   Enter the amount from line 24 . . . . | **27** |

28   Subtract line 27 from line 26. If zero or less, enter -0- and go to line 34 | **28** |

29   Enter your qualified 5-year gain, if any, from line 7 of the worksheet on page D-8 . . | **29** |

30   Enter the **smaller** of line 28 or line 29 . . . . | **30** |

31   Multiply line 30 by 8% (.08) . . . . | **31** |

32   Subtract line 30 from line 28 . . . . | **32** |

33   Multiply line 32 by 10% (.10) . . . . | **33** |

    If the amounts on lines 23 and 28 are the same, skip lines 34 through 37 and go to line 38.

34   Enter the **smaller** of line 20 or line 23 . . . . | **34** |

35   Enter the amount from line 28 (if line 28 is blank, enter -0-) . . . | **35** |

36   Subtract line 35 from line 34 . . . . | **36** |

37   Multiply line 36 by 20% (.20) . . . . | **37** |

38   Add lines 25, 31, 33, and 37 . . . . | **38** |

39   Figure the tax on the amount on line 20. Use the Tax Table or Tax Rate Schedules, whichever applies | **39** |

40   **Tax on all taxable income (including capital gains). Enter the smaller of line 38 or line 39 here and on Form 1040, line 40** . . . . | **40** |

✺

Supplemental Income and Loss

(From rental real estate, royalties, partnerships, S corporations, estates, trusts, REMICs, etc.)

▶ Attach to Form 1040 or Form 1041.   ▶ See Instructions for Schedule E (Form 1040).

OMB No. 1545-0074

2001

Attachment
Sequence No. **13**

Name(s) shown on return

Edward G. and Linda C. Dezine

Your social security number

234 56 7890

Part I **Income or Loss From Rental Real Estate and Royalties** Note. If you are in the business of renting personal property, use **Schedule C** or **C-EZ** (see page E-1). Report farm rental income or loss from **Form 4835** on page 2, line 39.

1	Show the kind and location of each **rental real estate property:**		2	For each rental real estate property listed on line 1, did you or your family use it during the tax year for personal purposes for more than the greater of:	Yes	No
A	....			• 14 days **or** • 10% of the total days rented at fair rental value? (See page E-1.) A		
B	....			B		
C	....			C		

Income:			Properties			Totals (Add columns A, B, and C)
			A	B	C	
3 Rents received	3					3
4 Royalties received	4					4
Expenses:						
5 Advertising	5					
6 Auto and travel (see page E-2) .	6					
7 Cleaning and maintenance . . .	7					
8 Commissions	8					
9 Insurance	9					
10 Legal and other professional fees	10					
11 Management fees	11					
12 Mortgage interest paid to banks, etc. (see page E-2)	12					12
13 Other interest	13					
14 Repairs	14					
15 Supplies	15					
16 Taxes	16					
17 Utilities	17					
18 Other (list) ▶	18					
19 Add lines 5 through 18	19					19
20 Depreciation expense or depletion (see page E-3)	20					20
21 Total expenses. Add lines 19 and 20	21					
22 Income or (loss) from rental real estate or royalty properties. Subtract line 21 from line 3 (rents) or line 4 (royalties). If the result is a (loss), see page E-3 to find out if you must file **Form 6198** . . .	22					
23 Deductible rental real estate loss. **Caution.** Your rental real estate loss on line 22 may be limited. See page E-3 to find out if you must file **Form 8582.** Real estate professionals must complete line 42 on page 2	23	(	)(	)(	)	

24	**Income.** Add positive amounts shown on line 22. **Do not** include any losses	24	
25	**Losses.** Add royalty losses from line 22 and rental real estate losses from line 23. Enter total losses here	25	( )
26	**Total rental real estate and royalty income or (loss).** Combine lines 24 and 25. Enter the result here. If Parts II, III, IV, and line 39 on page 2 do not apply to you, also enter this amount on Form 1040, line 17. Otherwise, include this amount in the total on line 40 on page 2	26	

For Paperwork Reduction Act Notice, see Form 1040 instructions.   Cat. No. 11344L   Schedule E (Form 1040) 2001

Name(s) shown on return. Do not enter name and social security number if shown on other side.	Your social security number
Edward G. and Linda C. Dezine	234 : 56 : 7890

Note. If you report amounts from farming or fishing on Schedule E, you must enter your gross income from those activities on line 41 below. Real estate professionals must complete line 42 below.

Part II   **Income or Loss From Partnerships and S Corporations**   **Note.** If you report a loss from an at-risk activity, you **must** check either column **(e)** or **(f)** on line 27 to describe your investment in the activity. See page E-5. If you check column **(f)**, you must attach **Form 6198.**

27	(a) Name	(b) Enter **P** for partnership; **S** for S corporation	(c) Check if foreign partnership	(d) Employer identification number	(e) All is at risk	(f) Some is not at risk
A	Designs by Dezine, Inc.	S		41-1234567	x	
B						
C						
D						
E						

	Passive Income and Loss		Nonpassive Income and Loss		
	(g) Passive loss allowed (attach **Form 8582** if required)	(h) Passive income from **Schedule K–1**	(i) Nonpassive loss from **Schedule K–1**	(j) Section 179 expense deduction from **Form 4562**	(k) Nonpassive income from **Schedule K–1**
A	0		26,031		
B					
C					
D					
E					
28a Totals					
b Totals			26,031		

29	Add columns (h) and (k) of line 28a	**29**	
30	Add columns (g), (i), and (j) of line 28b	**30** (26,031)
31	Total partnership and S corporation income or (loss). Combine lines 29 and 30. Enter the result here and include in the total on line 40 below	**31** (26,031)

Part III   **Income or Loss From Estates and Trusts**

32	(a) Name	(b) Employer identification number
A		
B		

	Passive Income and Loss		Nonpassive Income and Loss	
	(c) Passive deduction or loss allowed (attach **Form 8582** if required)	(d) Passive income from **Schedule K–1**	(e) Deduction or loss from **Schedule K–1**	(f) Other income from **Schedule K–1**
A				
B				
33a Totals				
b Totals				

34	Add columns (d) and (f) of line 33a	**34**	
35	Add columns (c) and (e) of line 33b	**35** ( )
36	Total estate and trust income or (loss). Combine lines 34 and 35. Enter the result here and include in the total on line 40 below	**36**	

Part IV   **Income or Loss From Real Estate Mortgage Investment Conduits (REMICs)—Residual Holder**

37	(a) Name	(b) Employer identification number	(c) Excess inclusion from **Schedules Q,** line 2c (see page E-6)	(d) Taxable income (net loss) from **Schedules Q,** line 1b	(e) Income from **Schedules Q,** line 3b

38	Combine columns (d) and (e) only. Enter the result here and include in the total on line 40 below	**38**	

Part V   **Summary**

39	Net farm rental income or (loss) from **Form 4835.** Also, complete line 41 below	**39**	
40	**Total** income or (loss). Combine lines 26, 31, 36, 38, and 39. Enter the result here and on Form 1040, line 17 ▶	**40**	
41	**Reconciliation of Farming and Fishing Income.** Enter your **gross** farming and fishing income reported on Form 4835, line 7; Schedule K-1 (Form 1065), line 15b; Schedule K-1 (Form 1120S), line 23; and Schedule K-1 (Form 1041), line 14 (see page E-6)	**41**	
42	**Reconciliation for Real Estate Professionals.** If you were a real estate professional (see page E-4), enter the net income or (loss) you reported anywhere on Form 1040 from all rental real estate activities in which you materially participated under the passive activity loss rules . . .	**42**	

✱   Schedule E (Form 1040) 2001

Exhibit 7.7 U.S. Income Tax Return for an S Corporation

| Form **1120S**
Department of the Treasury
Internal Revenue Service | **U.S. Income Tax Return for an S Corporation**
▶ Do not file this form unless the corporation has timely filed
Form 2553 to elect to be an S corporation.
▶ See separate instructions. | OMB No. 1545-0130
2001 |

For calendar year 2001, or tax year beginning _April 29_, 2001, and ending _December 31_, 20 01

A Effective date of election as an S corporation 4-29-01	Use IRS label.	Name Designs by Dezine, Inc.	**C** Employer identification number 41 : 1234567
B Business code no. (see pages 29–31) 233200	Other- wise, print or type.	Number, street, and room or suite no. (If a P.O. box, see page 11 of the instructions.) 9425 Norwood Avenue	**D** Date incorporated 4-29-01
		City or town, state, and ZIP code Hometown, MN 55378	**E** Total assets (see page 11) $ 63,017

F Check applicable boxes: (1) ☐ Initial return (2) ☐ Final return (3) ☐ Name change (4) ☐ Address change (5) ☐ Amended return
G Enter number of shareholders in the corporation at end of the tax year . . . . ▶

*Caution: Include **only** trade or business income and expenses on lines 1a through 21. See page 11 of the instructions for more information.*

Income

1a Gross receipts or sales _384,332_ **b** Less returns and allowances _____ **c** Bal ▶	**1c**	384,332
2 Cost of goods sold (Schedule A, line 8)	**2**	329,976
3 Gross profit. Subtract line 2 from line 1c	**3**	54,356
4 Net gain (loss) from Form 4797, Part II, line 18 *(attach Form 4797)*	**4**	
5 Other income (loss) *(attach schedule)*.	**5**	
6 **Total income (loss).** Combine lines 3 through 5 . . . . ▶	**6**	54,356

Deductions (see page 12 of the instructions for limitations)

7 Compensation of officers	**7**	42,700
8 Salaries and wages (less employment credits)	**8**	
9 Repairs and maintenance	**9**	
10 Bad debts	**10**	
11 Rents.	**11**	786
12 Taxes and licenses	**12**	6,428
13 Interest	**13**	3,414
14a Depreciation *(if required, attach Form 4562)* **14a** 11,866		
b Depreciation claimed on Schedule A and elsewhere on return . . **14b**		
c Subtract line 14b from line 14a	**14c**	11,866
15 Depletion **(Do not deduct oil and gas depletion.)**	**15**	
16 Advertising	**16**	592
17 Pension, profit-sharing, etc., plans	**17**	
18 Employee benefit programs.	**18**	2,353
19 Other deductions *(attach schedule)*	**19**	12,248
20 **Total deductions.** Add the amounts shown in the far right column for lines 7 through 19 . ▶	**20**	80,387
21 Ordinary income (loss) from trade or business activities. Subtract line 20 from line 6. . . .	**21**	(26,031)

Tax and Payments

22 **Tax: a** Excess net passive income tax *(attach schedule)* . . . **22a**		
b Tax from Schedule D (Form 1120S) **22b**		
c Add lines 22a and 22b (see page 16 of the instructions for additional taxes)	**22c**	
23 **Payments: a** 2001 estimated tax payments and amount applied from 2000 return **23a**		
b Tax deposited with Form 7004. . . . . **23b**		
c Credit for Federal tax paid on fuels *(attach Form 4136)* . . . **23c**		
d Add lines 23a through 23c	**23d**	
24 Estimated tax penalty. Check if Form 2220 is attached . . . . ▶ ☐	**24**	
25 **Tax due.** If the total of lines 22c and 24 is larger than line 23d, enter amount owed. See page 4 of the instructions for depository method of payment . . . . ▶	**25**	
26 **Overpayment.** If line 23d is larger than the total of lines 22c and 24, enter amount overpaid ▶	**26**	
27 Enter amount of line 26 you want: **Credited to 2002 estimated tax** ▶ _____ Refunded ▶	**27**	

Sign Here ▶

Under penalties of perjury, I declare that I have examined this return, including accompanying schedules and statements, and to the best of my knowledge and belief, it is true, correct, and complete. Declaration of preparer (other than taxpayer) is based on all information of which preparer has any knowledge.

Linda Dezine	*3/20/01*	*President*	May the IRS discuss this return with the preparer shown below (see instructions)? ☒ **Yes** ☐ **No**
Signature of officer	Date	Title	

Paid Preparer's Use Only	Preparer's signature ▶		Date	Check if self-employed ☐	Preparer's SSN or PTIN
	Firm's name (or yours if self-employed), address, and ZIP code	▶		EIN	
				Phone no. ( )	

For Paperwork Reduction Act Notice, see the separate instructions.   Cat. No. 11510H   Form **1120S** (2001)

Schedule A	**Cost of Goods Sold** (see page 16 of the instructions)		
1	Inventory at beginning of year	**1**	0
2	Purchases	**2**	329,104
3	Cost of labor	**3**	
4	Additional section 263A costs *(attach schedule)*	**4**	
5	Other costs *(attach schedule)*	**5**	872
6	**Total.** Add lines 1 through 5	**6**	329,976
7	Inventory at end of year	**7**	
8	**Cost of goods sold.** Subtract line 7 from line 6. Enter here and on page 1, line 2	**8**	329,976

9a Check all methods used for valuing closing inventory:

    (i) ☐ Cost as described in Regulations section 1.471-3

    (ii) ☐ Lower of cost or market as described in Regulations section 1.471-4

    (iii) ☐ Other (specify method used and attach explanation) ▶ ....

  b Check if there was a writedown of "subnormal" goods as described in Regulations section 1.471-2(c) . . . . ▶ ☐

  c Check if the LIFO inventory method was adopted this tax year for any goods *(if checked, attach Form 970)* . . . . . ▶ ☐

  d If the LIFO inventory method was used for this tax year, enter percentage (or amounts) of closing inventory computed under LIFO **9d**

  e Do the rules of section 263A (for property produced or acquired for resale) apply to the corporation? . . . . ☐ Yes ☒ No

  f Was there any change in determining quantities, cost, or valuations between opening and closing inventory? . . ☐ Yes ☒ No
    If "Yes," attach explanation.

Schedule B	**Other Information**	**Yes**	**No**
1	Check method of accounting: **(a)** ☐ Cash **(b)** ☒ Accrual **(c)** ☐ Other (specify) ▶................................		
2	Refer to the list on pages 29 through 31 of the instructions and state the corporation's principal: **(a)** Business activity ▶ Service .... **(b)** Product or service ▶ Remodeling		
3	Did the corporation at the end of the tax year own, directly or indirectly, 50% or more of the voting stock of a domestic corporation? (For rules of attribution, see section 267(c).) If "Yes," attach a schedule showing: **(a)** name, address, and employer identification number and **(b)** percentage owned.		X
4	Was the corporation a member of a controlled group subject to the provisions of section 1561?		X
5	Check this box if the corporation has filed or is required to file **Form 8264,** Application for Registration of a Tax Shelter . . . . ▶ ☐		
6	Check this box if the corporation issued publicly offered debt instruments with original issue discount . . ▶ ☐ If so, the corporation may have to file **Form 8281,** Information Return for Publicly Offered Original Issue Discount Instruments.		
7	If the corporation: **(a)** filed its election to be an S corporation after 1986, **(b)** was a C corporation before it elected to be an S corporation **or** the corporation acquired an asset with a basis determined by reference to its basis (or the basis of any other property) in the hands of a C corporation, and **(c)** has net unrealized built-in gain (defined in section 1374(d)(1)) in excess of the net recognized built-in gain from prior years, enter the net unrealized built-in gain reduced by net recognized built-in gain from prior years (see page 17 of the instructions) . . . . . ▶ $		
8	Check this box if the corporation had accumulated earnings and profits at the close of the tax year (see page 17 of the instructions) . . . . ▶ ☐		

Note: *If the corporation had assets or operated a business in a foreign country or U.S. possession, it may be required to attach Schedule N (Form 1120), Foreign Operations of U.S. Corporations, to this return. See Schedule N for details.*

Schedule K	**Shareholders' Shares of Income, Credits, Deductions, etc.**		

	(a) Pro rata share items		**(b)** Total amount
Income (Loss)	1 Ordinary income (loss) from trade or business activities (page 1, line 21)	**1**	(26,031)
	2 Net income (loss) from rental real estate activities *(attach Form 8825)*	**2**	
	3a Gross income from other rental activities **3a**		
	b Expenses from other rental activities *(attach schedule)* . **3b**		
	c Net income (loss) from other rental activities. Subtract line 3b from line 3a	**3c**	
	4 Portfolio income (loss):		
	a Interest income	**4a**	3
	b Ordinary dividends	**4b**	
	c Royalty income	**4c**	
	d Net short-term capital gain (loss) *(attach Schedule D (Form 1120S))*.	**4d**	
	e (1) Net long-term capital gain (loss) *(attach Schedule D (Form 1120S))*.	**4e(1)**	
	(2) 28% rate gain (loss) ▶ .... (3) Qualified 5-year gain ▶..................		
	f Other portfolio income (loss) *(attach schedule)*.	**4f**	
	5 Net section 1231 gain (loss) (other than due to casualty or theft) *(attach Form 4797)* . .	**5**	
	6 Other income (loss) *(attach schedule)*	**6**	

Form **1120S** (2001)

| Schedule K | Shareholders' Shares of Income, Credits, Deductions, etc. (*continued*) | | |

		(a) Pro rata share items		**(b)** Total amount	
Deductions	7	Charitable contributions (*attach schedule*)	7		
	8	Section 179 expense deduction (*attach Form 4562*)	8		
	9	Deductions related to portfolio income (loss) (itemize)	9		
	10	Other deductions (*attach schedule*)	10		
Investment Interest	**11a**	Interest expense on investment debts	**11a**		
	b (1)	Investment income included on lines 4a, 4b, 4c, and 4f above	**11b(1)**		
	(2)	Investment expenses included on line 9 above	**11b(2)**		
Credits	**12a**	Credit for alcohol used as a fuel (*attach Form 6478*).	**12a**		
	b	Low-income housing credit:			
	(1)	From partnerships to which section 42(j)(5) applies	**12b(1)**		
	(2)	Other than on line 12b(1).	**12b(2)**		
	c	Qualified rehabilitation expenditures related to rental real estate activities (*attach Form 3468*) .	**12c**		
	d	Credits (other than credits shown on lines 12b and 12c) related to rental real estate activities	**12d**		
	e	Credits related to other rental activities	**12e**		
	13	Other credits	13		
Adjustments and Tax Preference Items	**14a**	Depreciation adjustment on property placed in service after 1986	**14a**	2,966	
	b	Adjusted gain or loss	**14b**		
	c	Depletion (other than oil and gas)	**14c**		
	d (1)	Gross income from oil, gas, or geothermal properties	**14d(1)**		
	(2)	Deductions allocable to oil, gas, or geothermal properties	**14d(2)**		
	e	Other adjustments and tax preference items (*attach schedule*)	**14e**		
Foreign Taxes	**15a**	Name of foreign country or U.S. possession ▶			
	b	Gross income from all sources	**15b**		
	c	Gross income sourced at shareholder level	**15c**		
	d	Foreign gross income sourced at corporate level:			
	(1)	Passive	**15d(1)**		
	(2)	Listed categories (*attach schedule*)	**15d(2)**		
	(3)	General limitation	**15d(3)**		
	e	Deductions allocated and apportioned at shareholder level:			
	(1)	Interest expense	**15e(1)**		
	(2)	Other	**15e(2)**		
	f	Deductions allocated and apportioned at corporate level to foreign source income:			
	(1)	Passive	**15f(1)**		
	(2)	Listed categories (*attach schedule*)	**15f(2)**		
	(3)	General limitation	**15f(3)**		
	g	Total foreign taxes (check one): ▶ ☐ Paid ☐ Accrued . . .	**15g**		
	h	Reduction in taxes available for credit (*attach schedule*)	**15h**		
Other	16	Section 59(e)(2) expenditures: **a** Type ▶ .... **b** Amount ▶	**16b**		
	17	Tax-exempt interest income	17		
	18	Other tax-exempt income	18		
	19	Nondeductible expenses	19		
	20	Total property distributions (including cash) other than dividends reported on line 22 below	20		
	21	Other items and amounts required to be reported separately to shareholders (*attach schedule*)			
	22	Total dividend distributions paid from accumulated earnings and profits	22		
	23	**Income (loss).** (Required only if Schedule M-1 must be completed.) Combine lines 1 through 6 in column (b). From the result, subtract the sum of lines 7 through 11a, 15g, and 16b .	23	(26,028)	

Form **1120S** (2001)

Schedule L — Balance Sheets per Books

Assets	Beginning of tax year (a)	(b)	End of tax year (c)	(d)
1 Cash				6,053
2a Trade notes and accounts receivable . .			8,000	
b Less allowance for bad debts				8,000
3 Inventories				8
4 U.S. Government obligations				
5 Tax-exempt securities				
6 Other current assets (attach schedule) .				
7 Loans to shareholders				
8 Mortgage and real estate loans . . .				
9 Other investments (attach schedule) . .				
10a Buildings and other depreciable assets .			60,822	
b Less accumulated depreciation . . .			11,866	48,956
11a Depletable assets				
b Less accumulated depletion				
12 Land (net of any amortization)				
13a Intangible assets (amortizable only) . .				
b Less accumulated amortization				
14 Other assets (attach schedule)				
15 Total assets			0	63.025
Liabilities and Shareholders' Equity				
16 Accounts payable				
17 Mortgages, notes, bonds payable in less than 1 year				
18 Other current liabilities (attach schedule) .				2,520
19 Loans from shareholders				46,172
20 Mortgages, notes, bonds payable in 1 year or more				40,064
21 Other liabilities (attach schedule) . . .				
22 Capital stock				300
23 Additional paid-in capital				
24 Retained earnings				(26,031)
25 Adjustments to shareholders' equity (attach schedule)				
26 Less cost of treasury stock	(	)	(	)
27 Total liabilities and shareholders' equity . .			0	63,025

Schedule M-1 — Reconciliation of Income (Loss) per Books With Income (Loss) per Return (You are not required to complete this schedule if the total assets on line 15, column (d), of Schedule L are less than $25,000.)

1 Net income (loss) per books	(26,037)	5 Income recorded on books this year not included on Schedule K, lines 1 through 6 (itemize):		
2 Income included on Schedule K, lines 1 through 6, not recorded on books this year (itemize):		a Tax-exempt interest $		
3 Expenses recorded on books this year not included on Schedule K, lines 1 through 11a, 15g, and 16b (itemize):		6 Deductions included on Schedule K, lines 1 through 11a, 15g, and 16b, not charged against book income this year (itemize):		
a Depreciation $		a Depreciation $		
b Travel and entertainment $				
	9	7 Add lines 5 and 6.		
4 Add lines 1 through 3.	(26,028)	8 Income (loss) (Schedule K, line 23). Line 4 less line 7		(26,028)

Schedule M-2 — Analysis of Accumulated Adjustments Account, Other Adjustments Account, and Shareholders' Undistributed Taxable Income Previously Taxed (see page 27 of the instructions)

	(a) Accumulated adjustments account	(b) Other adjustments account	(c) Shareholders' undistributed taxable income previously taxed
1 Balance at beginning of tax year . . .			
2 Ordinary income from page 1, line 21 . .			
3 Other additions	3		
4 Loss from page 1, line 21	(26,031)		
5 Other reductions	(9)	( )	
6 Combine lines 1 through 5	(26,037)		
7 Distributions other than dividend distributions .			
8 Balance at end of tax year. Subtract line 7 from line 6	(26,037)		

✪   Form **1120S** (2001)

SCHEDULE K-1
(Form 1120S)

Department of the Treasury
Internal Revenue Service

Shareholder's Share of Income, Credits, Deductions, etc.

▶ See separate instructions.

For calendar year 2001 or tax year
beginning _____ , 2001, and ending _____ , 20___

OMB No. 1545-0130

2001

Shareholder's identifying number ▶ 123-45-6789	Corporation's identifying number ▶ 41 1234567
Shareholder's name, address, and ZIP code	Corporation's name, address, and ZIP code
Linda C. Dezine 9425 Norwood Avenue Hometown, MN 55378	Designs by Dezine, Inc. 9425 Norwood Avenue Hometown, MN 55378

A   Shareholder's percentage of stock ownership for tax year (see instructions for Schedule K-1) . . . . . . ▶ ____100__ %

B   Internal Revenue Service Center where corporation filed its return ▶ Ogden, UT 84201 ....

C   Tax shelter registration number (see instructions for Schedule K-1) . . . . ▶ ....

D   Check applicable boxes: **(1)** ☐ Final K-1   **(2)** ☐ Amended K-1

	(a) Pro rata share items		(b) Amount	(c) Form 1040 filers enter the amount in column (b) on:
Income (Loss)	1 Ordinary income (loss) from trade or business activities . . .	1	(26,031)	See page 4 of the Shareholder's Instructions for Schedule K-1 (Form 1120S).
	2 Net income (loss) from rental real estate activities	2		
	3 Net income (loss) from other rental activities	3		
	4 Portfolio income (loss):			
	a Interest	4a		Sch. B, Part I, line 1
	b Ordinary dividends	4b		Sch. B, Part II, line 5
	c Royalties	4c		Sch. E, Part I, line 4
	d Net short-term capital gain (loss).	4d		Sch. D, line 5, col. (f)
	e (1) Net long-term capital gain (loss).	4e(1)		Sch. D, line 12, col. (f)
	(2) 28% rate gain (loss)	4e(2)		Sch. D, line 12, col. (g)
	(3) Qualified 5-year gain	4e(3)		Line 4 of worksheet for Sch. D, line 29
	f Other portfolio income (loss) *(attach schedule)*	4f		(Enter on applicable line of your return.)
	5 Net section 1231 gain (loss) (other than due to casualty or theft)	5		See Shareholder's Instructions for Schedule K-1 (Form 1120S).
	6 Other income (loss) *(attach schedule)*	6		(Enter on applicable line of your return.)
Deductions	7 Charitable contributions *(attach schedule)*	7		Sch. A, line 15 or 16
	8 Section 179 expense deduction	8		See page 6 of the Shareholder's Instructions for Schedule K-1 (Form 1120S).
	9 Deductions related to portfolio income (loss) *(attach schedule)* .	9		
	10 Other deductions *(attach schedule)*	10		
Investment Interest	11a Interest expense on investment debts	11a		Form 4952, line 1
	b (1) Investment income included on lines 4a, 4b, 4c, and 4f above	11b(1)		See Shareholder's Instructions for Schedule K-1 (Form 1120S).
	(2) Investment expenses included on line 9 above	11b(2)		
Credits	12a Credit for alcohol used as fuel	12a		Form 6478, line 10
	b Low-income housing credit:			
	(1) From section 42(j)(5) partnerships	12b(1)		Form 8586, line 5
	(2) Other than on line 12b(1)	12b(2)		
	c Qualified rehabilitation expenditures related to rental real estate activities	12c		
	d Credits (other than credits shown on lines 12b and 12c) related to rental real estate activities	12d		See pages 6 and 7 of the Shareholder's Instructions for Schedule K-1 (Form 1120S).
	e Credits related to other rental activities.	12e		
	13 Other credits	13		

For Paperwork Reduction Act Notice, see the Instructions for Form 1120S.   Cat. No. 11520D   **Schedule K-1 (Form 1120S) 2001**

Form **4562** (Rev. March 2002) Department of the Treasury Internal Revenue Service (99)	**Depreciation and Amortization** **(Including Information on Listed Property)** ▶ **See separate instructions.** ▶ **Attach to your tax return.**	OMB No. 1545-0172 20**01** Attachment Sequence No. **67**
Name(s) shown on return Designs by Dezine, Inc.	Business or activity to which this form relates Remodeling	Identifying number 41-1234567

Part I   Election To Expense Certain Tangible Property Under Section 179
Note: *If you have any listed property, complete Part V before you complete Part I.*

1	Maximum amount. See page 2 of the instructions for a higher limit for certain businesses	**1**	$24,000
2	Total cost of section 179 property placed in service (see page 3 of the instructions)	**2**	
3	Threshold cost of section 179 property before reduction in limitation	**3**	$200,000
4	Reduction in limitation. Subtract line 3 from line 2. If zero or less, enter -0-	**4**	
5	Dollar limitation for tax year. Subtract line 4 from line 1. If zero or less, enter -0-. If married filing separately, see page 3 of the instructions	**5**	

(a) Description of property	(b) Cost (business use only)	(c) Elected cost	
6			

7	Listed property. Enter the amount from line 29 . . . . **7**		
8	Total elected cost of section 179 property. Add amounts in column (c), lines 6 and 7	**8**	
9	Tentative deduction. Enter the **smaller** of line 5 or line 8	**9**	
10	Carryover of disallowed deduction from line 13 of your 2000 Form 4562.	**10**	
11	Business income limitation. Enter the smaller of business income (not less than zero) or line 5 (see instructions)	**11**	
12	Section 179 expense deduction. Add lines 9 and 10, but do not enter more than line 11	**12**	
13	Carryover of disallowed deduction to 2002. Add lines 9 and 10, less line 12 ▶ **13**		

Note: *Do not use Part II or Part III below for listed property. Instead, use Part V.*

Part II   Special Depreciation Allowance and Other Depreciation (Do not include listed property.)

14	Special depreciation allowance for certain property (other than listed property) acquired after September 10, 2001 (see page 3 of the instructions)	**14**	
15	Property subject to section 168(f)(1) election (see page 4 of the instructions)	**15**	
16	Other depreciation (including ACRS) (see page 4 of the instructions)	**16**	

Part III   MACRS Depreciation (Do not include listed property.) (See page 4 of the instructions.)

Section A

17	MACRS deductions for assets placed in service in tax years beginning before 2001	**17**	
18	If you are electing under section 168(i)(4) to group any assets placed in service during the tax year into one or more general asset accounts, check here . . . . ▶ ☐		

Section B—Assets Placed in Service During 2001 Tax Year Using the General Depreciation System

(a) Classification of property	(b) Month and year placed in service	(c) Basis for depreciation (business/investment use only—see instructions)	(d) Recovery period	(e) Convention	(f) Method	(g) Depreciation deduction
19a 3-year property						
b 5-year property		55,595	5.0	HY	200DB	11,119
c 7-year property		5,227	7.0	HY	200DB	747
d 10-year property						
e 15-year property						
f 20-year property						
g 25-year property			25 yrs.		S/L	
h Residential rental property			27.5 yrs.	MM	S/L	
			27.5 yrs.	MM	S/L	
i Nonresidential real property			39 yrs.	MM	S/L	
				MM	S/L	

Section C—Assets Placed in Service During 2001 Tax Year Using the Alternative Depreciation System

20a Class life					S/L	
b 12-year			12 yrs.		S/L	
c 40-year			40 yrs.	MM	S/L	

Part IV   Summary (See page 6 of the instructions.)

21	Listed property. Enter amount from line 28.	**21**	
22	**Total.** Add amounts from line 12, lines 14 through 17, lines 19 and 20 in column (g), and line 21. Enter here and on the appropriate lines of your return. Partnerships and S corporations—see instr.	**22**	11,866
23	For assets shown above and placed in service during the current year, enter the portion of the basis attributable to section 263A costs . . **23**		

For Paperwork Reduction Act Notice, see separate instructions.   Cat. No. 12906N   Form **4562** (2001) (Rev. 3-2002)

Exhibit 7.8 Personal Financial Statement Comparison— Edward G. and Linda C. Dezine (000s omitted)

	2000	2001	Change
Assets			
Cash	$ 40	$ 45	$ 5
Non-readily marketable securities	0	100	100
Real estate	600	700	100
Automobiles	20	35	15
Personal property	50	50	0
Total	710	930	220
Liabilities			
Banks	0	15	15
Others	0	0	0
Unsecured	0	0	0
Accounts payable	3	3	0
Real estate	300	410	110
Total	303	428	125

Prepared as of December 31, each year.

Calculating Personal Cash Flow

Use a form like the one in Exhibit 7.9 to compute personal cash flow. The form lists either the line number of the individual tax return or the personal financial statement as the source.

Net personal cash flow is calculated as:

$$
\begin{aligned}
&\text{Net personal income available for debt service} \\
&\pm\ \text{total business and investment income} \\
&\underline{-\ \text{total personal expenses}} \\
&=\ \text{net personal expenses}
\end{aligned}
$$

Analysis of personal cash flow includes examining net wages received; net other personal income, net business/investment activity, personal expenses, and debt service requirements and borrowing.

Net Wages Received

To calculate the amount of **net wages** received, add all sources of personal income and subtract taxes. Exhibit 7.10 on page 246 summarizes how to calculate net wages received. The line numbers are from 2001 tax schedules. The lender verifies that the line numbers on the tax schedules have not changed from year to year.

Exhibit 7.9 Personal Cash Flow Form

Net Wages Received
    Wages, salaries (line 7, 1040) _____
Less Taxes Paid
    Federal tax withheld (Line 66, 1040) _____
    Estimated tax payments (Line 60, 1040) _____
    State/local taxes paid (Schedule A, Line 5) _____
    Social Security tax withheld (W-2) _____
    Net personal income from wages _____

Net Other Personal Income
    Interest income (Line 8a, b, 1040) _____
    Dividends (Line 9, 1040) _____
    State/local income tax refund (Line 10, 1040) _____
    Alimony received (Line 11, 1040) _____
    Other income (Line 21, 1040) _____
    Miscellaneous income _____
    IRA, pension distributions (Line 15a, 16a, 1040) _____
    Unemployment compensation (Line 19, 1040) _____
    Social Security benefits (Line 20a, 1040) _____
    Net personal income available for debt service _____

Net Business and Investment Activity
    Business income or loss (Line 12, 1040) _____
    Plus depreciation (Line 20, Schedule E) _____
    Plus depreciation (Line 13, Schedule C) _____
    Sale and purchases of securities (Schedule D) _____
    Partnership contributions (K-1) _____
    Partnership withdrawals (K-1) _____
    Purchase of investments (PFS changes) _____
    Total business and investment income _____

Personal Expenses
    Personal living expenses (provided or best estimate) _____
    Real estate taxes (Line 6, Schedule A) _____
    Interest paid (Line 14, Schedule A) _____
    Interest paid on loans not deductible _____
    Principal paid (changes in PFS last year) _____
    Medical expenses (Line 1, Schedule A) _____
    Cash contributions (Line 15, Schedule A) _____
    Personal insurance (best estimate) _____
    Other expenses (Line 23, Schedule A, plus best estimate) _____
    Lease payments (PFS) _____
    Revolving accounts _____
    Total personal expenses _____

Exhibit 7.10 Net Wages Received

Wages, salaries (Line 7, 1040) less taxes paid _____

Federal tax withheld (Line 59, 1040) _____

Estimated tax payments (Line 60, 1040) _____

State/local taxes paid (Line 5, Schedule A) _____

Social Security tax withheld (W-2) _____

Net personal income from wages _____

Net Other Personal Income

Net other personal income includes all other income except W-2 wages. The lender needs to determine whether the income will continue, what the sources of income are, and whether the income is available for future debt service. To calculate net other personal income, begin with net personal income from wages and add the sources of other income, as illustrated in exhibit 7.11.

Exhibit 7.11 Net Other Personal Income

Interest income (Line 8a, b, 1040) _____

Dividends (Line 9, 1040) _____

State/local income tax refund (Line 10, 1040) _____

Alimony received (Line 11, 1040) _____

Other income (Line 21, 1040) _____

Miscellaneous _____

IRA, pension distributions (Line 15a, 16a, 1040) _____

Unemployment compensation (Line 19, 1040) _____

Social Security benefits (Line 20a, 1040) _____

Net personal income available for debt service _____

For Edward G. and Linda C. Dezine, the net personal income available for debt service is calculated as:

Wages, salaries (Line 7, 1040)	$ 159,588
− federal tax withheld (Line 59, 1040)	29,289
− state/local taxes paid (Line 5, Schedule A)	8,866
− Social Security tax withheld (W-2)	11,800
+ interest income (Line 8a, 8b, 1040)	2,428
+ dividend income (line 9, 1040)	8
+ other income (Line 21, 1040)	8,900
= net personal income from wages	120,969

The Dezines have slightly more than $120,000 to support their debt, business investments, and personal expenses.

Net Business and Investment Activity

The calculation of net business and investment activity can be complicated, depending on the number of tax schedules involved. Net business and investment activity includes line 12 from 1040, schedule D, schedule E, and K-1 from partnerships and S corporations, as well as the calculation of the changes between two personal financial statements. In addition, consider any depreciation and amortization listed in the various schedules. Using a form similar to exhibit 7.12, calculate for net business and investment activity.

Exhibit 7.12 Net Business and Investment Activity

Business income or loss (Line 12, 1040)	_____
Plus depreciation (Line 20, Schedule E)	_____
Plus depreciation (Line 13, Schedule C)	_____
Sale and purchases of securities (Schedule D)	_____
Partnership contributions (K-1)	_____
Partnership withdrawals (K-1)	_____
Purchase of investments (PFS changes)	_____
Total business and investment income	_____

The Dezines' business and investment activity is summarized as:

Net Business and Investment Activity

Business income or loss (Line 12, 1040)	$39,518
Sale and purchase of securities (Schedule D)	(1,324)
Total business and investment income	38,194

Personal Expenses

Personal expenses include all personal living expenses, debt payments, interest payments, and any other expenses not previously considered. Personal living expenses vary, depending on lifestyle. Some lenders use a set percentage of gross income to avoid subjectivity. Either the applicant provides this information or the lender estimates it using personal financial statement trends. For example, if the statement indicates no personal liquidity but good income, the applicant probably spends all income or invests it in nonliquid assets. If the earlier analysis reveals any investment income, assume that it is spent on personal living expenses. Exhibit 7.13 illustrates the calculation for personal expenses.

Exhibit 7.13 Personal Expenses

Personal living expenses (provided or best estimate) _____

Real estate taxes (Line 6, Schedule A) _____

Interest paid (Line 14, Schedule A) _____

Interest paid on loans not deductible _____

Principal paid (changes in PFS last year) _____

Medical expenses (Line 1, Schedule A) _____

Cash contributions (Line 15, Schedule A) _____

Personal insurance (best estimate) _____

Other expenses (Line 23, Schedule A, plus best estimate) _____

Lease payments (PFS) _____

Revolving accounts _____

Total personal expenses _____

The calculation of total personal expenses for the Dezines is:

Personal living expenses (provided or best estimate)	$ 30,000
Real estate taxes (Line 6, Schedule A)	3,221
Interest paid (Line 14, Schedule A)	29,410
Interest paid on loans not deductible (credit cards estimate)	360
Principal paid (changes in PFS last year)	0
Medical expenses (Line 1, Schedule A)	1,318
Cash contributions (Line 15, Schedule A)	30,530
Personal insurance (personal financial statement)	8,000
Other expenses (Line 23, Schedule A, plus best estimate)	355
Lease payments (PFS)	0
Revolving accounts	0
Total personal expenses	103,194

The estimated $30,000 personal living may be under or overstated. The lender can best determine this expense from a personal interview. No amounts were listed for principal paid because the Dezines refinanced their home when the remodeling was completed. Also, the auto debt was refinanced when the new car was purchased in 2002. Therefore, the amounts of principal payments are unknown. The insurance was taken from the current personal financial statement and the revolving accounts were the lender's best estimate.

Net Personal Cash Flow

A lender's concern is the availability of income that can service future debt. To determine the amount of cash available to service additional debt, calculate net personal cash flow by adding and subtracting the sources and uses of income.

The Dezines' net personal cash flow calculations are:

Net wages and salaries	$ 120,969
± net business and investment activity income	38,194
− personal expenses	103,194
= net personal cash flow	55,969

It appears the Dezines have more than sufficient income to service their debt. Exhibit 7.14 on the following page illustrates the completed personal cash flow form for the Dezines.

GLOBAL PERSONAL CASH FLOW AND DEBT-TO-INCOME RATIO

When lending to small companies, many banks calculate global personal cash flow. Global personal cash flow includes all personal and company debt and income. Be careful not to double count income when calculating global cash flow. For example, income received from S corporations is taxed on the personal tax return but does not flow to the individual. Do not count the income for both the business and the individual. The Dezines' net personal cash flow was $55,969. However, Linda Dezine lent Designs by Dezine, Inc., $46,172, which would make the personal cash flow much tighter.

The Dezines' global debt-to-income ratio is:

Total gross income (Line 22, 1040)	$ 183,087
+ Non-cash depreciation for 1120S	11,866
= Total gross cash income	194,953
Monthly income	16,246
× Allowable maximum percentage	40%
= Maximum monthly debt payments	6,498

The Dezines' debt was calculated as:

Residence mortgage payments	$ 45,600
+ auto loans	4,800
+ credit cards (5% of amount owed)	150
= total annual payments	50,550
Monthly payments	4,213
+ company debt payments (auto loans $1,100 per month and interest on shareholder debt)	1,400
= total global debt payments	5,613
Global debt-to-income (5,613/16,246)	35%

Exhibit 7.14 Completed Personal Cash Flow Form

Net Wages Received

Wages, salaries (line 7, 1040)	$ 159,588

Less taxes paid

Federal tax withheld (Line 66, 1040)	29,289
Estimated tax payments (Line 60, 1040)	0
State/local taxes paid (Schedule A, Line 5)	8,866
Social Security tax withheld (W-2)	11,800
Net personal income from wages	109,633

Net Other Personal Income

Interest income (Line 8a, b, 1040)	2,428
Dividends (Line 9, 1040)	8
State/local income tax refund (Line 10, 1040)	0
Alimony received (Line 11, 1040)	0
Other income (Line 21, 1040)	8,900
Miscellaneous income	0
IRA, pension distributions (Line 15a, 16a, 1040)	0
Unemployment compensation (Line 19, 1040)	0
Social Security benefits (Line 20a, 1040)	0
Net personal income available for debt service	120,969

Net Business and Investment Activity

Business income or loss (Line 12, 1040)	39,518
Plus depreciation (Line 20, Schedule E)	0
Plus depreciation (Line 13, Schedule C)	0
Sale and purchase of securities (Schedule D)	(1,324)
Partnership contributions (K-1)	0
Partnership withdrawals (K-1)	0
Purchase of investments (PFS changes)	0
Total business and investment income	38,194

Personal Expenses

Personal living expenses (provided or best estimate)	30,000
Real estate taxes (Line 6, Schedule A)	3,221
Interest paid (Line 14, Schedule A)	29,410
Interest paid on loans not deductible	360
Principal paid (changes in PFS last year)	0
Medical expenses (Line 1, Schedule A)	1,318
Cash contributions (Line 15, Schedule A)	30,530
Personal insurance (best estimate)	8,000
Other expenses (Line 23, Schedule A, plus best estimate)	355
Lease payments (PFS)	0
Revolving accounts	0
Total personal expenses	103,194

The global debt-to-income ratio is higher than the personal debt-to-income ratio calculated earlier. However, the global calculation includes interest on $46,000 of shareholder debt that would not be paid in the event of liquidation.

A lender monitors how much personal liquidity will need to be used to fund future cash flow needs of the business.

SUMMARY

Personal financial statements summarize all assets, liabilities, net worth, income, expenses, and contingent liabilities of the individual providing the statement. The borrower usually prepares the statement on a bank-approved form or a computer-genererated form, which is attached to the bank form after all key questions on the bank form are answered. All personal financial statements are addressed to the lending bank, signed, dated, and checked for mathematical errors.

The balance sheet lists assets in order of liquidity. When listing assets, the lender determines the liquidity, solvency, and marketability of the asset. Assets are evaluated using ownership criteria. Supporting schedules in the statements provide ownership information and other supporting data. The balance sheet must balance, with assets equaling liabilities plus net worth. The lender calculates the adjusted net worth. Adjusted net worth is calculated by reducing assets in value or availability. The statement must include a representation and warranty that it is true and correct.

Personal cash flow is calculated using the U.S. Individual Tax Form 1040 and supporting schedules. Income is analyzed based on its type, source, and frequency. Net wages received, net other personal income, net business and investment activity, and personal expenses are calculated to determine personal cash flow to service debt.

QUESTIONS FOR DISCUSSION

1. When analyzing the personal income of a loan applicant, what are the key issues?
2. What are the differences among liquidity, solvency, and marketability of a personal asset?
3. If a personal financial statement listed non-readily marketable securities valued at $200,000, what type of questions would you ask?
4. If a borrower has gross income of $6,000 per month and total monthly payments of $1,500, what is the debt-to-income ratio?
5. What types of noncash transactions may be found on a tax return?

Exercise

Using the blank form in the *Master Case Book*, construct a personal financial statement for Michael Richards as of September 30, 20xx, using the following information. Calculate the adjusted personal net worth.

Residence mortgage	$155,000
Value of privately held company	$200,000
Credit cards	$ 5,000
Boat	$ 20,000
Autos owned	$ 25,000
Mutual fund	$ 20,000
Due from parents	$ 10,000
Auto debt	$ 15,000
Personal property	$ 35,000
401(k)	$135,000
Cash	$ 15,000
Boat loan	$ 12,000
Home	$225,000
Receivable due from friends	$ 10,000

8

CONSTRUCTING AND ANALYZING CASH BUDGETS

LEARNING OBJECTIVES

After studying *Constructing and Analyzing Cash Budgets*, you will be able to

- describe the primary uses of cash budgets,
- construct and analyze a cash budget,
- determine which borrowers should prepare a cash budget,
- explain the application of cash budgets, and
- define the key terms that appear in **bold** in the text.

INTRODUCTION

A cash budget is a tool that helps forecast a company's short-term financing needs. Most companies report net income on an accrual-basis income statement, but that does not reflect the amount of cash generated. Consequently, lenders trying to make a decision on a short-term loan request might have difficulty determining the borrower's ability to generate cash and repay debt.

A cash budget provides an estimate of a company's short-term cash position and funding requirements. It is particularly useful in determining the credit needs of start-up companies, expanding companies, or those with seasonal variations in operations. A cash budget is used to estimate the flow of cash through the company's accounts during a designated time period. Lenders use cash budgets to review the periods between the origination and repayment of loans. Companies develop cash budgets to control monthly, weekly, or daily cash requirements. By projecting a company's schedule of receipts and disbursements on a monthly, weekly, or daily basis, a lender can identify the cause, timing, and magnitude of a company's peak borrowing needs and its repayment capabilities for short-term debt.

CASH BUDGET OVERVIEW

Ideally, most companies should use cash budgets as a part of their own internal financial planning process. If the borrower does prepare a cash budget, lenders must examine the underlying assumptions of the company's forecast. Assumptions are reviewed on the basis of their realism. For example, lenders should ask the following questions:

- Has the past performance of the company supported the projections?
- Are the projections conservative and dependable, with proper consideration given to external factors (such as the economy, the industry, or government regulations)?
- Are the assumptions within management's control?
- Are the past data reliable?

Many small companies are not able to provide a cash budget for analysis because they do not employ a comptroller who would prepare one. The cost of having the company's accountant prepare this analysis might be too great in relation to the amount of the loan requested. Larger companies may not need to prepare a cash budget because they employ comptrollers to manage the day-to-day cash needs. In many cases, lenders prepare a cash budget based on interviews, historical financial statements, accounts receivable turns, inventory management, and accounts payable terms. Lenders must be able to take the information derived from accrual-basis financial statements and convert it to cash-basis information. However it is prepared, whether by the borrower, comptroller, or lender, a cash budget is only a rough estimate of cash needs. This is because the person preparing the budget is working with estimates and numerous variables that could easily change.

A cash budget is used to examine a company's inflows and outflows on a cash, rather than an accrual, basis. The timing of these cash flows and the company's actual cash requirements are taken into account. This means that although a company's income statement recognizes sales at delivery, a cash budget recognizes cash sales or collections of accounts receivable. If a company makes credit sales on 30-day terms, a cash budget recognizes the collection of cash 30 days after the sale (assuming the customer pays in 30 days), rather than on the day of sale.

An accrual income statement recognizes expenditures as an expense when a purchase is delivered or, in the case of cost of goods sold, when a sale is made. This does not necessarily mean that the cash has been paid. The amount due can be charged to accounts payable and eventually paid when the cash is available. The time in which the expenditure is paid is the focus in a cash budget. The issue of recognizing it as an expense is not important. For example, an insurance premium paid annually, rather than expensed evenly throughout the year, is entered as a cash expenditure during the month it is paid.

To construct a cash budget for an existing company, lenders use the common-sized analysis of the income statement and balance sheet to identify days ratios on receivables, inventories, and payables. One of the primary assumptions in a cash budget is that the past days ratios in accounts receivable, inventories, and accounts payable will remain steady. Lenders must be able to rely on the relationship between a company's various current asset and current liability accounts to its sales. If alterations were to be made in these relationships, as would occur in a change in collection payment terms, lenders need to know of them to properly complete the budget.

A cash budget also is based on detailed cash flow information about the timing of the acquisition of equipment, the repayment of long-term debt, and when interest and principal payments on a loan come due.

Simply put, companies use cash budgets to keep their checking accounts from running out of cash. Lenders use cash budgets to determine when customers are likely to need to borrow and to assure themselves that borrowers will be able to repay short-term loans. Sometimes the lender will want to rework the cash budget to determine how unexpected changes in cash-flow assumptions affect it. This procedure, commonly referred to as **scenario analysis**, could enable the lender to uncover financing needs not foreseen by the company.

In simple terms, projected receipts and projected disbursements represent a company's projected cash flow—positive or negative. By evaluating the likely timing and magnitude of these cash inflows and outflows, lenders can determine the company's cash needs for its operating cycle. When cash flow produces less than the company's minimum cash requirement, the company needs to borrow money.

A cash budget enables management to control the company's performance on an interim basis and allows a lender to analyze that performance by identifying the various components of cash flow. Management can react quickly if the actual cash flow varies significantly from the expected cash budget. Management's effectiveness in dealing with such deviations depends on the time increment (monthly or weekly) that is used to prepare the cash budget and how often the company's performance is reviewed. Obviously, a company can react to problems more quickly if its cash flow is monitored monthly rather than quarterly or semiannually.

To summarize, cash budgets forecast a company's cash receipts and disbursements between statement dates, usually monthly. The most common sources of cash are cash sales, the collection of accounts receivable, and proceeds from new loans. The most common uses of cash include operating expenses, payments of accounts payable (for inventories), interest, taxes, labor (payroll), and capital expenditures.

Use of Cash Budgets

When considering a loan request from a company with seasonal sales, lenders find the cash budget to be a critical tool of financial statement analysis. Seasonal financing requirements are spurred by increases in inventory and accounts receivable, which are associated with periodic peaks in sales, production, or purchasing. This interim need might not be apparent in a company's year-end financial statements because a true short-term need will be self-liquidating. The assets being financed will convert to cash to repay debt. For example, a company purchases lawn mowers during the winter. The repayment source is the sale of the asset purchased (lawnmowers) during the spring. The company should be able to pay the interim loan during the course of an operating cycle. The operating cycle defines the time period during which cash converts into inventory, then into accounts receivable (or cash), and, finally, through the collection of accounts receivable, back into cash. If the company cannot pay its interim loan by converting its assets into cash during the operating cycle, its borrowing need is not short-term. Since seasonal borrowing is self-liquidating, the company does not have to be profitable to repay the debt, provided its cash flow is not negative and the accounts receivable are collected.

For start-up companies, a cash budget is essential in the early months. New companies typically have one-time expenses, such as rental deposits. Start-up companies that provide a product or service on credit also are not able to collect cash from accounts receivable in the early weeks. Therefore, the company will have expenses that are due during a time when little cash is collected.

When approving a short-term loan request, the lender must have confidence in the company's cash budgets. For established companies, this confidence is a direct result of how well management has performed against its previous plans and how dependable the company's cash flows have been in the past. For start-up companies, the quality of the supporting information, the assessment of management, and the amount of initial capital assist in providing the confidence needed. A cash budget shows absolute cash needs; however, because the budget is only a forecast and a single short-term event could delay a receipt of cash, the lender should be ready to finance more than the budget estimates.

CASH BUDGET FORMAT

When a cash budget is completed, the lender's job is to check the timing and magnitude of the company's projected cash flows based on other available financial information. Prior to the preparation or interpretation of a cash budget, the lender reviews all of the information, including income tax information. The assumptions behind the cash budget projections are a critical part of the cash budget.

Whether constructing a cash budget or reviewing an existing one, a lender must identify

- the timing and amount of the company's cash sales revenues, credit sales, and conversion of accounts receivable to cash inflows;
- the company's days accounts receivable compared with its established credit terms;
- the suppliers' credit terms and the company's payment practices, with respect to purchased materials;
- the magnitude and timing of the company's direct labor and overhead costs and of its various operating expenditures, including its general and administrative expenses and selling expenses; and
- the company's non-operating expenditures (dividend payment policies, loan repayment schedules, and interest payments).

The specific format that companies use for their monthly cash budgets varies. A typical format is located in the *Master Case Book*, and exhibit 8.1 on the next page includes the following elements:

- beginning cash (including marketable securities) at the start of each period (line 1);
- receipts, including cash sales, collections of accounts receivable, new loan proceeds, injection of owner's equity, and other cash proceeds (line 2);
- total cash available, the sum of lines 1 and 2 (line 3);
- operating cash paid out, including inventory (raw material) purchases; labor and overhead expenses; selling, general and administrative expenses; owner's salary; and interest expense (lines 4–8);
- total disbursements—the sum of lines 4 through 8 (line 9);
- other cash outflows, including loan principal payments; capital expenditures; and dividends (lines 10–12);
- total cash paid out, the sum of lines 9 through 12 (line 13);
- net cash position (total cash available [line 3] minus projected total cash paid out [line 13] equals line 14;
- minimum cash position (the amount required for ongoing operations, line 15);
- loan required—the amount needed to bring the company's cash position up to its minimum cash requirement;
- negative funding requirements indicate amounts available for repayment of previous funding needs (line 16); and
- cumulative borrowing/reduction—the amount of current short-term debt plus or minus any additional funds needed (line 17).

Exhibit 8.2 on page 259 illustrates the application of cash budget analysis to a start-up company for the first six months.

Exhibit 8.1 Cash Budget

	Jan	Feb	Mar	Apr	May	June	Jul	Aug	Sept	Oct	Nov	Dec
1 Beginning cash	—	—	—	—	—	—	—	—	—	—	—	—
2 Receipts	—	—	—	—	—	—	—	—	—	—	—	—
3 Total cash available	—	—	—	—	—	—	—	—	—	—	—	—
4 Material purchases	—	—	—	—	—	—	—	—	—	—	—	—
5 Labor (non-S, G, & A)*	—	—	—	—	—	—	—	—	—	—	—	—
6 S, G, & A*	—	—	—	—	—	—	—	—	—	—	—	—
7 Owner's salary	—	—	—	—	—	—	—	—	—	—	—	—
8 Interest expense	—	—	—	—	—	—	—	—	—	—	—	—
9 Total disbursements	—	—	—	—	—	—	—	—	—	—	—	—
10 Loan principal	—	—	—	—	—	—	—	—	—	—	—	—
11 Capital expenditures	—	—	—	—	—	—	—	—	—	—	—	—
12 Dividends	—	—	—	—	—	—	—	—	—	—	—	—
13 Total cash paid out	—	—	—	—	—	—	—	—	—	—	—	—
14 Net cash position	—	—	—	—	—	—	—	—	—	—	—	—
15 Minimum cash	—	—	—	—	—	—	—	—	—	—	—	—
16 Loan required	—	—	—	—	—	—	—	—	—	—	—	—
17 Cumulative borrowing/reduction	—	—	—	—	—	—	—	—	—	—	—	—

* Selling, general, & administrative expenses

Basic Subtotals of the Cash Budget: Service Inc. Example

The owners of Service, Inc., provided the following information in the interview portion of the lending process.

Service, Inc., is a new dental practice in the community. Two recent graduates who majored in general dentistry are starting up the practice. The initial capitalization of the practice will be $100,000, contributed by the dentists and outside investors. The initial expenditures consist of $200,000 for equipment and $50,000 for leasehold improvements. Management projects initial revenues of $30,000 per month for the first year. Other expenses that will be incurred monthly include:

- owner's salary $10,000 ($5,000 per owner)
- purchases $1,000 (for raw materials)
- selling, general, and administrative expenses (including other employee payroll) $6,000

The collections of the accounts receivable will take 60 days, due to insurance claims. Raw materials will be purchased on terms of net 30 days. The minimum cash needed each month is $3,000. The company has requested a $25,000 line of credit and a term

Exhibit 8.2 Service, Inc., Cash Budget (000s omitted)

		Month 1	Month 2	Month 3	Month 4	Month 5	Month 6
1	Beginning cash	100	3	3	3	3	3
2	Cash receipts	150	0	30	30	30	30
3	Total cash available	250	3	33	33	33	33
4	Material purchases	0	1	1	1	1	1
5	Labor (non—S, G, & A)	0	0	0	0	0	0
6	S, G, & A	6	6	6	6	6	6
7	Owner's salary	10	10	10	10	10	10
8	Interest expense	0	1	1	1	1	1
9	Total disbursements	16	18	18	18	18	18
10	Loan principal	0	2	2	2	2	2
11	Capital expenditures	250	0	0	0	0	0
12	Dividends	0	0	0	0	0	0
13	Total cash paid out	266	20	20	20	20	20
14	Net cash position	(16)	(17)	13	13	13	13
15	Minimum cash	3	3	3	3	3	3
16	Loan required	19	20	0	0	0	0
17	Cumulative borrowing/reduction	19	39	29	19	9	0

loan of $150,000 to fund the equipment purchases. Beginning in month 2, Service, Inc., is projecting to repay principal on the requested loan at $2,000 per month.

The lender is not sure whether the financing requested is the correct amount and, therefore, prepares a cash budget. Exhibit 8.2 shows the cash budget prepared from the interview assumptions.

Beginning Cash

The first step in filling out the cash budget is to show the amount of cash on hand at the beginning of the time period being forecast (exhibit 8.2, line 1). For cash budget purposes, cash and marketable securities are considered cash. For an existing company, information about the amount of cash available can be obtained from bank statements, broker statements, company financial statements, or a tax return. The cash budget for Service, Inc., begins with the initial capitalization of $100,000. The cash on hand at the beginning of each month thereafter is either the minimum cash required, $3,000, or the amount of excess cash produced from operations (line 15).

Receipts

The first entry in the receipts section is cash collected from sales, which is collections from accounts receivable and other proceeds (such as cash sales and loan proceeds).

The managers of Service, Inc., reported that sales are not highly seasonal. The company must list its cash sales and its credit sales separately for the lender. Service, Inc., has reported that its sales are all credit sales on 60-day terms. Therefore, the company's first-month sales of $30,000 show up on the cash budget as $30,000 in cash receipts in month 3; the credit sales of $30,000 in month 2 are collected in month 4, and so forth. It is assumed that the term loan proceeds of $150,000 will be received in month 1.

Total Cash Paid Out

The cash-paid-out figures are estimates based on the expenses calculated from the company's interview. Expenditures also might be based on company-provided estimates or the historical financial statements.

The amount of inventory a company purchases is based on anticipated sales, and the lender normally analyzes the rate of inventory turnover to assess how far in advance of sales those purchases occur. Unfortunately, the inventory turnover calculation is inaccurate in the Service, Inc., case because the inventory being looked at will be used to start the company. If Service, Inc., were an established business whose sales were seasonal, the lender would obtain monthly financial statements during the peak season.

The lender may assume from the interview that Service, Inc.'s, purchases are $1,000, provided by management, and payable net 30 days. This amount is entered on line 4, beginning in month 2.

The next item on the cash budget is non-selling, general, and administrative (S, G, & A) labor. For some companies, labor expense is included in cost of goods sold. The lender may need to ask the company for a detailed summary of the historical cost of goods sold. For established companies lenders analyze the costs of labor as a historical percentage of sales whether the expense is in cost of goods sold or S, G, & A. The lender determines future wage increases, management overhead changes, and future needs, based on sales increases. For Service, Inc., there is no cost of goods labor expense because all labor costs are included in the S, G, & A expenses and owner's salary.

S, G, & A expenses are based on historical percentages of net sales. But within these expenses, some might be fixed (to an extent) and some variable. For example, utilities are more fixed than advertising expenses. The lender determines the mix of expenses and what will change in the coming time frame of the cash budget. Most of the time, the historical percentage of net sales can be used for the cash budget. Service, Inc., has estimated expenses of $6,000 per month for rent, utilities, full- and part-time employees, and other expenses. These are paid in the month they are incurred. Line 6 reflects the $6,000 per month needed to pay S, G, & A expenses.

The two owners of Service, Inc., need $5,000 per month in salary. This amount will be drawn immediately and is entered on line 7 of the cash budget. If the owners could delay a payment, or if salaries were paid on a delayed basis, this amount would be less the first month. For example, if wages were paid one week in arrears, then the first month only would have three weeks of wages, and the entire month of wages would begin in month 2.

Interest expense is based on the historical cost, changes in the amount borrowed, potential changes in interest rates, and projected debt reduction. Service, Inc., has requested a $150,000 loan at 8 percent interest and is not expected to use the requested line of credit. Projected interest expense would be $12,000 for one year ($150,000 × 0.08). Interest expense is paid each month, beginning in month 2 and entered on line 8 as $1,000 (the amount expected to be paid monthly on the equipment loan). Of course, this is slightly overstated, since the loan should reduce by the principal paid as payments are made. The cash budget reflects the best guess at this time.

Total disbursements are the sum of lines 4 through 8. These expenses reflect the total cash paid for cost of goods sold, operating expenses, and interest expense from the income statement.

The loan principal is the amount the company is expecting to pay on existing term debt. This amount is the current maturities long-term debt divided by 12. The lender then adds any additional projected amounts to be borrowed. Service, Inc. has requested a five-year term loan for $150,000. This would be repaid at $30,000 per year or $2,500 per month if the loan were written at principal plus interest. Most loans require a fixed principal and interest payment. In the early stages of the loan, more is paid on interest and less on principal. Service, Inc., is projecting to repay $24,000 in principal during the first twelve months. Line 10 reflects this amount, divided by 12, beginning in month 2.

Capital expenditures are amounts the company expects to pay for fixed-assets purchases. These amounts might or might not be financed. Some companies pay cash for small fixed-asset purchases and others finance all purchases. The current operating capacity, age of the current fixed assets, projected sales growth, and changing technology are factors that affect fixed-asset purchases. Service, Inc., is projecting equipment purchases of $200,000 and leasehold improvements of $50,000. Line 11 reflects these amounts in month 1 because they are needed to start the business. No other capital expenditures are forecast for the first six months.

Dividends are amounts paid to the owners. If dividends are needed to pay estimated taxes, then a dividend is usually paid out in January, April, July, and October. Dividends for personal use can be paid at any time. Service, Inc., is not forecasting any dividends for the first six months because it is a new company. Total cash paid out (line 13) is the sum of lines 9 through 12. This line should total all expected cash payments during the month.

The net cash position is the net cash available after paying all expenses. Line 14 is the sum of subtracting line 13 from line 3.

Minimum Cash

Every company needs a **minimum cash** amount to operate. This is based on historical cash balances, compensating balance requirements, and projected sales growth. For new companies, the projected minimum cash is management's best guess as to what will be needed to operate the business each day.

The owners of Service, Inc., have projected minimum cash of $3,000, which is entered on line 15. The size of the loan required is the difference or sum of lines 14 and 15. If line 14 is negative, or less than the minimum cash needed, then line 16 will be the sum of lines 14 and 15. If line 14 is positive, and greater than the minimum cash needed, line 16 is zero. Line 17 is the cumulative borrowing need or debt reduction need as a result of line 16. Service, Inc., needs more than the $25,000 line of credit requested for the first three months. But by month 4, the line of credit should be below the $25,000 requested. The borrowing on the line of credit should be repaid within the first six months of operation, according to the cash budget.

CASH BUDGET FOR A GROWING COMPANY (DESIGNS BY DEZINE, INC.)

This section uses Designs by Dezine, Inc., as an example to show a cash budget for a growing company with some seasonality. Exhibit 8.3 reflects Designs by Dezine, Inc.'s, historical and projected sales for the years 2001 and 2002, on a monthly basis.

On January 2, 2002, the company requested bank financing for a new computer system that costs $10,000. Designs by Dezine, Inc., plans to pay $5,000 down and finance the balance over five years (the depreciable life of the equipment). The company requested a loan with a five-year amortization of principal plus interest.

The bank's examination of Designs by Dezine, Inc.'s, financial statements made the lender wonder if the company also might need permanent funding or revolving credit to support the growth in sales projected for the second year. The lender decided to construct a new cash budget.

Exhibit 8.4 summarizes the major accounts from Designs by Dezine, Inc.'s, 2001 company tax returns. These figures provide the basis for the development of the company's 2002 cash budget. The 2002 monthly cash budget for Designs by Dezine, Inc., is shown in exhibit 8.5 on page 265. A discussion of each line of the budget follows.

Beginning Cash

On Designs by Dezine, Inc.'s, 2001 income tax return (exhibit 7.7, page 241) balance sheet, the cash account at year-end 2001 totaled $6,053. The lender enters this amount on line 1 as beginning cash. Line 15 on the cash budget shows the minimum cash balance required for ongoing operations as $5,000. If cash is higher than the $5,000 at the end of any month, it is because all short-term debt has been repaid.

Receipts

As summarized in exhibit 8.3, Designs by Dezine, Inc., projects a sales increase for 2002. The growth is from one full year of operations and projected larger contracts. The company is somewhat seasonal, with large sales levels in the summer and fall. As a construction company, Designs by Dezine, Inc., obtains a 50 percent down payment with the contract. Most contracts are completed in 30 to 45 days. The remaining 50 percent is collected on completion. The company ended 2001 with $8,000 of accounts receivable. The first month's receipts would include $10,000 of down payments for the projected January sales. The company also will be taking out a loan for $5,000 to purchase the new computer system. However, since the company is putting $5,000 down on the purchase, the two entries offset one another. Therefore, the receipts are $18,000 ($8,000 accounts receivable and $10,000 down payments). Therefore, line 2 reflects the accounts receivable collections and sales down payments, totaling $18,000.

Exhibit 8.3 Historical and Projected Sales—Designs by Dezine, Inc.

Designs by Dezine, Inc

Monthly sales for 2001 (000s omitted)

Month	Sales	Month	Sales
January	$ 0	July	$ 40
February	0	August	55
March	0	September	60
April	0	October	74
May	15	November	90
June	30	December	20
		Total	384

Designs by Dezine, Inc

Projected sales for 2002 (000s omitted)

Month	Sales	Month	Sales
January	$ 20	July	$ 60
February	25	August	70
March	40	September	80
April	50	October	90
May	60	November	110
June	60	December	35
		Total	700

Total Cash Available

Total cash receipts in line 3 equal:

- $24,000 for January ($6,000 cash, $8,000 accounts receivable collections, and $10,000 down payment of projected January sales)
- $27,000 for February ($10,000 collected on the balance of January sales, 50 percent down on projected February sales $12,000, plus beginning cash $5,000)
- $38,000 for March ($13,000 collected on the balance of February sales, 50 percent down on projected March sales $20,000, plus beginning cash of $5,000)

and the amount from the schedule below (exhibit 8.5, page 265) for each month thereafter (receipts from down payments and the balance of sales from the previous month plus beginning cash or excess net cash position).

	2001	Common-sized
Income Statement		
Sales	$ 384	100.0%
Raw material purchases	330	85.9%
Depreciation	12	3.1%
Owner's salary	43	11.2%
Selling, general, and administrative (S, G, & A)	22	5.7%
Interest	3	0.8%
Net profit before tax	(26)	(6.7%)
Balance Sheet Assets		
Cash	6	9.5%
Accounts receivable	8	12.7%
Total current assets	14	22.2%
Net fixed assets	49	77.8%
Total assets	63	100.0%
Liabilities		
Other current liabilities	3	4.8%
Notes payable shareholder	46	73.0%
Long-term debt	40	63.5%
Net worth	(26)	(41.3%)
Total liabilities and equity	63	100.0%

Total Cash Paid Out

The cash-paid-out figures usually are estimated expenditures, using expenses as a percentage of sales, which is calculated from the company's previous income statement. The lender might wish to discuss with the borrower what affect the new equipment and projected sales growth will have on the financial performance of the company. Moreover, the lender must analyze the expense categories to determine which of them are fixed and might remain stable in the face of growing sales. Cash budget expenditures might also be based on company-provided estimates of proposed expenditures.

Material Purchases and Labor

Because the analysis shows growing sales for Designs by Dezine, Inc., it is logical for the lender to assume that many of the company's costs will grow. The next step is to calculate material purchases and labor expenses. Designs by Dezine, Inc.'s, material expenses were 85.9 percent of sales last year. This amount also includes labor for each job. The company is projecting 75 percent of sales material and labor expenses. After a discussion with the owners, the lender calculates the amount of material costs at 40 percent and labor costs at 35 percent.

When creating a cash budget, a lender must take into account the actual timing of a company's accounts payable for raw material or inventory payments. Designs by Dezine, Inc.'s, accounts payable for materials are paid 30 days after the start of a job. Generally, raw materials are delivered early in the job with payment due 30 days after receipt of the raw materials. Therefore, January purchases are paid in February, February purchases are paid in March, and so forth. Labor expenses are paid in the month incurred. Therefore, January material purchases are $0 and labor expenses are $7 (projected sales of $20 × 0.35). February material purchases are $8 (January projected sales of $20 × 0.40) and labor expenses are $ 8.75 (February projected sales of $25 × 0.35). For each month following, material purchases will continue to be 40 percent of the previous month's sales and labor will be 35 percent of the current month's sales.

Selling, General, and Administrative Expenditures

A company's income statement often lists the individual expense categories that make up its S, G, & A expenses. These categories include office employees' salaries, office supplies, advertising, transportation, accounting, and so on. Expenditures that vary with sales should be incurred in the same month as the sales and paid for in that same month. It is not necessary to expect these expenditures to take place in advance of the sales date. S, G, & A expenses are calculated as a percentage of sales if no major changes

Exhibit 8.5 Cash Budget—Designs by Dezine, Inc. (000s omitted)												
	Jan	Feb	Mar	Apr	May	June	Jul	Aug	Sept	Oct	Nov	Dec
1 Beginning cash	6	5	5	5	5	5	5	5	5	6	15	28
2 Receipts	18	22	33	45	55	60	60	65	75	85	100	72
3 Total cash available	24	27	38	50	60	65	65	70	80	91	115	100
4 Material purchases	0	8	10	16	20	24	24	24	28	32	36	44
5 Labor (non—S,G, & A)	7	9	14	18	21	21	21	25	26	32	39	12
6 S, G, A	4	4	4	4	4	4	4	4	4	4	4	4
7 Owner's salary	5	5	5	5	5	5	5	5	5	5	5	5
8 Interest expense	1	1	1	1	1	1	1	1	1	1	1	1
9 Total disbursements	17	27	34	44	51	55	55	59	64	74	85	66
10 Loan principal	1	2	2	2	2	2	2	2	2	2	2	2
11 Capital expenditures	10	0	0	0	0	0	0	0	0	0	0	0
12 Dividends	0	0	0	0	0	0	0	0	0	0	0	0
13 Total cash paid out	28	29	36	46	53	57	57	61	66	76	87	68
14 Net cash position	(4)	(2)	2	4	7	8	8	9	14	15	28	32
15 Minimum cash	5	5	5	5	5	5	5	5	5	5	5	5
16 Loan required	9	7	3	1	0	0	0	0	0	0	0	0
17 Cumulative borrowing/reduction	9	16	19	20	18	15	12	8	0	0	0	0

are anticipated. For 2001, Designs by Dezine, Inc.'s, S, G, & A expenses were 5.7 percent of sales. However, this number is distorted because 2001 was a partial year and sales are projected to increase substantially. Designs by Dezine, Inc., is projecting S, G, & A expenses of $48,000 per year. After discussing this with the owner, the lender determines that this amount is reasonable. Therefore, the cash budget uses $4,000 per month on line 6.

Owner's Salary

Last year, Linda drew officer's compensation of $42,700 for 8 months. She is expecting to draw up to $80,000 this year if the company is profitable. However, she has agreed to take a $5,000 salary each month until the company can afford to pay her more. The $5,000 draw is listed on line 7 of the projected cash budget. Because the cash budget shows excess cash in November and December, it is likely she will increase her salary sometime during those months.

Interest Expense

The new $5,000 loan and a shareholder's loan taken out late last year will increase interest expense and the cash flow required for principal repayment. The amount of the shareholder's loan is obtained from the company tax return. Assuming that the interest will be at an 8 percent rate, the new interest expense would be $400 per year for the computer loan. The amount on line 8 is calculated as current interest expense on the autos ($40,064 × 0.08) and the shareholder's loan ($46,172 × 0.09) plus the interest on the new loan. This amount is then divided by 12 to reflect the amount paid monthly. Because the cash budget is presented in even thousands, this amount has been rounded up and therefore is overstated

Total Disbursements

The sum of lines 4 through 8 equals total disbursements on line 9. This sum should total the cash expenditures for cost of goods sold; selling, general, and administrative expenses; and interest expense.

Loan Principal

Designs by Dezine, Inc.'s, balance sheet shows long-term debt of $40,064 for autos in 2001. For cash budgeting, assume that there will be level principal payments throughout the year for the existing loan, which amounts to monthly payments of approximately $650. Payments on the requested loan will begin in February (calculated with a loan amortization table), accounting only for the principal portion ($5,000/5 years = $1,000 per year). Beginning in February, the company is hoping to begin repaying shareholders $1,000 per month on the principal portion of the debt. Both loan payments are listed on line 10, which has been rounded to $2,000 per month beginning month two. For month one, the principal payments are rounded to $1,000 to reflect the amount of the current payments.

Capital Expenditures

Computer equipment is the company's only projected capital equipment purchase for 2002 (line 11), which is scheduled to be purchased in January (assuming the loan request is approved) at an estimated cost of $10,000.

Income Taxes and Dividends

Income taxes can be a problem for companies preparing cash budgets. Designs by Dezine, Inc., is an S corporation. Linda Dezine is the sole owner and is personally liable for the income taxes. Therefore, the company will show no taxes paid. However, most S corporations pay a dividend to the owner to fund taxes. Because the company showed an operating loss last year, the amount of dividend for this year needs to be based on projected earnings. Linda Dezine hopes to operate the company at break-even this year. Therefore, no dividends are projected.

Total Cash Paid Out

The lender has now accounted for all of Designs by Dezine, Inc.'s, anticipated cash expenditures for each month. The company's projected total cash outlays are listed for each month on line 13 of exhibit 8.5.

Net Cash Position

This line of the cash budget is calculated by subtracting total cash paid out (line 13) from total cash available (line 3). It shows that Designs by Dezine, Inc.'s, net cash position does not exceed its minimum cash required (line 15) until May.

Loan Required

This is the amount of cash the company needs to maintain its stated minimum cash position of $5,000. From January until April, the company needs a loan. In May, the net cash position is $7. With a minimum cash need of $5, this net cash position allows the company to repay $2 of the loan. In June, the net cash position is $8, which allows the company to repay $3 of the loan (after the minimum cash of $5 is met). Finally, in September the net cash position is $14, which allows the company to repay the remaining $8 of the loan and start October with $6 in cash.

The amount of a loan required is calculated by subtracting the company's net cash position (line 14) from its minimum cash requirement (line 15). The company is able to accumulate excess cash because of the 50 percent down payment obtained on each project. The company does not have to pay for material purchases for 30 days, so the company has excess cash until the purchases need to be paid.

CASH BUDGET ANALYSIS

The lender analyzes the cash budget to determine the affect on the operating cycle, working capital, and capital expenditures. Each of these items affects the cash flow, profit margins, and amount of debt needed.

Interrelationship Between the Operating Cycle and Cash Needs

As mentioned before, the cash conversion (or operating) cycle will help determine a company's need for a cash budget. For example, a restaurant probably will not need a cash budget because its operating cycle is short, possibly only a few days. The distinction between its accrual income and its cash income will be slight. Further, a review of its monthly statements is practically mandatory for a lender because the capability of generating income can change quickly.

The long operating cycles of manufacturing and certain wholesaling companies can be a problem because they require sizable working capital. A considerable amount of cash is needed to acquire raw materials inventories, pay employee wages, and maintain an inventory of finished goods. For these companies, cash budgets are essential.

Interrelationship Between Working Capital and Capital Expenditures

Sales growth or replacement of capital expenditures requires careful planning. When sales grow, accounts receivable and inventory also grow. Working capital is defined as current assets minus current liabilities. With accounts receivable and inventory being the primary current assets, the cash budget will help determine the affect on the company's working capital requirements.

When a company needs to replace or add fixed assets, sales usually grow. Again, if sales grow, the related current assets grow. If the company can schedule repayment of a loan in accordance with the useful life of the equipment, then the working capital cash needs can be addressed by drawing a cash budget.

The cash budget also addresses the issue of separating financing for permanent expansion of fixed assets from financing for working capital needs. The focus on cash flow makes a cash budget an exceptionally good demonstration of the difference between accounting for income and determining debt repayment capacity. Convincing borrowers to use this approach for their own understanding would be invaluable. If a company has a substantial profit margin, it frequently can finance most, if not all, of its working capital needs.

SUMMARY

The monthly cash budget is an important tool of financial statement analysis because it helps identify the cause, timing, and magnitude of a company's peak borrowing needs during interim periods that may not show up on financial statements. For example, financing needed to purchase inventory for seasonal sales increases can be identified. In addition, the company's ability to repay the additional debt requirement would be apparent.

Cash budgets also are used to determine if borrowing needs are truly short-term or if they represent permanent funding needs. In self-liquidating loans, the assets being financed are converted to cash to repay the debt. In long-term loans, the debt is repaid from the net cash flow of the business. A cash budget can help lenders avoid the pitfall of inadvertently lending for the short term when the borrower actually has a long-term need.

The timing of receipts and expenditures is a crucial component of a company's cash flow and must be taken into consideration when developing a cash budget. Receipts and expenditures must be in line with the company's past performance and with management's plans for the year (such as making capital purchases, tightening up the company's credit policies, or carrying more or less inventory). In addition, lenders' assumptions should be consistent with their review of the company's financial statements.

QUESTIONS FOR DISCUSSION

1. If raw material purchases needed to be paid at the time of purchase, how would Designs by Dezine, Inc.'s, cash budget be affected?
2. What types of cash are included in calculating total receipts?
3. What issues should be considered in calculating interest expense?
4. For what types of companies is a cash budget useful?
5. How is the amount of minimum cash determined?

Exercise

If Service, Inc., had sales of $40 per month beginning month 3 and increased its S, G, & A expenses to $9 (because of the increased sales), what effect would this have on the cash budget by month 6?

9

CALCULATING AND INTERPRETING PRO FORMA FINANCIAL STATEMENTS

LEARNING OBJECTIVES

After studying *Calculating and Interpreting Pro Forma Financial Statements*, you will be able to

- describe the primary uses of a pro forma forecast as a financial statement analysis tool,
- construct and analyze pro forma forecasts of income statements and balance sheets,
- explain the importance of properly interpreting pro forma forecasts, and
- define the key terms that appear in **bold** in the text.

INTRODUCTION

Some companies prepare forecast financial statements as part of routine financial planning. Pro forma forecast income statements and balance sheets represent management's best guess about how a company will perform in the future. A forecast considers the expected economic, competitive, and regulatory environments in which the company will operate. Lenders typically require commercial term loan applicants to submit forecast financial statements that show the company's projected financial results for one to three years or the term of the loan, whichever is shorter. The number of years covered in a pro forma forecast is entirely up to the lender. Some lenders forecast for only one year because a particular business environment might be too uncertain to put any reliability in a longer forecast. This module uses a one-year forecast for convenience, but the principles expressed can be extended easily for up to five years.

Lenders also request copies of past forecast statements so that they can compare management's past predictions with the company's actual results. Lenders prepare pro forma balance sheets and income statements based on the company's past performance and expectations of the future.

Even at their best, pro forma forecast statements have shortcomings. No one can predict the future with certainty, and many unforeseen factors dramatically affect a company's projected financial plans.

REVIEWING THE ASSUMPTIONS

One of the lender's first tasks in reviewing a loan applicant's forecasts is to determine how optimistic the loan applicant's plan is. Hastily reviewing an optimistic plan from a company could draw the lender into a problem loan. Lenders need to consider for themselves whether the company's pro forma seems to be realistic.

Lenders use conceptual and mechanical tools to decide whether a company's pro forma is reasonable. Lenders also use these tools to create pro formas about their clients. The conceptual part of the analysis is based on analyzing the company's past performance, as evidenced by its prior financial statements, statements of cash flows, and ratio analyses. The pro forma forecast, taking into consideration both internal and external forces that affect the loan applicant's business, must assess the financial consequences of management's plans and strategies and how they are likely to affect the company's borrowing needs, repayment capacity, and general credit worthiness. One method lenders use to be objective in their analysis is to think in terms of most likely (best) and least likely (worst) scenarios.

A tool lenders use to improve the likelihood of creating realistic assessments is constructing multiple one-year forecasts, either manually or on a computer program. A good computer program allows the lender to change assumptions and easily fit various scenarios into a spreadsheet. A good computer program also allows the lender to run simulations of changes in important variables to see the results. The same computer program used to spread financial statements usually can be used to prepare a forecast.

PRO FORMA FRAMEWORK

The basic framework for forecasting financial statements involves paying attention to

- the company's past performance, its continued reliability, and the consistency of past projections;
- the external factors that affect the company's operation, such as the economy, industry trends, the market, competition, and government regulations; and
- the internal factors that affect the company's operation, such as management, physical plant, financial controls, marketing strategy, and managerial reports.

A lender who considers these elements will be able to determine not only if a company's financial projections are technically correct, but also if the projections are based on reasonable assumptions.

Realistic Assumptions

A lender reviewing a company-prepared forecast will not rely totally on the company's assumptions, but will introduce other assumptions that might be more realistic. The company's and lender's forecast results are compared in a process that is similar to analyzing financial statements. The basis of both sets of projections and the resulting analysis is the company's past financial results and its plans for sales, expense controls, capital equipment, and plant expenditures for the coming years.

In addition to reviewing the financial documents submitted by the company, a lender often visits the company in person to meet key personnel and see the company's operations. The lender also should get references from outside sources, such as suppliers, customers, and trade associations. If the company is a start-up, the lender may need to call suppliers to determine what type of credit will become available.

Financial Statement Background

To ensure that a forecast analysis is comprehensive and credible, a lender must have on hand

- a complete set of income statements, balance sheets, and statements of cash flows for the past three to five years,
- the company's debt schedule, and
- the company's projections created during past periods (if available).

Dependability of Performance

A thorough understanding of a company, its industry, and its market helps the lender determine the reliability of a company's financial projections and assumptions. Long-term forecasts are most dependable for companies that have established consistent performance trends and have closely tracked the industry. Much of this information will have been derived from analyzing the company's balance sheets and income statements, industry trends, and ratios. At this point in the review, the lender should have a solid grasp of the company's operations and its past and current performance.

Creating a meaningful forecast analysis for new companies and those with brief records or a record of inconsistent performance is exceedingly difficult. For example, a company that provides products or services for a competitive market can be subject to a rapid loss of the market share. For new companies, lenders obtain information on the products or services to determine what level of sales may be expected.

Time Intervals

The time interval represented by the company's forecast statements should match the purpose and the repayment period for the proposed loan. For example, in projecting seasonal borrowing needs, the company constructs a cash budget and not a pro forma financial statement.

Projections that support long-term financing requests should indicate the company's ability to repay the debt and extend far enough into the future to reassure the lender that current trends will continue. These projections should be consistent with trends established over the same period of time in the past. The lender compares past projections to the past performance of the industry. If the projections are not consistent with trends established over the same period of time in the past, the owner or senior management should provide substantive explanations for these discrepancies.

External Factors

External factors affect a company's operations and thus the analysis of its forecast statements. A lender considers how these various factors might change over time and thereby influence the company's future performance in unexpected ways.

Although a company's management cannot control the external factors that make up the company's operating environment, it must anticipate and plan for such factors if the company is to reach its financial objectives. In making or analyzing projections, the company or lender takes into consideration such major external factors as

- the economy—predictions for general business conditions, interest rates, and economic fluctuations

- the industry—its growth or stagnancy, the ease of entry into it, its degree of competitiveness and number of competitors, and the company's position in the industry (whether it is a leader or a marginal producer)

- the market—its degree of diversification (number of buyers), the cost of entry into it, the basis of competition (price, quality, technology), the competition from complementary products, and sociological trends (consumer preferences, environmental concerns, and so on)

- government regulations—prospects for regulatory changes (deregulation), particular environmental issues, and future vulnerability to imports or protection by import restrictions

- labor—the future availability and cost of labor; if nonunionized, prospects for unionization; if unionized, likelihood of strikes and anticipated costs of new contract negotiations

Companies using price-sensitive products, such as the airline and travel industry, can have their entire inventory source or service process disrupted by an unforeseen event. Even well-established companies can be affected by unanticipated events. For example, the U.S. airlines and the travel industry were hurt financially after the terrorist attacks on September 11, 2001.

Internal Factors

Internal factors include the human, financial, and physical resources available to the company. Management can control these factors and use them to enhance the company's operational performance. The major internal factors to consider are

- management—experience, past performance, ability to project performance and to perform according to projections, ability to achieve objectives, and ability to grow with the company

- physical plant and equipment—capacity, condition, and efficiency compared to that of competitors; technological sophistication

- financial controls—accounts receivable systems (approval and collection), inventory and purchasing systems, accounts payable systems, expense controls, and budgetary provisions

- marketing strategy—the company's niche marketing plan and market territory, adequacy of financial and human resources to support the plan distribution system

- managerial reports—quality and adequacy of financial and other managerial reports, which are the basis for decision making

The essence of good management is the ability to plan for an uncertain future, react to adverse or favorable events, and employ the company's resources to achieve its objectives. This requires a thorough knowledge of both the external and internal factors that affect a company and the requirements and limitations these factors impose.

CASE INTRODUCTION—DESIGNS BY DEZINE, INC.

Designs by Dezine, Inc's., financial statements, summarized in exhibit 9.1, will be used throughout this chapter to illustrate the forecasting process. On January 2, 2002, the company requested bank financing for a computer system that cost $10,000. Designs by Dezine, Inc., plans to pay $5,000 down and finance the balance over five years. The company has requested a loan with a five-year amortization of principal plus interest. A one-year forecast will be used to demonstrate pro forma analysis.

Management has provided the bank with a forecasted income statement and balance sheet (exhibit 9.1). The bank has provided various services to the Designs by Dezine, Inc. owners for several years. As part of the commercial relationship, the company provides the bank with copies of its monthly and annual financial statements. Because of these past dealings, the lender has a good feel for the company's strengths and weaknesses and knows a number of its officers. The company's borrowings traditionally have been term loans for vehicles. To supplement the company's financial statements, the lender also has obtained industry information from the company's trade association.

External Factors

The economy is currently weak. All economic indicators are flat or down and are projected to remain so for the next year. Monetary growth and inflation appear stable for the immediate future. Industry predictions show that the value of residential real estate will increase by 5 percent in the current year.

The remodeling industry is expected to do well as individuals will likely remodel their existing homes rather than move during an economic down turn. The remodeling industry expects to grow by 15 percent next year. Federal government regulations have little direct effect on the remodeling industry. State regulations vary by state with most states raising air quality levels in homes and requiring better insulating materials and better built homes.

Internal Factors

Designs by Dezine, Inc.'s, management team's goal is for the company to become a leader in the industry. For its first year, the company performed satisfactorily. Now the management wants to direct a growth-oriented company with quality projects that are larger in size. Management's primary weakness lies in its lack of a sales manager. The president currently functions in that position. The company also will need to consider renting its own facility in the coming year.

Although the company's management intends to take an aggressive position in the market, it is unwilling to lower price in order to achieve an increased market share. This approach requires the company to hire very skilled laborers and to compensate them well.

PRO FORMA FORECASTING ANALYSIS

Forecasting analysis enables the company's management and the bank's loan officer to anticipate the financial consequences of the company's plans and strategies. It has been said that the "the past predicts the future." By analyzing the past performance, forecasting the future can begin.

Past Performance

A company's past performance is an important indicator of the predictability of the future. The company's past history offers a basis on which to judge the reasonableness

(000s omitted)

Income Statement	Amount ($)	%
Net sales	700	100.0
Cost of goods sold	525	75.0
Gross profit	175	25.0
Selling, general, and administrative expenses	46	6.6
Owner's salary	60	8.6
Depreciation	14	2.0
Total operating expenses	120	17.1
Operating profit	55	7.8
Interest expense	10	1.4
Net profit before tax	45	6.4
Taxes	0	0.0
Net profit after tax	45	6.4
Dividend for taxes	15	2.1

Balance Sheet

Assets	Amount ($)	%
Cash	22	25.3
Accounts receivable	18	20.7
Inventory	2	2.3
Total current assets	42	48.3
Gross fixed assets	71	81.6
Depreciation	26	29.9
Net fixed assets	45	51.7
Total assets	87	100.0

Liabilities	Amount ($)	%
Bank debt short term	0	0.0
Accounts payable	14	16.1
Long-term debt	33	37.9
Shareholder debt	35	40.2
Total liabilities	82	94.2

Net Worth	Amount ($)	%
Common stock	1	1.1
Retained earnings	4	4.6
Total net worth	5	5.7

of the assumptions used to construct the projected statements. Exhibit 9.2 summarizes Designs by Dezine, Inc.'s, common-sized balance sheet and income statement for 2001.

Past Income Statements

Designs by Dezine, Inc., had only eight months of sales last year, during which it generated sales of $364,000. The income statement also shows that the company's gross margin was 14.1 percent. The gross profit varies, depending on the mix of products sold. For example, the company makes more money on decks and custom cabinets than it does on large additions. Selling, general, and administrative expenses were 5.7 percent of sales. The company had an operating loss its first year, which is not unusual.

Exhibit 9.2	Financial Statement Summary for Year Ending December 31, 2001—Designs by Dezine, Inc.	

	(000s omitted)	
Income Statement	20x1 Amount ($)	Common-sized (%)
Net sales	384	100.0
Cost of goods sold	330	85.9
Gross profit	54	14.1
Selling, general, and administrative expenses	22	5.7
Owner's salary	43	11.2
Depreciation	12	3.1
Interest expense	3	0.8
Net profit before tax	(26)	(6.7)

Balance Sheet		
Assets	20x1 Amount ($)	Common-sized (%)
Cash	6	9.5
Accounts receivable	8	12.7
Total current assets	14	22.2
Net fixed assets	49	77.8
Total assets	63	100.0
Liabilities	20x1 Amount ($)	Common-sized (%)
Other current liabilities	3	4.8
Notes payable shareholder	46	73.0
Long-term debt	40	63.5
Net worth	(26)	(41.3)
Total liabilities and equity	63	100.0

Past Balance Sheets

An examination of past years' balance sheets should help to create expectations for the company's future financing needs. Designs by Dezine, Inc.'s, balance sheet shows the company's financial position is funded primarily by the owner.

The company's sales terms are 50 percent down at signing of the contract and the balance on completion of the project. Most work is done in 30 to 45 days. During 2001, receivables were collected on completion of all work. The company's inventory is nominal, consisting of nuts, bolts, nails, and lumber. The fixed assets consist of two company trucks.

FORECASTING AN INCOME STATEMENT

The income statement is the first statement forecasted because the income statement largely drives the balance sheet. Examples of how the balance sheet is based on the income statement include:

- net profit and dividends are used to calculate retained earnings,
- accounts receivable are calculated from projected credit sales,
- inventory is calculated using cost of goods sold, and
- fixed assets are lowered by the amount of depreciation.

Sales

The sales projection is the cornerstone of the entire forecasted financial statement. An unrealistic sales figure causes the rest of the projections to be of questionable value, since the forecast income statement accounts are usually calculated as a percentage of sales. The sales projection also affects many balance sheet accounts, such as accounts receivable and inventory. The basis for the estimation of sales can vary. Sales can be projected on the basis of a very precise, detailed sales budget or as a percentage increase over the previous year's figures.

Designs by Dezine, Inc., has projected a large sales increase for the next year. This is based on the company's operating for a twelve-month period and completing some larger projects. Based on eight months' sales in 2001 of $384,000 and now forecasting a full year of operations, management predicts sales to be in the $700,000 range for 2002. Exhibit 9.3 on the following page summarizes historical and projected sales by month.

From comments in the credit file, the lender notes that first year sales were originally projected to be $500,000. Because the company did not achieve its first year sales, the lender feels sales in the $650,000 range are more appropriate than the $700,000 listed in the company's forecast. For the first year, sales averaged about $50,000 per month. With the company operating for a full year, this allows an approximated increase of 8 percent, which the lender feels is more realistic.

Exhibit 9.4 on page 281 shows the company's forecast income statement as well as that of the bank.

Exhibit 9.3 Historical and Projected Sales—Designs by Dezine, Inc. (000s omitted)

Designs by Dezine, Inc

Monthly sales for 2001 (000s omitted)

Month	Sales	Month	Sales
January	$ 0	July	$ 40
February	0	August	55
March	0	September	60
April	0	October	74
May	15	November	90
June	30	December	20
		Total	384

Designs by Dezine, Inc

Projected sales for 2002 (000s omitted)

Month	Sales	Month	Sales
January	$ 20	July	$ 60
February	25	August	70
March	40	September	80
April	50	October	90
May	60	November	110
June	60	December	35
		Total	700

Cost of Goods Sold

Cost of goods sold usually ranks second behind sales in importance on the forecast income statement. It is usually calculated as a percentage of projected sales, taking into consideration both the company's past and anticipated performance. When a company must trim its selling prices to remain competitive, the cost of goods sold as a percentage of sales increases. Therefore, if the number of units sold remains the same, the cost of goods sold, as a percent of sales, will increase.

Management's projected cost of goods sold should be consistent with the previous year's figures. The company is projecting a 10 percent improvement. Designs by Dezine, Inc.'s, cost of goods sold ranged from 82 to 90 percent per project last year. The percentage varies depending on the product sold. Management projects cost of goods sold at 75 percent of projected sales for the following year. Management hopes to achieve this by keeping its labor busy on a more consistent basis.

Exhibit 9.4 Comparison Forecast Income Statement—Designs by Dezine, Inc. (000s omitted)

Income Statement	Company		Bank	
	Amount ($)	%	Amount ($)	%
Net sales	700	100.0	650	100.0
Cost of goods sold	525	75.0	510	78.5
Gross profit	175	21.5	140	21.5
Selling, general, and administrative expenses	46	6.6	58	8.9
Owner's salary	60	8.6	60	9.2
Depreciation	14	2.0	14	2.1
Total operating expenses	120	17.1	132	20.3
Operating profit	55	7.9	8	1.2
Interest expense	10	1.4	10	1.5
Net profit before tax	45	6.4	(2)	(0.3)
Taxes	0	0.0	0	0.0
Net profit after tax	45	6.4	(2)	(0.3)
Dividends	15	2.1	0	0.0

The lender believes that the company's projected cost of goods sold as a percentage of its sales is not realistic and reasonable because it is not consistent with past performance. Also, the company has stated it does not make as much on larger projects yet is targeting larger projects to achieve the sales growth. Therefore, the lender applies 78.5 percent to the cost of goods sold projected by the bank. At this point, the forecast income statements already differ, as illustrated in exhibit 9.5.

The bank's conservative forecast of lower sales and higher cost of goods sold produces a gross profit of $35,000 less than the customer's projection. Each one-percent change on the banker's forecast in the cost of goods sold lowers the gross profit by $6,500.

Exhibit 9.5 Forecast Cost of Goods Sold—Designs by Dezine, Inc. (000s omitted)

Income Statement	Company		Bank	
	Amount ($)	%	Amount ($)	%
Net sales	700	100.0	650	100.0
Cost of goods sold	525	75.0	510	78.5
Gross profit	175	25.0	140	21.5

Operating Expenses

Designs by Dezine's operating expenses include selling, general, and administrative expenses, depreciation, and officers' salaries. These expenses differ from those included in the cost of goods sold because they are not directly related to the purchase or production of goods or services. However, the operating expenses are usually more difficult to control when sales change rapidly. A company normally projects its operating expenses as a percentage of projected sales or as a percentage change from the previous year's operating expenses.

Selling expenses include the cost of advertising, market research, sales training, promotion, and commissions. Management can vary these expenses at its discretion, as warranted by changing conditions in the marketplace. For instance, when a company introduces a new product or encounters increased competition in the industry, management might increase its sales commissions or promotional outlays.

The general and administrative (G&A of S, G, & A) expenses include rent, utilities, real estate, taxes (other than income taxes), depreciation of assets not used in production (such as administrative offices and equipment), telephones, staff and officers' salaries and benefits, and subscriptions. If the company anticipates no dramatic changes, these items can be calculated as a percentage of sales based on past history. The lender should evaluate the assumptions behind each figure in this category.

In the past, management consistently held selling, general, and administrative expenses to 5.7 percent of sales. The company is forecasting these expenses at 6.6 percent of sales for next year. A modest increase in expenses is due to increased advertising cost. The bank projects these expenses at 8.9 percent of sales because of its lower sales forecast and a possible need to rent space next year.

The owner has forecasted a personal salary of $60,000 per year. This is close to the annualized amount taken last year. The bank agrees with this amount. The depreciation expense was $12,000 (rounded up) last year. Depreciation expense is expected to be $12,000 on the existing trucks and $2,000 for the new computer for a total of $14,000.

Operating Profit

After the operating expenses have been subtracted from the gross revenues, the company's operating profit remains. The company projection of sales and expense figures results in an operating profit of $55,000, or 7.9 percent of sales. The bank's projections result in an operating profit of 1.2 percent of sales, or $8,000. The increased cost of goods sold percentage and increased selling, general, and administrative expenses have caused a difference of $47,000 between the two forecasts.

Other Income and Expense

Income statements often include other income and other expense items that do not result from the company's normal business operations. Although these accounts normally are quite small, the lender must determine what specific items are included and whether they are recurring or nonrecurring. These accounts are not usually predictable as a percentage of a company's sales. Designs by Dezine, Inc., has not had other income in the past and does not anticipate any in the coming year. Its only nonoperating expense is interest.

Interest expense is often listed separately on the income statement. This is a relatively predictable expense, because a range of interest rates can be assumed for term debt and short-term (seasonal) borrowings. It is estimated by the average amount of term and seasonal debt outstanding during the year.

The increased interest expense for the new loan is added to the historical interest expense. The historical interest expense is low. The shareholder advanced about $46,000 late in the year. This loan was to fund the company during the first year of operation. The forecast includes interest expense on the existing auto debt of $4,000, shareholder debt of $5,500, and the new computer loan of $400. Although it appears the company might need more money to fund its growth, the amount is unknown until the balance sheet is constructed. Therefore, the lender has forecasted $10,000 for interest expense.

Income Taxes

Income taxes often are projected using current Internal Revenue Service income tax tables. But because of tax incentives associated with fiscal tax policies, this may not be a realistic assumption. Few, if any, growing companies are paying the current corporate tax-schedule rate. The problem is complicated because accrual accounting, according to GAAP, requires that the provision for taxes be at the standard rate. Designs by Dezine, Inc., is an S corporation and has forecasted a $15,000 dividend to be used to pay the taxes. The loan officer is forecasting a net loss, so the bank's income statement for Designs by Dezine, Inc., does not indicate a dividend.

FORECASTING THE BALANCE SHEET

After analyzing and reworking Designs by Dezine, Inc.'s, forecast income statement, the lender constructs the pro forma forecast balance sheet (see exhibit 9.6 on the following page). This exhibit, like the income forecast, is a comparison of the customer forecast submitted with the loan application and the one made by the lender. The assumptions made and conclusions reached in projecting the various income statement accounts affect several entries on the forecast balance sheet. Therefore, the assumptions used in composing and analyzing the forecast balance sheet must be consistent with those used for the income statement.

The cash account in the assets section of the balance sheet or the notes payable short term to bank account in the liabilities section is the plug figure used to balance the forecast balance sheet. In other words, one of these accounts is used to balance the statement after all of the other accounts have been calculated. After the forecast balance sheet has been calculated—if assets exceed total liabilities and net worth (stockholders' equity)—any differences are shown by increasing the notes payable to bank account. However, if total liabilities and net worth exceed assets, the difference is added to the cash account to balance the statement or subtracted from the notes payable if any loans are outstanding.

Exhibit 9.6　Forecast Balance Sheet—Designs by Dezine, Inc.

Balance Sheet

	Company		Bank	
Assets	*Amount ($)*	*%*	*Amount ($)*	*%*
Cash	22	25.2	5	7.1
Accounts receivable	18	20.7	18	25.7
Inventory	2	2.3	2	2.9
Total current assets	42	48.3	25	35.7
Gross fixed assets	71	81.6	71	101.4
Depreciation	26	29.9	26	37.1
Net fixed assets	45	51.7	45	64.3
Total assets	87	100.0	70	100.0
Liabilities	*Amount ($)*	*%*	*Amount ($)*	*%*
Notes payable bank short term	0	0.0	15	21.4
Accounts payable-trade	14	16.1	14	20.0
Long-term debt	33	37.9	33	37.9
Shareholder debt	35	40.2	35	50.0
Total liabilities	82	94.2	97	138.6
Net worth	*Amount ($)*	*%*	*Amount ($)*	*%*
Common stock	1	1.1	1	1.4
Retained earnings	4	4.6	(28)	(40.0)
Total net worth	5	5.7	(27)	(38.6)

The changes on the balance sheet will help the lender determine the level of capital expenditures, long-term debt, and debt structure. In addition, the lender will be able to identify certain liquidity, leverage, and profit ratios and test the relationship of those ratios to past figures and those within the industry.

Assets

Asset forecasts are based on past trends and estimated changes. For example, a company might install a new collection system, which would reduce the accounts receivable. The fixed-asset account normally grows in relationship to the plant and equipment capacity. The fixed assets also can grow to replace outdated equipment. Each asset account should be compared to past trends.

Cash and Marketable Securities

Every company needs a minimum cash balance. For forecasting purposes, cash and marketable securities accounts are combined. The forecast is based on past cash balances, since certain cash balances from the level of operations result in check float.

In the borrower's loan agreement, it is possible that additional balances will be required as compensating balances. In that case, they should be added to the above-calculated amount. The company forecasts its minimum cash needs at $5,000. Management attributes its ability to live within the projected cash rate to its improved management of inventory and receivables. The lender agrees with Designs by Dezine, Inc.'s, assessment of its minimum cash needs.

Because the company is projecting greater profits, the company forecast has plugged cash at $22,000. The bank is forecasting an operating loss so the minimum cash of $5,000 is used.

Accounts Receivable

Accounts receivable reflects the amount owed to the company by its customers at the end of the period covered by the forecast-income statement. The company's past performance with respect to receivables days, that is, the average collection period, is used to assess a company's projected accounts receivable.

The lender should thoroughly understand management's sales and collection policies. Credit terms should be compared with actual collection periods to determine the effectiveness of a company's collection policies. A company's sales posture will be the most important factor to affect accounts receivable. For example, management could try to increase sales by offering longer credit terms, by offering credit terms for products formerly sold for cash only, or by lowering prices.

The accounts receivable calculation is done considering trends from previous statements. For most companies, the calculation for accounts receivable uses the following formula:

$$\frac{\text{(Projected days accounts receivable} \times \text{Projected sales)}}{365 \text{ days}} = \text{Projected accounts receivable}$$

For example, if Designs by Dezine decided to not obtain down payments and allow credit terms of 45 days after completion, the calculation for accounts receivable would be:

$$\frac{45 \times \$700}{365} = \$86$$

Sometimes, the average collection period for receivables analysis alone can be misleading and can fail to reveal problems with uncollectible receivables or disputed bills. By comparing several months of accounts receivable, the lender can determine new accounts and predict collection times of existing accounts. This is particularly helpful if a company has a concentration of sales to one company. A listing of accounts receivable should be used to evaluate management's assumptions for future receivables because the aging reflects management's actual practices and successes with respect to collecting receivables.

Designs by Dezine, Inc., requires payment when the project is completed. Accounts receivable represent the 50 percent of the sales not collected at the time of the signing of the contract. For example, December sales are projected to be $35,000. The company will collect $17,500 at the signing of the contract. The balance of the December sales will be listed as accounts receivable of $17,500 ($18,000 rounded) on the forecasted statement. This is the estimated amount of work that will be done on December sales but not paid. This is an estimate only and is likely to be on the high side because the company probably will not complete all the December sales prior to the end of the month.

Inventory

The inventory account on a forecast balance sheet usually is calculated on the basis of the company's past days inventory ratio. For most companies, the calculation of inventory is:

$$\frac{(\text{Projected days inventory} \times \text{projected cost of goods sold})}{365 \text{ days}} = \text{Projected inventory}$$

For example, if a retail lumber yard carried 90 days of inventory and had projected cost of goods sold of $1,200,000, the projected inventory calculation would be:

$$\frac{90 \times \$1,200,000}{365} = \$295,890$$

In addition to considering past performance, lenders preparing inventory predictions should take into account anticipated changes in the company's sales and purchasing policies. For example, if a supplier changes the minimum purchase requirement from one case to ten cases per order, the amount of inventory forecasted on the balance sheet must be changed.

Designs by Dezine, Inc., carries a nominal inventory consisting of nails, screws, and other small items. Both the company and bank forecast inventory of $2,000.

Fixed Assets

Many companies routinely prepare a capital expense or acquisitions budget, which lists planned projects, their costs, and anticipated sources of funding. If no such budget exists, company management provides a schedule of fixed assets and depreciation to the bank. This information also can be included in the notes of a company's financial statements. The fixed asset schedule includes the purchase date, useful life, cost, method of depreciation, and depreciation taken to date for each principal asset. Any projected increases in fixed assets (that is, anticipated purchases) are shown in the acquisitions budget.

Companies usually need to replace their fully depreciated assets (which are carried at zero) at a cost higher than the original cost. Lenders should know the age and useful life of the company's fixed assets to determine the replacement needs. A manufacturing facility with considerable excess capacity distorts the need, since the company can increase sales without a corresponding increase in the size of its fixed assets. Thus, the capacity of the company's existing plant and equipment, relative to projected production and space needs, must be taken into consideration. Some companies show no fixed assets on their balance sheet (or a very small amount relative to sales) because they lease their equipment or the company's principals own the fixed assets and rent them back to the company.

Designs by Dezine, Inc.'s, assumptions for its fixed assets account are:

Beginning fixed assets	$ 61
+ new purchases	10
= total gross fixed assets	71
− previous years depreciation	12
− depreciation per year for existing fixed assets	12
− new depreciation	2
= net fixed assets (book value)	45

The new depreciation is calculated using the purchase price and is based on the depreciable life of the equipment which is five years ($10,000/5).

Depreciable fixed assets are evaluated by using one or both of the following methods:

- Asset usage—measures loss of useful life

$$\frac{\text{Accumulative depreciation}}{\text{Fixed assets at cost}} = \text{Percent used}$$

- Remaining useful life—measures number of years of depreciable life remaining

$$\frac{\text{Net book value}}{\text{Annual depreciation}} = \text{Remaining life}$$

For Designs by Dezine, Inc., these calculations for 2001 are

Asset usage

$$\frac{\text{(Accumulated depreciation) } 12}{\text{(Gross fixed assets) } 61} = 20\% \text{ used}$$

Interpretation: 20 percent of the fixed assets have been depreciated. The company should not have to provide funds to replace the company vehicles and maintain productivity.

Remaining life

$$\frac{\text{(Net book value) } 49}{\text{(Annual depreciation) } 12} = 4.1 \text{ years}$$

Interpretation: This tells the lender the average useful life of the company vehicles is more than 4 years.

Total Assets

The loan officer forecasts total assets of $70,000, compared to the company's forecast of $87,000. The difference in the current assets affects the total assets. The company will have to increase liabilities or equity to fund this difference.

Liabilities and Net Worth

Having completed the review of the asset side of the company's forecast balance sheet, the first item on the liability side of the balance sheet—notes payable short term to banks—will be considered.

Notes Payable Short Term to Banks

As mentioned previously, notes payable short term to banks serves as a plug figure in balancing forecast statements. Therefore, other projected liability accounts are completed before calculating this figure. The lender is forecasting a net operating loss and therefore notes payable short term are plugged at $15,000. The company is forecasting excess cash and therefore indicates that no short-term debt is needed.

Accounts Payable and Accruals

The amount of accounts payable is a function of the amount and terms of trade credit that is extended by suppliers as well as the company's actual payment practices. The company's forecasted days payable is verified to the past days payable. Accruals are estimated based on past trends.

It is often difficult for a lender to obtain a listing of purchased raw materials, which is needed to calculate a payables turnover ratio and enter it onto a balance sheet forecast. Usually, the best the lender can do is relate the accounts payable to the cost of goods sold. For most companies the calculation for accounts payable is:

$$\frac{\text{Projected days accounts payable} \times \text{projected cost of goods sold}}{365} = \begin{array}{l}\text{Projected accounts payable or} \\ \text{raw material purchases (if known)}\end{array}$$

Designs by Dezine, Inc., is expecting to pay its suppliers on the completion of each job. Materials are estimated to be 40 percent of each sale. The projected accounts payable of $14,000 represent 40 percent of the forecasted December sales of $35,000. Therefore, the lender agrees with the company forecast for accounts payable.

Current Maturities of Long-term Debt

Current maturities represent the principal amounts of long-term debt due in the next 12 months. This figure can be calculated with the schedule of debt in the footnotes of a company's financial statement or using the previous year's current maturities. Any current maturities resulting from the proposed loan also should be included. The current maturities for the new loans might be principal payments, a custom-designed schedule, or payments (including interest and principal, like installment loans) in which amortization tables would be used.

Last year's taxes for Designs by Dezine, Inc., did not break out the current maturities long-term debt. Therefore, the forecast does not use this account. This is misleading because some portion of the existing term debt and the new computer loan will be due in the coming year.

Long-term Debt

Long-term debt represents the portion of the debt schedule with maturities in excess of one year. Designs by Dezine, Inc., and the bank use the same calculation for long-term debt.

Existing long-term debt	$ 40,000
+ new long-term debt	5,000
− projected payments	12,000
= projected long-term debt	33,000

The company has projected long-term debt payments of $21,000 on the company vehicles and shareholder loan and $1,000 on the new computer loan. The existing debt has two years remaining on the amortization. The new computer loan will be financed for five years.

Net Worth

Generally, the equity section of the balance sheet is easily projected. Common stock figures (for preferred and common stock) can be picked up from previous balance sheets unless additions or deletions to the stock were made in the current year. As exhibit 9.7 illustrates, the retained earnings account is increased by the amount of projected after-tax profits from the forecast income statement, less projected dividends.

Exhibit 9.7 Summary of Retained Earnings		
	Company	*Bank*
Previous retained earnings	$ (26)	$ (26)
+ projected profit (loss)	45	(2)
− less dividends	(15)	0
= new retained earnings	4	(28)

The Plug Accounts

As discussed previously, the notes payable short term account is one of two possible plug (balancing) figures on the balance sheet. The cash account is the other one. If assets exceed liabilities and net worth on the forecast balance sheet, the difference is added to the notes payable short term to banks in order to balance the statement. But if liabilities and net worth exceed assets, the difference is added to cash to balance the statement. The company plugs the cash account and the bank plugs the notes payable short term.

The mere balancing of amounts into notes payable short term should not be considered a realistic alternative to this procedure unless it accurately balances the balance sheet, but the financing needed might be long term rather than short term. The company might need a permanent working capital loan and, therefore, might need long-term financing. The lender will make the decision after preparing a statement of cash flows and reviewing the overall financial condition of the company. In addition, the interest expense on the plug has not been calculated, causing a slightly lower expense and lower need for funds.

ANALYZING EACH SCENARIO

When a multiple-year forecast statement is prepared at the low point in the company's operating cycle, any need for seasonal debt to finance a seasonal buildup in accounts receivable and inventory will not be apparent. Companies that have seasonal sales or production peaks should prepare cash budgets. It would be most desirable for the lender or company to prepare a cash budget before preparing the long-term forecast. By preparing a cash budget first, the amount of peak debt needed and the potential loan structure can be determined—regardless of whether the company needs short-term or long-term debt and how much.

Designs by Dezine, Inc., and the bank's lender have composed two different sets of forecast financial statements, as presented in exhibits 9.4 and 9.6. The bank's projections show that the company needs more debt than it has requested. Some of the more significant changes made by the lender to the company's forecast statements include the following:

- The bank projects less in sales revenues than the company does.
- The bank projects more cost of goods sold expense than the company does.
- The bank projects more in general and administrative expenses than the company does.
- The bank projects significantly less cash flow compared with the company's projection because the bank projects lower net profits.

Because cash and only cash repays loans, a projected cash flow statement should also be prepared. Exhibit 9.8 leads you step-by-step through the process of creating an abbreviated-method cash flow statement for the company-prepared forecast. Exhibit 9.9 that follows shows the abbreviated-method cash flow statement for the bank-prepared forecast. According to the company's projection, the cash flow is sufficient to fund the next year. The company-prepared cash flow indicates short-term debt will not be needed. The lender's projection indicates that cash flow is not sufficient. The bank-

Cash Sources—"Inflows"			Cash Uses—"Outflows"	
Cash profit (net income plus depreciation expense)	59	OR	Cash loss (net loss, offset by depreciation expense)	0
Decrease in accounts receivable	0	OR	Increase in accounts receivable	10
Decrease in inventories	0	OR	Increase in inventories	2
Increase in accounts payable	14	OR	Decrease in accounts payable	0
Increase in short-term debt	0	OR	Decrease in short-term debt	0
			Cash dividends	15
Disposals of fixed assets	0	OR	Fixed asset additions	10
New long-term debt	5		Long-term loan payments	22
New capital stock issued	0		Increase in treasury stock	0
Decrease in cash balance	0	OR	Increase in cash balance	16
Decrease in all other assets	0		Increase in all other assets	0

prepared cash flow indicates the company will need to borrow $15,000 in short-term debt. The bank currently does not have a line of credit approved for the company. The projected net loss by the lender indicates the company is not expected to have the ability to service its debt. The lender will need to discuss the two scenarios with the company. The primary concern is to determine how the company will fund its growth if the profits do not materialize as the company projects.

The company cash flow statement calculations for exhibit 9.8 are:

Cash profit plus depreciation	$45 + $14
Increase in accounts receivable	8 to 18
Increase in inventory	0 to 2
Increase in accounts payable	0 to 14
Cash dividends	15
Fixed asset additions (computer)	10
New long-term debt (computer)	5
Long-term debt payments on existing debt plus new computer	22
Increase in cash balance	6 to 22

Each of the numbers used came from the historical and projected financial statements discussed earlier.

Exhibit 9.9 Abbreviated Cash Flow Statement—Designs by Dezine, Inc., Bank Forecast for 2002

Cash Sources—"Inflows"			Cash Uses—"Outflows"	
Cash profit (net income plus depreciation expense)	12	OR	Cash loss (net loss, offset by depreciation expense)	0
Decrease in accounts receivable	0	OR	Increase in accounts receivable	10
Decrease in inventories	0	OR	Increase in inventories	2
Increase in accounts payable	14	OR	Decrease in accounts payable	0
Increase in short-term debt	15	OR	Decrease in short-term debt	0
			Cash dividends	0
Disposals of fixed assets	0	OR	Fixed asset additions	10
New long-term debt	5		Long-term loan payments	22
New capital stock Issued	0		Increase in Treasury stock	0
Decrease in cash balance	10	OR	Increase in cash balance	0
Decrease in all other assets	0		Increase in all other assets	0

The lender-prepared cash flow statement was calculated as:

Cash profit plus depreciation	($2) + $14 = $12
Increase in accounts receivable	8 to 18
Increase in inventory	0 to 2
Increase in accounts payable	0 to 14
Increase in short-term debt	0 to 15
Fixed asset addition (net computer)	10
New long-term debt	5
Long-term debt payments	22
Decrease in cash	6 to 5

UNCERTAINTIES IN FORECASTS

Forecast statements attempt to estimate a company's financial future in an uncertain environment. These uncertainties include the economy, competition, government regulations, technological change, and management's ability to perform effectively. Although uncertainty increases the more the projection extends into the future, the offset is that feedback received by management in the interim allows the plan to be changed.

Another shortcoming of forecast analysis is that it can result in overlooking the company's interim financing needs. Because the multiple-year forecast balance sheet reflects the company's financial state at a given point in time (usually the fiscal year-end), it does not reveal any funding needs that might arise between fiscal year-end balance sheet dates. These hidden funding needs typically involve the need for seasonal asset buildups in preparation for heavy sales periods.

SUMMARY

Long-term forecast analysis must be based on accurate knowledge of the company's past performance, as well as on knowledge of the external and internal factors that affect the company's operations. It is particularly difficult to make accurate projections for young companies and for companies that have had erratic operating results in the past.

A long-term forecast analysis enables the lender to reach conclusions about a company's probable financing needs and repayment ability. However, the forecast results are only as good as the underlying assumptions on which the projections are based. Therefore, the lender must closely examine the validity of the company's assumptions, making adjustments to the company's forecast statements as deemed necessary. In general, the lender will favor more conservative or realistic assumptions than will company management.

The single most important element of long-term forecast financial statements is the sales projection. Without a reliable sales figure, the entire forecast process is of questionable value. A change in sales can affect projected profits, accounts receivable, inventory, accounts payable, and the perceived borrowing needs of the company. Even a small miscalculation in this key assumption can dramatically affect many areas of the forecast analysis. Therefore, the lender should use scenario analysis to understand how a one percent change in the net margin or a one-day change in accounts receivable and inventory could affect the various statements and the cash flow of the company.

In constructing a forecast balance sheet, assets are made to equal liabilities and net worth by using a plug figure—either cash and marketable securities (on the assets side) or notes payable short term to banks (on the liabilities side). The latter is not to be taken literally, however, since the company might need long-term rather than short-term financing.

When forecasting accounts receivable, inventory, and accounts payable, the past average collection period, selling time, and payment time are generally used. The fixed assets are adjusted for new purchases and the new depreciation. Other assets and liabilities are forecast based on historical amounts.

Forecast analysis has a number of limitations, such as its failure to reveal seasonal financing needs. Because the future is unpredictable, all forecast projections should be tempered with appropriate conservatism.

QUESTIONS FOR DISCUSSION

1. A company requests financing for its seasonal inventory. What type of long-term forecast should be prepared?
2. What is the most important part of a long-term forecast?
3. What should be considered when forecasting accounts receivable and inventory?
4. What are the two possible balance sheet accounts to plug in a forecast?
5. Who should prepare pro forma financial statements?

GLOSSARY

accounts payable—Those amounts due from a company to its vendors that must be paid within one year or less.

accounts receivable—Amounts due to a company for goods or services sold on credit. These are generally current assets.

accrual accounting—A method of accounting in which revenue is recognized when earned, expenses are recognized when incurred, and other changes in financial condition are recognized as they occur, without regard to the timing of the actual cash receipts and expenditures.

accrued expenses—Obligations resulting from the recognition of an expense prior to the payment of cash.

adjusted personal net worth—The amount of an individual's net worth after making adjustments for the overstated value of assets and understated amount of liabilities.

adverse opinion—An accounting opinion expressing that the statements do not fairly present the financial position or results of operations in conformity with generally accepted accounting principles.

agricultural business—A business engaged in the production of crops or livestock.

AICPA—American Institute of Certified Public Accountants.

allowance(s)—Allowances result when customers are compensated for faulty goods by receiving credit on future bills.

allowance for doubtful accounts—The balance sheet account that measures the amount of outstanding accounts receivable expected to be uncollectible.

Annual Statement Studies—A summary of industry averages published annually by The Risk Management Association.

assets—Anything owned by a business or individual that has commercial, exchange, or book value. Assets may consist of specific property or claims against others, in contrast to obligations due to others (liabilities). They may be tangible (physical in character), such as land, buildings, and machinery, or intangible (characterized by legal claims or rights), such as amounts due from customers (accounts receivable) and patents (a protected right). Under generally accepted accounting principles, an asset is defined as the probable future economic benefits obtained or controlled by a particular entity as a result of past transactions or events.

audit—An official examination and verification of accounts.

average collection period—The average number of days required to collect accounts receivable.

B

balance sheet—A detailed list of assets, liabilities, and owners' equity (net worth) showing a company's financial position at a specific time. A bank's balance sheet is generally called a statement of condition.

BCIP—Business Credit Information Package.

break-even analysis—Calculation of the sales needed to cover total costs (that is, to break even). Break-even analysis provides management with information necessary to determine whether a proposed new product can reasonably be expected to become profitable.

brokerage firm—A company in the business of arranging contracts for the purchase and sale of securities.

buildings—The value of real estate owned not including the value of the land.

BCIP—A form of the compilation statement used to bridge the information shortfall of nondisclosure compilations. The BCIP is a tripartite agreement among the banker, accountant, and borrower to address issues not normally addressed in a compilation statement.

C

capital—(1) The funds invested in a company on a long-term basis. These funds are obtained by issuing preferred or common stock, retaining a portion of the company's earnings from the date of incorporation, and long-term borrowing. (2) The funds invested in a firm by the owners for use in conducting business. (3) The owners' original investment, plus any profit reinvested in the business, that appears on the balance sheet.

capital expense budget—Management's estimate of the amount of fixed assets to be purchased in the coming year.

cash—The actual amount of cash in the bank, petty cash, and cash on hand.

cash accounting—An accounting system in which revenues and expenses are recorded and realized only when the accompanying cash inflow or outflow occurs, without regard to the actual period to which the transactions apply. Also called cash basis accounting. Compare with accrual basis accounting.

cash budget—A monthly or quarterly schedule of cash receipts and expenses.

cash flow cycle(s)—The cycle through which a firm's cash passes as it is converted into raw materials to manufacture a product, or purchase inventory or provide a service; which are sold on credit to create accounts receivables, and when collected are converted back into cash.

cash flow statement (statement of cash flows)—A statement of a company's cash receipts and payments during a given period.

cash flows from financing activities—The amount of cash that directly relates to the external financing of the business, involving debt or equity.

cash flows from operations—The amount of cash generated from a business enterprise's normal, ongoing operations during an accounting period.

cash receipts—A schedule of cash collected, such as cash collected from sales, as opposed to accounts receivable, which are accrued sales.

cash value life insurance—The amount of cash available on a life insurance policy if the policy were canceled, less any policy loans outstanding.

collateral—Specific property, securities, or other assets pledged by a borrower to a lender as security on a loan.

commercial paper—A negotiable, short-term, unsecured promissory note in bearer form, issued by well-regarded businesses. Commercial paper is generally sold at a discount and has a maximum maturity of nine months.

commercial finance companies—Companies that specialize in making working capital or investment capital loans to small businesses.

commercial sales finance companies—Companies that finance large industrial or agricultural equipment.

common-sizing—A form of financial ratio analysis that allows the comparison of companies with different levels of sales or total assets by introducing a common denominator. A common-size balance sheet expresses each item on the balance sheet as a percentage of total assets; a common-size income statement expresses each item as a percentage of net sales.

common stock—A security (or securities) that represents ownership in a corporation. Common stock is the one type of security that must be issued by a corporation. The two most important common stockholder rights are voting and dividend rights. Common stockholder claims on corporate assets are subordinate to those of bondholders, preferred stockholders, and general creditors.

compilation—The degree of work performed by a public accounting firm in conjunction with the issuance of financial statements of a nonpublic entity that is less in scope than a review or audit. As such, the accountant does not express an opinion or any other form of assurance on the financial statements.

contribution margin—A component of break-even analysis. The portion of sales available to cover fixed costs and contribute to net profit. It is calculated as net sales minus variable costs.

corporation(s)—A business organization(s) that is treated as a single legal entity and is owned by its stockholders, whose liability is generally limited to the extent of their investment. The ownership of a corporation is represented by shares of stock that are issued to people or to other companies in exchange for cash, physical assets, services, and goodwill. The stockholders elect the board of directors, which then directs the management of the corporation's affairs.

cost of goods sold—The costs to manufacture a product including raw material, labor, and manufacturing overhead or the cost of inventory for wholesale and retail companies.

coverage ratios—A measure of a corporation's financial ability to meet recurring expenses. Earnings are compared to interest or scheduled debt service, and the resulting ratio is referred to as the coverage ratio.

current assets—Cash, marketable securities, accounts receivable, and inventory readily convertible into cash, usually within one year or within the normal operating cycle of the business.

current maturities of long-term debt—The principal portion of long-term debt that will be repaid during the upcoming year.

current ratio—A liquidity ratio used to analyze the amount of current assets available to pay current liabilities.

D

days ratios—also called activity ratios, are indicators of liquidity and measure the days accounts receivable, inventory, and accounts payable.

days accounts payable—A liquidity or activity ratio used to analyze the average time it takes a company to pay its vendors.

days accounts receivable—A liquidity or activity ratio used to analyze the average time it takes to collect credit sales due to the seller.

days in inventory—A liquidity or activity ratio used to analyzed the average time it takes a business to sell its inventory.

debt-to-capitalization ratio—A financial leverage ratio used to assess the permanent capital of a company. This ratio shows what percentage of a company's

permanent capital is financed with debt as opposed to shareholders' investments.

debt-to-worth ratio—A financial leverage ratio used to measure the risk of the creditors versus the owners.

debt service coverage ratio—A coverage ratio that shows what proportion of a company's net profit and non-cash expenses will be needed to pay the principal due on long-term debt in the coming year.

deferred charges—Services that already have been performed and on which payment has been made.

deferred income—Income received but not yet earned. Deferred income appears on the balance sheet as a liability.

deferred taxes—Result when the tax consequences attributable to items that are included in book income but excluded from computation of taxable income during that period. The tax consequence will be recognized in a future period.

depreciation—(1) In accounting, a process of allocating the cost of a fixed asset less salvage value, if any, over its estimated useful life. A depreciation charge is treated as a non-cash expense. (2) In economics, a loss of value in real property caused by age, physical deterioration, or functional obsolescence. (3) In foreign exchange, a decline in the value of a nation's currency or gold because of market factors.

direct method (of the cash flow statement)—A method to calculate the cash flow of a business. The direct method starts with net sales and balances to the change in cash. To calculate the direct method, two years of financial statements are needed.

disclaimer opinion—A financial statement provided by the accountants in which no opinion can be expressed because of limitations in the scope of the auditing firm's engagement, uncertainties about the future that cannot be resolved, or the effect of which cannot be estimated.

discount(s)—A price reduction provided to a purchaser for early payment of goods or services.

dividend—The portion of profit paid out to the stockholders.

dividend payout ratio—A ratio used to analyze the portion of profit paid out to stockholders.

due from affiliates—The amount owed to a company from a related business or entity.

due to affiliates—The amount owed to a related company.

E

equipment—Fixed assets used in the business to produce a product or provide a service, such as machinery, vehicles, and office furniture.

equity—The value of the stockholders' ownership of a corporation, which equals the difference between the company's total assets and its total liabilities. Equity includes preferred stock, common stock, retained earnings, and other surplus reserves. Also called book net worth or total capital.

external factors—Those things that are not controlled by the borrower but influence their business, such as government regulation, the economy, technology, and the industry in which they operate.

F

FASB—Financial Accounting and Standards Board.

FIFO—First in, first out.

Financial Accounting and Standards Board (FASB)—Organization that coordinates the preparation of and changes to generally accepted accounting principles (GAAP).

financial leverage ratios—Relationships among balance sheet values that measure the extent to which owners, rather than creditors, finance a business.

financing activities—Measures the cash flows from debt, its repayment, proceeds from and payments to shareholders.

finished goods—Products for which the manufacturing process is complete.

first-in, first-out (FIFO)—A system of inventory valuation that assumes that a firm's operations will use first those items purchased earliest. Thus, on the firm's financial statements, the cost of the items purchased most recently is assigned to ending inventory. In a period of rising prices, FIFO accounting overstates earnings.

fiscal year-end statements—A financial statement prepared as of the company's legal year end. For proprietorships, partnerships and S corporations, the legal year end is December 31 of each year. The financial statements are for a twelve-month period unless it is the business's first year of operations or the business changed its year end during the last year.

fixed assets—Those items of a long-term nature required for the normal conduct of a business and not converted into cash during a normal operating period. Fixed assets include furniture, land, buildings, leasehold improvements, vehicles, and machinery.

forecast analysis—Projecting income statement and balance sheets based on historical financial statements.

G

GAAP—Generally accepted accounting principles.

generally accepted accounting principles (GAAP)—The rules, conventions, practices, and procedures that form the foundation for financial accounting.

general partnership(s)—A company or companies formed by two or more people joining as co-owners. All co-owners are liable for company debts to the full extent of their personal assets.

goodwill—(1) An intangible asset that is the present value of expected future income in excess of a normal return on an investment. Goodwill arises from considerations, such as a company's strong reputation, favorable location, and good relations with its customers. (2) Under GAAP, goodwill is not recorded unless it is purchased as part of a business combination transaction and represents the excess of the cost of an acquired company over the sum of identifiable net assets.

gross margin—The expression of gross profit as a percentage of net sales. It is the average percentage of markup on goods sold.

gross profit—Sales revenues less the cost of goods sold, excluding selling, general, and administrative, and other expenses.

I

income statement—A financial statement that shows a summary of a company's or individual's income and expenses for a specific period. Also called profit and loss statement, operating statement, and earnings statement.

indirect method (of the cash flow statement)—A method used to calculate cash flow of a business. The indirect method starts with net profit and balances to the change in cash. To calculate the indirect method, two years of financial statements are required.

intangibles—Assets that have no physical existence, such as patents, trademarks, copyrights, franchises, and goodwill.

interim statements—Financial statements issued for periods shorter than one year.

inventory—The materials owned and held by a business, such as raw materials, intermediate products and parts, work-in-progress, and finished goods. These materials may be intended for either internal consumption or sale.

investing activities—Measures long-term increases in fixed assets, other long-term investments, and proceeds from disposing of these assets.

IRS—Internal Revenue Service.

L

land—A fixed asset which values on the amount of acreage owned at cost, excluding any building value.

last-in, first-out (LIFO)—A method of inventory valuation that assumes that the most recent purchases are used first in determining the cost of goods sold. As such, ending inventory is valued assuming the earliest purchases remain in ending inventory. Compare with first-in, first-out (FIFO).

leasehold improvements—Improvements made to property that is leased or rented by the borrower.

lease(s)—A contract(s) in which one party grants to another party the right to use or occupy property owned by the former. The granting party is the lessor. The party using the property is the lessee.

lender prepared direct method (of the cash flow statement)—A method to calculate the cash flow of a business. The direct method starts with net sales and balances to the change in cash. To calculate the direct method, two years of financial statements are needed.

letter(s) of credit—An engagement by a bank or other person made at the request of a customer that the issuer will honor drafts or other demands for payment upon compliance with the conditions specified in the credit. The credit may be revocable or irrevocable. The engagement may be either an agreement to honor or a statement that the bank or other person is authorized to honor. Under a direct-pay letter of credit, the bank pays off all maturing obligations and obtains reimbursement from the borrower.

liability—An amount owed.

LIFO—Last in, first out.

limited liability company (LLC)—A variation of the corporation, it offers tax advantages and limited personal liability to the owners. LLCs have a limited life, however, and ownership interests are not freely transferable.

LLC—Limited liability company.

LLP—Limited liability partnership.

long-term debt—Generally, debt maturing in one or more years.

long-term forecast—A projection of a company's financial statements for longer than one year.

M

management letter—A letter sent to the management of a company expressing operational concerns or deficiencies not expressed in the audit.

manufacturer—A company engaged in producing a product for sale to other manufacturers, wholesalers, retailers, or service companies. The company purchases raw material and adds labor to produce a finished good, which is then sold on credit terms.

marketable securities—Cash not needed immediately in the business and temporarily invested to earn a return.

minimum cash—The least amount of cash a business needs to fund daily operations.

N

net profit—The excess of total revenues over total expenses.

net wages—The amount of all sources of personal income minus taxes.

net working capital—A liquidity measure calculated as current assets minus current liabilities.

net worth—Assets minus liabilities of a business. This is the owner's equity. Also called shareholders' equity.

note(s) payable short-term—An amount owed by a business to a bank or other lender in the form of a loan due in one year or less. A note payable entails a written promissory note given by the borrower to the lender.

note(s) receivable—The amount owed to a business on a promissory note from a customer or other debtor.

O

operating activities—Cash generated from activities normally involved in producing goods or delivering services, such as collection of accounts receivable, cash payment for inventory, and interest expense.

operating cycle(s)—The time required to purchase or manufacture inventory or provide a service, sell the product, or provide the service and collect the cash.

operating expense(s)—An expense incurred as a result of a company's normal operations. Also commonly called selling, general, & administrative expenses.

operating leverage—The relationship of fixed costs to total costs in a company's operation. The higher the fixed costs, the higher the operating leverage.

operating profit—Earnings from a company's normal business operations. This figure generally excludes other income and other expense. Also called operating income.

other expenses—Other expenses in the financial statement that are not included in general, selling, and administrative expenses. These other expenses include losses on sales of assets, losses do to one time events, and interest expense.

other income—Sources of revenue for a business not included in net sales. These sources include interest income, gains on sales of assets, and rental income.

P

paid-in surplus—The contributions of capital received by a corporation that are not credited to capital stock. Paid-in surplus results from the sale of Treasury stock at a price greater than its purchase price; issuance of par value stock at a price greater than par value, issuance of non-par stock at a price greater than stated value, forfeited payments made on subscribed stock, and contributions by stockholders and people outside the corporation.

permanent working capital—A loan for the purpose of meeting a company's working capital requirements. A permanent working capital loan is most often used to finance current assets long-term that have already been financed on a short-term basis.

personal expenses—The sum of all personal living expenses, debt payments, and interest payments.

personal financial statement—Statement of an individual's personal financial resources and obligations, comparable to a balance sheet for business.

plug figures—The amount needed to balance a projected balance sheet. If the assets exceed the liabilities and net worth, then notes payable short-term are used. If liabilities and net worth exceed the assets, then cash is used to balance the statement.

preferred stock—One of the two major types of equity securities (common stock is the other type). Preferred stock receives dividends before common stock, and the dividend rate for most preferred stock is fixed at the time of issuance. If a corporation is liquidated, preferred stockholders are given preference to the company assets ahead of common stockholders. Unlike common stock, preferred stock does not usually entail voting rights.

prepaid expenses—A non-current asset classification of expenditure made to benefit future periods. Prepaid expenses include prepaid rent, certain taxes, royalties, and unexpired insurance premiums.

pro forma forecast— A financial statement that assumes future events in order to project conditions of the company as a result of those events. For example, a pro forma statement may assume future sales to project anticipated income.

proprietorship(s)—A business entity owned and operated by a single individual. The owner is fully liable for all debts incurred by the business.

Q

qualified opinion—An opinion rendered by an independent auditor of financial statements stating that the statements in some way do present fairly the financial position, the results of operations, and/or the changes in financial position for the company.

quick ratio—A liquidity ratio that lenders use to measure a company's ability to meet its current obligations. The ratio is calculated by dividing current assets minus inventory by current liabilities. Also called acid-test ratio.

R

ratios—The comparison of various figures found on a company's financial statements, for purposes of analysis.

raw materials—Basic commodities or natural resources that will be used in the production of goods.

receivables aging—A listing of customer accounts and the amounts due by billing dates in aging categories.

retailer—A business engaged in selling finished products to consumers, generally for cash or cash equivalents or, on occasion, for credit.

retained earnings—Earnings, not distributed to stockholders, that have not been transferred to the surplus account. Retained earnings are a part of the company's net worth.

returns—Finished goods that have been returned to the seller. The amount of returns is deducted from gross sales in arriving at net sales.

return-on-assets ratio (ROA)—A profitability ratio. Return on assets is net income divided by total assets. Return on assets indicates how efficiently assets are employed.

return-on-equity ratio (ROE)—A profitability ratio that shows the profit earned on each dollar of equity. Return on equity measures the income earned on each dollar of the shareholder's investment.

return-on-sales ratio (ROS)—A profitability ratio that shows the profit earned on each dollar of sales. Expressed as net profit divided by sales. Return on sales measures how many pennies the company earned for each dollar of sales.

review—The degree of work performed by a public accounting firm in conjunction with the issuance of financial statements of a nonpublic entity that is greater in scope than a compilation but less in scope than an audit and does not provide a basis for the expression of an opinion on the financial statements. However, the accountant's report would generally state that, based on his or her review, the accountant is not aware of any material modifications that need to be made to the financial statements for them to conform to generally accepted accounting principles.

revolving line of credit—A specified maximum line of credit on which a borrower may draw for a limited period. The balance may fluctuate from zero up to the maximum amount.

RMA—The Risk Management Association

S

S corporation—A variation of the corporation, it arose with the enactment of the Tax Reform Act of 1986. The most significant difference between S corporations and regular corporations is in the treatment of income. With an S corporation, all net income from the corporation is taxed at individual tax rates and not at corporate rates.

sales projection—The amount of revenue a company forecasts for a coming period. It is the foundation of preparing a company budget.

sales volume—The amount of revenue a company receives over a given period of time. It is measured in the total number of units sold and the mix of units sold.

SEC—Securities and Exchange Commission.

scenario analysis—The use of various assumptions to prepare a cash budget or pro forma financial statement. Scenario analysis is used to determine the impact of various assumptions on the company's financial statements.

scope of auditor's engagement—Term used to describe the extent of an accountant's action, inquiry, and preparation of financial statements.

seasonal line of credit—A line of credit used to finance a periodic increase in current assets, such as inventory, in anticipation of a seasonal surge in sales volume.

Securities and Exchange Commission (SEC)—The SEC publishes regulations pertaining to financial information submitted by businesses reporting the results of their financial condition and their operations.

selling, general, & administrative expenses—The expenses in a business that relate to operations. Also called operating expenses. These expenses include advertising, utilities, and office salaries, as opposed to cost of goods sold, which relates to expenses to produce or sell the product.

service(s) company—A company which does not sell a tangible product, such as the medical, accounting, and legal professions.

SFAS No. 95 (statement of cash flows)—An accountant-prepared statement of cash flows prepared according to GAAP and using a GAAP-prepared financial statement.

SIC—Standard Industrial Classification.

sources of cash—All revenues readily available to a business; these include collections of accounts receivable, sales of inventory for cash, selling fixed assets for cash, accounts payable and other borrowings.

special commitment loans—Loans used for the purpose of supporting an isolated increase in current assets necessitated by a special circumstance.

SFAS—Statement of cash flows.

subordinated debt—Debt that ranks lower than other liabilities in the priority of its claim on the issuer's assets or payment.

T

term loan(s)—A loan scheduled to run for more than one year, usually repayable in annual or more frequent installments.

times-interest-earned ratio—A leverage ratio indicating the relationship between interest expense and net profit, used to determine whether a business can meet its periodic interest payments.

U

unqualified opinion—An opinion rendered by an independent auditor of financial statements asserting that the financial statements present fairly the financial position, the results of operations, and the changes in financial position for the company.

U.S. Individual Tax Return Form 1040—Form required by the Internal Revenue Service which summarizes an individual's income and expenses for the reporting period.

W

wholesaler—A business engaged in selling a finished product. The company usually purchases the product from a manufacturer and sells the product to a retailer.

work-in-process—Products for which the manufacturing process is only partially completed.

working assets—Those assets that are used primarily to generate revenue or that are the largest dollar amount on the balance sheet.

working capital—A company's investment in current assets, namely, cash, marketable securities, accounts receivable, and inventory. The difference between a company's current assets and current liabilities is known as net working capital.

working investment—The amount of cash held in accounts receivable, inventory, accounts payable, and accrued expenses. The difference between these two categories of current assets and current liabilities is known as gross working capital.

working investment ratio—The ratio of working investment (working assets and working liabilities) to net sales.

INDEX

I

illiquidity, 100
income analysis, for personal financial
    statement, 211-212, 224-227
income statement
    accrual-basis, 12
    break-even point, 24
    cash-basis, 12
    forecasting of, 279-283
income statement analysis, 24, 63-97
    break-even analysis and, 84-89
    expense analysis and, 72-84
    external factors and, 66
    forecasting analysis and, 278
    management objectives and, 66
    method of accruing revenue, 66-67
    operating leverage and, 89-90, 91
    other expenses and, 90, 92, 93-95
    other income and, 92-93
    period of income statement and, 67
    sales analysis and, 67-72
    spreadsheet concept and, 64-65
    types of businesses and, 66
income taxes
    cash budgets and, 267
    deferred, 126, 127
    expense analysis and, 94-95
    income statement forecasting and,
        267
    payable, 123
indirect method SFAS NO. 95
    Statement of Cash Flows, 174,
        186, 187
industry information, sources of, 138
insurance companies, 60
intangibles, 118-119
interest expense, 94, 266
interest income, 92, 224
interim financial statements, 7, 15, 67
internal factors, and forecasting, 275
internally prepared financial statements,
    13-15
interpretive analysis, 5
inventory
    analysis of, 24
    cash flows and, 176, 192

components of, 107-108
days inventory ratio and, 148-150
finished goods as, 108
forecasting and, 286
physical count of, 75-76
raw materials as, 107
valuation of, 76-78
work-in-process as, 108
inventory holding gains profit, 76
investing activities
    calculation of cash flows from,
        183-184
    personal financial statement and,
        247
investments in affiliated companies,
    17-18
IRA accounts, 219
IRA distributions, 225
itemized deductions, 226

K

Keogh accounts, 219

L

labor, 264-265
large nonrecurring sales, 71
last-in, first-out (LIFO) method, 76-77
    change in valuation method and,
        79-80
    compared with FIFO, 77
lease financing, 59
leasehold improvements, 111
leases as liabilities, 126, 128
leasing companies, 60
legal structures, 31-33, 34
    corporation, 32, 34
    general partnerships, 31-32, 34
    limited liability company, 33
    S corporation, 32-33, 34
    sole proprietorship, 31, 34
lender-prepared direct method cash
    flow analysis, 186, 188-195, 204
letter of credit, 59
leverage ratios, 151-153
    debt-to-capitalization ratio,
        152-153, 154

Improve Your Performance with these ABA Products & Services

ABA Web Sites. The ABA has been the connecting link for bankers for more than 125 years. Now, technology allows us to put the world of banking right on your desktop through the Internet. Explore www.aba.com for more information about these and other products and services.

Products

ABA Retail Banking Survey Report. Information issues shaping today's retail banking landscape form the core of ABA's Retail Banking Survey Report. The survey presents detailed data about retail banking operations, performance management, deposit and other banking services, stratified by two asset categories: less than $500 million and $500 million or more. Divided into three main sections—an analysis of Internet banking, a management summary and detailed data tables—the report contains information on both traditional and special services that banks offer to individuals and small businesses, including: branch automation, automated teller machines, employee training and compensation, POS debit cards, package plans, and online banking.

Banking and Finance Terminology. The most reliable source for banking and finance terminology, the 4th edition of this industry resource will help you read with greater comprehension and write with greater authority in the such areas as accounting, asset and liability management, commercial and consumer lending, credit cards, economics and global banking, human resources management, insurance, investments and securities, law and regulatory compliance, marketing and sales, operations and payment systems, electronic funds transfers, real estate finance, trust and private banking, and more. The book presents a total of more than 7,000 definitions, with more than 1,000 new entries! Much more than a dictionary, this compact reference contains information that reflects today's expanding financial services industry, including appendices on industry acronyms and abbreviations, key performance ratios, economic indicators, Federal Reserve regulations, important banking legislation, and federal and state regulatory agency addresses.

Law and Banking Principles. Your legal aid for the fundamentals of banking law, this highly informative, revised and up-to-date, text outlines and illustrates in plain English how laws affect the business of banking. You will learn the fundamentals of banking law from the point of view of employees in direct contact with customers. This is a powerful information tool that will give you the confidence to grasp the legal and regulatory requirements of banking. You will be able to explain the regulatory system governing banks; identify the major laws that affect the business of banking today; describe differences between crimes and torts, and list those that affect banking today; and list property ownership types and how banks obtain an interest in customer property. Also in this edition are detailed chapters about the Uniform Commercial Code as it relates to banking and information on internet banking.

Reference Guide to Regulatory Compliance. Keep one copy of this easy-to-carry publication in your briefcase and keep another on your desk top. Updated annually, this comprehensive desktop reference book offers detailed information on more than 34 regulatory areas affecting banks, arranged by bank function—deposits, lending, information reporting, bank operations, safety and soundness, and social responsibility. Developed as an extended outline, the guide covers federal regulations, consumer legislation, and all the rules you need to know to meet all the demands of today's compliance requirements. The *Guide* also includes pertinent regulatory citations and self-study/review questions and answers.

Services

American Institute of Banking. ABA's American Institute of Banking (AIB) is a continuing education curriculum for the financial services industry. AIB courses are instructor guided, include learning measurements, and are designed to increase job skills and knowledge. Completion of prescribed courses can lead to industry-recognized AIB diplomas and certificates, or assist in professional licensing requirements. AIB courses are offered in flexible formats. In addition to traditional classroom instruction, today's AIB offers Internet delivery for many of its courses.

Performance Training Series. The ABA Performance Training Series addresses vital skills that every banker needs today. All training materials clearly outline objectives and all use interactive techniques, promoting group discussions and activities for reinforcement. The seminars are grouped in topic clusters: Business Fundamentals, Compliance, Managing People, Retail Banking (Product Knowledge and Sales), and Small Business (Product Knowledge and Sales).

ABA eLearning. Now there's a training solution that moves faster than your world does. Combining ABA's knowledge of the financial services industry with the technical expertise of the e-learning leaders, Digital Think, ABA eLearning delivers training faster, more effectively, and more efficiently than ever before. More than 50 individual courses support the curriculum in these areas: Basic Banking Knowledge, Fundamental Business Skills, Management and Leadership, Regulatory Compliance, Retail Banking Fundamentals, Retail Banking Sales Skills, Small Business Banking Fundamentals, Small Business Banking Sales Skills, Trust and Investments, as well as eBusiness fundamentals and Microsoft Application courses.

ABA Telephone Briefings. Get real-time expert information on your business challenges without leaving the office. No need to invest travel time and expense to participate. Educate 1 or 100 employees for the same low price. Each seminar provides a participant's guide. You may ask questions directly to leading experts on the issues. New topics are added all the time. Check *www.aba.com* for the latest schedule.

Payment Systems Today. This 15-hour short course provides you with a high level overview of the systems that power our nation's economy. The course shares with you basic information about the most common payment systems available today, their use in the economy, and regulatory and security concerns in the process. Topics include cash, checks, electronic checks, debit cards, credit cards, smart cards, stored value cards, prearranged and preauthorized ACH and funds transfers, inter-bank settlement, global payment systems, security and the laws and regulations governing payments.

For more information, call **1-800 BANKERS** or visit our web site, *www.aba.com.*

STUDENT SURVEY

Thank you for participating in this American Bankers Association/American Institute of Banking course/seminar. Your responses on the following evaluation will help shape the structure and content of future courses. After completing the evaluation, please fold, staple, and mail this postage-paid response form.

TELL US ABOUT YOURSELF:

Name _____ Phone # _____

Title_____ E-mail_____ Fax no. _____

Department_____ Bank/Company _____

Address _____

City _____ State _____ Zip _____

Your education　❑ high school　❑ some college　❑ BA/BS degree　❑ advanced degree _____

TELL US ABOUT YOUR EMPLOYER

Your employer's business is in　❑ banking　❑ other
(specify)_____

Number of years you've worked for financial services industry:
❑ 0-2　　❑ 3-5　　❑ 6-10　　❑ more than 10

Your employer's asset size:　❑ up to $250mm
❑ $251mm - $500mm　❑ $501mm - $5 B　❑ $5 B plus

Number of employees:
❑ up to 100　❑ 101 to 300　❑ 301 to 1,000　❑ 1,001 plus

Does your employer have an in-house training department?
❑ yes　　❑ no

If the answer is *yes*, who manages that department?
Name: _____

Title: _____

TELL US ABOUT YOUR AIB EXPERIENCE

Number of courses/seminars taken in last 3 years:
❑ 0　　　❑ 1-2　　❑ 3-5　　❑ 6 or more

AIB course taken through (please check all that apply):
❑ Local ABA Training Provider
❑ AIB online program
❑ AIB correspondence study
❑ other　(specify _____)

Are you working on another degree? ❑ yes ❑ no
(specify)_____
_____

Are you working on an AIB certificate/diploma program?
❑ yes (please specify)　❑ no
❑ Bank Operations　　　❑ Banking & Finance
❑ General Banking　　　❑ Bank Marketing
❑ Performance Training Series Certificate
❑ Lending Diploma [❑ Commercial　❑ Consumer　❑ Mortgage]

Please list any other training providers you have used and the courses/seminars you have taken.

_____

_____

_____

TELL US YOUR OPINION OF THE COURSE MATERIALS
Please indicate your degree of agreement with the following:

	Strongly Disagree			Strongly Agree
Materials covered all important topics.	1	2	3	4
Learning objectives were clear.	1	2	3	4
Graphics well illustrated course content.	1	2	3	4
Theory and practical applications were well balanced.	1	2	3	4
Examples/case studies helped achieve learning objectives.	1	2	3	4
Exercises gave ample opportunity to apply learning.	1	2	3	4

Overall, how would you rate the following?

	Poor			Excellent
Course/seminar materials	1	2	3	4
Your experience with the course/seminar	1	2	3	4

Did your instructor use any supplemental materials to teach this course/seminar? ❑ Yes (What? _____)❑ No

TELL US WHAT OTHER SUBJECTS IN THE FINANCIAL SERVICES INDUSTRY YOU WOULD LIKE TO STUDY

Are there other banking areas you want to learn about? Please specify: _____
_____
_____

What course(s) would help you improve your performance in your current job? Please specify: _____
_____
_____

What type of courses best suit your needs?
❑　Instructor led classroom training
❑　Courses presented over the Internet
❑　Courses presented on CD-ROM multimedia
❑　Printed correspondence courses
❑　Other (please specify):_____
_____

Please provide additional comments about the course/seminar, the materials, other training topics, ABA/AIB, and/or your training needs so that we may better serve you in the future:

_____
_____
_____
_____
_____
_____
_____

TELL US WHAT INFORMATION WE SHOULD SEND TO YOU   (check all that apply)
❑ AIB diploma programs   ❑ ABA conferences   ❑ AIB online programs
❑ ABA schools   ❑ ICB certification program ❑ other products and services   (describe: _____)
May we contact you about courses/seminars under development for your input?   ❑ yes ❑ no

Thank you for completing this survey.
For more information about the ABA/AIB, please visit our Internet Web site at **www.aba.com** or call our Member Service Center at **1-800-BANKERS**.

- - - - - - - - - - - - - PLEASE FOLD ALONG DOTTED LINE - - - - - - - - - - - - - - -

BUSINESS REPLY MAIL
FIRST-CLASS MAIL PERMIT NO. 10579 WASHINGTON, DC

POSTAGE WILL BE PAID BY ADDRESSEE

AMERICAN BANKERS ASSOCIATION
ATTN: PRODUCTS PRODUCTION COORDINATOR
1120 CONNECTICUT AVENUE NW
WASHINGTON DC 20077-5760

NO POSTAGE
NECESSARY
IF MAILED
IN THE
UNITED STATES

NOTES

NOTES

NOTES

NOTES